Publications of the
# Carnegie Endowment for International Peace
## Division of Economics and History
John Bates Clark, Director

# THE CONTINENTAL SYSTEM

## An Economic Interpretation

BY

ELI F. HECKSCHER, D.Phil.

Professor of Political Economy at the University College of Commerce, Stockholm
Fellow of the Royal Economic Society, London

EDITED BY

HARALD WESTERGAARD

Professor of Political Science in the University of Copenhagen

GLOUCESTER, MASS.
PETER SMITH
1964

First Published 1922
Reprinted, 1964

# EDITOR'S PREFACE

THE author of the present inquiry into the Continental System during the beginning of the last century is known as one of the most prominent political economists in Scandinavia and as a thorough investigator of the history of commerce. Among other things he has done very useful work by his suggestive researches concerning the economy of the World War.

When the Carnegie Endowment for International Peace publishes the book, the obvious explanation is that the Continental blockade in many ways throws light on the economic blockade among the belligerent powers involved by the World War.

That the Napoleonic Continental System could by no means have such far-reaching effects as those of the World War already appears from the great difference in dimensions, and from the fact that the separate nations at that time were far more independent of each other economically than they are at the present time with its extraordinary degree of international division of labour. But the author further shows how powerless the governments were at that time compared with those of the present day in the face of attempts at breaking the blockade, and to how slight an extent the measures were supported by the populations themselves. These great changes in the conditions of power and in the general view are highly interesting from a sociological point of view. But even if Napoleon had been in possession of sufficient power his own policy shows to how slight an extent a real international blockade was aimed at by the Continental System.

HARALD WESTERGAARD.

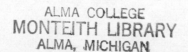

# AUTHOR'S PREFACE

For the aim and character of this short study the reader is referred to the Introduction and the Bibliographical Note. A few words may be added, however, as to the conditions under which it was written.

The book represents a sort of synthesis of earlier studies of the mercantile system and its outgrowths, on the one side, and the result of extensive theoretical and practical work—private, academic, and government—in the field of present-day war economics, on the other. In its original form it was written very rapidly during the winter of 1917–18, under strong pressure of other work, and was presented to my history teacher, Professor Harald Hjärne, on the seventieth anniversary of his birth, at the beginning of May 1918. Probably the atmosphere of a rather strict blockade in a neutral country will be found to pervade it as a more or less natural consequence of the time of its production.

When the Carnegie Endowment for International Peace, through its representative for Scandinavia, my esteemed colleague, Professor Harald Westergaard, proposed that I should treat the subject for its series, I overhauled my earlier text, changing its outward arrangement in several respects and making a number of additions, partly based on new materials. As before, however, I was restricted to such information as was to be found in my own country, and consequently I cannot hope to have escaped error altogether, especially as the field is very large and some of my sources not above suspicion. But what I hope is that the leading ideas of the book, that is, the interpretation of the Continental System, will prove substantially correct.

As the book appears in an English translation, it may be

well for me to point out that I have not had American readers principally in mind. Had that been the case, the brief outline of American policy with regard to the Continental System (part II, chapter IV) would have been either enlarged or omitted altogether, since it cannot contain, in its present form, much that is unknown to educated American readers.

The British Orders in Council of 1807 have been reproduced in an appendix, as they are far more inaccessible than the Napoleonic decrees, and are, moreover, very often misunderstood and sometimes even misquoted.

The English text is, in the main, the work of my colleague Mr. C. S. Fearenside, M.A. (Oxford), Junior Lector in English at the University College of Commerce. There can be no question about the desirability of writing a book from the beginning in the language in which it is to appear, since the association of ideas with language, at least in political and social sciences, is far too close to allow a text to pass entirely unscathed through the ordeal of a translation. But in this case too much was already written in Swedish to leave more than one course open to me. Mr. Fearenside has found it the best plan to follow the Swedish original very closely, instead of attempting to recast the sentence structure on English lines. I am very grateful to him, not only for the work of translation, but also for numerous valuable suggestions regarding the outward arrangement of the text.

My wife has been my best helpmate throughout the work, and to the Carnegie Endowment I am deeply indebted for the reading of the proof.

ELI F. HECKSCHER.

UNIVERSITY COLLEGE OF COMMERCE,
STOCKHOLM, *July 4, 1919.*

# CONTENTS

## PART I

### ANTECEDENTS OF THE CONTINENTAL SYSTEM

# PART II

ORIGIN AND EXTERNAL COURSE OF THE CONTINENTAL SYSTEM

# PART III

INTERNAL HISTORY AND WORKING OF THE CONTINENTAL SYSTEM

## PART IV

### EFFECTS OF THE CONTINENTAL SYSTEM ON THE ECONOMIC LIFE OF GREAT BRITAIN AND THE MAINLAND

# CONTENTS

# CHRONOLOGICAL TABLE

1678    Beginning of Anglo-French commercial war
1713    Anglo-French commercial treaty of Utrecht
1776    Publication of Adam Smith's *Wealth of Nations*
1780    League of Armed Neutrality
1786    Anglo-French commercial treaty (Eden Treaty)
1788    French industrial crisis
1789    Convocation of French States General
1791    New French protective tariff
1793 (Feb.)    Outbreak of Anglo-French war
                Captures authorized by Great Britain
    (Mar.)    French prohibitive customs law
    (June)    British food blockade directed against France
    (Sept.)    French Navigation Act
    (Oct.)    Truculent French prohibitive measure
    (Nov.)    British naval instructions against French colonial trade
1794 (Mar.)    Scandinavian League of Armed Neutrality
    (Aug.)    Revocation of British food blockade
1796 (July)    French enactment against neutral trade
1797 (Feb.)    British bank restriction
1798 (Jan.)    New British naval blockade (*entrepôt* principle)
                Passage of French ' Nivôse Law '
1799 (Dec.)    Repeal of ' Nivôse Law '
1800 (Dec.)    New League of Armed Neutrality
1801 (Mar.–Apr.)    Battle of the Baltic ; collapse of Armed Neutrality
1802 (Mar.)    Peace of Amiens
1803 (Apr.)    French duties on cotton goods
    (May)    Renewal of Anglo-French war
    (June–July)    British blockade of Elbe and Weser
1804 (beginning)    Confiscation of British goods in Holland
    (Apr.)    Blockade of French ports
1805 (May)    Restriction of American carrying trade (*Essex* case)
    (Oct.)    Battle of Trafalgar
                Publication of James Stephen's *War in Disguise*
    (Oct.–Dec.)    Collapse of Austria ; Peace of Pressburg
1806 (Jan.)    Death of William Pitt ; Ministry of ' All the Talents '
    (Feb.–Apr.)    Codification of French prohibitive customs duties

1806 (Apr.)   American Non-importation Act
    (May)   North Sea blockade instituted by Fox
    (Sept.)   Death of Fox
    (Oct.)   Collapse of Prussia
    (Nov.)   Berlin decree
    (Dec.)   Execution of the Continental System in Hamburg
1807 (Jan.)   ' First ' (Whig) Order in Council
    (Mar.)   ' All the Talents ' succeeded by Portland Ministry
    (June)   Anglo-American affair of the *Chesapeake*
    (Sept.)   Bombardment of Copenhagen ;   British occupation of Heligoland
    (Nov.)   New (Tory) Orders in Council
    (Nov.)   First Milan decree
    (Dec.)   Second Milan decree
    (Dec.)   American Embargo Act
    (end)   French occupation of Etruria ;  Leghorn in French hands
1808 (Apr.)   Bayonne decree against America
    (May–June)   Spanish insurrection ;  opening-up of new transmarine markets to Great Britain
    (Sept.)   Closing of French-Dutch frontier
1809 (Mar.)   American Non-intercourse Act
             Diminished vigilance along North Sea coast
    (Apr.)   New (formally milder) Order in Council
    (Jan.–July)   British occupation of French colonies
    (July)   French Schönbrunn decree ;  new customs cordon in western Germany
    (Oct.)   Peace of Vienna ;  Trieste in French hands
1810 (Jan.)   French prize decree
    (Mar.)   Rambouillet decree against America
    (Mar.–July)   Incorporation of Holland with the French Empire
    (May)   Freedom of American trade
    (July)   French licence decree
    (July–Aug.)   Outbreak of grave crisis in Great Britain and France
    (Aug.)   Trianon tariff
             Fictitious revocation of French Continental decrees
    (Oct.)   Fontainebleau decree
             Great British mercantile fleet in the Baltic
    (Dec.)   Incorporation of the North Sea coast with the French Empire
    (Dec.)   Rupture between France and Russia (new Russian tariff)
             Rest of French colonial empire lost
1811 (Mar.)   American Non-importation Act
             Continuation of crisis in Great Britain and France

# THE CONTINENTAL SYSTEM

## AN ECONOMIC INTERPRETATION

# INTRODUCTION

HISTORY has rightly been called of old *magistra vitae*, which function is incompatible with that of *ancilla fidei* or even *ancilla pietatis*. The fact is that historical research can offer us knowledge only by bringing forward its conclusions quite irrespective of their value as a support for any practical aims, howsoever lofty. The endeavours which have been going on all over the world in recent years to transform scientific work into a species of propaganda with a great show of learning, are related not only to the conditions of the moment, but also to the deeper spiritual influences which themselves have done much to bring those conditions about. They are in this way easy to explain; but their tendency to endanger and to create indifference for true research is not lessened thereby.

In the present inquiry I have pursued, to the best of my humble ability, a purely scientific aim, in the meaning of the term that has just been indicated. I have not sought to take sides in the struggles that are barely finished, but only to make use of the experiences of former times, in combination with the experiences of to-day, in order thereby to make room for a better understanding of the entire course of developments. As a matter of fact, it is difficult to imagine a task within the sphere of economic history which is more worth while taking up just now than a consideration of the last great commercial blockade. As will appear from the following account, both the resemblances and the differences of the Napoleonic wars with respect to the recent World War are instructive in the highest degree. But it can scarcely be expected that the matter will be treated in a purely objective manner, that is to say, exclusively on the basis of its own inherent conditions, by those who, metaphorically speaking, have been in the midst of the conflict; for the possibilities of utilizing the lessons of the past as a spear to cast at the joints of the enemy with the laudable purpose of the warrior to wound and kill—to adapt the words of Victor Rydberg—are here, quite naturally, legion.

An even approximately exhaustive treatment of the Continental System, however, lies beyond what has here been attempted. Neither time nor strength was available for so much. It was intended that the following survey should be, first and foremost, economic in character; and the aim of objective treatment was thereby considerably simplified. For economy, as is well known, simply means housekeeping—the directing of outward means to a given end. The moral content of the means in themselves, and still more the expediency of the end in itself, fall outside the confines of economic research. All examination of the one or of the other will therefore be avoided. Instead of this, we will have before us two objects : first, the purely historical one of determining how the means and the end came into being; secondly, the economic one of inquiring into the suitability of the means for their task and the effects of the policy in general.

More clearly stated, there are three principal questions to be examined :

1. In what economic ideas did the Continental System originate ?
2. What was its actual economic bearing ?
3. In what manner did it correspond to its aim ?

The first of these three questions is very richly illustrated, from a purely external point of view, in the literature already existing on the Continental System; for the third there is likewise abundant, though not completely worked-up, material ; the second, however, seems to have suffered from the fact that no economist, so far as is known, has yet subjected it to scientific treatment. On all three questions, and especially on the last two, a clearer light is thrown by comparison with the recent blockade.

A French student of Napoleonic times, M. Marcel Dunan, has declared in an engrossing and very subjectively written bibliography of the Continental System (1913), that the time has not yet come for general surveys of this gigantic undertaking, because, according to his view, we do not yet know either its causes, its roots, its applications, or its effects. Absolute certainty, however, is not given to man ; and even though it is undoubtedly true that many years of research must elapse before positive judgment can be passed on certain important points—as will, indeed, appear from what follows—the agreement in the results of the different investigations is so surprisingly great that even now it seems possible to say a great deal without much danger of error. Otherwise, one may wait in vain for investigations on all the necessary points, if no efforts have been made beforehand to summarize the conclusions already reached.

In a supplement to this exposition the most important materials for a more detailed study of the Continental System have been brought together for the benefit of those who may feel impelled to push deeper into this fertile and interesting field of inquiry.

# PART I

# ANTECEDENTS OF THE CONTINENTAL SYSTEM

# FOREWORD

THE Continental System is a unique measure to which a country resorts for the purpose of crushing a political enemy by economic means and at the same time building up its own commercial and industrial prosperity to an extent previously undreamt of. The will to injure one's enemy and to benefit one's own country is, therefore, a matter to be taken for granted beforehand, and consequently does not require much elucidation. That will is seldom lacking in the life of nations, least of all when they are at war, and was evidently bound to attain an unusual intensity in a statesman of the character of Napoleon, who throughout his career renounced all moral traditions and made self-assertion his loftiest lodestar. What we have here to investigate and elucidate, therefore, is not mainly these simple aims of policy, but rather, if one may put it so, the means to those ends; or, to express it more clearly, what friends and foes conceive to be gain and loss in the sphere of economics, that is, what kind of economic changes they regard as beneficial and as detrimental. These matters are very far from self-evident even at the present time, although they have been the subject of protracted scientific treatment; and they were obviously still less self-evident a hundred years ago. If we wish to understand the nature of the Continental System, therefore, we must first consider the body of ideas whence it proceeded; and if we wish to understand its effects, we must further consider those ideas with reference to their true economic connexions. Only in that way, too, can we form a clear idea of the similarities and dissimilarities of the Continental System with respect to the blockade policy pursued during the recent World War; for the aim to injure the enemy and benefit the home country is to be taken for granted as much in our own time as it was in the time of Napoleon.

In order to form a correct understanding of the antecedent conditions of the Continental System, in the meaning just given, we must point especially to one feature of the mercantilist point of view whence it sprang, namely, to what we may call its static conception of economic life.  If, for instance, we refer to one of the most clear-headed and consistent of the mercantilist statesmen, namely, Colbert, we learn from many of his writings that he conceived the industry, trade, shipping, and bullion resources of the world as quantities given once for all, which, therefore, could not be appreciably increased or decreased by human activity.  Under such a conception it is obvious that there can be but one conclusion, viz., that the economic prosperity of a country depends on its power to deprive its competitors of their shares of the given quantity, and not on its power to increase the total quantity.  That is to say, only at the expense of others can a country be rich.[1]

It is not difficult to understand to what kind of economic policy such a conception would naturally lead.  It led to the policy of commercial war ; and without any great exaggeration we may say with the well-known German economic historian, Professor Schmoller, that the trade policy of former times consisted of an unbroken series of commercial blockades.[2]

[1] *Lettres, instructions et mémoires de Colbert* (Paris, 1861–73), vol. II, p. cclxvii ; vol. VI, pp. 264–5, 269 ; vol. VII, p. 239 ; *et al.* As this side of mercantilist opinion does not appear to be at all generally understood, we may give a somewhat full quotation from Colbert's *Dissertation sur la question : quelle des deux alliances, de France ou de Hollande, peut estre plus avantageuse à l'Angleterre* (March, 1669), where the point of view is brought out with all the incisive logic of which Colbert was master : ' L'on peut avancer certainement que le commerce de toute l'Europe se fait avec le nombre de 20,000 vaisseaux de toute grandeur ; et l'on demeurera facilement d'accord que ce nombre ne peut estre augmenté, d'autant que les peuples sont toujours égaux dans tous les Estats, et que la consommation est pareillement toujours égale.' Finding that one of England's chief considerations in deciding for or against an alliance must be the increase of her shipping, he goes on to say : ' Cette augmentation ne peut provenir que par la découverte de quelque nouveau commerce jusqu'à présent inconnu, ou par la diminution du nombre des vaisseaux de quelqu'une des autres nations.  La découverte de quelque nouveau commerce est fort incertaine, et il n'est pas permis de raisonner sur une chose si casuelle, ou, pour mieux dire, si certaine qu'elle n'arrivera pas. . . . Il faut donc que ce soit par la diminution du nombre des vaisseaux de quelqu'une des autres nations.' *Lettres*, &c., vol. VI, pp. 264–5.  Cf. Sombart, *Der moderne Kapitalismus* (2nd ed., Munich and Leipzig, 1917), vol. II, p. 918.

[2] Schmoller, *Umrisse und Untersuchungen zur Verfassungs-, Verwaltungs- und Wirtschaftsgeschichte* (Leipzig, 1898), p. 95.

This, then, was the body of ideas in which the Continental System originated, in so far as commercial wars, in the current view of that time, were bound to seem economically profitable to an extent that can scarcely be appreciated by any tolerably clear-minded person of to-day.

All this, however, does not explain of what the benefit and profit of commercial war, on the one hand, and the injury and loss on the other, were supposed to consist. But on this point, too, the mercantilist conception gave all the guidance necessary. Profit was supposed to consist in the augmentation of exports, in forcing the goods of one's own country on other countries; loss, in allowing other countries to force goods on one's own country. Industry, trade, navigation, that is, economic activity in general, were in a way regarded as ends in themselves. The goods that were their fruits, so to speak, were to be exported so far as possible, if they belonged to one's own country, and to be kept out so far as possible, if they belonged to other countries. The verdict of the balance of trade—including, however, the balance of payments for freightage, &c.—determined the result. Modern economists are far more familiar with this trend of thought than they are with the static conception of things. Even in our own day 'the natural man' reasons in this way; and this reasoning, so far as one can see, is substantially a fruit of the ideas contributed to history during the mercantilist period.[1]

All this makes clear, not only the existence, but also the tendency, of commercial wars. Their object was necessarily to force the greatest possible amount of one's own goods into the enemy's country, and, so far as possible, to prevent the enemy from introducing goods into one's own country. Inasmuch as this, precisely because of the conception indicated, was the object of trade policy even in time of peace, the transition from peace to war was very easily effected; and for that reason

---

[1] This subject is obviously too comprehensive for incidental treatment in this connexion. What the writer has in mind is the signal reversal from the mediaeval eagerness to keep goods within reach to the opposite eagerness to dispose of goods which has been the predominant trait both of mercantilist and of popular present-day opinion.

we undoubtedly meet with a consistency in the trade policy of that time which, strictly speaking, is lacking in our own time. Nowadays, as in the days of mercantilism, most states, guided by the economic perceptions of the average man, labour in time of peace to render difficult the importation of foreign goods, and at the same time to force their own products on the world market, (although in reality this is incompatible with the former aim). In time of war, however, they suddenly swerve around, either to the inverted standpoint of encouraging imports and hampering exports, or, in general terms, of preventing all trade with the enemy. This statement does not, of course, imply any judgment as to which policy has the greater justification; it is merely an assertion of the at least seemingly greater inconsistency of our present procedure.

An important part of what follows will be devoted to the investigation of the question as to whether and to what extent the older procedure may be expected to accomplish its purpose—the crushing of the enemy by economic means. And in that connexion it will be shown that, while the older tendency in war time was in close harmony with commercial policy in peace time, its relation to the generally observed rules and methods of naval warfare was far more inconsistent.

# CHAPTER I
## COMMERCIAL POLICY

To begin with, however, it seems expedient to trace in some detail the evolution of commercial policy during the century before the Continental System, with special reference to the development of that sphere of activity to which the great trade blockade was especially to be applied, namely, the commercial relations between Great Britain and France.

### BEGINNING OF ANGLO-FRENCH COMMERCIAL WAR (1660–1786)

England and France, as is well known, had been adversaries, with certain more or less lengthy intervals, from the early Middle Ages; and after mercantilism had become firmly established in both countries, it was inevitable that the commercial policy of both should come to be marked by the efforts and tendencies to which we have just referred. To go back no further than the middle of the seventeenth century, we find evidences of antagonism in the customs regulations at least from 1660 on; and after 1678, when the two countries were on the verge of actual war, we may regard commercial war and mutual embargo simply as the normal state of relations between them. After the deposition of the House of Stuart and the outbreak of war between England and France in 1689, there was a further intensification of the antagonism; and with the outbreak of the War of the Spanish Succession, in 1701, the commercial war may be said to have assumed its definitive form. In connexion with the Peace of Utrecht, in 1713, a famous attempt was made to settle the commercial conflict, as well as the political differences, by means of a commercial treaty; and good-will was not wholly lacking either on the French side or on the side of the

Tory government then established in Great Britain. But in other British circles, especially among merchants and manufacturers, the opposition was too strong, and the treaty was consequently deprived of the two clauses which gave it its importance, that is, the clause concerning mutual treatment as the most favoured nation and the clause concerning the mutual abolition of all prohibitions and customs restrictions introduced since 1664, or, in certain cases, since 1699. The result was that the embargo was maintained on both sides, without any noteworthy interruptions, throughout the greater part of the eighteenth century, or for a period of more than a hundred years.

An elucidation of the nature of this hundred years' commercial war between France and Great Britain is essential to a correct understanding of the origin and development of the Continental System. In England, for instance, all importation of French wine, vinegar, brandy, linen, cloth, silk, salt, and paper, and also of all manufactures containing French silk, thread, wool, hair, gold, silver, or leather, was prohibited in 1678.[1] The law itself condemned importation from France, in principle, as ' a common nuisance ', and provided that the French goods were to be destroyed and not allowed to enter, even if they had been captured by English war-ships or privateers. After 1685, however, when this direct persecution of French goods was abandoned and replaced by the establishment of a large number of additional customs duties,[2] a number of severe measures followed on the part of France. Accordingly, when war actually broke out, in 1689, England returned to the principles of 1678. In due form she introduced a general prohibition on the importation of French goods and ordered that all liquid goods that were captured should be poured into the rivers or the sea, or be ' staved, spilt, and destroyed' at the place where they were stored ; also that all cloths, paper, salt, &c., should be publicly burned.[3]

It is unnecessary to dwell upon the protectionist nature of

[1] 29 & 30 Char. II, c. 1, s. 70.    [2] 1 James II, cc. 3 & 5.
[3] 1 W. & M., c. 34, s. 1.

these measures, the main object of which was to prevent French products from competing with domestic products in the English market. Later on, France, which as a rule seems to have been somewhat slower to act, proceeded to adopt similar measures, especially after the outbreak of the new war in 1701. Thus when Adam Smith, who among other things was a Scottish commissioner of customs, entered into a detailed discussion of Anglo-French trade policy in the third edition of his famous work more than eighty years afterwards, he felt justified in stating that, quite apart from the multitude of import prohibitions, especially on all kinds of textiles, the majority of the French imports before the outbreak of the new war in 1778, were assessed by the British customs to the extent of at least 75 per cent. of the value of the goods involved, and that, as a rule, this was equivalent to a formal prohibition.[1]

## SMUGGLING

Such, then, was the nature of commercial policy in the eighteenth century, in so far as it is revealed in the customs regulations of that time. But no idea of the economic conditions of former days could be more erroneous than that which is conveyed by the content of such prohibitions and restrictions. The regulations, as a matter of fact, constitute merely an expression of what the holders of power wished to see realized, and accordingly may be said to illustrate, primarily, nothing more than the economic views of the time. As regards the actual situation, we may safely assume that it was quite different from what the authorities had in view, since otherwise the regulations would not have been necessary ; and if we find them repeated at short intervals, as is usually the case, we may further assume that this was due to the fact that they were not complied with. In point of fact, the only exceptions to this

[1] *Statutes of the Realm*, vol. v, pp. 862 *et seq.* ; vol. vi, pp. 98 *et seq.*, *et al.* Ashley, *The Tory Origin of Free Trade Policy*, in *Surveys Historic and Economic* (London, 1900), pp. 277 *et seq.* ; Levasseur, *Les traités de commerce entre la France et l'Angleterre*, in *Revue d'économie politique* (1901), vol. xv, pp. 964 *et seq.* ; Adam Smith, *The Wealth of Nations* (Cannan ed., London, 1904), vol. i, pp. 432, 437–8.

principle are certain codifications of an already established system of law. These often express a phase that has already passed, it is true, but they nevertheless always have something to correspond to them in the world of realities, which is by no means the case with the innumerable ordinances of the regulative or creative type.

In the sphere of trade policy it is well known that smuggling played a very important rôle. We do not know, for obvious reasons, the exact extent to which it was carried on, but there can be no doubt that it was of frequent and widespread occurrence. According to contemporary opinion, indeed, it was almost as extensive as legitimate trade; and Adam Smith calculated that the commercial intercourse between Great Britain and France, which was exceptionally hampered by the customs regulations, was even principally carried on by smugglers. Thus it hardly entered people's minds that the prohibited foreign goods should be really unobtainable in the countries concerned. After the Peace of Versailles in 1783, for instance, everything English came into fashion in France, and prohibited goods were imported in great quantities, in spite of the fact that the French customs officials, according to the French economic historian, Emile Levasseur, carried their strictness so far as to seize the wearing apparel of travellers and hold it pending their departure from the country.

## Licences

But it was not due entirely to the demands of economic life that recourse was had to this very radical and illegal practice, which in many cases was not only tolerated, but actually facilitated by the authorities themselves. This was usually accomplished by means of a system of licences, which assumed larger or smaller dimensions, according to circumstances, but which were almost always of importance. This licence system, therefore, must almost always be taken into account as an ever-present means of circumventing the nominally valid ordinances. The licences undoubtedly often originated in favouritism, bribery, and similar forms of corruption ; but not infrequently their origin lay deeper.  Partly they were intended to satisfy the insatiable demands of trade, which made themselves felt either within or in opposition to the law, and which, accordingly, it was often considered best to satisfy silently beforehand ; but partly also, and at least as often, they arose from the constant need of money on the part of the government.  This latter consideration gave rise to what one might call fiscalism, that is, to the tendency to change a policy with a certain economic aim—whether rightly or wrongly conceived—under the pretext of bringing revenue into the coffers of the state.  On this rock a great deal of the economic policy of the mercantilist period, to say nothing of that of earlier mediaeval times, had suffered shipwreck ; and this, too, was to be of fundamental importance in relation to the Continental System.  As a characteristic example of the combined effect of smuggling and the licence system, it may be mentioned that in the last decade of the seventeenth century there were discovered in England traces of a great conspiracy organized to facilitate the importation of prohibited French silks under false or stolen labels of the kind prescribed to indicate the fact that the goods involved had either been imported under licence or else had been manufactured within the country.[1]

The actual intercourse between two countries thus followed a course which diverged considerably from that laid out by their professed policies.  But if this was always the case at times of more or less state interference in the economic domain, it was especially the case in the eighteenth century.  During that period, in fact, the old policy was exposed to undermining currents flowing from two different quarters, namely, from the general transformation in all conditions of production which had received the nowise exaggerated name of Industrial Revolution, on the one side, and from the new social philosophy which was slowly paving the way for economic liberalism, on the other. Both of these factors were destined gradually to put an end to

[1] W. R. Scott, *The Constitution and Finance of English, Scottish, and Irish Joint-Stock Companies* (Cambridge, 1911), vol. III, pp. 80 *et seq.*

the old economic order ; but in the long run it was the change in the conditions of production that may be said to have exerted the greater influence. In spite of that, however, a direct influence on commercial policy came from the new social philosophy. Curiously enough, this impulse originated in France, where the new ideas were very far from being common property, as the following development should show very clearly. But just as Turgot, in his capacity of minister of finance under the autocratic King Louis XVI, succeeded in 1776 in carrying through a quite revolutionary reform of internal industrial legislation—a reform which by no means had any favourable public opinion behind it—so one of his pupils, as foreign minister, succeeded ten years later in bringing about a change in external trade policy, just because there was no representative assembly to oppose his measures.

### ANGLO-FRENCH COMMERCIAL TREATY OF 1786 (EDEN TREATY)

The author of this departure from the century-old commercial policy was the Comte de Vergennes. He was *quelque peu disciple des philosophes,* and it was especially because of the physiocratic views he shared with certain politically influential circles in France that he was able to accomplish his purpose. For as physiocracy attached foremost importance to agriculture, it was only natural that French statesmen were able to create substantial facilities for the importation of the industrial products which England was eager to sell, in return for facilities for the exportation of the agricultural products which she was no less eager to buy. Vergennes, undoubtedly of set purpose, neglected to find out the opinion of French industrial circles ; and there is no doubt that this was later on one of the starting-points of the disapproval of his work. In England the efforts to establish better trade connexions between the two countries met with great sympathy, and that, too, precisely among those elements of the population which had brought to naught the commercial treaty of 1713. As was shown by a far-reaching inquiry conducted in Great Britain, the representatives of almost all industries were eager for increased sales in the French market, especially because of their desire to make up for the loss which they believed themselves—incorrectly, as a matter of fact—to have sustained through the cutting off of the American market by the secession of the colonies ; and with very few exceptions they scoffed at the idea of danger arising from French competition in the home market. The British statesmen were naturally much impressed by this attitude, but at the same time they were by no means uninfluenced by the views of the economic theorists.

It was in England that the new ideas, which had gradually gained more and more predominance in both countries in the course of the eighteenth century, received their for all time classical synthesis in Adam Smith's *The Wealth of Nations* (1776), which riddled with criticism the unreasonableness and inconsistency of the old system that existed on paper, especially in the form it assumed in the commercial relations between Great Britain and France. Adam Smith's thesis was that ' a nation that would enrich itself by foreign trade is certainly most likely to do so when its neighbours are all rich, industrious, and commercial nations ', inasmuch as the international exchange of goods was thereby rendered all the more profitable. The applicability of this to France is apparent, and of special interest is the comparison drawn between the trade with the large and near-by French market, on the one hand, which permitted a turnover of business capital several times a year, and the boasted and until then in every way favoured trade with the thinly populated and remote North American colonies, on the other, where the return from invested capital was not made until after the lapse of several years. Through the American War of Independence this comparison received an appositeness which Adam Smith himself certainly did not foresee.[1]

There can be no doubt that Adam Smith's book exerted great influence on William Pitt, who was the leading statesman of Great Britain from 1783. According to a famous

[1] Adam Smith, *op. cit.*, vol. i, pp. 458 *et seq.*

anecdote, Smith once arrived at a dinner somewhat later than the other guests, who rose to receive him. He begged them to remain seated, whereupon Pitt remarked that it was only right for them to rise, since they were all his pupils. While this anecdote is perhaps just as little deserving of unqualified belief as are other similar anecdotes, yet one may place implicit confidence in a statement which Pitt is authentically credited with having made in Parliament after the death of Adam Smith, namely, that he (Smith) had offered the world the best solution of all economic and commercial questions.[1]

The result of these new forces was the Anglo-French commercial treaty of 1786 (often called the Eden Treaty, after the name of its English negotiator), which put an end to the hundred years' commercial war between the two western powers. During the negotiations Pitt had stood firmly on his ground, with the result that in the final settlement the British forced compliance with practically all their demands, while the French allowed nearly all theirs to drop. Customs duties were lowered all along the line, usually down to 10 or 15 per cent. of the value of the goods, and prohibitions on imports were abolished. On the other hand, almost the only British industry which was still uneasy about French competition, namely, the silk industry, had its demands respected to the extent of nothing less than a total prohibition on the importation of French silks into England.

But it was soon to prove that this somewhat belated breach with the century-old restrictive policy had no support in French public opinion, least of all in industrial circles. Indeed, one may go so far as to say that it was precisely this departure from the tradition of commercial war that led to a renewal of the old policy after the French Revolution. The Eden Treaty, which was

---

[1] On this and what follows, cf. Rose, *William Pitt and the National Revival* (London, 1911), pp. 183 *et seq.*, 322 *et seq.* ; Salomon, *William Pitt der jüngere* (Leipzig and Berlin, 1906), vol. I, pt. II, pp. 205 *et seq.* ; Levasseur, *Histoire des classes ouvrières et de l'industrie en France avant 1789* (Paris, 1901), vol. II, pp. 546 *et seq.* ; Levasseur, *Histoire du commerce de la France* (Paris, 1911), vol. I, pp. 535 *et seq.*, 542 *et seq.* ; also, *Histoire de France* (Lavisse ed., Paris, 1910), vol. IX, pt. I, pp. 221 *et seq.* On the situation just after the Eden Treaty, cf. Schmidt, *La crise industrielle de 1788 en France*, in *Revue Historique* (Paris, 1908), vol. 97, pp. 78 *et seq.* The work of F. Dumas, *Etude sur le traité de commerce de 1786* (Paris, 1904), was not accessible.

signed less than three years before the convening of the French
States General on May 5, 1789, in fact occupied almost from
the very beginning a foremost place in the long list of sins
imputable to the *ancien régime*. The French textile industries,
especially the cotton industry, had as early as the 'eighties
managed to benefit by the great technical revolution in England,
mainly by attracting British foremen and machinery to French
mills ; but, naturally enough, they were not yet anything like
equal to their teacher. Besides this, it was alleged by the French
that the value of British wares declared at the customs was so
much understated that the duty fell from the nominal 10 or
15 per cent. to an actual 2 or 3 per cent.; and at the same time
British manufacturers were said to increase the prices of raw
materials in France through the making of extensive purchases
there. The French calico, woollen, pottery, steel, and leather
industries complained bitterly of British competition and of
the general unemployment for which it was held responsible.
Even the Lyons silk industry worked under great difficulties,
which could not be attributed to any British competition, to
be sure, but which at all events were in no manner lessened
by the treaty with its retention of the British prohibitions. Bit-
terest of all were the complaints that emanated from the textile towns in the north of France—Amiens, Abbeville, Sedan,
Rouen, Rheims, Châlons-sur-Marne. Their protests were also
embodied in the famous *cahiers*, in which the French people
in 1789 gave expression to their feelings in all branches of
activity. Moreover, it has been observed that Robespierre, one
of the sworn enemies of Great Britain during the Revolution,
was a representative of the province of Artois and in such
capacity voiced the dislike that was there fostered against
British competition. But the feeling against the Eden Treaty
was by no means confined to these regions. It is really only
with regard to the wine district that we meet with any attitude
of satisfaction toward the new policy ; and it is highly significant that the *cahiers* of the city of Paris, for instance, contained
a demand that the treaty should be submitted to the States
General because of the revolutionary changes it had involved

and the vigorous protests it had evoked from all parts of the country. Public opinion, indeed, was unanimous in attributing the severe industrial crisis of 1788 to the Eden Treaty, which was called the death-warrant of French industry. An inspector of manufactures even went so far as to compare its detrimental effects with those that had followed the revocation of the Edict of Nantes in 1685, which had played havoc with a great deal of the work done by Colbert and his predecessors.

Thus there could be scarcely any doubt as to the political effects of this first departure from the policy of commercial war ; and it is this aspect of the matter which is of prime importance in this connexion. It is quite another question whether the Eden Treaty, even for the moment, was actually responsible for the placing of French economic life upon the low level where it was destined to remain, with a short interruption, during the revolutionary and Napoleonic periods. Severe as was the crisis to which it gave rise, there can be little doubt that precisely the last years of the *ancien régime* were characterized by exceptional prosperity especially, but by no means exclusively, for French trade, and that during the following ten or fifteen years Frenchmen looked back to this period as the zenith of their country's economic development. Even as regards industry, it is a fact that not even the flourishing period of the Consulate (1799–1804) elevated it to anything like the same height that it had attained under the *ancien régime*.[1] Moreover, the difficulties created by free intercourse consequently appear to have been exaggerated. There are positive evidences of certain wholesome effects on French industry which must be connected with the increased intercourse with Great Britain. Thus, in 1787, the year of the ratification of the treaty, there was set up in France (Orléans)—naturally by an Englishman—the first steam-driven cotton spinning mill.[2] Moreover, in the Constituent Assembly

---

[1] Chaptal, *De l'industrie françoise* (Paris, 1819), vol. I, p. xvi ; Levasseur, *Histoire des classes ouvrières et de l'industrie en France de 1789 à 1870* (Paris, 1903), vol. I, p. 405.

[2] Schmidt, *Les débuts de l'industrie cotonnière en France, 1760–1806,* in *Revue d'histoire économique et sociale* (Paris, 1914), vol. VII, pp. 26 *et seq.* ; Ballot, *Les prêts aux manufactures,* in *Revue des études napoléoniennes* (Paris, 1912), vol. II, p. 45.

we find a muslin manufacturer from Versailles (1790), as well as a silk manufacturer from Lyons (1791), stating that the development of French industry, after the difficulties of the first years, had increased apace under the stimulus of British competition, and that in many cases French manufacturers had succeeded in imitating and, by means of cheaper labour, in actually underselling their British competitors. This may or may not be a more faithful picture of the actual situation than that created by the innumerable complaints ; but at all events it seems only natural that a more lively intercourse with Great Britain should have facilitated the spread of new ideas and inventions. But to this, as to other things, there applies a truth which is far too often overlooked, namely, that the economic policy of a country is not determined by actual economic conditions but by the popular ideas concerning those conditions—which is manifestly quite another matter.

The commercial policy of the Revolution, therefore, very soon returned to the traditions established before 1786. Of recent investigators we may refer especially to M. Albert Sorel, who in his monumental work, *L'Europe et la révolution française* (1885–1904), seeks with exhaustive, though somewhat exhausting, persistence to maintain and emphasize the consistency of French policy before and after the Revolution. In nearly all the departments of foreign policy he represents the French revolutionaries of different shades as unconscious successors of Richelieu, Mazarin, and Louis XIV, and as equally unconscious predecessors of Napoleon, whose ideas and measures are therefore also represented as almost entirely in line with the traditional policy of France. Sorel has undoubtedly exaggerated the predestination of this development, as Professor Hjärne has pointed out in his noteworthy book, *Revolutionen och Napoleon* (Stockholm, 1911) ; and in general it is undoubtedly true that the deepest conception does not consist in representing the same *dramatis personae* as constantly reappearing in different costumes. But in the economic sphere—which does not stand out very much in Sorel's work, with its marked bias in favour of foreign policy—the connexion with the past is very strongly emphasized. As is well known, the men of the Revolution derived their strongest impressions from Rousseau, and, so far as one can see, they were very little impressed either by physiocracy or by British liberalism. Consequently they stood, unconsciously, but almost entirely, under the all-pervading influence of the old economic conception. Thus it was almost in the nature of things that the Eden Treaty not only should be treated as an isolated episode, but should positively hasten a return to the old system—especially inasmuch as the commercial reconciliation with Great Britain was the work of none other than the discredited and despised *ancien régime*.

Naturally enough, however, it was the general political situation which was chiefly responsible for the return to the policy of commercial war ; and consequently some few years elapsed before the change was made. In 1791 the Constituent Assembly adopted a new tariff, which, after great protectionist preparations, ultimately came to offer only a very moderate amount of actual protection. France and Great Britain were then at peace, and both were respecting the Eden Treaty. But the new tendency was even then asserting itself in France, not only in the form of recurring complaints against British competition, but also in the form of an actual raising of the customs rates on woollens and other textile goods manufactured in the Duchy of Berg—the even then flourishing textile region on the eastern side of the Rhine, which was destined to play an important part in the history of the Continental System. In justification of these measures, whereby the importation of textiles into France from the east was cut off, there was asserted the need of ' alleviating the detrimental effects ' of the Anglo-French treaty of 1786.[1]

Great Britain, under Pitt's leadership, had as long as possible stood aloof from the struggle against the French Revolution. But toward the end of 1792 the relations between the two countries became very strained. Great Britain held up cargoes bound for French ports, whereupon France retaliated by

[1] Levasseur, *Histoire des classes ouvrières*, &c., *de 1789 à 1870*, vol. I, pp. 38 *et seq.* ; Schmidt, *Le Grand-duché de Berg, 1806–1813* (Paris, 1905), pp. 326–7.

denouncing the Eden Treaty. This was shortly after the beginning of 1793; and on February 1 of that year, less than two weeks after the execution of Louis XVI, war actually broke out. This precipitated both countries into a policy of economic strangulation which was destined to last for more than twenty years and soon to leave all its predecessors far behind. Under the Revolution, and to a certain extent under Napoleon as well, this policy had two very closely interwoven sides, which, however, must be kept separate for the present. One side consists of the blockade measures and the generally rude treatment of maritime intercourse, in which Great Britain decidedly led the way, but was very closely followed by France; and the other side consists of the compulsory measures that were adopted specifically in the sphere of commercial policy. The latter measures were of real importance only on the French side, as a matter of fact, since similar measures on the British side would have been meaningless for the reason that French goods could hardly have reached England without English co-operation. It is the latter policy which we will first consider.

RENEWAL OF ANGLO-FRENCH COMMERCIAL WAR (1793–1799)

On March 1, 1793, only a month after the outbreak of war, the measures of prohibition began, and within a few months the Convention had passed almost all the laws that were possible along that line. The first law of this kind passed by the Convention, which also annulled all treaties previously entered into with enemy countries, prohibited indiscriminately the importation of a large number of textile, metal, and earthenware goods which were regarded as normally coming from England—it was, of course, the home manufacturers of these articles who had especially complained of British competition—but did not restrict the prohibition to goods coming from any specified country. With respect to all goods not expressly exempted, however, it was stipulated that evidence should be furnished that they did not come from an enemy country. This rendered necessary the use of certificates of origin for certain goods, even though they were indispensable to French consumers and could not be obtained from neutral countries (especially sugar). Two or three months later (May 19), accordingly, such goods had to be exempted. But the whole of this first law was a mild warning in comparison with the outbreak of fury, harmonizing completely with the spirit of the Reign of Terror, which on October 9 of the same year (Vendémiaire 18, year II) appeared in the form of a law bearing the title : *Loi qui proscrit du sol de la république toutes les marchandises fabriquées ou manufacturées dans les pays soumis au gouvernement britannique.* Its express application to Great Britain, one of the enemies of France, is in itself significant, the whole law, as its title indicates, being a straightforward proposal to persecute all British goods in the most drastic manner. It imposed on every holder of British goods the obligation to declare them and hand them over to the authorities, and provided that any customs official who allowed such goods to enter the country would be liable to twenty years' imprisonment in irons ; and the same punishment was assigned to any person who imported, sold, or bought them. But even this was not enough. The law further provided that anybody who wore or used British goods was to be regarded as *suspect* and to be punished as such in accordance with the notorious *loi des suspects* ; that is to say, he might be arrested and imprisoned at any time. All posters or notices couched in English and referring to stocks of British goods or containing British trade marks or appellations, as also all newspapers announcing the sale of British goods, were ' proscribed ' ; and the punishment in this case also was twenty years' imprisonment in irons.

After the crisis of Thermidor and the fall of Robespierre early in 1795, the legislators again retraced their steps to some extent by slightly lowering the duties on non-British goods. This did not last long, however, since they were raised again by the Directory at the close of the following year. On the whole it may be said that the rule of the Directory, from the autumn of 1795 to the autumn of 1799, marked a return to the policy of the Reign of Terror, though in a somewhat modified form, throughout the entire economic domain. As a sign of welcome to Lord Malmesbury, who visited Paris to negotiate peace, there was accordingly passed on October 31, 1796 (Brumaire 10, year V), a law prohibiting the importation and sale of British goods on an even larger scale than that established by the laws of 1793, inasmuch as the prohibition was extended to cover goods that were derived, not only from British industry, but also from British trade. And at the same time there was adopted so far as is known for the first time, but certainly not for the last time—the somewhat clumsy expedient of declaring certain groups of goods to be British, quite irrespective of their real origin. Even such goods as were brought into the country from captured or stranded vessels were not allowed to remain there, but had to be promptly re-exported. The resemblance between this and the above-mentioned regulations of the seventeenth century is unusually striking. Moreover, nearly all the regulations of the year 1793 were renewed in substance, although the provision concerning certificates of origin had again to be limited after a few months. Only in regard to penalties was there a very considerable modification. Among the goods which were always to be regarded as British was refined sugar ; but now again, as in 1793, its exclusion proved to be impossible, and the smuggling to which it gave rise finally resulted, in 1799, in the prohibition being replaced by a high customs duty. Evidence of the extent to which French legislators thought it possible to carry the persecution of everything British is furnished by the fact that the importation of Geneva watches was prohibited on the ground that they contained a small amount of steel presumed to be of British origin.

Another link in the policy of commercial war was formed by the Navigation Act, which was brought forward with great oratorical fanfare and was passed by the Convention on September 21, 1793, the anniversary of the overthrow of the monarchy. In exact imitation of the famous corner-stone of English maritime policy, the Navigation Act of the Commonwealth of 1651, and also of earlier French ordinances, it forbade foreign vessels to import any products other than those of their own country or to carry on coasting trade in France. Moreover, by a supplementary law of October 18 (Vendémiaire 27, year II), all foreign vessels were saddled with dues about ten times as high as those imposed on French vessels. There is a close analogy between these measures and those that were adopted during the seventeenth and early part of the eighteenth centuries. The latter were directed chiefly against the principal carrying country of the time, the Netherlands; and in the same manner the law of the Convention was directed against the new commercial nation, Great Britain. *Perfide Albion* came to occupy the same position in the popular imagination as its predecessor, only it was regarded as still more dangerous owing to the great development of its industries and political power.

All these trade laws of the Revolution manifestly had the same double character as their forerunners of the seventeenth and eighteenth centuries; that is to say, they were intended to injure Great Britain by excluding her goods and vessels, and at the same time to serve as an ultra-protectionist measure calculated to benefit French industries. According to the official statement, the Directory's law of 1796 was designed to 'give new life to trade, restore manufactures, and re-establish the workshops', and, on the other hand, 'to deprive our enemies of their most important resource in waging war against us' and compel them to make peace. In complete analogy with this, Barère, the trumpeter in ordinary of the Convention, speaking in the name of the Committee of Public Safety, had justified the Navigation Act partly on the ground that 'Carthage would thereby be destroyed'—'let us decree a solemn Navigation Act,' he said, ' and the isle of shopkeepers will be ruined '—and partly on the ground that France would thereby multiply her industries, stimulate the consumption of domestic products, create her own ship-building yards, build up a flourishing mercantile marine, &c., &c. This, so to speak, dualistic character the Continental System was destined to retain but at the same time to lead to an irremediable self-contradiction.

Naturally it is true of the commercial blockades of the Revolution, as of those of earlier times, that they were not even approximately maintained; the result was that smuggling once more became one of the principal means of Anglo-French intercourse.  Notwithstanding the law of 1796, the practice seems to have grown up of importing British and other prohibited goods on a large scale as captured goods.  Disordered as every department of the public administration was, one can not doubt that the authorities merely winked at all this; and besides they were often obliged to mitigate the laws, as we have already seen, in order to ensure some observance of them.  An example of this was given by the Navigation Act, which was introduced with such high-sounding words and a month later repealed for the most part by a number of supplementary regulations providing that certain raw materials and enemy goods might be imported in time of war by neutral vessels; shortly afterwards such vessels also received the right to carry on coasting trade.[1]

[1] *Lois et actes du gouvernement* (Paris, 1807), vol. VI, pp. 434–5; vol. VII, pp. 83, 409–10, 464–5, 492 *et seq.*; *Bulletin des lois de la république française*, 2d ser., bull. 86, no. 825; bull. 105, no. 1002; *Le Moniteur*, Sept. 23 and 24, 1793; Oct. 21, 1796; Levasseur, *Histoire des classes ouvrières*, &c., *de 1789 à 1870*, vol. I, pp. 38 *et seq.*, 87 *et seq.*, 260; Sorel, *L'Europe et la révolution française* (Paris, 1893), vol. III, pp. 476–7; vol. V, pp. 116, 124; Schmidt, *Le Grand-duché de Berg*, pp. 326 *et seq.*; Chapuisat, *Le commerce et l'industrie à Genève pendant la domination française, 1798–1813* (Geneva and Paris, 1908), Annexe XIV; Rose, *William Pitt and the Great War* (London, 1911), pp. 103–4; Kiesselbach, *Die Continentalsperre in ihrer ökonomisch-politischen Bedeutung* (Stuttgart and Tübingen, 1850), pp. 55–6.

# CHAPTER II

## MARITIME BLOCKADE

It has already been intimated that, parallel with the commercial blockade, which came principally from the French side, there was taking place, mainly on the British side, a systematic persecution of trade with enemy countries, and that both of these lines of development came to be united in the Continental System. Seemingly and on paper these two lines of policy were not only separate, but also, in part, absolutely conflicting; this, in fact, has led many observers astray. But if we consider the policy of the maritime blockade with reference to its actual application, as opposed to its outward form, we find that its character, in spite of all inconsistencies and lack of precision, easily reveals as merely an outcome of the mercantilist commercial policy. In this way, consequently, the aim of the commercial war of a hundred years ago was altogether unlike that pursued in the recent World War. On this point, however, scarcely any of the usual accounts give us clear information. The majority of them take the policy of blockade as a more or less self-evident matter without inquiring into its aims. The only writer who, so far as I know, has embarked on a deeper analysis is the foremost naval historian of our time, the late Admiral Mahan of the United States Navy, who has undoubtedly cast much light on the history of the Continental System in his books, *The Influence of Sea Power upon the French Revolution and Empire* (1893), and *Sea Power in its Relations to the War of 1812* (1905). In general, however, it may be said that Admiral Mahan is too much concerned with sea-power in itself to devote sufficient attention to its connexion with economic policy and economic activity, which after all have also a non-naval side.

In the external system of the maritime blockade the actual blocking of the enemy's ports and coasts unquestionably forms the central point. Characteristic of the system, however, was the practice adopted by Great Britain of establishing a so-called 'paper blockade', that is to say, of declaring in a state of blockade long stretches of coast which she could not or would not effectively blockade by means of sufficient naval forces, and on the strength of this declaration capturing neutral vessels bound for well-nigh any enemy port. This practice received its most extreme statement in an *obiter dictum* attributed to the British Admiralty Judge, Sir James Marriott, who in 1780, during the war with France and Spain, the European allies of the American colonies, declared that the ports of those countries were *ipso facto* blockaded by virtue of their geographic position.[1] It was perhaps chiefly to this central point in the naval policy of Great Britain that the neutrals demurred. The demand that the blockade should be effectual, that is to say, that it should apply only to places which were so well guarded that vessels could not reach them without imminent danger of capture, consequently played an important rôle among the five celebrated points enunciated in 1778 by the Danish statesman, A. P. Bernstorff, and used as the foundation of the unusually successful Swedo-Dano-Russian Armed Neutrality of 1780.

## MERCANTILIST IMPORT OF THE BLOCKADE

The blockade undoubtedly had its root in the idea of siege, as the Swedish international jurist, Dr. Nils Söderqvist, has pointed out ; and like the siege, accordingly, it aimed in principle at a real cutting-off of the enemy's territory, especially as regards the exclusion of supplies. Here, therefore, the external contrast with the mercantilist commercial policy is very marked ; for the latter, as we have seen, aimed to encourage the forcing of goods upon the enemy and would consequently have regarded a consistent application of the blockade principle as a direct advantage to the enemy country in so far as its supplies were crippled, and as an advantage to

---

[1] Söderqvist, *Le blocus maritime* (Stockholm, 1908), pp. 44–5.

the home country only in so far as the blockade impeded the foreign sale of the enemy's own goods.  This peculiar and important but usually overlooked inconsistency can be explained only by the fact that the practice of blockade arose in the pre-mercantilist period.  But with the development and spread of mercantilist ideas the practice necessarily had to reshape itself;  and this, in fact, was what actually happened.

The result was twofold.  In the first place, blockade measures were employed to accomplish other purposes than those formally intended;  and, in the second place, the regulations existing on paper were annulled, either by exceptions or by deliberate laxity in their enforcement, to such an extent as to create an order of things quite different from that which was officially prescribed.

## FUNCTION OF CAPTURE AT SEA

First, then, we have to consider the employment of blockade measures for purposes other than those formerly intended.  Here primary importance attaches to the fact that seizures or captures may be said to have been ends in themselves.  To some extent this appears even in the relative importance of the paper blockade as compared with the effective blockade;  for the former gave much greater chances of capture but, at the same time, was a far less safe means of preventing intercourse with the enemy.  Moreover, two of the most important methods of blockade are largely explained when we come to consider the importance of captures—namely, the arbitrary extension of the idea of contraband and the persistent refusal of Great Britain to acknowledge the proposition that ' free ships make free goods ' or that ' the flag covers the cargo ', which implies that enemy goods are immune from capture on neutral vessels.

The object of this encouragement of captures for their own sake was scarcely in any notable number of cases what one would nowadays be most inclined to expect, that is, the procurement of goods for one's own use in this convenient manner. It is true that Pitt, according to a statement of the then Swedish envoy in London, Lars von Engeström—a statement, however, which is not confirmed by the brief parliamentary reports— referred in the House of Commons on November 3, 1795, to seizures of corn cargoes bound for French ports as a means of overcoming the exceptional shortage of foodstuffs in England;[1] and there is also a later utterance of Napoleon to the same effect.[2] But these cases would seem to be almost unique, as one might expect beforehand in view of the fact that the object of the seizures was not, as a rule, to acquire goods, but rather to dispose of them. An explanation must be found elsewhere, namely, in the fact that captures were a means of encouragement to the captors themselves; and to this point there was ascribed the greatest importance. To begin with, it applied to the great horde of privateers, who were regarded as forming a very important augmentation to the fighting forces of the country, but who manifestly could not embark on that career except with some prospect of profit. In a highly characteristic manner a well-known English international jurist, William Manning, towards the middle of the nineteenth century explained the benefit of these privateers on *laissez-faire* lines. ' They increase the naval force of a state,' he said, ' by causing vessels to be equipped from private cupidity, which a minister might not be able to obtain by general taxation without much difficulty '.[3]

EVIDENCE OF JAMES STEPHEN IN ' WAR IN DISGUISE '

But this held good, not only of the privateering fleet, but also of the Royal Navy itself, in which captures formed a source of income to commanders and crew that was of the greatest importance in stimulating their willingness and zeal. How deeply rooted this opinion still was only a hundred years ago is best illustrated by a book of that time which perhaps, on the whole, gives a clearer notion of the pre-conditions of the policy of blockade than any other, namely, James Stephen's *War in*

---

[1] Lydia Wahlström, *Sverige och England under revolutionskrigens början* (Stockholm, 1917), pp. 192–3; *Parliamentary History*, vol. XXXII, pp. 235–6.

[2] See p. 94.

[3] Manning, *Commentaries on the Law of Nations* (London, 1839), p. 117.

1569.43

*Disguise ;   or, the Frauds of the Neutral Flags*, which was published the same day as the battle of Trafalgar (October 21, 1805) and within four months appeared in three British and two American editions.

The importance of this book—which, significantly enough, was republished during the recent World War as a contributory aid to the solution of its problems—will appear in several places later on, and a few words about its author, therefore, seem in order.   James Stephen, father of Sir James Stephen (nicknamed ' Mr. Over-Secretary Stephen ') and grandfather of Sir James Fitzjames Stephen and Sir Leslie Stephen, was a barrister practising in the Prize Appeal Court of the Privy Council, the highest prize court in England.   Both in this capacity and earlier as a lawyer in the West Indies, he had acquired an intimate knowledge of the conditions of trade during the long naval war, as well as of the application of the principles of law to them.   Thus not only was he thoroughly familiar with matters in this department, but he was also far from representing any extreme jingo view.   This is perhaps best shown by the fact that, like his brother-in-law, William Wilberforce, the great emancipator of the slaves, he was a decidedly religious person, belonging to the Clapham Sect, and devoted a large part of his life to the struggle for the abolition of negro slavery.   This fact gives his utterances on captures their proper background.   He dwells long on the injustice which would be inflicted on ' our gallant and meritorious fellow subjects, the naval captors,' when they were compelled to see valuable cargoes, ' their lawful game,' passing continually under their sterns.   ' It is painful to reflect,' he says, ' that these brave men lose the ancient fruits of distant service, while enduring more than its ordinary hardships.'   His account of the importance of capture as an inducement for seamen may be quoted *in extenso* :

Let us give full credit to our gallant officers, for that disinterested patriotism, and that love of glory, which ought to be the main springs of military character, and which they certainly possess in a most eminent degree. But it would be romantic and absurd, to suppose that they do not feel the value of that additional encouragement, which his Majesty and the legislature hold out to them, in giving them the benefit of the captures they make. What else is to enable the veteran naval officer, to enjoy in the evening of his life, the comforts of an easy income ; the father to provide for his children ; or the husband for an affectionate wife, who, from the risques he runs in the service of his country, is peculiarly likely to survive him ? By what other means, can a victorious admiral, when raised, as a reward of his illustrious actions, to civil and hereditary honours, hope to support his well-earned rank, and provide for an ennobled posterity ? . . . It is from the enemies of his country, therefore, that he hopes to wrest the means of comfortably sustaining those honours, which he has gained at their expence.

As to the common seamen and mariners, the natural motives of dislike to the naval service, are in their breasts far more effectually combated by the hope of prize money, than by all the other inducements that are or can be proposed to them. The nautical character is peculiarly of a kind to be influenced by such dazzling, but precarious prospects.[1]

## ATTACKS ON ENEMY EXPORTS, NOT IMPORTS

With this encouragement of captures for their own sake, however, there was undoubtedly coupled a desire to cut down the enemy's trade. But this desire, too, has to be conceived in a strictly mercantilist spirit. To inflict military injury on the enemy, either directly or indirectly, was not—at least not to any notable extent—the object of the interference with his trade. On the contrary, the primary object was that of waging commercial war against him, *i. e.*, of depriving him of a source of gain, or, in other words, beating him off the field; and, parallel with this, it was aimed to extend a country's own trade—which could be done, and was constantly attempted, at the expense, not only of the enemy country, but also of neutral countries. This brought it about that the establishment of a blockade dealt the latter a much harder blow than is the case at the present time. The intention was to prevent them from receiving any profit either from the enemy country or from other countries, and so far as possible to expel them, as well as the enemy, from

[1] Stephen, *War in Disguise: or, the Frauds of the Neutral Flags* (Piggott ed., London, 1917), pp. 106–7.

sources of gain which had previously been open to them.  It is perhaps not altogether clear whether considerations of this nature influenced some of the measures of the recent blockade.  But however that may be, it is true that such a policy has no connexion whatsoever with the blockade of the enemy as such, but may be pursued, as actually happened a hundred years ago, purely as an end in itself.  The objection to the proposition that 'free ships make free goods' was rooted in this object much more than in the inclination to encourage captures for their own sake ;  for as goods belonging to subjects of enemy countries were liable to seizure on neutral vessels, the neutrals were prevented from taking over the traffic which the enemy himself had been able to carry on before he was driven from the sea, as the British historian Lecky has well observed.[1]  And this was still more the case with the fourth of the great disputed questions concerning the law of war at sea, namely, that of *commerce nouveau*, or, in British terminology, the rule of 1756, the wording of which, as elaborated by British jurists, was that ' a neutral has no right to deliver a belligerent from the pressure of his enemy's hostilities, by trading with his colonies in time of war in a way that was prohibited in time of peace.'  This principle prevented the neutrals from pushing their way either into the enemy's coasting trade or—and this was more important— into what might be regarded as a special form of coasting trade, namely, trade with the enemy's colonies.  In time of peace both of these were jealously guarded preserves of the trade and navigation of the home country ;  but in time of war the belligerent power that was debarred from the sea willingly turned them over to neutrals with the double object of maintaining the traffic and of preventing it from falling into the hands of the enemy.

The characteristic difference between the policy of that time and the policy of to-day is that, when the masters of the sea a century ago tried to prevent neutrals from carrying on a certain kind of trade, their object was not to kill that trade altogether, as is the case nowadays, but to seize it for themselves.

[1] Lecky, *History of England in the Eighteenth Century* (original library edition, London, 1882), vol. IV, p. 157.

It is therefore indisputable, as the neutrals complained and as
Stephen himself admits, that British vessels were allowed to
trade with France, while neutral vessels were overhauled and
seized.[1] In full accord with this and with mercantilist trade
policy, it was sought first and foremost to cut off all kinds of
exports from the enemy to the neutrals, especially if they competed with those of the home country. In complete contrast
with the efforts of the recent war, the endeavours of that time
were aimed, on the one side, at getting rid of the excess of export
goods in the home country and, on the other side, at preventing
the enemy from selling his products. This was in part due to
the fact that apprehensions were always felt of low prices on
these goods in the home country and also of high prices in the
enemy country. On the one side, therefore, the whole of
Stephen's account is permeated by anxiety lest the price of
British colonial goods should decline as a result of their being
kept out of the continental markets by French and Spanish
colonial goods. In previous wars, according to his view, the
British home market, ' relieved by a copious exportation from
temporary repletions,' gave them (the colonies), ' in its large and
ever-advancing prices, some indemnity for the evils of the war,'
while at that time, according to his statements, the prices were
sinking on the Continent in consequence of the importation of
goods from the enemy's colonies. On the other hand, he is
dominated by dislike of the idea that the same neutral trade
should provide access to America of the textile and iron goods
of the Continent in competition with those of Great Britain
herself. What troubled him, therefore, was not that the Continent should get colonial goods, but that it should get them
from the enemy colonies, which, like the mother country itself,
should be cut off from exports, he thought, but not from imports.

Finally, therefore, all this implies that no cutting-off of
imports to the enemy could come into the line of the policy
pursued. It denotes merely an effort to place those imports
under the control of the naval power itself, so that the country

---

[1] Holm, *Danmark-Norges udenrigske Historie fra 1791 til 1807* (Copenhagen,
1875), vol. I, p. 231 ; Stephen, *op. cit.*, p. 170.

might thereby give preference, so far as possible, to its own products and those of its colonies, and also so that it might take over trade and navigation with the enemy mainland. The latter consideration, however, took a secondary place, as Great Britain often had need of neutral shipping to supplement her own overworked mercantile marine ; and it is especially note-worthy that the neutrals' supply of the enemy's (e. g., the French) market with the belligerent's (e. g., Britain's) own products was an all but self-evident matter, against which there was really no objection to raise from a British point of view. Manifestly, such a blockade policy diverged funda-mentally from that of the recent World War.

The only substantial exception to this general tendency—and even that a very partial one—concerned import goods of purely military importance, that is too say, military supplies, naval stores, and sometimes, at least in principle, foodstuffs for the enemy's fighting forces on land and sea. These items were emphasized by Pitt, for instance, in the great speech which he delivered before the House of Commons on February 2, 1801, immediately before his retirement, in defence of the policy of maritime blockade that he had introduced. In the actual execution of the policy, however, it is difficult to find any marked traces of this ; and, significantly enough, it was coolly stated in Parliament, in 1812, that the clothing of the French army came from Yorkshire, and that ' not only the accoutre-ments, but the ornaments of Marshal Soult and his army ' came from Birmingham. The reservation was made, however, that they had not been ordered directly by the French govern-ment ! [1]

It may be remarked in passing that Edward III, four and a half centuries earlier, had already given licences for the exportation of corn to the enemy, though the ruling thought at that time was that of procuring revenue for the Crown.[2]

---

[1] Stephen, *op. cit.*, pp. 60 *et seq.*, 90, 195, *et al.* ; Emory Johnson and others, *History of the Domestic and Foreign Commerce of the United States* (Washington, 1915), vol. II, p. 23 ; *Parliamentary History*, vol. XXXV, p. 916 ; Hansard's *Parliamentary Debates*, vol. XXIII, pp. 8, 42–3.

[2] Brodnitz, *Englische Wirtschaftsgeschichte* (Jena, 1918), vol. I, p. 140.

## Colonial Trade

The colonial trade, which at that time was conducted in all countries on the lines of the Old Colonial System, deserves special attention in this connexion. The fundamental idea of that system was that the mother country and the colonies should constitute an economic whole, with a strict division of labour between them, so that the mother country alone supplied the colonies with the industrial products and other things they needed, and in exchange received alone, or practically alone, the raw materials, precious metals, foodstuffs, and stimulants that the colonies produced, all with national vessels and through national merchants. In this case, therefore, not only were exports to the colonies regarded as economically profitable to the mother country, but the same also held good of imports from the colonies. Accordingly, it was considered a great triumph if a country succeeded, by means of the maritime blockade, in conveying the products of enemy colonies also to its own shores, and at the same time in preventing those products from competing with the products of their own colonies on the mainland of Europe. A great many, not to say the majority, of the controversies that arose in those days regarding the matter of the commercial blockade, especially in Great Britain and America, turned precisely on the question of colonial trade, which also quantitatively played a surprisingly great part in the total commercial intercourse of the sea-trading countries, especially through the re-exportation of colonial goods that arose out of it. Thus, according to the so-called 'official values' in the statistics of trade, the British exports of foreign goods (which means substantially colonial goods) rose uninterruptedly in the course of the revolutionary wars from 21 per cent. of the total in 1792 to $36\frac{1}{4}$ per cent. in 1800. Likewise, the French re-exportation to Europe of goods from the West Indies immediately before the Revolution was greater than the whole of French exportation of domestic staple products of the textile and liquor industries. On the other hand, the transit trade of the United States in French, Spanish, and

British West Indian products increased prodigiously during the same period, representing in 1806 a value of no less than $60,000,000, or one and a half times the value of the exports of the domestic goods of the United States.[1]

## TRADING WITH THE ENEMY

Such, then, were the purposes that the policy of blockade was intended to serve. But as has already been mentioned, the curious thing about its practical application did not lie exclusively in this alteration of its objects, but also in the fact that the policy actually pursued was in reality quite different from that which held good on paper. To some extent this was true of the measures that pertained strictly to the law of war at sea, especially to blockades; but to a still greater extent it was true of trading with the enemy. The prohibition of this was regarded, especially in Great Britain, as an indispensable principle of international law and was therefore rigorously maintained on paper; and this notion was also strengthened by the desire of every country to mark the moral gulf that should separate its own subjects from the enemy, or, as the phrase ran, ' to prevent treasonable and improper intercourse '.[2] But there was not the slightest idea of carrying out this fundamental principle in practice. With almost grotesque force the contrast between theory and practice is brought out in one passage in Stephen's book in which he discusses the objection that might be raised against his pleadings in favour of measures against neutral trade, namely, that they would plunge Great Britain into war with the then neutrals and thereby impede her exports. He goes on to say :

Is it asked, ' Who would afterwards carry our manufactures to market ? ' I answer, ' Our allies, our fellow subjects, our old and new enemies themselves.' In the last war (1778–1783—when Spain and Great Britain were enemies) nothing prevented the supplying of Spanish America with British manufactures, in British bottoms, even when they

[1] Hansard, vol. IX, app., col. xv ; Levasseur, *Histoire des classes ouvrières*, &c., *avant 1789*, vol. II, p. 554 note ; Johnson and others, *op. cit.*, vol. II, p. 20.

[2] Stephen in the House of Commons, Mar. 3, 1812, Hansard, vol. XXI, p. 1136.

were liable to confiscation by both the belligerent parties for the act, but that the field of commerce was preoccupied, and the markets glutted by the importations under neutral flags.

But would I advise a toleration of these new ' modes of relieving the hostile colonies ' ?  Its toleration would not be necessary.  Even your own hostilities would not be able to overcome the expansive force of your own commerce, when delivered from the unnatural and ruinous competition, of its present privileged enemies.  You might often capture the carriers of it and condemn their cargoes ; but the effect would chiefly be to raise the price upon the enemy, and the difference would go into the purses of your [prize-taking] seamen.  The prize goods themselves, would find their way from your colonies into the hostile territories.[1]

It would be difficult to find a more typical example of the capacity to ' make the best of both worlds '.  The legal principle of prohibiting trade with the enemy was constantly maintained, while at the same time full provision was made for exports above all to the enemy, which according to the deeply rooted ideas of the time was of vital interest to the country.  The same combination of incompatible views is revealed in almost every utterance that has come down from that time ;  and when the will existed, it was not difficult to find means for its realization. One of these means was the system of licences, of which Stephen says that ' papal dispensations were not more easily obtained in the days of Luther '.  Another means was the system called ' neutralization,' whereby vessels and cargoes that in reality belonged to one or another of the belligerents were declared on sworn—that is to say, perjured—evidence, to belong to neutrals. These tactics—which, however, were sometimes turned against the belligerents themselves, and in such cases were combated both by the law courts and by the supporters of the official policy—were employed on a strictly business basis, commonly with a commission of 1–2 per cent. for the firm that handled the transaction.  Especially Emden, in East Friesland, which belonged to Prussia and was consequently neutral, was a centre for transactions of this nature, and there were loud complaints against British marine insurance firms which bound themselves,

[1] Stephen, *War in Disguise*, p. 168.

against a special premium of 1 per cent., not to urge the legally valid plea against the enemy origin of the cargoes, which by law always involved the invalidity of the insurance. Besides this, moreover, there always remained the possibility of winking at an illegal practice which there was no intention of preventing ; and it is characteristic of the situation that in the year 1794 Swedish captains openly declared to the British customs officers that their vessels were bound for a French port.

Trading with the enemy also appears as a fairly self-evident practice in nearly all accounts of the commercial conditions then prevailing. This is revealed, for instance, by the British trade statistics themselves, which show that the share of the enemy countries, France and the Netherlands (northern and southern), in the total exports of Great Britain declined only from 15 to 12 per cent. in the years 1792–1800. This, too, is conclusive evidence in support of Stephen's proposition as to the impossibility of war measures adopted by Great Britain to the end of overcoming the expansive force of her own trade.[1]

Following this hasty sketch of the general character of the maritime blockade policy of that time, it seems expedient to show in a more concrete form the development of those measures during the years from the intervention of Great Britain in the revolutionary wars in 1793 down to the Peace of Amiens in 1802. It contains, indeed, a good deal which may be of value, not only in throwing light on the general situation at that time, but also in furnishing a background for what was to come later.

---

[1] Stephen, *War in Disguise*, pp. 39, 70 *et seq.*, 169, *et al.* ; Rose, vice president of the Board of Trade in the House of Commons, March 3, 1812, Hansard, vol. XXI, p. 1122 ; Mahan, *Influence of Sea Power upon the French Revolution and Empire, 1793–1812* (London, 1893), vol. II, pp. 252 note, 309; *The Laws of England* (Halsbury ed., London, 1907), *s.v.* Aliens, vol. I, pp. 311–12 ; Wahlström, *op. cit.*, pp. 62–3. In this connexion it may not be irrelevant to refer as a parallel to a well-known passage in the *Pickwick Papers* (ch. 40) : ' What, am I to understand that these men earn a livelihood by waiting about here to perjure themselves before the judges of the land, at the rate of half a crown a crime ! ' exclaimed Mr. Pickwick, quite aghast at the disclosure. ' Why, I don't know exactly about perjury, my dear sir,' replied the little gentleman. ' Harsh word, my dear sir, very harsh word indeed ! It's a legal fiction, my dear sir, nothing more.'

## British Measures (1793–1802)

The measures adopted at the beginning of the maritime blockade in 1793 exhibit marked resemblances to the corresponding measures adopted during the recent World War, and are therefore of especial interest and importance. As early as February 14, that is to say, a fortnight after the outbreak of the war, Great Britain authorized the capture of all vessels and goods belonging to France; and in the following month she proceeded to work. On April 4 she proclaimed all her most advanced principles concerning the law of war at sea, and on June 8 she introduced the most famous of her measures, namely, the instructions of 1793, whereby fleet commanders and privateers were authorized ' to stop and detain all vessels loaded wholly or in part with corn, flour, or meal, bound to any port in France or any port occupied by the armies of France ', with the understanding that the British government would purchase the cargo with the proper allowances for freight, called ' pre-emption '. This measure took the form of a plan to starve out France. Count Axel von Fersen, the chivalrous young Swedish nobleman who, as is well known, was one of the most active allies of the French *émigrés*, had emphasized this, as early as April 29, in a letter addressed to the Regent of Sweden, Charles Duke of Södermanland; and in a notification of the measure addressed to the Baltic powers, especially one to Denmark in July, Great Britain justified her June instructions in a manner very similar to that in which the policy of starving out Germany was justified during the recent war. The notification declared that the war was being conducted in a manner contrary to the principles of international law, that France had no recognized government, and that the corn trade had been taken over by the French authorities themselves, that is to say, had become an act of the enemy's own government; and, finally, the blockade against imports was represented purely as an important means of forcing the enemy to make peace. Lars von Engeström hit the mark in describing the tendencies of that time—as also those of the

World War—when he wrote that the struggle ' had passed into a kind of political war of religion '.

A genuine blockade of the importation of foodstuffs into France might therefore have been expected, that is, a ' starving-out scheme' similar to that of the World War. In a way such a plan might even have been made to harmonize fairly well with the continental economic policy of that time, at least until the French Revolution ; for as a matter of fact, the prevailing note on the subject of foodstuffs continued to be the pre-mercantilist tendency to prevent exports, rather than the mercantilist one to encourage domestic production by hampering imports and facilitating exports. As has been already mentioned, however, Pitt's justification for the seizures was not based on this notion, but on Britain's own quite temporary need of foodstuffs— according to Lars von Engeström's statement ; [1] and evidence of how deeply rooted the notion of the inexpediency of pre-venting imports to the enemy was is furnished by the fact that the ensuing developments did not at all follow along the lines which were indicated in the first measures. Only fourteen months afterwards, on August 18, 1794, the previously cited article in the June instructions of 1793 was repealed, and this meant that the importation of corn into France was again permitted. It is true that in the following April a new attempt was made to put the instructions of 1793 into force, but this was done chiefly with the object of forcing the United States into a ratification of the celebrated Jay Treaty of 1794. That, however, wound up the whole of this episode, so that through-out the entire period of the twenty years that still remained before Europe obtained a lasting peace, not a single attempt at starving out France was made, so far as we know, nor were there any further efforts to stop her imports on the part of the power that had the command of the sea. Against only one small country, Norway, did Great Britain occasionally make use of her ability to prevent the introduction of supplies, for reasons which will be discussed in due time.

In contrast with these sporadic attempts to prevent importa-

[1] See p. 33.

tion into France, the regulation of the trade with the French and Spanish colonies continued throughout the war, that is, until the Peace of Amiens in 1802; and this became the starting-point of the events that were to take place during the period of the Continental System proper. Here, too, there was a certain amount of wavering on the part of Great Britain, but the general principles were maintained with a consistency wholly different from that shown in the other case. A beginning was made with the celebrated instructions of November 6, 1793, which aroused the particular animosity of the neutrals, especially the United States, for the reason that they prescribed the capture of all vessels carrying the products of the French colonies or conveying supplies to them. Shortly afterwards, however, these draconic orders were revoked as a concession to the United States, and their place was taken by the new instructions of January 8, 1794. These restricted the order concerning capture to vessels proceeding directly from the West Indian colonies of the enemy to a European port; and this, in turn, opened up the possibility of a so-called ' circuitous voyage ' *via* some neutral extra-European port, that is to say, primarily an American port, but also possibly a Danish or Swedish colonial port. Nevertheless, it was provided that the products of enemy colonies should have become neutral property in order to be loaded, and that blockade-running vessels, as well as vessels conveying naval stores or munitions of war to the enemy colonies, would be liable to capture. These regulations were further modified by the new instructions of January, 1798, which both abolished the requirement that the colonial goods should have become neutral property and also, and above all, permitted direct traffic to a European port, that is, a port belonging to the British Empire or to the home land of the neutral vessel. This stipulation in favour of a British port is of especial interest in that it furnishes evidence of the British design to attract to Great Britain the trade even in the products of enemy colonies. As Admiral Mahan has rightly remarked, it was an outcome of the effort characteristic of the old colonial system to create in the home country a staple or *entrepôt* for colonial goods. In point of fact, the instructions of 1798 remained in force until the termination of the revolutionary wars in 1802.[1]

In comparison with the treatment of neutral shipping in the recent war, these orders do not present a very strict appearance; for at the present time the belligerent that is dominant on the seas tries to cut off practically every sort of neutral intercourse with the enemy over such waters as it commands and even, to some extent, over other waters.   But one must not overlook the fact that privateering, which it was in many ways almost impossible to distinguish from piracy pure and simple, and even the private interests of the crews of war-ships in effecting captures, brought about an arbitrariness and a brutality in the treatment of maritime commerce which is unknown to-day. This has been copiously illustrated by the recently deceased Danish historian, Professor Edvard Holm, whose account undeniably gives one the impression that the trials and troubles of neutral trade, even during the first years of the revolutionary wars, in practice exceeded even those of the present time, even though its chances of profit, as far as we can judge, were greater. Nevertheless, the acts of the belligerents during those first years were almost deeds of mercy in comparison with what was to come;   and the new departure was the work of the new French policy.   Like most of the measures of the French revolutionary governments, the measures against maritime trade were marked by a combination of violence and impotence;   but they were so far explicable because the British application of the laws of war at sea rendered French navigation all but impossible.   As usual, the principal sufferers in the end were the neutrals, and this time the measures of violence against them were carried to the most extreme limit that had yet been reached.

---

[1] Martens, *Recueil des principaux traités* (2d ed., Göttingen, 1826), vol. v, pp. 596–604; *Annual Register*, 1793, State Papers, pp. 176 *et seq.*; Stephen, *op. cit.*, p. 175 note, 18 *et seq.*, 33;   Holm, *op. cit.*, vol. I, pp. 106–15, 171 *et seq.* ;   Mahan, *op. cit.*, vol. II. pp. 233 *et seq.* ;   also, *Sea Power in its Relations to the War of 1812* (London, 1905), vol. I, pp. 27, 89–90, 93; Wahlström, *op. cit.*, pp. 10 *et seq.*, 62–3, 99, 126; Bassett, *The Federalist System, 1789–1801*, in *The American Nation : A History* (New York and London, 1906), vol. II, pp. 122–3, 129 ; Klinckowström, *Le Comte de Fersen et la cour de France* (Stockholm, 1878), vol. II, p. 419; Lars von Engeström, *Minnen och anteckningar* (Stockholm, 1876), vol. I, pp. 235 *et seq.*

## French Measures (1793–1799)

At first the measures of France had been considerably milder than those of Great Britain; and this was natural enough in view of the fact that France stood in great need of the help of neutrals. By a law passed on May 9, 1793—that is to say, before the British instructions of June 8, but after the declaration of April 4—the Convention ordered that all neutral vessels conveying foodstuffs to an enemy port or carrying goods belonging to the enemy should be captured and conducted into a French port. Such vessels were to be fair prizes, and their cargoes were to be purchased on behalf of France. But the French purchase regulations themselves were more favourable to the neutrals than the corresponding British ones; and at the same time it was declared, in the same way as afterwards under Napoleon, that the orders would be abolished as soon as the enemy on his part granted the unrestricted importation of foodstuffs into France.

At first the practice, too, was milder on the French side. Gradually, however, French policy turned completely around; and it was not long before the new tendency acquired official form. On July 2, 1796 (Messidor 14, year IV), the Directory categorically declared in an ordinance of only a few lines that British methods were to be applied against the neutrals in every respect. The culmination, however, was reached in the notorious law of January 18, 1798 (Nivôse 29, year VI), which laid down that the nationality of a vessel should be determined by its cargo, so that if any vessel was carrying goods of any kind coming from England or its possessions, no matter who was the owner, this fact alone should justify the confiscation, not only of these goods, but also of the vessel itself and its entire cargo. Moreover, any vessel that had touched at a British port was forbidden to put in at any French port; and earlier it had already been made a practice to seize vessels bound for a British port.

It would have been difficult to go farther; and this time actions were not milder, but still more violent, than words.

From the two years or so during which the law of Nivôse was in
force come all the wildest examples of high-handed procedure
on the part of belligerents on the seas.  It was especially Scandinavian vessels that were exposed to this reign of terror, while
the only important neutral power besides Sweden and Denmark
and Norway, namely, the United States, began what was
practically a privateering war against France without any
formal declaration of war.  The French law came into force
without any preliminary warning, so that vessels which had
sailed without knowledge of its provisions fell helplessly into
the hands of captors ;  and once seized, their chances of escape
were very small indeed.  With the importance that British
industry had now acquired, in fact, it was almost impossible for
a vessel to sail without having on board some article of British
origin ;  and it was not at all necessary that these articles
should constitute its cargo, in the strict sense of the term, to
seal its fate.  A woollen blanket on the skipper's berth, a few
sacks of British coal for the ship's stove, British earthenware
used by the crew, the British metal buttons of the skipper's
coat, etc., were sufficient to lead to confiscation.  Indeed, the
old Hamburg economist Büsch gives us in one of his last
works, that bearing the exquisite title of *Ueber das Bestreben der
Völker neuerer Zeit, einander in ihrem Seehandel recht wehe zu
thun* (1800), such an example as this :  Once when a French
captor, quite exceptionally, did not succeed in finding anything
British on board a captured vessel, two of the sailors were
bribed to disclose the alleged fact that the skipper had had a pair
of English boots which he had thrown overboard on the
approach, of the captor ; and that, says Büsch, was enough to
bring about the confiscation of the cargo.[1]  In a suit against
five Danish East Indian vessels bearing rich products obviously
of Danish origin, the captors succeeded in having the cargoes
condemned on the ground that Lascars included in the crews
were British subjects ;  and in other cases vessels and cargoes
were condemned on the ground that the former had been built
in a British shipyard and had been bought after the outbreak

---

[1] Büsch, *Sämmtliche Schriften über die Handlung* (Hamburg, 1825), vol. v,
pp. 278-9.

of the war—in spite of the fact that the vessel was a French prize and had been sold to its then Danish owner by the French captor.

Justice was indeed a parody. Those who acted as judges were ordinarily the consuls in the most important haunts of the privateers, with whom they often acted in collusion ; nay, some of them were themselves ex-privateers or even still commercially interested in the captures—an example which one of Napoleon's governors was destined to follow in the fullness of time.[1] The abuses increased to such an extent that they completely outgrew the control of the weak government of the Directory. On one occasion, for example, Reubell, one of the members of the Directory, informed the Danish minister in Paris that a French prize court had condemned and caused to be sold for the benefit of the captor, a Swedish vessel with a cargo destined for the French government itself. Moreover, the privateers worked into each other's hands in various ways. Thus one of them might rob a neutral vessel of its ship's papers in order that another might seize it with impunity ; for without papers its condemnation was certain.

What is peculiar in the policy of the Directory, and at the same time significant for the ensuing developments, is the fact that it had the effect of a French self-blockade. It is indeed manifest, as Admiral Mahan points out, that the power which was excluded from the sea was the one which really had need of the neutrals for the procurement of its supplies, and which, therefore, from a purely material point of view at least, had the most to lose by a course of violent action against them. ' Every blow against a neutral,' he says, ' was really, even though not seemingly, a blow for Great Britain.' During the period of scarcely two years in which the law of Nivôse was in force, it practically did away with that neutral trade and navigation with France which was to some extent independent of Great Britain. Neutral vessels, in fact, did not venture there, so that even during the year 1798 their coasting trade in France declined by

[1] *Correspondance de Napoléon Ier* (Paris, 1858–1869), no. 18,491 (Feb. 8, 1812).

two-thirds and their foreign trade with the same country by one-fourth. Moreover, the obstacles that French captures placed in the way of free navigation brought it about that neutrals in general were pushed back ; and this, of course, was an advantage to Great Britain, which was enabled by her command of the sea to protect her trading vessels by means of convoys. The latter obstacle in the way of neutral shipping was of less importance than the former, however, because the two neutral Scandinavian states also fitted out convoys in common on the basis of the League of Armed Neutrality of 1794. This had excellent commercial results, at least for Denmark, but the French policy caused it to be of very little benefit to France. Nor did the latter country receive any compensations whatever for its own shipping, for according to the Directory's own declaration, in 1799, the British blockade had been maintained so strictly that not a single vessel was sailing the seas under a French flag.

It was therefore quite natural that Napoleon, as early as December, 1799, that is, shortly after his accession to power, should repeal, or cause to be repealed, the law of Nivôse and revive the more moderate regulations of 1778 (law of Frimaire 23 and ordinance of Frimaire 29, year VIII) ; and at the beginning of the following year he did away with some of the worst abuses in the administration of prize-court justice by instituting a Supreme Prize Court in Paris. In principle, however, his later policy was to be a faithful reflection of that of the Directory, as will be shown in due course.[1]

[1] *Lois et actes*, &c., vol. vii, pp. 52–3 ; *Bulletin des lois*, &c., 2d ser., bull. 178, no. 1,678 ; bull. 235, no. 2,118 ; Martens, *op. cit.*, 2d ed., vol. v, pp. 388–9, 398–9 ; vol. vi, pp. 743–4 ; Büsch, *op. cit.*, chs. viii–ix ; Holm, *op. cit.*, vol. i, pp. 69, 175–6, 195, 222 *et seq.*, 232–50, 258, 266–7, 307, 313 ; Mahan, *Influence of Sea Power*, &c., vol. ii, pp. 219–20, 243 *et seq.*, 255 *et seq.* ; Bassett, *op. cit.*, pp. 220–21. For the whole of this part of the subject, cf. also Söderqvist, *op. cit.*, pp. 18–49 ; *Report of the Fourth Special Committee of the Swedish Second Chamber for 1902*, no. 8, pp. 54–61 ; *The Armed Neutralities of 1780 and 1800*, edited by James Brown Scott (Carnegie Endowment for International Peace, Division of International Law. New York, 1918) ; Hugo Larsson, *Sveriges deltagande i den väpnade neutraliteten, 1800–1801* (Lund, 1888) ; Clason, *Gustaf IV Adolf och den europeiska krisen under Napoleon* (Stockholm, 1913).

# CHAPTER III
## CONTINENTAL BLOCKADE

THE Continental System originated, therefore, on the one side, in a blockade that followed the general lines of mercantilist trade policy, especially on the part of France, and, on the other side, in a maritime blockade dominated by the same ideas which proceeded from Great Britain but was imitated in still more intensified forms by France, where, owing to the British mastery of the seas, it acquired the character of a self-blockade. To complete the antecedent conditions of the Continental System, consequently, there is only one feature lacking; but it is the feature which has given the policy itself its name, that is, the combination of the European countries to the exclusion of Great Britain, which, supposing that the same conditions held good as before, means a common self-blockade of the Continent as against Great Britain.

This feature did not become significant until the time of Napoleon, for until then the external means of exercising power, as well as the great political personality it demanded, were still lacking; but recent Napoleonic research has taken great pains to demonstrate that it was significant even during the preceding period. From the beginning of history the community of nations has always looked upon commercial countries with a certain jealousy and suspicion; and in this respect, as has already been said,[1] *perfide Albion* inherited the feeling which had once been fostered against its rival, the United Netherlands. This feeling was further intensified by the unpalatable experiences of both enemies and neutrals during the incessant wars, on account of Great Britain's ruthlessly applied methods of naval warfare. There is nothing surprising, therefore, in the fact that plans were formed for the exclusion of Great Britain. What is remarkable, on the contrary, is the fact that nobody, so far as is known, has yet succeeded in showing the existence of any

[1] See p. 32.

such plans other than those emanating directly or indirectly from French sources.   Examples of this kind have a great interest of their own ; but they are too patent to call for any detailed investigation.

As early as 1747 we know that proposals were brought forward in the French *Bureau de Commerce* to unite France, the Hanse Towns, Prussia, and the Scandinavian powers for the purpose of crushing the maritime power of Great Britain— probably a mere incident in the long-standing Anglo-French duel.[1]   But it was not until after and in consequence of the outbreak of war between Great Britain and France in 1793 that this tendency acquired any lasting significance.   The attitude took one or another of two forms, according to circumstances : either all the continental countries were regarded as commercially dependent on England, and therefore as necessary objectives in the military and economic war waged by the French republic against its foremost enemy ; or else, contrariwise, they all had the same interest in crushing the power of England and were thus the natural allies of France.

The attitude appears in the first of these two forms in a great speech which the Girondist naval officer, Kersaint, delivered in the Convention on January 1, 1793—that is to say, before the outbreak of war—and in which he exhorted his countrymen, with the usual revolutionary eloquence, to face the struggle with the whole world.   In his opinion, France alone had her own industry and wealth, while Spain, Portugal, Holland, and the Italian republics worked largely with British capital and British goods.   The New World and Asia, he said, were likewise economically dependent on Great Britain ; nay, even the trade of Denmark (*i.e.*, Norway), Sweden, and Russia in naval stores was made possible by the co-operation of British capitalists.   'One cannot find on the face of the globe,' he declared, ' any lucrative branch of trade which has not been exploited to the profit of that essentially shop-keeping people.' In consequence of this, he argued, the injuries inflicted on the states of the Continent fell finally on Great Britain, for whose

[1] Schmidt, *Le Grand-duché de Berg*, p. 418.

benefit that economic life was carried on, a view which Napoleon was afterwards destined to push to the extreme. Asia, Portugal, and Spain were regarded by Kersaint as the most important markets for British industry, and they were to be closed to Great Britain by being opened to the rest of the world ; Lisbon and Brazil were to be assailed ; support was to be given to the old adversary of the British in India, Tippoo Sahib, &c.[1]

Thus Kersaint not only passed over the United States, the undiminished importance of which for British trade does not appear to have been fully recognized in France, but also disregarded Germany and the European mainland proper, as distinguished from the coastal and peninsular fringes referred to above. As a rule, however, Germany was a factor of considerable importance in these efforts. To begin with, the prohibition of 1796 against British goods was extended in March, 1798, to the left shore of the Rhine, which was then united with the French republic ; and this prohibition was applied with a strictness which, in an account of the situation written in 1798 and ascribed to Napoleon, was alleged to presage (*ébaucher*) the Continental System.[2] For the rest, it was mainly a matter of paper projects and pious wishes, not of effective measures, and the majority of them concerned the German North Sea littoral. Here, as a rule, it was the other side of the policy that was turned outwards, that is, the common interests of all the continental states against Great Britain. A writer of German birth, Ch. Theremin, who was later to serve Napoleon in various posts in Germany, published in Paris in the year III (1794-5) a pamphlet with the significant title *Intérêts des puissances continentales relativement à l'Angleterre*, in which the afterwards well-known doctrine of the natural and inevitable conflict between Great Britain and the Continent was developed at length, and the hostility of the other continental states to France was shown consequently to be contrary to their

---

[1] *Le Moniteur*, Jan. 3, 1793 ; Sorel, *op. cit.*, vol. III, pp. 244-5.

[2] *Commentaires de Napoléon Ier* (Paris, 1867), vol. III, p. 413. As the essay is not included in the *Correspondance*, the authorship of the Emperor does not appear to be above doubt.

own best interests. A year or two later, at the beginning of the
Congress of Rastadt in 1797, plans were made to bar the mouths
of the Elbe and the Weser to the British ; and at the same time
it was proposed, in a paper now preserved in the archives of the
French Foreign Office, that Hanover and Hamburg should be
transformed into a republic allied with France, which afterwards was to be joined with the great North German rivers by
an extensive system of canals. Aside from its strategical
advantages, it was thought that this would establish a commercial combination which would lead to increased sales for French
goods and to an embargo on British industrial products. In
the same year (1797) this project called forth a refutation
published by an anonymous German ' citizen of the world ',
who turned out to be a true prophet in his exposition of the
futility of all efforts to shut out the British. In his opinion,
which subsequent experience was destined fully to confirm,
the British, under the protection of Heligoland, would divert
their trade to Tönning in Holstein and thereby ruin Hamburg
and Bremen. He also reminded his readers that the pro-
hibitory measures of the French republic against British goods
had so far led to nothing more than an immense system of
smuggling.

It was precisely Hamburg that was the central point of the
early French efforts to exclude England. The French envoy
there, Reinhard, the son of a Swabian clergyman, spoke as
early as 1796 of the necessity of preventing the importation of
British goods, the exclusion of which from the French market
alone he considered at that time sufficient to ruin England.
At the beginning of 1798, however, shortly before his removal
to Tuscany, Reinhard—chiefly, it is true, in order to protect
the Hanse Towns, the prosperity of which he had several
reasons to promote—emphasized the necessity of combining
all the continental states in such a policy of exclusion. That
object would be attained through the active co-operation of
Denmark and Prussia with the passive support of Russia ; but
that would not be possible so long as only the Hanse Towns
took part, for in that case the goods might come in across

Holstein, that is to say, from the Danish side, through Altona, which was quite close to Hamburg.

About the time of Reinhard's departure, in 1798, there arrived in Hamburg an emissary from the Directory's Minister of Police charged with the mission of combining the many French republicans there in the adoption of measures against British trade. This agitator, a well-known Jacobin named Léonard Bourdon, aroused the horror of the Hamburg city fathers by assembling his fellow countrymen and exhorting them to boycott British goods and also to act as spies upon the commercial activities of Great Britain. Moreover, the draconic French prohibitions on the importation of British goods, to which we have already referred,[1] had effect outside the boundaries of France. Thus Reinhard speaks of the consternation that the prohibitions of 1796 aroused in the Hanse Towns, which had been wont to supply France with those goods.[2]

The importance, for the general policy of the French revolutionary governments, of all of these plans for the exclusion of Great Britain from the European Continent, forms, as one may easily surmise, a principal theme in Sorel's book.[3] He seeks to show that the French programme of foreign policy—the ' natural frontiers ' (the Atlantic Ocean, the Rhine, the Alps, and the Pyrenees)—necessarily involved a recognition of these conquests on the part of all other powers, and that the acquiescence of Great Britain could not be enforced except by attacks on her trade ; and that this, in its turn, could be effected only by a continental blockade, ' a formidable and hyperbolical measure, out of all proportion to the object that necessitates it, but nevertheless the only one that can be adopted '. One

[1] See pp. 31–32.
[2] Zeyss, *Die Entstehung der Handelskammern und die Industrie am Niederrhein während der französischen Herrschaft* (Leipzig, 1907), p. 94 ; Schmidt, *Le Grand-duché de Berg*, pp. 339 *et seq.* ; Servières, *L'Allemagne française sous Napoléon Ier* (Paris, 1904), pp. 128–9; Wohlwill, *Neuere Geschichte der Freien und Hansestadt Hamburg insbesondere von 1789 bis 1815*, in *Allgemeine Staaten-Geschichte* (Gotha, 1914), Abt. III, Werk x, pp. 181 *et seq.*, 197, 202 note 2 ; also, *Frankreich und Norddeutschland von 1795 bis 1800*, in *Historische Zeitschrift* (1883), pp. 424–5.
[3] Sorel, *op. cit.*, vol. IV (1892), pp. 176, 183, 213, 266 *et seq.*, 359, 387 *et seq.*, 392, 464 ; vol. v (1903), p. 102.

need not accept the logic of this argument as irrefutable—the point about the imperative necessity of British recognition of the new conquests seems particularly weak—to admit that such thoughts must have occupied the minds of the French politicians who, under various names, guided the destinies of France during the six or seven years that intervened between the outbreak of war in 1793 and Bonaparte's definitive accession to power in 1799. There can be no doubt, therefore, that notions of that character had lain at the foundation of the majority of the legislative measures previously treated. Thus Lecouteulx, the representative who in 1796 reported to the *Conseil des Anciens* upon the legislative proposal for the exclusion of British goods, justified the measure on the ground that the flags of France and her allies floated from Emden to Trieste, and that almost all the ports on the coasts of the European ocean were closed to Great Britain. Consequently, he concluded, ' we must put an end to the voluntary subsidies which consumers of British goods are paying to that country '.[1]

With regard to foreign policy proper, Sorel has brought forward a multitude of examples bearing witness to the same tendency, some of the more significant of which may be mentioned here. Thus about 1794 Caillard, a French diplomatist, proposed that the Continent should be closed by a series of alliances. ' From the Tagus to the Elbe,' he declared, ' there is no point on the mainland where the British should be allowed to set foot.' In 1795 efforts were made to hand Portugal over to Spain, in order thereby ' to deprive England of one of her most valuable provinces '; and the closing of the continental ports was now to affect the whole coastline from Gibraltar to the island of Texel, outside the Zuider Zee. The same tendencies, moreover, determined French policy with regard to Naples and Belgium. In the early part of 1797 Haugwitz, the Prussian

---

[1] *Le Moniteur*, Nov. 4, 1796; Mahan, *Influence of Sea Power*, &c., vol. II, pp. 248 *et seq.* Dupont de Nemours combated the proposal, as might have been expected of an orthodox economist; but when the President announced that the motion of Lecouteulx had been carried another member exclaimed : ' Nous sommes sauvés ! ' *Le Moniteur*, Nov. 6 (Brumaire 16).

foreign minister, wrote in a memorandum intended for the Russian government that there could be no doubt as to the intention of the Directory to seize the coast of the North Sea as far as the mouth of the Elbe, as its plans were known to be to isolate England, separate her from the Continent and exclude her shipping from the ports of the Mediterranean, the Atlantic and the North Sea. About the same time the American minister in London reported—incorrectly at the time, it is true, but evidently in accord with current rumours—that France had demanded the cessation of trade between the Hanse Towns and England and, its demand having been refused, had recalled its minister there.[1] The Baltic Sea was also to be closed to the British in 1795 by playing Sweden and Denmark against Russia, which for the moment was on friendly terms with Great Britain. But the most characteristic example of all these forerunners to the policy of Napoleon can be found in the instructions (cited by Sorel) to the French envoy at The Hague, dated Fructidor 6 and 7, year III (August 23-4, 1795). This deserves to be cited verbatim :

> The alliance with Holland offers the most important result of all, namely, to exclude the British from the Continent, to shut them out in war time from Bayonne to north of Friesland and from access to the Baltic and North Seas. The trade with the interior of Germany will then return to its natural channels. . . . Deprived of these immense markets, harassed by revolts and internal disturbances which will be the consequence, England will have great embarrassments with her colonial and Asiatic goods. These goods, being unsaleable, will fall to low prices, and the English will find themselves vanquished by excess (*vaincus par l'abondance*), just as they had wished to vanquish the French by shortage.

In this utterance the familiar policy of strangling exports finds clear expression, and its agreement with the whole of Napoleon's motives for the Continental System is very striking.

---

[1] *Preussen und Frankreich von 1795 bis 1807*, in *Publicationen aus den K. Preussischen Staatsarchiven*, VIII (Bailleu ed., Leipzig, 1881), vol. I, p. 113 ; Mahan, *Influence of Sea Power*, &c., vol. II, pp. 247-8. Admiral Mahan, however, appears to believe in the truth of this altogether unfounded rumour, for the facts of which cf. Wohlwill, *Neuere Geschichte*, &c., pp. 161, 188-9.

An excellent parallel, for instance, is exhibited by the boastful survey that was laid before the *Corps législatif* in 1807.[1] But this process of thought must also be examined in connexion with the views of the French revolutionaries, afterwards taken over by Napoleon, as to the implications and foundations of the economic strength of Great Britain; and the instructions of 1795 thus form a convenient transition to that instructive chapter.

[1] See *infra*, p. 74.

# CHAPTER IV

## ECONOMIC POSITION OF GREAT BRITAIN

'THE Causes of the Rise and Decline of Cities, Countries, and Republics,' *Die Ursachen des Auff und Abnehmens der Städt, Länder und Republicken*—to quote the title of a book by the German mercantilist, Johann Joachim Becher—have always formed, and still form, a very obscure chapter in economic history, and one which has been far from fully elucidated by economic inquiry. During the period with which we are now concerned the stability of the position of England as the leading maritime and colonial nation, after the relative decline of the Netherlands, formed a constant source of speculation and doubt. It was perhaps natural that this mistrust was most prevalent in French circles, and particularly among the French revolutionaries; for to those who had been trained in the school of Rousseau it was necessarily quite obvious that an organization so completely detached from the land was unnatural and, therefore, not durable—all the more so for the reason that physiocracy, so far as its influence was to be taken into account at all, might also lead to the same conclusions. The hollowness of the English economic system is also the burden of the often quoted official speech in which Brissot, the leader of the Girondists, on January 12, 1793, laid before the National Convention the whole argument in favour of a war with England, in terms which were to be re-embodied in the final declaration of war. ' We must tear asunder,' he declared, ' the veil that envelops the imposing colossus of England. . . . When the well-informed observer regards this imposing scaffold of English greatness, he is able to penetrate to its internal vacuity. . . . Say, then, if it will not be an easy matter to overturn a power whose colossal stature betrays its weakness and calls for its overthrow.' [1]

[1] *Le Moniteur*, Jan. 15, 1793.

This representation of 'perfidious Albion' as a colossus with feet of clay is of frequent occurrence, whether it signifies merely what people wished or what they actually believed, or—what is most likely—something betwixt and between.   In Napoleon, too, it was based on a general economic conception, namely, that a country's trade is of slight value in comparison with its industry and agriculture; and this could not fail to react on his conception of the strength of the foremost commercial nation.   The well-known French chemist, Jean Antoine Chaptal, Minister of the Interior under the Consulate, and afterwards closely connected with the industrial policy of the Empire, describes in his memoirs Napoleon's dislike of merchants, who only exchanged goods, he said, while manufacturers produced them, and who with a turnover of a million gave employment to only two or three assistants, while manufacturers with the same turnover supported five or six hundred families.   And that Chaptal is here correctly reporting Napoleon's conception—which, in that case, would not greatly diverge from that which is still popular—seems all the more probable when one considers the perfect coolness with which the Emperor from the very first prophesied that the Continental System would ruin, under his direct or indirect rule, such commercial towns as Lyons, Amsterdam, and Rotterdam.[1]

## BRITISH NATIONAL DEBT

But the belief in the instability of the position of Great Britain arose not only from general economic conceptions of this nature, but also from numerous actual conditions and developments which could not but denote the beginnings of economic decay.   It cannot be sufficiently emphasized how long people had believed they had seen signs of this.   One of the most important of these signs was the rapid increase in the British national debt during the time with which we are concerned—especially when considered in the light of the generally

[1] Chaptal, *Mes souvenirs sur Napoléon* (Paris, 1893, but written shortly after 1815), pp. 274–9; *Lettres inédites de Napoléon Ier* (Lecestre ed., Paris, 1897), no. 134.

current notion that such a development must inevitably lead to national bankruptcy.  The economic literature of England herself during the eighteenth century is full of Kassandra-like prophecies as to the impending ruin of the state owing to the augmentation of its liabilities.  In fact, Lord Macaulay says in a well-known passage that, with the exception of Burke, no author since the founding of the English debt had perceived the security which the general economic development of the country provided against these dangers.  Especially interesting in this connexion is Adam Smith's gloomy representation of the state of affairs, the view of the European national debts presented in the *Wealth of Nations* being throughout remarkably pessimistic for so optimistic a writer.  In Adam Smith's opinion, the funded debts ' will in the long run probably ruin all the great nations of Europe ', as they had already steadily weakened them.  And even though he believes that England, owing to her better system of taxation, is in a better position than most countries to stand the strain, he warns his readers ' not even to be too confident that she could support, without great distress, a burden a little greater than what has already been laid upon her '.

When this was written, in 1775, the funded British debt was £124,000,000, and the war with the American colonies, which intervened between the first and third editions of the *Wealth of Nations*, served nearly to double that amount.  When Great Britain plunged into the revolutionary wars at the beginning of 1793, in fact, her national debt amounted to £230,000,000. Afterwards the war was financed to such an extent by means of loans that the funded debt for Great Britain and Ireland at the time of the Peace of Amiens, in 1802, had risen to what was, for the conditions of that time, the truly astounding sum of £507,000,000—a figure the significance of which is perhaps best made clear when one reflects that the funded debt of England at the outbreak of the World War in 1914 amounted to no more than £587,000,000.  Under these circumstances Adam Smith's warning could not fail to make an impression ; and indeed we find it employed as a main weapon against Great Britain in a pamphlet published in 1796 with the significant title, *The Decline and Fall of the English System of Finance*. The author was the well-known republican and free-thinker, Thomas Paine, who had some years previously fled to France and become a member of the National Convention. In the French journalism of the period dealing with this subject, which has been sketched by an English woman historian, Miss Audrey Cunningham, an impending British state bankruptcy figures as a fairly self-evident prospect in the future. This is especially the case in a very measured paper, *Des finances de l'Angleterre*, written in 1803 by the French *littérateur*, Henri Lasalle, and reproduced by Miss Cunningham *in extenso*.[1]

It is true that we must beware of overestimating the importance of these views. It would be hard to discover, as a matter of fact, anything more hopelessly shattered than the finances of France herself during the Revolution; and her capacity to develop a great military power, despite the most thorough-going national bankruptcy, might rather be expected to have implanted doubts as to far-reaching political consequences arising from financial difficulties. But the thoughts of leading French statesmen did not move in that direction. Whether because of sincere conviction or because of the effect on public opinion, therefore, it became in due time an axiom of Napoleon that his finances both in war and in peace must be managed as much as possible without loans; and his ministers of finance, greatly against their will, had consequently to resort to the most dubious means of raising funds—not only increasing the annual deficits in the national budget, but also sanctioning measures of downright dishonesty against the purveyors to the state—rather than negotiate public loans. Thus the accumulation of debt represented to Napoleon, at least officially, the one great danger to a state's existence.

---

[1] Macaulay, *History of England* (1st ed., London, 1855), vol. IV, ch. XIX, pp. 327–9; Burke, *Observations on a late publication intituled ' The Present State of the Nation '* (1769); Adam Smith, *op. cit.*, vol. II, pp. 396, 407–8, 414–15; *The National Debt, 1786–1890* (Blue Book, C. 9010, London, 1891), p. 72; Kiesselbach, *op. cit.*, p. 70 note; Miss Cunningham, *British Credit in the Last Napoleonic War* (Cambridge, 1910), pp. 17–18, 27 *et seq.*

From the pedestal of public financial virtue he could then condemn the heavily indebted Great Britain ; and he naturally did not neglect the opportunity to do so.

But the belief in the dangers of piling up debt were scarcely due to this contrast alone, the deceptiveness of which can hardly have escaped Napoleon's notice. It was also rooted, we may be sure, in a deeper conviction, namely, in the notion of the artificiality, the unnaturalness, of the economic system of Great Britain, in comparison with the well-grounded prosperity of France. Especially typical of the French view is a passage in Brissot's previously cited speech, in which he says that England had no security—' not a single hypothec '—to offer for her loans, while France, to begin with, had three milliards in properties recovered by the Crown, as well as in the riches of the land and of industry, ' the enormous resources which have long since been consumed by the claims of British ministers '. The fact that these ' hypothecs ', which formed the guaranty of the French paper currency (*assignats*), had already, at the time of Brissot's speech, allowed the currency to decline to one-half of its nominal value, and did not prevent it from sinking to less than one three-hundredth thereof, did not serve to destroy the belief in their importance for the national credit. The intangibility of a credit system like that of Great Britain caused French observers quite honestly to doubt its staying power ; and, as usual, this held good of Napoleon quite as much as of the revolutionary politicians. As a matter of fact, Napoleon's amateurishness in dealing with matters of credit is revealed in practically every line he wrote on that subject and is also confirmed by the evidence of the people around him.[1]

---

[1] *Correspondance* : Communications as regards Finances and the Banque de France ; *e. g.*, on the former, no. 21,020 (Dec. 19, 1813) ; on the latter, no. 6,040 (Apr. 15, 1802), no. 14,305 (Sept. 8, 1808), nos. 16,438, 16,448, 16,471 (May 5, 9, 15, 1810) ; Mollien, *Mémoires d'un ministre du trésor public, 1780–1815* (Gomel ed., Paris, 1898), vol. ii, pp. 411–33, 465 *et seq.*, *et al.* Less weighty in this connexion are the utterances of the great speculator Ouvrard, *Mémoires sur sa vie et ses diverses opérations financières* (Paris, 1827), vol. i, pp. 73, 135, 195, 201 ; G. Weill, *Le financier Ouvrard*, in *Revue Historique* (Paris, 1918), vol. 127, p. 47 ; Sorel, *op. cit.*) vol. vi, pp. 212, 242.

### British Credit System

To all this, however, must be added the fact that there were not lacking signs calculated to arouse genuine doubts, even in fairly penetrating observers, as to the durability of the British system of credit.  The main cause of this was the Bank Restriction Act of 1797, whereby the Bank of England was released from the obligation to redeem its notes, an obligation which it did not resume for a period of twenty-two years.  Thus Great Britain had a paper currency throughout the whole of the revolutionary and the Napoleonic periods.  That this was a great and unexpected blow, especially for admirers of the British credit system, is fully substantiated by what Mollien, Napoleon's future minister of finance, writes about the matter in his *Mémoires d'un ministre du trésor public*.  The fact is that Mollien, through impressions received partly from Turgot's most faithful collaborator, Malesherbes, and partly from his father, a French manufacturer, was entirely dominated by economic liberalism, and that to a far greater extent in the English form, as embodied in Adam Smith, than in the French form as embodied in physiocracy.  In his memoirs, which were begun in 1817, but which were founded, according to his own statement, on almost daily jottings, he refers to the strong impression which the British Bank Restriction Act had made on him when he was a man of forty and experienced both as a financial official and as a practical manufacturer.  Inasmuch as the Bank of England was solvent, he believed that it was in a position to meet its liabilities without loss to its creditors ; but in that case, he says, its notes would decline in value, the British Exchequer would have to close, &c. ;  and he adds : ' Those who have long prophesied disturbances and ruin for England have never had greater reasons for their gloomy forebodings.'  The remarkableness of the situation made such an impression on Mollien that at the close of the following year he went so far as to make a flying journey of observation to the enemy's territory, *via* Germany, with the *Wealth of Nations* as his only companion.[1]

[1] Mollien, *op. cit.*, vol. I, pp. 185 *et seq.*, &c.

During the first decade of the British paper currency, that is, from 1797 to about 1808, the depreciation of the bank-notes, as measured by the price of bullion and the rates of foreign exchange, was only intermittently (principally in the years 1800–2) of any very great importance. During that period, therefore, there was no great danger to be seen in the irredeemability of the notes, and least of all any danger to the public finances of Great Britain or to her credit system in general. But ideas on this subject being as thoroughly misty as they were, it is perhaps almost natural that the situation should have been misunderstood. In Great Britain not only the politicians, but also the bankers and business men, obstinately refused to recognize any real depreciation of the notes, even when it became, in the course of time, very considerable. In France, on the other hand, the people, under the influence of the woful history and far-reaching injuries done by their own *assignats*, saw a peril overhanging England in the mere existence of an irredeemable paper currency. The contemporary literature previously cited [1] abounds with such views; and during his reign Napoleon never failed to boast it as absolutely inconceivable that a government so extremely well organized as his should ever have to fall back upon such a disastrous expedient as the use of paper money, ' the greatest foe to the social order (*l'ordre social*),' of which ' the history of all times confirms that its fatal experiences occur only under emasculated governments '.[2]

But all this could at the most show the weakness of the economic position of Great Britain, and thus inspire a general hope of success in the struggle against such an enemy. It had apparently no direct connexion with that special kind of tactics in commercial war which is called continental blockade. Such a connexion does not appear until we come to consider the importance that the trade of Great Britain, and especially her exports to the Continent, were regarded as having for her credit system, and in general the conception of the effect of the continental connexions on British currency.

[1] See p. 62.
[2] *Correspondance*, nos. 9,929 (Mar. 5, 1806), 14,413 (Oct. 25, 1808), 21,020 (Dec. 19, 1813), &c.

In this respect, too, Kersaint's previously cited speech of January 1, 1793, is significant, as was pointed out as far back as 1850 by the first historian of the Continental System, Kiesselbach, and has been emphasized in our own time by the English historian, Dr. J. Holland Rose. 'The credit of England', says Kersaint, 'rests on fictitious riches. The real riches of that people are scattered everywhere and essentially mobile. On her own soil the national wealth of England is to be found almost exclusively in her Bank, and the whole of that structure is supported by the prodigious activity of her maritime commerce.' With such an idea it was evidently easy to arrive at the thought of ruining the whole credit system of England by an attack on her trade. The same line of thought—the dependence of the credit system on foreign trade—is followed more completely in several papers of French authorship referred to by Kiesselbach and made the subject of an interesting investigation by Miss Cunningham. The writer was a Chevalier De Guer (or Deguer), who had gone to England as a Royalist *émigré* and had there made a special study of the British system of finance. He is of especial interest in this connexion, for the reason that Napoleon, in a letter of 1803, expresses great satisfaction with his work, and desires from him a more detailed account of the position of British finances. On the whole, he regarded that system as well worthy of imitation, even as regards the circulation of bank-notes, but at the same time he believed that it had certain weak points. He brought out his results, for the enlightenment of his countrymen, especially in a paper entitled *Essai sur le crédit commercial comme moyen de circulation*, which was originally printed in Hamburg in 1801, but was afterwards reprinted in France, and also in other articles, one of which Napoleon caused to be inserted in his official organ, *Le Moniteur*, for 1803.

The discussions in question were connected especially with the questions of the gold reserve of the Bank of England and the British rates of exchange; and these connexions are of great interest here.  As every one knows, Great Britain supported the struggle of the Continental powers against France by means of subsidies of varying magnitude.  From the beginning of the revolutionary wars down to the Peace of Amiens in 1802, the sum total of these subsidies, according to the official statement, amounted to about £14,300,000, including one loan of £4,600,000 to the Roman Emperor in 1795.  The total amount of extra-ordinary payments on the Continent, however, was much larger than that, exceeding £41,000,000 for the three years 1794–6 alone.  The ability of Great Britain to continue these subsidies during the later phase of the Napoleonic wars, supplemented by her ability to maintain her own troops on the mainland, was manifestly one of the points in the economic position of Great Britain which, politically speaking, was bound to take a fore-most place in the eyes of the French statesmen.  It was impor-tant, therefore, to see how strong the connexion of those sub-sidies was with the British system of credit.[1]

In this respect, also, Adam Smith's representation of the case is highly illuminative.  In his famous criticism of the mer-cantile system as he conceived it, he is led to discuss the question—which is also well known in connexion with the recent war—as to the importance of gold reserves for carrying on war and consequently also as to their necessity for British payments on the Continent.  He thus gets an opportunity to show that the expenses of war are defrayed ' not with gold and silver, but with consumable goods ', and that these goods may be acquired by exporting from the belligerent country some

---

[1] Rose, *Napoleon and British Commerce* (1893), reprinted in *Napoleonic Studies* (London, 1904), p. 167; also in his chapter on ' The Continental System ' in *The Cambridge Modern History* (Cambridge, 1906), vol. IX, p. 363; *Correspondance*, no. 6,611; Kiesselbach, *op. cit.*, ch. III; Miss Cunningham, *op. cit.*, ch. IV; Porter, *The Progress of the Nation* (new ed., London, 1851), sec. IV, ch. IV, p. 507 (on the basis of a return to the British Parliament in 1815); Tooke, *A History of Prices from 1793 to 1837* (London, 1838), vol. I, pp. 208–9; Hawtrey, *The Bank Restriction of 1797* in the *Economic Journal* (1918), vol. XVIII, pp. 52 *et seq.*, rept. in *Currency and Credit* (London, 1919). ch. XVI.  The figures of Mr. Hawtrey (p. 56) agree with those of Tooke, if they are taken to include the loan to the Emperor, though they are said to exclude it.  The total of Tooke (£42,174,556) is wrong by one million, accord-ing to his own figures.  I have followed him with the necessary correction, not having had access to the *Parliamentary Paper* from which he secured his data.

part either of 'its accumulated gold and silver', or of 'the annual produce of its manufactures', or of 'its annual rude produce'. After a clear discussion of the first of these alternatives, he lays it down that 'the enormous expense of the late war (Seven Years War) must have been chiefly defrayed, not by the exportation of gold and silver, but by that of British commodities of some kind or other '; and he makes the weighty observation that, as a consequence of this, the exports of Great Britain had been unusually great during the war, without yielding any corresponding imports in return. But in so far as payment for the continental war was effected by means of precious metals, 'the money of the great mercantile republic,' those metals must also have been purchased with British export goods, since neither the accumulated bullion reserves nor the annual production of gold and silver was anything like sufficient to cover the huge sums in question. In general, therefore, he concludes that it is the exports of England that enable her to wage war on the Continent, and chiefly the exports of finer and more fully manufactured industrial articles, which are able to bear high transportation charges. 'A country whose industry produces a great annual surplus of such manufactures, which are usually exported to foreign countries, may carry on for many years a very expensive foreign war, without exporting any considerable quantity of gold and silver, or even having any such quantity to export.' Adam Smith also describes how this works out in practice. The government arranges with a merchant to remit the necessary supplies to the theatre of war, and the merchant, in order to establish a claim there, sends out goods either to that country or to another country where he can buy a draft on the former.[1]

To what extent this in itself absolutely conclusive statement—the capacity of which to throw light on the Continental System has not, to my knowledge, been observed—rightly leads to the conclusion that the exports of Great Britain were a necessary pre-condition for her capacity to carry on a war against France on the mainland, is a question which must be

[1] Adam Smith, *op. cit.*, vol. I, pp. 407–11.

entirely reserved for later discussion.[1]  The only thing it is
necessary to point out here is how very obvious such a consequence must have seemed.  In De Guer's writings, as summarized by Miss Cunningham, that conclusion is reached without
reference to Adam Smith, it is true, perhaps without his being
known and, in any case, without any of his lucidity of thought.
De Guer points out that, when war was waged in Westphalia or
the Netherlands a hundred years earlier, as in Marlborough's
time, England had no difficulty either in providing her own
troops with what they required or in paying subsidies, for she
could send goods there and thereby obtain balances to her credit
on the spot.  But as the Belgian ports had now been closed,
and the theatre of war had also been moved to the Upper Rhine
and the Danube, great credit difficulties had arisen in the paying
of subsidies.  Thus De Guer's way of putting things might
inspire still greater hopes than that of Adam Smith as to the
difficulty of maintaining the continental war if the exports of
the subsidizing power were cut off from the Continent.  Indeed,
the French *littérateur* seems to have simplified the problem to
the extent of having left out of account what is called ' triangular
trade ', which means that the exports to one country are used
in order to buy drafts on, *i.e.*, to pay debts to, another country.
With such a conception the mere closing of the Continent might
seem sufficient for the purpose, even if British trade as a whole
were left undisturbed.

In his practical conclusions De Guer approaches the view
that Adam Smith undertook to controvert.  When England
cannot pay subsidies by exporting goods abroad, the consequences, in De Guer's opinion, will be one or the other of the
following : either she must export gold ; and with the great
circulation of paper currency within the country, as contrasted
with the small increase of its supplies of metallic currency, this
exposes all the note-issuing banks to the danger of collapse ;
or, on the other hand, she must neglect to export precious
metals ; and as she has not sufficiently large balances to her
credit on the Continent to correspond with her payment of

[1] See pt. IV, ch. IV.

subsidies, the rates of exchange will then go against her to such an extent as to be ruinous to her trade.  As usual, external phenomena, more or less correctly conceived, here affected the train of thought.  There had been a heavy decline in the metallic reserves of the Bank of England (almost down to £1,000,000) which had led to its suspending payments in February 1797 ; and the attention excited by this event seems to have over- shadowed the fact that the reserves only the next year rose again to £6,500,000, or even £7,000,000, and that during the following years, despite considerable fluctuations, they never again went down to the point where they were at the time of the suspension of payments.  The British rates of exchange, especially on Hamburg, had fluctuated violently, and had been particularly 'unfavourable' to England, as has already been partially hinted,[1] in the years 1794 and 1800–1801 ; and this was popularly connected with the great payments on the Continent, which undoubtedly coincided to some extent in time with these phenomena.[2]  De Guer's view was consequently very easily explained ; to what extent it was correct, is a question which does not appertain to this stage of our inquiry.

What does concern us here, on the other hand, is the excel- lent basis for an attack on British exports created by such a theory.  On the one hand, the conception of the rates of exchange and the supplies of precious metals, as effects of the balance of payment abroad, and, on the other hand, the con- ception of the general solvency of Great Britain as dependent on the bullion reserves of the banks, had carried people forward (or back) to a justification of the old mercantilist trade policy on a much stronger basis than before.  For the commercial policy of the mercantile system also built on the doctrine of the balance of trade, on the danger of 'insufficient weight in the scales of trade'; but in the sixteenth and seventeenth centuries, unlike the Napoleonic period, there had been no system of note circulation with a metallic covering which might be assumed to be ruined by an unfavourable balance of payments.

[1] See p. 42.
[2] Tooke, *op. cit.*, vol. I, pp. 197–207, 239–52 ; vol. II, p. 384.

## EXPORTS OF GOLD

Such trains of thought were certainly not foreign to Napoleon, as will appear from his observations at a later period, to be treated in their proper place ; but in the main it may be said that he was dominated by simpler economic notions. Judging from his own utterances, as well as from the evidence of his assistants, indeed, we cannot easily doubt that, thanks to his contempt for the ideologues, he was still in the pre-mercantilist or bullionist stage, which saw something unfortunate for a country in the exportation of the precious metals and good fortune in the importation of gold as such. Thus, for instance, in a highly characteristic letter of May 29, 1810, to Gaudin, his Minister of Finance, Napoleon writes how smuggling with England is to be arranged. 'My object', he says, 'is to favour the exportation of foodstuffs from France and the importation of foreign money.' In another letter, of April 3, 1808, to his brother Louis of Holland, he gives instructions as to how to export gin to England by means of smugglers, ending in the bullying apostrophe : ' They must pay with money, never with goods, never, do you understand ? ' In accordance with this idea licences were issued which authorized voyages to England against exports from there of gold and silver in specie and bullion, but nothing else ; and in a report to the Emperor dated November 25, 1811, Gaudin gives as the object of the licensing system 'the extraction of metallic money from England, the exportation of French goods, and activity in our ports.' His colleague, Mollien, also mentions as an explanation of an extremely curious business with enormous advances from the French treasury to the financiers, whose business, on the contrary, would have been to advance the taxes (*les faiseurs de service*), that a thing of that kind could never have taken place unless those gentlemen had undertaken to obtain precious metals from the Spanish colonies, which were regarded as being of incalculable value.[1] With such a conception, the war against British exports justified itself as soon as it caused Great Britain to export gold.

---

[1] *Correspondance*, nos. 16,508, 13,718 ; Servières, *op. cit.*, p. 136, note 3, pp. 138–9 ; Mollien, *op. cit.*, vol. I, p. 493. The letter to King Louis is printed in the

One might be inclined, beforehand, to doubt Napoleon's interest in these questions, but such a view would be an immense mistake. What was at once the strength and the weakness of Napoleon was that he wished himself to understand every detail of his government better than any of his assistants, and this is particularly true as regards finances. I do not know whether this is a characteristic trait of the French revolutionaries in general, but the same feature, as a matter of fact, is to be found in Bernadotte, concerning whom Trolle-Wachtmeister, an acute Swedish observer, tells us in his diary (1816) that the then Crown Prince did not at all dispute the possibility that Sweden had three hundred more efficient soldiers than he, but declared that with regard to high finance he would yield to nobody, as he had long made it a subject of special study. Possibly this was simply an imitation of Napoleon, with whose remarkable financial measures the later efforts of his old rival had many points in common. It is certain that Napoleon's fantastic but immensely laborious summaries, often made in the field and always by his own hand, of the tables given him by his ministers of finance, reveal an almost inconceivable attention to precisely these questions, although the results bear no proportion to his toil or his ingenuity. A study of his letters easily reveals this, especially when it is observed from where the writings date. Mollien's memoirs are a running commentary on the same tendency. He says that ' two months of discussions in council and private conferences, which were almost daily repeated at Paris or Saint-Cloud after the return of the Emperor from the banks of the Niemen (in 1807), had not exhausted that curiosity, that passion for details, which he felt especially in questions of finance. His imagination created at every moment new combinations of figures, which he took for the creation of new resources. His errors of this kind were the more difficult to confute because the figures in which he expressed them gave to the mistakes the appearance of mathematical verities.'

*Correspondance* from the *Mémoires de Ste-Hélène*, and is dated from a place where the Emperor arrived only a fortnight later ; but there does not appear to be any reason for doubting its authenticity.

Consequently, it is not at all unlikely that Napoleon ascribed to his notions on the credit system and the precious metals a decisive influence on his great policy against England.[1]

### ECONOMIC DISLOCATIONS

Probably, however, other matters also played a part. One of these was the rather self-evident idea which has already been incidentally mentioned, *viz.*, that of causing dislocations in the economic life of England, especially in her industry. He caused one of his penmen, d'Hauterive, in a paper published in 1800, *De l'état de la France à la fin de l'an VIII*, to dwell on the thorough division of labour, on which the economic life of England was built, as a specially detrimental circumstance in every ' sudden change in the channels of trade ', to use Ricardo's famous expression. As far as we can judge, it was especially unemployment, and consequent labour unrest, that Napoleon hoped to bring about in England through his policy of exclusion. At any rate, it is a fact that few matters in his own domestic policy occupied his thoughts to the extent that this did. The system of grants which he introduced for the benefit of industry in the crises of 1807 and 1810–11 he justified with his usual, and in this case very sensible, lack of sentimentality in a letter which he addressed on March 27, 1807, to his Minister of the Interior, Champagny, on the ground that he was anxious not to save certain business men from bankruptcy, but to prevent great numbers of workmen from being without work ; and for the opposite reason no help was to be obtained for handicraftsmen and petty manufacturers on whom only a few workmen were dependent. Mollien, who entertained an orthodox *laissez-faire* dislike of this entire system of grants, also describes in detail how a large wool manufacturer, Richard Lenoir, who was in his opinion insolvent, succeeded in obtaining a loan of 1,500,000 francs owing to the fact that he was the owner of a large factory in one of the most populous suburbs of Paris, Faubourg St.

[1] Trolle-Wachtmeister, *Anteckningar och minnen* (Tegnér ed., Stockholm, 1889), vol. II, p. 74 ; Mollien, *op. cit.*, vol. II, p. 155, *et al.*

Antoine.  And Chaptal, whose views scarcely ever coincided with Mollien's, tells us, in full accordance with this, that the Emperor said to him : ' I fear these disturbances based on lack of bread : I should have less fear of a battle against 200,000 men '.

How Napoleon pictured to himself the purely external workings of the Continental System appears perhaps most distinctly from the already cited *Survey of the Position of the Empire* on August 24, 1807, which the Minister of the Interior laid before the *Corps législatif*.  This purports to be a picture of the workings of the system ; but as the latter had scarcely yet been put into execution at that time, it is mainly useful as giving evidence concerning its purpose.

England sees her merchandise repulsed from the whole of Europe, and her vessels laden with useless wealth wandering around the wide seas, where they claim to rule as sole masters, seeking in vain from the Sound to the Hellespont for a port to open and receive them.[1]

It now remains to be seen how this policy was put into execution, and what effects it involved.

[1] *Correspondance*, no. 12,187;  Ballot, *loc. cit.*, vol. II, pp. 48–9;  Mollien, *op. cit.*, vol. III, pp. 19–25 ; Chaptal, *Mes souvenirs*, &c., p. 285 ; *Correspondance*, no. 13,063.

# PART II
## ORIGIN AND EXTERNAL COURSE OF THE CONTINENTAL SYSTEM

# CHAPTER I

## COMMERCIAL WAR BEFORE THE BERLIN DECREE

### Military War (1799–1802)

As everybody knows, the accession of Napoleon to power at the close of 1799 did not lead to general peace, certainly not to peace with Great Britain; and the tendencies which have been described above consequently continued on both sides. The principal novelty was an increased activity on the part of the neutrals, resulting in the organization of the League of Armed Neutrality in December, 1800, between Sweden, Denmark, and Russia, with Prussia as a somewhat reluctant fourth party. It was based on the same principles as the Armed Neutrality of 1780, but with further guaranties against capture under blockade, in the form of a provision for previous warning on the part of the war-ships on guard, and also of a prohibition against the searching of trading vessels under convoy. The impulse had been given by the fact that the Scandinavian convoys had been continued even after France had annulled the law of Nivôse in December 1799, as has already been mentioned; and consequently it is apparent that the new League was directed mainly against Great Britain. The consequence of this was a succession of encounters with British war-ships; and in September 1800 Great Britain was guilty of an act of unusually flagrant aggression, when British privateers just outside the port of Barcelona seized a Swedish vessel and, under the protection of its neutral flag, succeeded in capturing the Spanish ships lying there at anchor.

The League of the Neutrals thus became an extremely welcome moral and political support for Napoleon against Great Britain; and some of his earlier utterances concerning the cutting-off of the Continent from England are due to its short career.  For instance, we have his pronouncement to his assistant, Roederer (December 1800), as to the necessity of ' blockading the English on their island' and ' turning to their confusion that insular position which causes their insolence, their wealth, and their supremacy '.[1]  Napoleon already posed as a champion of the freedom of the seas, and in a treaty with the United States, signed in 1800 and ratified in 1801, he laid down the same principles as had been championed by the Armed Neutrality.  But, as is well known, the Armed Neutrality came to an end after some few months with the murder of the Czar Paul I and the Battle of the Baltic, in March and April 1801 ;  and the only result of the action of the neutrals was an Anglo-Russian navigation convention (June 5/17 of the same year), with the belated and somewhat reluctant adhesion of Denmark and Sweden.  By this convention Great Britain succeeded in establishing the principle that free ships should not make free goods, and that war-ships, but not privateers, should be allowed to search convoyed trading vessels, in return for the abandonment, in theory, of the paper blockade and for restrictions in the definition of contraband, which was further limited by an agreement with Sweden in 1803.  Napoleon, however, followed up his plans of cutting off England in other quarters by means of what the English historian, Dr. Rose, making use of an expression of Napoleon himself, has called his ' coast system ', that is to say, the adoption of the French policy of the 'nineties of excluding Great Britain from access to the mainland by making himself master of its coasts in some form or other.  After Austria had concluded formal peace at Lunéville, in February 1801, therefore, first Naples and the Papal States, and later on in the year Great Britain's own ally, Portugal, had to acquiesce in the closing of their ports to the British.

This phase of the blockade policy came to an end fairly

[1] Sorel, *L'Europe et la révolution française*, vol. VI, pp. 22-3 ; Holm, *Danmark-Norges Historie fra den store nordiske Krigs Slutning til Rigernes Adskillelse, 1720–1814* (Copenhagen, 1912), vol. VII, pt. I, pp. 42-3.  Cf. also de Watteville, *Souvenirs d'un douanier du Premier Empire* (*Boucher de Perthes*), in *Revue Napoléonienne* (N.S., Rome, 1908), vol. II, p. 71.

soon, however, owing to the fact that peace was at length concluded between Great Britain and France, namely, the preliminaries of London, in October 1801, and the formal Peace of Amiens, in March 1802.

## PEACE OF AMIENS (1802)

But the Peace of Amiens turned out to be merely a brief and feverish pause in the world struggle; and all modern investigators would seem to agree that a principal cause, not to say *the* principal cause, of its short duration was the continuation of the commercial war after the close of the military war, which, we may remark in passing, is a significant experience for those who wish to form a picture of the future of Europe after the recent great trial of strength. Napoleon, on the whole, adhered to his old policy of prohibitions, acting under the pressure of the French industrialists, who, according to Mollien, had never been as bent on protection as then. Confiscations continued under the old prohibitory laws of the Revolution; and these tendencies were the more unwelcome to Great Britain because Napoleon, during the short period of peace, extended or maintained his power over great non-French regions, including Holland, Switzerland, and Piedmont. The efforts made by Great Britain to bring about a renewal of the Eden Treaty were doomed beforehand to fail, since nothing was further from Napoleon's thoughts. In 1806, when peace with Great Britain was again under discussion, he is said to have declared in the *Conseil d'État* that within forty-eight hours after its conclusion he intended ' to proscribe foreign goods and promulgate a French navigation act which should close the ports for all non-French vessels. . . . Even coal and English milords would be compelled to land under the French flag.'

As regards the question of the influence of French policy on the economic position of Great Britain during the peace interval, the idea has spread, on the great authority of Dr. Rose, that the peace meant a change for the worse; but this, as far as one can judge, is a mistake. During the year

1802 the export figures show a rise on all points, especially for the value of domestic goods and for the re-exports of foreign and colonial goods, which rose by 15 and 23 per cent., respectively, as compared with the year before; and at the same time a lively, though somewhat speculative, trade with North and South America began. But in 1803 a great relapse occurred all along the line, the figures for which fall not only below those for 1802, but also below those for the last years of the war; and it is conceivable that one might have seen in this an effect of the French restrictions and the increased possibility of competition from other countries, which in certain quarters had been expected to be a consequence of the restored freedom of the seas.[1]

In any case the result of the politico-economic strain—as of various purely political matters which have nothing to do with our problem—was the outbreak of war as early as May 1803; the trial of strength between Great Britain and France was now to proceed without interruption until Napoleon's fall, and in its course to give rise to the most unlimited development of the ideas which we have previously traced.[2]

[1] The value of British exports in the years 1801-3 is shown by the following figures taken from Porter, *The Progress of the Nation*, p. 356.

| Year | United Kingdom produce and manufacture | | Foreign and colonial merchandise |
|------|------------|-----------------|------------------|
|      | Real values | Official values | Official values |
| 1801 | £39,730,000 | £24,930,000 | £10,340,000 |
| 1802 | 45,100,000 | 25,630,000 | 12,680,000 |
| 1803 | 36,130,000 | 20,470,000 | 8,030,000 |

The first column expresses the change in the value of the exports, while the other two express rather the change in their quantity. The figures in Hansard's *Parliamentary Debates* (vol. IX, app., cols. xv-xvi) differ somewhat from these, but show no divergence in their general tendency. Dr. Rose bases his conclusions on the shipping figures, which, however, according to his own statement, show a quite insignificant decline of 3·2 per cent., and, according to Porter's figures (pp. 397-8), even a slight rise of 6·5 per cent.

[2] Rose, in *Napoleonic Studies* (London, 1904), pp. 173 *et seq.*; Sorel, *op. cit.*, vol. VI, pp. 168, 190, 207, 211-12, 249-50; Levasseur, *Histoire des classes ouvrières, &c., de 1789 à 1870*, vol. I, pp. 465-6; Pelet, *Opinions de Napoléon sur divers sujets de politique et d'administration* (Paris, 1833), pp. 238-9; Cunningham, *The Growth of English Industry and Commerce in Modern Times* (3d ed., Cambridge, 1903), pp. 675-6; Smart, *Economic Annals of the Nineteenth Century, 1801-1820* (London, 1910), pp. 57, 72; Roloff, *Die Kolonialpolitik Napoleons I*, in *Historische Bibliothek* (Munich and Leipzig, 1899), vol. X, pp. 134 *et seq.*

## Blockade (1803–1806)

At first the commercial war continued on both sides, in the main, under its old forms ; and to certain details of it we shall have occasion to return later on.   Immediately after the outbreak of the war (May 17, 1803) England seized all French and Dutch vessels lying in British ports.   A month later (June 24) the neutral trade with enemy colonies was regulated on lines half-way between those of 1794 and 1798 ; and shortly afterwards (June 28 and July 26) there was taken what was at least for the moment the most effective of all the British measures, namely, the declaration that the mouths of the Elbe and the Weser were in state of blockade, whereby the entire trade of Hamburg and Bremen was cut off.   Again in the following year (August 9, 1804) all French ports on the Channel and the North Sea were declared under blockade. The British measures of the next two years are distinctly more difficult to summarize, not only because of the varying conditions of war, but also because of the different tendencies among the leading English statesmen.   On the whole, they applied partly to the colonial trade, particularly the trade of the Americans with the European mainland, and partly to the trade with the North Sea coast in general.   The colonial trade with the Americans was made the object of sweeping restrictions in 1805, not, however, through new ordinances, but through a new interpretation of the law on the part of British courts.   The North Sea coast was again treated in a greatly varying manner, inasmuch as the blockade of 1803 was annulled in the autumn of 1805 and was renewed in an extended form in April 1806, when it was applied also to the mouths of the Ems and Trave.   On May 16 of the same year a double blockade was proclaimed, including, in the first place, a strict blockade of the coast between the mouth of the Seine and Ostend, and, in the second place, a less strict blockade of the rest of the coast between the Elbe and Brest.   Neutral vessels, however, were allowed, under certain conditions, to put in at ports on the less strictly blockaded section.   Finally, the blockade between the Elbe and the Ems was annulled on September 25, 1806. Of course, these wobbling measures could not fail to hit the towns of North Germany especially very hard ; and their paper-blockade nature kept alive the unpopularity of British policy in naval warfare.[1]

Napoleon, on his part, had caused many thousands of Englishmen travelling in France to be arrested immediately after the outbreak of war, and shortly afterwards had extended this method of belligerency to Holland as well ; and he now proceeded to more comprehensive measures in two different directions. The first was the exclusion of England from all connexion with the mainland, especially with the North Sea coast. For this purpose he occupied Hanover, which, as is well known, belonged to the British royal house, and from there he extended his repressive measures to the great centres of maritime trade, Hamburg and Bremen. His general, Mortier, received orders to seize all British ships, goods, and sailors that were to be found there. And although this measure failed, the French largely made themselves masters of British trade to these points, both in general by the occupation of Hanover, and in particular by the seizure of the little Hamburg district of Ritzebüttel, which included its outport, Cuxhaven, at the mouth of the Elbe. The first of the above-mentioned British declarations of blockade formed the answer to this ; and the independence of the Hanse Towns was consequently subjected to new blows from both antagonists. In October 1804, for instance, Napoleon simply kidnapped the British envoy from Hamburg, that is to say, from neutral soil. Moreover, in the beginning of 1804 a double action was taken against the influx of British goods farther south. The imports through Emden, in Prussian East Friesland, up the Ems to the great market of Frankfurt-am-Main were barred by the occupation of the town of Meppen on the Ems ; and at the same time large quantities of British goods were confiscated in the vassal state of Holland. In May 1805, Napoleon resolved to intervene

---

[1] G. F. & C. Martens, *Nouveau recueil de traités* (Göttingen, 1817), vol. I, pp. 433-9; Smart, *op. cit.*, vol. I, pp. 70-1 ; Stephen, *War in Disguise*, p. 31.

against British goods in Holland by causing French patrols to confiscate them along the Dutch side of the frontier.  This led the Dutch legislature, in order to prevent such high-handed procedure in the future, to pass a law prohibiting all intercourse with Great Britain, to order the confiscation of all vessels that came from there, to prohibit the importation of British goods, and also to declare certain kinds of goods to be *ipso facto* British, and finally to lay down a line of demarcation within which the storing of goods was forbidden.  These measures undeniably in many respects presage the events of the following year.

Nevertheless, in the matter of the Continental blockade all these things bore the mark of mere skirmishes.  Meanwhile, however, Napoleon had also taken up a second line, which demands greater attention, because this side of his policy was pursued to its final goal during the first years after the outbreak of war.  The second line was confined, in the main, within the limits of French jurisdiction ; and its object was to close the French market to British industrial products, and at times to colonial goods of British origin.

## FRENCH CUSTOMS POLICY

As a link in his general colonial policy, which in the main scrupulously followed the lines of the Old Colonial System, Napoleon had already in 1802, during the year of peace, fixed a customs tariff on colonial goods in such a way that the duties were 50 per cent. higher for almost all specified goods, and 100 per cent. higher for unspecified goods, imported from foreign colonies than on goods imported from French colonies (Thermidor 3, year X—July 22, 1802).  In the new customs statute, which became a law immediately before the outbreak of war in 1803, this arrangement was kept practically unchanged ; but a high duty (8 francs per kg.) was established on cotton goods, which, of course, was aimed at the British textile industry (Floréal 8, year XI—April 28, 1803).  The outbreak of war immediately revived the old line of pure prohibition, well known from the days of the Convention and the Directory, against everything British (Messidor 1—June 20). Colonial goods and industrial products coming directly or indirectly from Great Britain or its colonies were to be confiscated, and neutral vessels had to furnish detailed French consular certificates showing that the goods were of innocent origin. Nevertheless, the characteristic concession was made that the master of a ship who, 'through forgetfulness of forms or in consequence of change of destination ', failed to provide himself with such certificates, might nevertheless be allowed to discharge his cargo on condition that he took French goods of corresponding value in return freight—an idea which Napoleon was destined to develop strongly in his later policy. In the new customs statute of the following year, the principle of prohibition was retained. On the one side, it is true, it was made milder, among other things by conceding the right to import certain classes of goods in vessels clearing from ports that had no French commercial representative ; but, on the other hand, it was made more strict by a further prohibition with a very wide range, namely, that vessels which had cleared from, or had unnecessarily put in at, a British port should not be admitted to French ports (Ventôse 22, year XII—March 13, 1804). This last regulation anticipated the great Berlin decree, which may be looked upon as the origin of the Continental System proper.

Nevertheless one may safely assume that the whole of this system of differentiation, with special prohibitions against British goods and vessels coming from Great Britain, was calculated to prove as impracticable at this time as it had in the preceding decade. Napoleon, therefore, quietly fell back on a policy of general prohibition which was not directed specifically against Great Britain, but struck at all non-French goods alike. In reality those measures which affected industrial products were felt most severely, not by Great Britain, but by her continental competitors, especially those in the then Duchy of Berg, or what is now the Ruhr district east of the Rhine. This was not the intended result, it is true, but it further strengthened the protection of French industry. The foundation was laid in the Customs Tariff of 1805, which substantially raised the duties on colonial goods and cotton goods (Pluviôse 17, year XIII—February 6, 1805), and the culmination was reached in two decrees issued in the early part of 1806 (February 22 and March 4). These decrees, which were incorporated in the great protectionist codification of the customs laws of the Empire on April 30 of the same year, developed tendencies in two directions. On the one side, there was an enormous increase in the customs rates on colonial goods, with substantially less distinction—in certain cases none at all—between French goods and foreign goods. This was manifestly connected with the fact that Napoleon, after the battle of Trafalgar, largely lost the power of communication with his colonies and had to take into account the fact that the colonial trade would fall more and more into the hands of the British. By way of example, we may observe that, while the customs rates on both brown sugar and coffee, as well as on cocoa, in 1802 and 1803 had been 50 and 75 francs per 100 kilograms for French and foreign goods, respectively, they now increased to 80 and 100 francs, respectively, for sugar, and to 75 and 100 francs, respectively, at first, and to 125 and 150 francs, respectively, later on, for coffee ; for cocoa they increased at first to 95 and 120 francs and afterwards to 175 and 200 francs, respectively. Thus the rates amounted to three and a half times as much as they had been three years before. But all this was a trifle compared with the most striking rise of all in the customs rates, namely, on an industrial raw material of such fundamental importance as cotton. Having previously paid 1 to 3 francs per 100 kilograms, it was burdened in 1806 with a duty of no less than 60 francs, which, at a low estimate, was 10 per cent. of the value, though it is true that 50 francs were allowed as a drawback on exports of cotton manufactures. Most revolutionary of all seemed the simultaneous prohibition of the importation of cotton cloths, calicoes, and muslins in February 1806 ; and the prohibition was extended in April to certain other kinds of cotton cloth as well.  Yet at this time cotton had already become an absolute necessity.  In later years, at St. Helena, Napoleon made out that the *Conseil d'État* had shrunk from this project, but that he had forced his will through by quoting the authority of Oberkampf, the leading man in the French textile industry.  Naturally, Napoleon had no difficulty in getting his support of a policy that protected his own particular industry.  At the same time the importation of cotton twist (*filés pour mèches*) was forbidden ; the customs duty on yarn was raised, especially for the lower numbers, *i. e.*, the coarser qualities ; and it was publicly stated that this article also would have been prohibited altogether if it had been thought possible to spin sufficiently high numbers in France.[1]

Southern Europe came under the same régime as early as 1806.  In Italy, during that year, Napoleon pursued a policy which was intermediate between the earlier and the later French method.  Thus in the Kingdom of Italy (North Italy), of which Napoleon was king, a number of articles, especially textile goods, were declared, in accordance with earlier examples, to be *eo ipso* British, and were consequently prohibited when they did not come from France—a declaration which in reality was directed principally against the continental rivals of France. On the other hand, in the Kingdom of Naples, which was ruled by Joseph Bonaparte, only really British goods were prohibited ; but in addition all British property was seized.  In the same year Switzerland was suddenly obliged to pass a law which, under severe penalties, prohibited all importation of British manufactures except cotton yarn.  This was an act of retribution because Swiss merchants, in the weeks just prior to the transfer of the principality of Neuchâtel to France, had been importing colonial goods and manufactures there and afterwards had been daring enough to complain when they were all confiscated by Napoleon.

By these measures Napoleon felt that he had effectively

[1] The principal changes in French customs duties on colonial produce from 1802 to 1810 are tabulated in app. II, from which a better view of the situation may perhaps be obtained than from the enumeration in the text.

closed the French, Italian, and Swiss markets to British industry and trade; but it now remained to close the rest of the continental markets in the same way. In doing this he fell back, in reality, on the old policy of prohibition directed especially against England, though without giving up the French customs policy, which was prohibitive against all; on the contrary, the latter policy went hand in hand with the former throughout his period of rule. But it was to the measures directed exclusively against Great Britain that Napoleon himself gave the name of the Continental System.[1]

[1] *Bulletin des lois*, &c., 3d ser., bull. 203, no. 1,849; bull. 276, no. 2,752; bull. 287, no. 2,822; bull. 353, no. 3,669; 4th ser., bull. 29, no. 483; bull. 74, no. 1,324; bull. 78, no. 1,371; bull. 89, no. 1,515; Wohlwill, *Neuere Geschichte*, &c., pp. 271 *et seq.*; Vogel, *Die Hansestädte und die Kontinentalsperre*, in *Pfingstblätter des Hansischen Geschichtsvereins* (Munich and Leipzig, 1913), vol. IX, pp. 12 *et seq.*; König, *Die sächsische Baumwollenindustrie am Ende des vorigen Jahrhunderts und während der Kontinentalsperre*, in *Leipziger Studien auf dem Gebiete der Geschichte*, 45th ser. (Leipzig, 1899), vol. III, pp. 30, 43–4; Legrand, *La révolution française en Hollande* (Paris, 1895), pp. 309, 311, 327, 353; de Cérenville, *Le système continental et la Suisse, 1803–1813* (Lausanne, 1906), pp. 36 *et seq.*; Levasseur, *Histoire des classes ouvrières*, &c., *de 1789 à 1870*, vol. I, pp. 467 *et seq.*, 422 note 4; Schmidt, *Le Grand-duché de Berg*, pp. 333 *et seq.*; Roloff, *op. cit.*, pp. 132, 205 *et seq.*; Darmstädter, *Studien zur napoleonischen Wirtschaftspolitik*, in *Vierteljahrschrift für Social- und Wirtschaftsgeschichte* (1905), vol. III, pp. 122–3; Rambaud, *Naples sous Joseph Bonaparte, 1806–1808* (Paris, 1911), p. 436.

# CHAPTER II

## THE BERLIN DECREE

THE years 1803–6 were notoriously full of world-overturning events : Napoleon's preparation for a descent on England (1803–5) ; the foundation of the French Empire (May–December 1804) ; the formation of the Third Coalition against France and its defeat at Ulm and Austerlitz (October and December 1805) ; as an immediate sequel to this, the Peace of Pressburg, with the extension of the ' coast system ' to the eastern shore of the Adriatic, but also the definitive overthrow of the French fleet at Trafalgar (October 21, 1805) ; and finally the formation of the Fourth Coalition and the crushing of Prussia at Jena and Auerstädt (October 14, 1806).

In the autumn of 1806, therefore, Napoleon's victory on the Continent was as complete as his defeat at sea. Consequently he was so far perfectly right when in later years he pointed to the battle of Jena as the natural antecedent to the execution of the Continental System, inasmuch as that battle placed into his hands the control of the Weser, Elbe, Trave, Oder, and all the coastline as far as the Vistula, although, naturally enough, he omitted to point to the battle of Trafalgar as a negatively operating factor.[1] The great manifestation consisted in the Berlin decree, issued November 21, 1806, from the capital of the power that had been last and most thoroughly vanquished. The external occasion was Great Britain's recently mentioned blockade declaration of May 16 of the same year ; but that was nothing more than a pretext. Sorel has brought to light some documents of July 1805, and February 1806, written by a certain Montgaillard, in which the Berlin decree is portended. In these documents there is the usual talk of how England is lost if it is only possible to enforce a prohibition of her industrial products in Europe, for to destroy her trade is to deal her a blow

[1] *Correspondance de Napoléon Ier*, no. 16,127 (Jan. 10, 1810).

in the heart and to attack her alliances at the same time as her continental intrigues. But the idea that peace with the different powers would have as a necessary pre-condition the closing of all the ports of the mainland to the British was evidently very widespread, as can be seen from a contemporary utterance of French industrialists. And, indeed, even before the issue of the decree we find Napoleon, both in one of his army bulletins (October 23) and in a letter to his brother Joseph (November 16), speaking of the continental blockade as a matter of course. At the same time as this last letter, another letter was addressed to the commander of North Germany, Marshal Mortier, instructing him to close the Elbe ' hermetically ', to confiscate all English goods, and even to arrest the English and Russian consuls at Hamburg.[1] In every respect, therefore, the Berlin decree stands out as a culmination of earlier thoughts and measures, although, despite all this, it had the effect of a bomb, thanks to Napoleon's masterly capacity as a stage manager.

### PREAMBLE

Like most of the measures of both parties, the Berlin decree purported to be a measure of reprisal rendered necessary by numerous aggressions of the adversary ; but its regulations were nevertheless solemnly proclaimed as embodying ' the fundamental principles of the Empire ', until England disavowed her false pretensions. In content the regulations, as is usual in French ordinances, are very clear, at least at first sight, although they were gradually to prove, intentionally or un-intentionally, rather ambiguous. The preamble states : (1) that England does not acknowledge international law ; (2) that she treats all enemy subjects as enemies (this is directed against her legislation against alien enemies); (3) that she extends the right of capture to merchant vessels and merchandise and private property ; (4) that she extends the blockade to

---

[1] Sorel, *op. cit.*, vol. VII, pp. 55, 104, 114 ; memorial printed in Tarle, *Konti-nental'naja blokada* (Moscow, 1913), vol. I, p. 706 ; *Correspondance*, nos. 11,064, 11,271, 11,267, 11,283 (Berlin decree).

unfortified places (a reproach which forms a reminiscence of the siege character of a blockade) and to places where she has not a single ship of war ; (5) that she uses the right of blockade with no other object than that of hampering intercourse between peoples and building up her own trade and industry on the ruins of the trade and industry of the Continent; (6) that trade in English goods involves complicity in her plans ; (7) that her proceedings have benefited her at the expense of everybody else ; (8) and, consequently, that retaliation is justifiable.   It is further stated, therefore, that the Emperor intends to use her methods against her, and accordingly that the regulations will remain permanently in force until England has acknowledged that the law of war is the same by land and by sea and cannot be extended to private property and unarmed individuals, and that blockade shall be restricted to fortified places guarded by sufficient forces.

## REGULATIONS

The fundamental regulations laid down on this basis fall into four categories.   First, the British Isles are formally declared in a state of blockade, and all trade or communication with them is prohibited (Articles 1 and 2).   Secondly, the decree turns against all British subjects in territories occupied by the French ;   they are declared to be prisoners of war, and all property belonging to them to be fair prize (Articles 3 and 4). Thirdly, war is made on all British goods ;   all trade in them is prohibited and all goods belonging to England or coming from her factories or her colonies are declared to be fair prize, half of their value to be used to indemnify merchants for British captures (Articles 5 and 6).   Fourthly and lastly, every vessel coming direct from ports of Great Britain or her colonies, or calling at them after the proclamation of the decree, is refused access to any port on the Continent (Article 7).

What was left undecided was the question of procedure at sea.   In later years (1810) Napoleon himself declared on two or three different occasions that the Berlin decree implied only ' continental blockade and not maritime blockade ', and that it was not to be applied to the sea, that is, to lead to captures ; but this only bears witness to that capacity of forgetfulness of which Napoleon was master on occasion. It is true that his naval minister, Admiral Decrès, in answer to a question from the American envoy, gave it as his opinion that a vessel could not be captured simply and solely because it was on its way to an English port. It is also true that captures or condemnations of captured or stranded vessels on the basis of the Berlin decree did not occur in 1806 or in the first seven months of 1807 ; and this caused shipping premiums to drop to 4 per cent. and in England formed the basis of the regular standing argument of the opposition against the government's measures of reprisal. But it is equally true that this state of affairs came to an end with a declaration made by Napoleon himself, after his return from Poland, and communicated to the Law Courts in September 1807 ; in point of fact, the practice had already been altered in August and consequently not, as Napoleon later gave out, by the new Milan decree of December 1807. The Emperor's exposition of the law states that English goods on board neutral vessels should be confiscated ; and in practice the decree was interpreted in such a way that an enemy destination was sufficient ground for the condemnation of a vessel. For that matter, this was in full accord both with the principles of blockade and with the practice of the period of the Directory.[1]

Even after this interpretation, however, the Berlin decree was so much milder than the Nivôse law of 1798 that the occurrence of British goods at least did not occasion the condemnation of the vessel itself and the rest of its cargo.

## SIGNIFICANCE

From a formal point of view there are at the most two novelties in the regulations of the Berlin decree. The one is the declaration of blockade against the British Isles, which could

---

[1] *Correspondance*, nos. 16,127, 17,014 (Jan. 10, Oct. 7, 1810) ; Hansard, vol. XIII, app., pp. xxxiii *et seq.* ; Mahan, *Influence of Sea Power*, &c., vol. II, pp. 273, 281–2 ; cf. also p. 245 ; also, *Sea Power in its Relations*, &c., vol. I, pp. 143, 189 note 1.

scarcely have occurred to anybody except Napoleon at a time when not a single war-ship held the sea against the British. Its principal object, indeed, was to form an effective and grandiose gesture ; and not without reason the famous British lawyer, Lord Erskine, could later (February 15, 1808) say in the House of Lords that Napoleon might just as well have declared the moon in a state of blockade.[1]  Presumably, however, Napoleon aimed not only at the theatrical effect, but also at reducing the British principle of a paper blockade to an absurdity.  The second novelty was the treatment of British subjects and their property on the Continent.  Like the former regulation, this came about as a continental parallel to the British system of capture at sea.  Its practical effect, as far as one can judge, was restricted to the moment of proclamation, as the law took by surprise many Englishmen and their enterprises, especially in the German territories governed by Napoleon.

The epoch-making character of the Berlin decree, therefore, is scarcely due to either of these formally new regulations. What is important is the wide range which from the time of the Berlin decree was given to a whole series of measures which for a long time had been applied more or less sporadically.  It was only now that it had become possible to elaborate the different methods of reprisal into a truly ' continental ' system, that is, one embracing the whole, or nearly the whole, of the European mainland.  And it was only now, too, that they were made the central point in the entire internal and external policy of France, around which everything else had to turn in an ever-increasing degree.  It was only now that the idea was seriously taken up by a ruler and statesman who had the unique capacity and ruthless consistency which were the necessary prerequisites for transforming the plan from a mere visionary programme into a political reality.  The interest surrounding the development of the Continental System, therefore, is connected with the fact that its idea now came to be followed up in deadly earnest, and that the entire content of the ideas

[1] Hansard, vol. x, p. 473.

was thereby given an opportunity to affect the life of Europe for better or for worse.

The content of this system should be sufficiently clear from what has already been said, but it may nevertheless be set forth here, when we are entering upon the further development of external events. As a declaration of blockade against Great Britain was little more than a theatrical gesture, and as Napoleon was almost entirely destitute of means to assert his will on the sea, the blockade had to be applied by land. This means that it was, and aimed at being, a self-blockade on the part of the Continent, just as had already been the case with the Directory's Nivôse law of 1798. With the object of preventing Great Britain from disposing of her goods on the Continent and thereby bringing her to her knees, the Continent itself was to renounce all importation of British goods and colonial wares, so far as the latter came from British colonies and British trade. The whole thing not only was, but was intended to be, a ' self-denying ordinance '. The privations to which the Continent was afterwards subjected were thus a designed effect of Napoleon's measures, and not at all the work of his enemy, who, on the contrary, devoted himself to relieving them, for the most part in principle and almost entirely in practice. Unless this starting-point, which to our way of thinking seems very paradoxical, is firmly grasped at the outset, the following development will appear inexplicable. To what extent Napoleon realized all the consequences of his measure, we have, it is true, no means of knowing ; but evidence is not lacking that he was conscious of their main features. Even when he issued the decree concerning the closing of the Hanse Towns (December 3, 1806), he wrote to his brother Louis of Holland that the serious obstacles in the way of intercourse with England would ' undoubtedly injure Holland and France ', but that they were necessary; and in a letter [1] addressed to the same correspondent a few days later he says that the system would ruin the great commercial towns. Moreover, in connexion with the intensification of the system by the second Milan decree

[1] Cited *ante*, p. 60.

he wrote a year later (December 17, 1807) to the minister of the interior, Cretet, and ordered him to encourage capturing as ' the only means by which the requirements of the country could be supplied '. On the same occasion, also, his minister of finance, Gaudin, in a report written in connexion with the Milan decree, pointed out the injury inflicted by the system on the French industries, which had already found it difficult to obtain colonial raw materials; but he considered that the injury to England was yet greater owing to her greater dependence on industry and foreign trade.[1]

Admiral Mahan, in his somewhat harsh criticism of Napoleon's policy, condemns the Continental System on the ground that it injuriously affected the neutrals, who were especially indispensable to France because she herself was excluded from the sea. 'The neutral carrier,' he says, ' was the key of the position. He was, while the war lasted, essentially the enemy of Great Britain, who needed him little, and a friend of France, who needed him much.'[2] This statement appears to involve the ignoring of all the motives behind this mode of warfare, the object of which was to conquer Great Britain economically; for that object Napoleon could never have attained by allowing neutral trade to continue. That Napoleon had to expect greater injury to Great Britain than to his own countries from the self-blockade of the Continent was a necessary consequence of the views which, as we have already seen, were common to him and his adversary; and from his standpoint, accordingly, the policy was sufficiently justified. Whether he and his opponents conceived the economic connexions aright, is quite another question, which belongs to a later chapter. It is a question, moreover, which can by no means be disposed of by a mere reference to his need of the help of the neutrals for supplies which he thought he could do without or replace from other sources.

---

[1] *Correspondance*, nos. 11,378, 13,395; Servières, *L'Allemagne française*, &c., pp. 129–30.

[2] Mahan, *Influence of Sea Power*, &c., vol. II, pp. 353 *et seq.*

## EXECUTION

Napoleon immediately proceeded to carry the Berlin decree into execution over as large a part of the Continent as possible. With significant openness one article incorporated in the decree itself (Article 10) instructed the French foreign minister to communicate it to the governments of Spain, Naples, Holland, and Etruria—all vassal states—and to the other allies of France ; and a letter of the same day from the Emperor to Talleyrand prescribes practically the same course. But the decree was to have its first political effects in the Hanse Towns, where, as we know, the foundation had been laid long beforehand, and where what were really executive measures had been ordered before the publication of the decree.

The Hanse Towns, and especially Hamburg, were perhaps of all places in Europe the most decisive points for the success or failure of the Continental System. During the last years of the *ancien régime* the flourishing French trade in goods from the French West Indies had chiefly gone to the Hanse Towns, where the French colonial goods had largely squeezed out their competitors, so that the Hanse Towns during these years absolutely came first among all European countries in the export trade of France. But the revolutionary wars put a sudden stop to all this, and that, too, not only for France, but also for Holland, which was occupied by the French. This was undoubtedly due in part to the fact that the policy of the Directory against the neutrals prevented them from maintaining the trade relations now that France could no longer maintain them herself. It was now that Great Britain came to the fore as by far the most important purveyor of colonial goods and industrial products to the Hanse Towns, and through them not only to the whole of Germany, but also to great parts of the rest of the Continent. At the same time Great Britain, on her part, had good use for the corn and other agricultural produce which were foremost among North German exports through Bremen. It is true that the statistics of the period must be used with great caution, and the figures from different sources, even official ones, are often irreconcilable. In this case, however, the general tendency is unmistakable, and some data may therefore be given. In 1789 only 49 vessels of 7,250 tons in all went to England from Hamburg and Bremen; but in 1800 there were 500 vessels of 72,900 tons in all. That is to say, the traffic increased ten times over. The value of British exports there is said to have risen between 1792 and 1800 from £2,200,000 to £13,500,000; in fact, the British minister at Hamburg stated in 1807 that during the twelve preceding years the exports of colonial produce, East India goods, and British manufactures to the Hanse Towns amounted to an average of £10,000,000—a figure the significance of which is shown by the fact that the entire British exports in 1807 were estimated at only a little more than £50,000,000.

Alongside this trade with Great Britain, however, there arose in the 'nineties an extremely lively, sometimes highly speculative, commercial intercourse between the Hanse Towns and the United States, which during that period sold more goods to Germany than to the entire British Empire. So long as the trade could be carried on without any great amount of British interference, it must have been far more favourable for France and her allies than the British trade, inasmuch as the American trade consisted, on the one side, of the importation of the products of the French and Spanish West Indies, and, on the other, in the exportation of German industrial products, which even managed to compete successfully with British goods in the United States. But it was one of Napoleon's deeply-rooted ideas, and one which was soon to assume the solemn form of the decrees, that nearly all textile goods and some sorts of colonial goods were in reality English, howsoever they might be disguised, and that all goods of maritime trade were at least ' suspect '. Consequently, he felt that almost the entire maritime trade of the Hanse Towns was a vital English interest; and this was certainly the case, at least to a large, if not to a predominant, extent.

As early as November 19, 1806, two days before the issue of the Berlin decree, therefore, Marshal Mortier seized Hamburg without further ado; and two days later (November 21) French troops likewise occupied Bremen and the Weser down to its mouth. Meanwhile, Lübeck had been taken by force as early as November 6, after Blücher had thrown himself into the town with his Prussian troops. Acting in accordance with his instructions, Mortier immediately ordered in Hamburg a statement to be made out of all money and goods arising from trade connexions with England. And in a magniloquent diplomatic note to the Senate of Hamburg, Napoleon's notorious ex-secretary and then minister there, Bourrienne, a few days later (November 24) gave as a motive of the measure the Emperor's feeling of obligation ' to seek to safeguard the Continent against the misfortunes with which it is threatened' through the machinations of England, inasmuch as a large number of the inhabitants of Hamburg were notoriously devoted to England ; and at the same time he emphasized the regulations of the Berlin decree. By an ordinance of December 2, and by letter after letter, Napoleon laid down, modified and intensified the customs cordon which was to be created along the entire North Sea coast and the river Elbe as far as Travemünde by a large military force operating in conjunction with the customs staff.[1]

[1] Vogel, *op. cit.*, pp. 4 *et seq.* ; Tarle, *Deutsch-französische Wirtschaftsbeziehungen zur napoleonischen Zeit*, in *Schmollers Jahrbuch für Gesetzgebung* (1914), vol. XXXVIII, p. 670; Schäfer, *Bremen und die Kontinentalsperre*, in *Hansische Geschichtsblätter* (1914), vol. XX, p. 414 *et seq.* ; Levasseur, *Histoire du commerce de la France*, vol. II, p. 19; Mahan, *Influence of Sea Power*, &c., vol. II, p. 251 ; Johnson and others, *History of the Domestic and Foreign Commerce*, &c., vol. II, pp. 20 *et seq.*

# CHAPTER III

## BRITISH COUNTER-MEASURES AND FRENCH RETORT

### Possible Lines of British Policy

The immediate question, after the bomb which Napoleon had exploded, was what attitude Great Britain would assume toward the new blow directed against the very foundation of her trade and industry. We are confronted here with one of the points in the history of the Continental System which both at that time and later have been most often misunderstood.

Napoleon's intention was to strangle British trade with the Continent. The most natural counterblow of Great Britain in resisting this attempt at strangulation, and one in strict accord with the conceptions of those times, was to maintain the connexion with the Continent in every conceivable way. Nor is there any doubt that this was in reality the main line of action pursued by her, that is to say, chiefly by the British merchants and manufacturers. Consequently, the main economic conflict lay between the French measures of self-blockade and the British endeavours to break through that blockade. But the efforts of the British public authorities along this positive line, which was in reality the decisive one, were very much restricted by natural causes, over and above the extremely important fundamental condition created by the supremacy of the British fleet at sea. And with the usual inclination of mankind in the sphere of economics to attach too great importance to state measures and very little importance to the work of economic machinery itself, the main stress has been laid on obvious but in reality subordinate matters. It is by no means intended to follow the same course in this book ; but what, from a deeper point of view, were the decisive matters on the British side do not belong—for reasons at which we have just hinted—to the external course of the Continental System and must therefore be left over for a later treatment.

It is true that one might regard one British measure as a positive counterblow, that is, an effort to compel the enemy, by economic or other pressure, to revoke his self-blockade decree. In form, indeed, this is what was attempted, inasmuch as all measures on both sides were represented as acts of reprisal, that is to say, as being caused by the aggressions of the enemy and as being intended to lead him into better ways. In the English official language the declared object was ' to restrain the violence of the enemy and to retort upon him the evils of his own injustice ', as it was expressed in the Order in Council of January 7, 1807. And undoubtedly these declarations were in many cases seriously meant. But if such pressure was to be exerted in the sphere of economics, it almost necessarily had to take the opposite form to penetrating into the continental market: it had to be an effectual (*i.e.*, import-preventing) blockade of the Continent. And this, as we well know, was just what people would not think of doing, for it would have implied, as was indeed said in Parliament, ' that France had shut the door against our commerce and that we had bolted it.' [1] Although this idea came up time and again, everything else contributed to put these positive counter-measures aside: Napoleon's obstinacy, which held out small hopes of any change in his tactics ; the slight prospects of giving any appreciable strength to such pressure ; and the direct disadvantages thereof for Great Britain's own industrial life. As before, therefore, nothing more was possible than a mere gesture, which was contradicted by every detail of actual trade life.

But by the side not only of attempting to break through the blockade, but also of placing obstacles in the way of imports with the object of bringing economic pressure to bear, there was a third, a negative line, namely, to try to injure the trade of France and her allies in the same way as Napoleon had sought to injure that of Great Britain. In other words, it was intended to cut off their exports, and in that way, according to the then prevailing view, to undermine the possibility of their economic prosperity, just as Napoleon intended to do as regards England. It was ' the policy of commercial rivalry ', as distinct from the policy of retaliation, to use Canning's expression.

[1] The expression was cited by Perceval in the House of Commons, Feb. 5, 1808. Hansard, vol. x, p. 328.

This could not create direct pressure, such as would compel the annulling of a self-blockade; but its purpose, here as on the opposite side, would have been a slow weakening of the enemy financially and economically. This third line, however, clearly led to measures quite different from those of the second line, that is to say, not to a cutting-off of the supplies of the Continent, but to an attack on the trade of the Continent, and especially on its exports.

This third line was, of course, quite in accordance with the general tendency we know, and to that extent had possibilities quite different from those of the second line. But the actual conditions strictly limited this third line too, in a way even more strictly than the former, simply because England's fourteen-year-old supremacy on the sea had not left much of the independent maritime trade with the Continent; and even during peace time, moreover, that trade had had nothing like the same importance for the continental states as British trade had for Great Britain. With these three lines, however, the possibilities of state counter-measures were all but exhausted. From this it follows that the political measures of Great Britain against Napoleon's Continental decree were not, as a whole, of primary importance for the issue of the economic trial of strength. In order to make the connexion clear, however, we must enter into a somewhat detailed study of the nature of British policy; and this is in every respect so peculiar and casts so much light on the driving forces, that such an investigation well repays itself, even apart from the international consequences of the British measures and reaction of these consequences on the economic conflict itself.

What was possible and remained to be done by means of state measures on the part of Great Britain had chiefly to do with colonial trade, and especially with the part played by the neutrals in that trade. In order that this may be comprehensible, however, it is necessary to turn back a little and glance at the connexion between the mainland of Europe and the colonies, especially the West Indies, during the war period down to 1807.[1]

[1] For the following account reference may be made, not only to the works previously cited, viz., those by Mahan, Roloff, Levasseur, Holm, Stephen (the

### Colonial Carrying Trade

The central point in the colonial trade at this time was formed by the West Indies, especially in their capacity as sugar producers; and among these the French and Spanish islands, especially Haiti and Cuba, were distinctly superior to the British islands, Jamaica, and the rest. The trade to the West Indian possessions of Napoleon and his Spanish ally, therefore, was regarded almost as the great prize of maritime commerce, which was sought after by the neutrals with the eager support of the European mother countries so long as they were powerless on the sea, while Great Britain wished to make use of her power to win this prize for herself. It is true that the foremost colony of all, Haiti, or, more correctly, its western or French third, St. Domingue, had suffered immensely from the many negro insurrections ever since the first years of the revolutionary wars; but sufficient was left to arouse the desire for gain. Furthermore, the remaining French colonies— Guadeloupe and Martinique in the West Indies, Guiana on the South American continent, Isle-de-France (now known as Mauritius) and Réunion and Senegal in Africa—were somewhat less damaged by the course of events during the war, while the Spanish possessions seem, on the evidence of outside witnesses, not to have suffered seriously. The country which lay handy to seize the trade with all these territories—which trade was jealously guarded in peace time—was clearly the United States. The latter had just begun its independent political existence and was seeking ways which might lead them away from the exclusive economic connexion with Great Britain that had been created and maintained during the colonial period. In this way there arose a triangular trade which was highly important for the Atlantic states of the American Union. Vessels

quotation on p. 107 comes from his pp. 81–2), Johnson (from whom is taken the table on p. 103), and Martens, as well as to the *Statutes at Large of the United Kingdom* and Hansard's *Parliamentary Debates*, but also to J. B. McMaster's chapter in the *Cambridge Modern History* (Cambridge, 1903), vol. VII, pp. 323 *et seq.*, and Channing, *The Jeffersonian System, 1801–1811*, in *The American Nation : A History* (New York and London, 1906), vol. XI, chs. 13–15. The quotation from McMaster on p. 104 is taken from his *History of the People of the United States*, vol. III, p. 225 (*ap.* Johnson, *op. cit.*, vol. II, p. 28).

proceeded with corn and timber to the French and Spanish West Indies, took on colonial goods there, especially sugar and coffee, which they conveyed to the European Continent, after which they returned, principally in ballast, but partly also with European industrial products. The balance of assets which the American merchants thus obtained on the Continent was used to liquidate the country's balance of liabilities to Great Britain for its textiles and iron goods, which continued to dominate the American market ; but a considerable part of it was also re-exported to the rest of America, chiefly the French and Spanish West Indies themselves.

The whole of this trade was in conflict with the ' rule of 1756 ',[1] and, therefore, could not be tolerated in principle by Great Britain. But as the rule was interpreted during the revolutionary wars proper by the great legal authority, the British Judge of Admiralty, Sir William Scott, afterwards Lord Stowell—still to-day the great name in the sphere of the law of war at sea—it offered various possibilities to the neutrals, and particularly to Americans. Especially in the famous case of the *Immanuel* (1799) he elaborated the idea, on the one hand, that the neutrals could make no claim whatever to trade with enemy colonies during war, because those colonies, owing to the Old Colonial System, had been as inaccessible to them before the war as if they had been situated in the moon, and had been thrown open to trade only through the British naval victories. But, on the other hand, he also emphasized the fact that these prohibitions on trade in the products of enemy colonies held good only so long as those products had not formed part of a neutral country's stock of goods ; and this he developed further in the case of the *Polly* in the following year, to the effect that the evidence of such a ' neutralization ' should consist in the unloading of the goods in a neutral port and there passing them through the customs. Such a demand for what was called a ' broken voyage ' was not difficult to fulfil, so much the less because the geographical position of the West Indies made it possible, with very little loss of time, for a vessel to put in at an American mainland port, especially Charleston, South

[1] See p. 36.

Carolina, on its way to Europe. It was undoubtedly with full
intention that the American government facilitated the matter
by granting permission that when the goods were passed
through the customs payment should be made by bond, and
that practically the whole of the duty, with a very small
exception ($3\frac{1}{2}$ per cent.), should be paid back on re-export.
Consequently, the customs' treatment furnished the smallest
possible guaranty that the goods had passed into neutral trade.
When the unloading of the goods was required, the vessels had
the possibility of going to a ship-building port in New England
and using the time for the completion of repairs while the cargo
was being discharged and reloaded. The trip thus became
a ' circuitous voyage '.

The result of this peculiar manipulation may be illustrated
in many ways. During the years of war the foreign trade of
the United States underwent an extraordinary increase, while
in the short peace interval there was an immediate decline ; and
the character of the trade is shown by the quite unique excess
of re-exports, *i.e.*, the exports of foreign products. It is true
that the figures are not in all respects above dispute, but they
are sufficiently reliable to merit reproduction.

FOREIGN TRADE OF THE UNITED STATES (1790-1807)

| Year | Exports | | | Imports | |
|---|---|---|---|---|---|
| | Domestic goods | Foreign goods | Total | Home consumption | Total |
| 1790 | $19,670,000 | $540,000 | $20,210,000 | $22,460,000 | $23,000,000 |
| 1791 | 18,500,000 | 510,000 | 19,010,000 | 28,690,000 | 29,200,000 |
| 1792 | 19,000,000 | 1,750,000 | 20,750,000 | 29,750,000 | 31,500,000 |
| 1793 | 24,000,000 | 2,110,000 | 26,110,000 | 28,990,000 | 31,100,000 |
| 1794 | 26,500,000 | 6,530,000 | 33,030,000 | 28,070,000 | 34,600,000 |
| 1795 | 39,500,000 | 8,490,000 | 47,990,000 | 61,270,000 | 69,760,000 |
| 1796 | 40,760,000 | 26,300,000 | 67,060,000 | 55,140,000 | 81,440,000 |
| 1797 | 29,850,000 | 27,000,000 | 56,850,000 | 48,380,000 | 75,380,000 |
| 1798 | 28,530,000 | 33,000,000 | 61,530,000 | 35,550,000 | 68,550,000 |
| 1799 | 33,140,000 | 45,520,000 | 78,670,000 | 33,550,000 | 79,070,000 |
| 1800 | 31,840,000 | 39,130,000 | 70,970,000 | 52,120,000 | 91,250,000 |
| 1801 | 47,470,000 | 46,640,000 | 94,120,000 | 64,720,000 | 111,360,000 |
| 1802 | 36,710,000 | 35,780,000 | 72,480,000 | 40,560,000 | 76,330,000 |
| 1803 | 42,210,000 | 13,590,000 | 55,800,000 | 51,070,000 | 64,670,000 |
| 1804 | 41,470,000 | 36,230,000 | 77,700,000 | 48,770,000 | 85,000,000 |
| 1805 | 42,390,000 | 53,180,000 | 95,570,000 | 67,420,000 | 120,600,000 |
| 1806 | 41,250,000 | 60,280,000 | 101,540,000 | 69,130,000 | 129,410,000 |
| 1807 | 48,700,000 | 59,640,000 | 108,340,000 | 78,860,000 | 138,500,000 |

We see here how the exports of foreign goods jumped from almost nothing to amounts which, at the close of the 'nineties, far exceeded the exports of domestic goods, and then during the peace year 1802–3 fell to little more than one-fourth of the amount for the last war year, but immediately after the outbreak of the new war rose to nearly half as much again as the exports of domestic goods in 1806.  The following figures (given by Mahan) showing the exports to Europe of the two most important West Indian products during the few typical war years and peace years are also highly illuminative.

| Product | 1792 (peace) | 1796 (war) | 1800 (war) | 1803 (peace) | 1804 (war) |
|---|---|---|---|---|---|
| Sugar (lbs.) | 1,122,000 | 35,000,000 | 82,000,000 | 20,000,000 | 74,000,000 |
| Coffee (lbs.) | 2,137,000 | 62,000,000 | 47,000,000 | 10,000,000 | 48,000,000 |

It may also be of interest to form a more graphic picture of this trade than can be given by figures.  A sketch by the American historian, Professor McMaster, gives a mere summary of the abundant data, based on proceedings in prize-court cases as found in Stephen's book to which we have so often had occasion to refer :

The merchant flag of every belligerent, save England, disappeared from the sea.  France and Holland absolutely ceased to trade under their flags.  Spain for a while continued to transport her specie and her bullion in her own ships, protected by her men-of-war.  But this, too, she soon gave up, and by 1806 the dollars of Mexico and the ingots of Peru were brought to her shores in American bottoms.  It was under our (the American) flag that the gum trade was carried on with Senegal, that the sugar trade was carried on with Cuba, that coffee was exported from Caracas, and hides and indigo from South America.  From Vera Cruz, from Cartagena, from La Plata, from the French colonies in the Antilles, from Cayenne, from Dutch Guiana, from the isles of Mauritius and Réunion, from Batavia and Manila, great fleets of American merchantmen sailed to the United States, there to neutralize the voyage and then go on to Europe.  They filled the warehouses at Cadiz and Antwerp to overflowing.  They glutted the markets of Emden, Lisbon, Hamburg and Copenhagen with the produce of the West Indies and the fabrics of the East, and, bringing back the products of the looms and forges of Germany to the new world, drove out the manufactures of Yorkshire, Manchester and Birmingham.

It was not to be expected that the British would look upon this development with approval. It took from them the trade with the enemy colonies, conveyed the products of these colonies to the enemy mother countries or gave them profitable sales in neutral markets, and consequently subjected the goods of the British colonies to an unwelcome competition on the Continent and at the same time created a market in America for the industrial products of the Continent which competed with those of Great Britain herself. Moreover, the shipping of the neutrals was considered to cause an enviable activity in the enemy ports; and, finally, it was considered to increase Napoleon's military power by relieving him of the necessity of providing convoys, which would have been necessary if the connexions had been provided by the French mercantile marine, and also by freeing him from the cares of supplying his colonies. These last matters implied a situation which the British would certainly have deprecated for their own part and which was also anything but welcome to Napoleon himself; but the other aspects of the situation involved many things which were bound to tempt Great Britain to interfere.

However, the British measures against the colonial trade of the Americans were comparatively mild for several years after the draconic law of November 6, 1793, regarding the confiscation of all vessels carrying products of the French colonies or conveying supplies to them had been revoked within two months. The absence of consistently maintained blockade declarations against the enemy colonies is especially striking. The instructions of 1794, 1798, and 1803, which we have previously mentioned,[1] aimed mainly at preventing only direct intercourse between the enemy mother countries and their colonies, and also, in the case of that of 1798, at drawing the trade through British ports. Beyond that, they wished to tolerate trade only in ' free goods ', that is to say, goods which had passed into neutral hands. Thus the instructions of 1794 forbade direct intercourse between the port of an enemy colony and a European port, as well as trade in products which

---

[1] See *ante*, pp. 45 and 81.

continued to be French property, while the instructions of 1798 allowed even direct intercourse with Europe provided a call was made at a European port belonging to Great Britain or the home country of the vessel.  The instructions of 1803 introduced a certain modification of this, in that, curiously enough, a British port is no longer approved but only a port in the vessel's home country ;  and it is further laid down that the goods must belong to a citizen of the same country.  Especially during the first years after the new outbreak of war in 1803 the treatment of the neutrals, both Americans and Danes, was unusually mild and their shipping was little disturbed.  The number of captured vessels incorporated with the British merchant fleet was also smaller in the years 1803–6 than it was in the preceding or following years.[1]

The ' neutralization ' of enemy property resulting from the trade war itself, as well as from Sir William Scott's exposition of the law, assumed enormous proportions ;  and Stephen's book is full of characteristic and well-documented examples of the extent to which the regulations were evaded.  These evasions, the number of which was legion, aimed at showing both that the trip was really (*bona fide*) begun in a neutral (American) port and that the goods were neutral property.  With the former object new ship's papers were procured in an American port, sometimes, indeed, a new crew ;  in fact, there were occasions when two vessels exchanged cargoes so that they might both truthfully say that the cargo had been taken aboard in a neutral port.  Moreover, separate insurances were taken for each trip, and the import duty was paid in the fictitious manner previously indicated.[2]  With regard to the neutral ownership of the cargoes, the most grotesque situations arose.  In this connexion an extract from Stephen's account, which is supported by references to the different legal cases, is well worth quoting :

[1] According to Porter (*op. cit.*, p. 396), the number of ships captured and incorporated with the British mercantile fleet was as follows :

| Year | Ships | Year | Ships | Year | Ships | Year | Ships |
|------|-------|------|-------|------|-------|------|-------|
| 1801 | 2,779 | 1804 | 2,533 | 1807 | 2,764 | 1810 | 3,903 |
| 1802 | 2,827 | 1805 | 2,520 | 1808 | 3,222 | 1811 | 4,023 |
| 1803 | 2,286 | 1806 | 2,564 | 1809 | 3,547 | 1812 | 3,899 |

[2] See *ante*, p. 103.

Merchants who, immediately prior to the last war, were scarcely known, even in the obscure seaport towns at which they resided, have suddenly started up as sole owners of great numbers of ships, and sole proprietors of rich cargoes, which it would have alarmed the wealthiest merchants of Europe to hazard at once on the chance of a market, even in peaceable times.  A man who, at the breaking out of the war, was a petty shoemaker in a small town of East Friesland, had, at one time, a hundred and fifty vessels navigating as his property, under Prussian colours . . . The cargoes of no less than five East Indians, all composed of the rich exports of Batavia, together with three of the ships, were contemporary purchases, on speculation, of a single house at Providence in Rhode Island, and were all bound, as asserted, to that American port ; where, it is scarcely necessary to add, no demand for their cargoes existed. . . .  Single ships have been found returning with bullion on board, to the value of from a hundred to a hundred and fifty thousand Spanish dollars, besides valuable cargoes of other colonial exports.  Yet even these daring adventurers have been eclipsed.  One neutral house has boldly contracted for all the merchandize of the Dutch East India Company at Batavia, amounting in value to no less than one million seven hundred thousand pounds sterling.

All this led, in the spring of 1805, to an alteration in the practice of the British law courts, which considerably damaged the possibilities of the American carrying trade.  The highest British prize court, the Prize Appeal Court of the Privy Council, in the famous case of the ship *Essex* with its cargo from Barcelona to Salem, Massachusetts, and thence to Havana, declared both the vessel and the cargo forfeited, despite the fact that the latter had been unloaded and passed through the custom-house in the usual way in the American port (May 22).  This precedent was immediately followed by two others in the Admiralty Court, whereby the intention of eluding the regulations was declared to be decisive as against the external criteria.  At the same time the British went a more direct way to the end of obtaining control over the American colonies of the enemy, namely, by passing a series of laws which were promulgated in April and June 1805, and in July 1806.  These were intended to encourage the importation of the products of those colonies either direct to England by licence or to the British West Indies, either to sixteen free ports established there or, with somewhat less liberty and on the basis of a licence, to other islands, with a somewhat varying right to be forwarded to the British home country. At the same time permission was given to send a return cargo from the British to the foreign colonies. To the sixteen free ports importation might be made in small vessels of any nationality whatsoever, that is to say, even of enemy nationality.[1]

This new application of the law as regards ' circuitous voyages ' aroused a great deal of feeling in the United States, and in April 1806, led to an American counter-measure ; and at the same time there were issued the British blockade declarations concerning the North Sea coast and the English Channel on which we have previously touched.[2] The most important of these in all respects was the blockade which was proclaimed on May 16, 1806, on the initiative of the then British foreign secretary, the celebrated Whig politician, Charles James Fox. This created a strictly blockaded region between Ostend and the mouth of the Seine—that is to say, practically Havre—and also two less strictly blockaded regions to the north and to the south thereof—from Ostend to the Elbe and from the mouth of the Seine to Brest, respectively. Neutral vessels were conceded the right to call at the ports on the last two stretches, on condition that their goods were not contraband of war and did not belong to enemy subjects, and on the further condition that they had not been loaded in an enemy port and were not, to begin with, bound to such a port.

Like most of the British blockade regulations, this was very obscure ; and it is not known to me how it was applied during the remainder of the year. Mahan's view that it liberated neutrals from the obligation laid down in the *Essex* case, honestly to import the goods of the enemy colonies before they were again exported to Europe, is not very satisfactory as an interpretation of the law ;[3] for the condition was absolutely binding by the

---

[1] 45 Geo. III, cc. 34 & 57 ; 46 Geo. III, c. 111.

[2] See *ante*, p. 81.

[3] Mahan, *Influence of Sea Power*, &c., vol. II, pp. 269–70 ; also, *Sea Power in its Relations*, &c., vol. I, p. 108.

' rule of 1756 ', even irrespective of the question whether any blockade had been ordered, and consequently it could not be regarded as annulled by the fact that the blockade had been made less strict on certain stretches.

Both in Great Britain herself and also in America and on the Continent of Europe, indeed, these different British measures during the years 1805 and 1806, especially the new exposition of the law in the prize courts, were regarded as serious blows against the neutral carrying trade. But the American trade statistics given above [1] do not point to this. On the contrary, they show a higher figure for exports of colonial goods during 1806 than during the year before or after; and the figures relating to captures do not show any considerable rise until the following year. It is possible, therefore, that in reality the application of the measures was such as Mahan has laid down. In any case, it may surely be considered clear that during 1806 Great Britain did not get rid of the neutral trade of which she disapproved or put an end to the advantages which, from a British point of view, this trade afforded to the enemy part of the Continent.

Then, at the close of the year, came Napoleon's Continental decree. Owing to the enormous emphasis with which it was proclaimed, as well as to the measures by which it was followed, this gave a tangible occasion for the discussion of new measures chiefly against the neutrals. The ministry which came to power in Great Britain after Pitt's death in January 1806, was under the leadership of Lord Grenville, who had for many years been Pitt's foreign secretary and fellow worker; and for the reason that it embraced many of the most gifted politicians in the country, it is known in history as the ' Ministry of All the Talents '. The foreign secretary at the start was Fox, the most Francophile of all British statesmen, and, after his death in the middle of September, the future leader of the Whig Party, the then Lord Howick, but better known under his later title of Earl Grey. This government was not inclined toward forcible measures; and the only British statesman after Pitt's death

[1] See *ante*, p. 103.

who was to some extent equal to Napoleon, but who did not belong to the Talents Ministry, namely, George Canning, somewhat later said disparagingly that the Grenville measures against the Berlin decree ' partook of all the bad qualities of half-measures '.[1]

### First Order in Council (January 7, 1807)

However, Lord Howick's governmental measure turned out to be the first step in the British counteraction which was to occupy the thoughts of the whole world during the following five years. Like its successors, it assumed the form of a measure by the King in Council, without the co-operation of Parliament, and it was therefore, from the point of view of public law, an Order in Council. Hence, this term became afterwards in the popular mind almost a proper name for regulations of this kind. The first Order in Council was issued on January 7, 1807, or a month and a half after the Berlin decree.[2] As a measure of reprisal against the Berlin decree and with the reference, previously quoted,[3] to the necessity of ' restraining the violence of the enemy and to retort upon him the evils of his own injustice ', trade between enemy ports was entirely forbidden, and also trade between other ports at which the Berlin decree prevented English ships from calling. The members of the Grenville government afterwards maintained that this was only an application of the ' rule of 1756 ', which included a prohibition of coasting trade along the territory of the enemy. But if that had been the case, there would have been no use of asserting an intention of reprisal; and the opponents of the government— e. g., Lord Eldon, the Lord Chancellor in the following Ministry— also observed that the order went outside the alleged principle, in that it prohibited, for instance, trade between French and Spanish ports. Trade between the enemy mother country and

[1] Hansard, vol. ix, p. 687 (June 30, 1807).

[2] All these Orders in Council of 1807 are printed in Hansard, vol. x, pp. 126–48; but as some of them are not readily accessible outside of Great Britain, and as they are, moreover, very often incorrectly summarized, they are reproduced in app. i from Hansard.

[3] See ante, p. 99.

her colonies was forbidden as a matter of course, but this implied nothing new.  On the other hand, as regards coasting trade proper, it was more difficult to get at than any other part of the enemy's shipping, a point to which the domestic opponents of the government did not fail to call attention.  On March 17, 1807, in a communication to J. G. Rist, the Danish *chargé d'affaires* at London at the time, Lord Howick amplified this further by declaring that there was no objection to neutral vessels carrying cargo to an enemy port, thence going in ballast to another port, and then carrying cargo from this last port to the home country.  It was just the flourishing Danish Mediterranean trade that was hit by the new law ; but apart from that the importance of the measure can not be regarded as great, except that to a certain extent it compromised the Whig Party with regard to the justifiability of measures of reprisal, and so far rendered difficult their position with regard to the more comprehensive measures of their successors in the same direction.[1]

It was quite natural, therefore, that those who were in favour of more forcible measures on the part of the government, either against Napoleon or against the neutrals, were not satisfied with the January order.  In this connexion we have first to think of Stephen and his supporters, who, according to the later evidence of his opponent, Brougham, constituted the great majority.  It is true that Stephen's book had appeared as far back as the autumn of 1805, or more than a year before the issue of the Berlin decree ; but there is nothing to indicate that either the man or his book had exerted any influence on the January order.  The positive demands of Stephen are not quite clear, it is true ; but in any case they can not be regarded as having been satisfied by the measure of the Grenville ministry. In many passages in his book Stephen assumes a negative attitude toward the thought of using the war as a pretext for

---

[1] Lord Eldon in the House of Lords, Feb. 15, 1808 (Hansard, vol. x, p. 475); Perceval in the House of Commons, Feb. 4, 1807 (Hansard, vol. viii, p. 629). Lord Howick's declaration is given in Hansard, vol. x, pp. 402 *et seq*. Linvald, *Bidrag til Oplysning om Danmark-Norges Handel og Skibsfart, 1800–1807*, in *Dansk Historisk Tidsskrift*, VIII (1917), vol. vi, pp. 409, 433–4.

commercial advantages, which he calls 'a morbid excess of sensibility to immediate commercial profit'; and as a warning example to his countrymen he mentions the action of the Dutch, during a siege, of selling powder to the enemy, whereby, he says, they 'preferred their trade to their political safety'. In accordance with this, he adopts for the most part a purely naval standpoint and urges that the neutrals, with very few exceptions, should be entirely prevented from dealing with enemy countries and in enemy goods, and especially with enemy colonies. In that way the enemy would be compelled to carry on his trade himself and to fetter his naval forces by convoying trading vessels and protecting his colonies and providing them with supplies; and by all these things the desired possibility of captures would also be secured to its fullest extent. Alongside all of this, however, we also find hints that more directly anticipate the following course of development, namely, that the goods of the enemy colonies might be conveyed to the British market and there taxed to such an extent as to prevent them from competing with those of the British colonies.

Stephen was closely connected with the English Tory politician, Spencer Perceval, who as prime minister was in company with Stephen at the time of his assassination by a lunatic in 1812; and it was from Perceval that there came the first positive criticism of the January regulations, *viz.*, in the House of Commons on February 4, 1807. In his speech, too, we have the first complete explanation of the motives that lay behind the definitive Orders in Council; and to judge by the speech it would seem that the detailed framing of those orders was due less to Stephen than to Perceval. The latter clearly takes his stand, from the very first, on what we have designated above [1] as the 'third line' of policy, namely, that of trade rivalry. After a criticism of the January regulations he comes to what he regards as two possible expedients for meeting the Berlin decree. The one would be 'to exclude certain necessary commerce' from the territory of the enemy. But if this leads us to expect a plea for an effective blockade, we are immediately

[1] See *ante*, p. 99.

disabused; for it refers to the importation of French and Spanish colonial goods into France, with the object of at least making them dearer and thus strengthening the competitive power of the British goods. The alternative expedient, and the one which was to acquire practical importance, consists in the previously treated ' third line ', namely, to turn the measures of France against herself by the order ' that no goods should be carried to France except they first touched at a British port. They might be forced to be entered at the custom-house and a certain entry fee imposed, which would contribute to enhance the price and give a better sale in the foreign market to your own commodities.' It is scarcely necessary to point out how faithfully the previously traced economic tendency of maritime blockade is here expressed, with sales on the enemy market as a self-evident aim. The second of these concrete proposals is somewhat influenced by the instructions of 1798, which in their turn stand in a certain connexion with the *entrepôt* or ' old colonial ' system.

Perceval's contribution to the discussion became of great practical importance owing to the fact that some few weeks later, in March 1807, the Grenville ministry resigned and was succeeded by a government with the Duke of Portland as a figurehead prime minister, Canning as foreign secretary, and Perceval himself as chancellor of the exchequer. The minister of finance soon found occasion to take up afresh the question of measures against the Berlin decree, and that occasion arose in the West Indian interest, which to some extent had also lain behind Stephen's action. A West Indian petition which had been presented to the House of Commons as early as February had been referred to a select committee, whose report was ordered to be printed in August. The report strongly emphasized the American trade between the enemy colonies and Europe as the cause of the fall in the price of sugar, and this was stated to have gone so far that it no longer covered even the expenses of cultivation except on the largest estates in the British West Indies. In the debate on this report Perceval promised a prompt treatment of the question. We may regard as a first step toward the fulfilment of this promise an Order in Council which was issued only a few days afterwards (August 19), whereby vessels sailing under the flags of Mecklenburg, Oldenburg, Papenburg, or Kniphausen were declared lawful prize if they touched at an enemy port unless they were going from or coming to a British port. As the colours of these somewhat dubious North German principalities were commonly used as neutral flags in the more risky cases, this measure implies a first application of the new principle to a part of the pretended neutral trade.[1]

### ORDERS IN COUNCIL (NOVEMBER 11–DECEMBER 18, 1807)

The decisive step, however, was taken by three Orders in Council of November 11, 1807, supplemented by one of November 18, five of November 25, and one of December 18 ; and to these there were afterwards added further new ones, so that in the end the number of them amounted to no less than twenty-four. It is this system of ordinances, and especially the fundamental ordinance of November 11, that formed the foundation of British policy during the following period—in form, it is true, only until the spring of 1809, but in reality until the collapse of the Continental System. It is also these, and not the January ordinance, that are usually meant when reference is made to the Orders in Council. They were further supplemented in the spring of 1808 by no fewer than six less important statutes governing such points of the system as could not be put into execution without the consent of Parliament.[2]

It is truly anything but easy to explain the purport of this far-reaching complex of regulations. The Orders in Council, in particular, are marvels of obscurity and rambling. We find the same matter scattered over several ordinances, which seemed

---

[1] Lord Brougham, *Life and Times of, written by himself* (2d ed., London, 1871), vol. II, pp. 5, 7; *Speeches of* (Edinburgh, 1838), vol. I, p. 404 ; Stephen, *War in Disguise*, &c., pp. 38 et seq., 116 et seq., 163 et seq., 171 ; Hansard, vol. VIII, pp. 620–56; vol. IX, pp. 85–101, 1152–3 ; app. pp. lxxxi et seq. ; Porter, *op. cit.*, p. 379.

[2] 48 Geo. III, cc. 26, 28, 29, 33, 34 and 37.

absolutely to contradict one another, of the same day or with only a few days' interval. This incomprehensibility not only holds good for the people of later generations, but also for the people of that time ; and the fogginess of the regulations was a standing butt for the jeers of the opposition. Thus, Lord Grenville declared his belief that the very persons who drafted them had scarcely understood their content ; and he also alleged that four points in the same ordinance contained four contradictions, and that he was not a little proud of having been able to understand the connexion at last.[1] The often confused and mutually conflicting explanations of the ministers did not, as a rule, help to clear matters ; and owing to the total lack of all special investigations, especially as to their connexion with general legislation regarding shipping and the colonies, certain points at the present time are not easy to interpret.[2] But this does not apply to the general line of thought, which is quite clear ; and the pretended object of the measures can be distinguished without any considerable difficulty from their real objects. The fundamental idea is to be found practically in the germ as early as Perceval's speech in February.

Seldom, however, has the contrast between the policy officially proclaimed and the policy actually pursued stood out in a more striking way than in the chief of the three Orders in Council of November 11, the one which can properly be called the blockade ordinance.[3] After a declaration that the January ordinance had not attained its object, either of compelling the enemy to revoke his measure or of inducing the neutrals to take action to the same effect, this ordinance simply proceeds to copy the most important points of the Berlin decree. Thus not only all enemy countries with their colonies, but also all places from which the British flag is excluded (this last point has nothing corresponding to it in the blockade declaration of the Berlin decree), are declared to be subject to the same rule as if they were really blockaded in the strictest manner ; and, further, all

---

[1] Hansard, vol. x, pp. 482-3 ; vol. xii, p. 774.
[2] The reader is here referred to the text of the Orders in Council in app. i.
[3] See app. i, no. v.

trade in their products is prohibited.  Every vessel trading to those countries shall be fair prize, as well as its cargo and all goods coming from there.

But immediately following these draconic regulations are exceptions which entirely nullify the rule and make possible the very trade so rigorously prohibited.  Out of alleged regard for the neutrals, in fact, it is declared that they shall still be allowed to provide themselves with colonial goods for their own consumption and even to carry on ' such trade with His Majesty's enemies as shall be carried on directly with the ports of His Majesty's dominions or of his allies '.  And in this the true fundamental principle has found expression.  Ignoring details, we may say that the real principal regulations, as distinct from the apparent ones, consists in permitting both direct trade between the home country of a neutral vessel and enemy colonies and also direct trade between the European British port and enemy ports.  What is prohibited in the first place, therefore, is direct intercourse between the enemy colonies and their mother countries.  But further, in the main, all direct intercourse between the enemy countries and other ports is prohibited, except when the ' other ports ' are either European British ports or ports in the vessel's own country.  That is to say, intercourse is also prohibited between enemy ports and neutral ports elsewhere than in the home country of the neutral vessels.

Thus the regulations left the intercourse of the neutrals, principally the Americans, with the enemy West Indian colonies so far undisturbed.  But by preventing the American vessels from conveying the products of those colonies direct to any port on the European mainland, neutral or enemy, the Orders in Council practically cut them off from almost the whole trade with the enemy colonies, except in so far as they were willing to put in at a British port ; for the intercourse which was still allowed between the enemy colonies and the United States itself was of no very great importance, the Union's requirements of West Indian products being quite insignificant.  Consequently, we can not deny the existence of a certain amount of consistency in these measures, despite their seeming aimlessness; and this showed itself in a number of details.

The principal thing in all respects was the obligatory call at a British port. The intention of this regulation was presumably, above all, to raise the prices on the products of the enemy colonies and the enemy parts of the European mainland in all ports where they might compete with goods of Great Britain or her colonies.[1] For this purpose it was laid down that both goods of enemy destination and goods of enemy origin, as well as goods which had been loaded in an enemy port, should be discharged on the arrival of the vessel at a British port. The only exceptions were corn, flour, and other unmanufactured natural produce brought direct from the producing country, where there was no competition with British goods, and where it was thought possible, without inconvenience, to show a certain consideration for the exportation by the United States of their own products, as opposed to their re-exportation of colonial goods. The whole of this exception, however, furnishes very significant evidence of the long distance that Great Britain had travelled from the temporary plan of 1793 to starve out the Continent.

When the goods were afterwards to be exported again, the majority of the foreign goods, but not the British colonial goods, nor the actual products of neutral countries just mentioned, were subjected to customs dues; and in complete accordance with the aim of the whole measure these duties attained a considerable height: for instance, for coffee, 28s. per cwt.; for brown sugar, 10s.; and for white sugar, 14s. At the prices then current these rates would seem to have corresponded to at least 20 or 30 per cent. of the value.[2]

What this meant for goods that had been brought under British control only by military pressure, appears from such a detail as the fact that a special provision in the most important

[1] Cf., for instance, the utterances of Lord Bathurst, the president of the Board of Trade, and Lord Hawkesbury (afterwards Lord Liverpool), the home secretary, in the House of Lords, Feb. 15, 1808 (Hansard, vol. x, pp. 471, 485).

[2] The figures relating to prices will be found in Tooke, *A History of Prices*, &c., vol. II, pp. 398, 414.

of the statutes had to concede to the owner of the goods the right to allow them to be destroyed in port without duty.[1] But besides this there were also certain restrictions in the right to re-export these goods at all, still without the slightest intention of cutting off the enemy's supplies, although it often might seem so, but only in the interests of commercial rivalry. The greatest relaxations, therefore, curious as it may seem, were made in the permission to export to European ports, inasmuch as everything might go there, even enemy property (to be distinguished, of course, from commodities of enemy origin); this was otherwise excluded from all toleration by reason of the British denial of the rule that ' free ships make free goods '. The reason, of course, was that British statesmen, as usual, wished to force upon a reluctant enemy goods *via* England. All British and East Indian commodities and captured goods were allowed to go to enemy colonies; and foreign goods imported to England might go there by a licence which would always still further increase their price ; while, finally, other places, chiefly, of course, the British colonies, might not, without special licence, receive six kinds of goods that played a special part in the colonial trade, namely, sugar, coffee, wine, brandy, snuff, and cotton.[2]

But there were two commodities concerning which there arose a very vehement struggle, namely, raw cotton and cinchona bark, usually called Jesuit's bark. The former was naturally of the greatest importance in the continental industry that competed with the British, while the latter, as is well known, was a *pièce de résistance* in the older pharmacopœia in all febrile maladies. After having originally thought of imposing an export duty on these goods too, the British government decided to prohibit their export. Here, at least, where an actual

---

[1] 48 Geo. III, c. 26, s. 16 (the Principal ' Orders in Council Act '). Cf. Lord Erskine in the House of Lords, Mar. 8, 1808 (Hansard, vol. x, pp. 966-7).

[2] This seems to the writer to be the only possible interpretation of the most obscure of all the ordinances, namely, the Order in Council of Nov. 25, 1807 (printed as no. IX in app. I), which is clearly the one alluded to by Grenville in his utterance previously cited (pp. 114-15), compared with the Order in Council of the same day (printed as no. X).

prohibition of export was created, one would expect to meet with an aim at the actual blockade of the Continent, which the opposition indeed often assumed, more or less *bona fide*, to be the real object of this measure. But, as a matter of fact, nothing was further from the thoughts of the government. Perceval, who in his capacity of chancellor of the exchequer introduced the bills on this subject, justified the prohibition on cinchona bark, it is true, by alleging that the greatest difficulties had already revealed themselves on the Continent, especially in Napoleon's armies, through the scarcity of medicaments, as was indeed shown by the fact that the price had increased sevenfold. But he went on immediately to say: ' The object of the prohibition in this instance was that it might ultimately be the means of introducing other articles into the Continent.' For these reasons the laws themselves authorized licences from the prohibitions, as Perceval again emphasized, in order to prevail on the enemy to receive British goods. ' There would be no difficulty,' he said, ' in obtaining any quantity of this article, the moment the enemy took off his prohibition from the importation of other articles.' [1] Thus the competition point of view was the deciding factor all along the line.

But it remained to regulate the control by seeing that the vessels went as a matter of fact to the British ports ; and the regulations on this subject were among those that attracted the greatest attention, although they are not of equal interest in principle. The commanders of British war-ships and privateers were instructed, before the new regulations became known, to warn vessels on the way to enemy or other forbidden ports, and also to order them to make their way to specially named ports. Vessels on their way to an American port which was not in their own country were to go to Halifax in Nova Scotia (which was also used for similar purposes during the recent war) or to a West Indian free port ; vessels south of the Equator were to go to Ceylon, to St. Helena or the Cape of Good Hope ; and

[1] House of Commons, Feb. 22 and 24, Mar. 16, 1808 (Hansard, vol x, pp. 695–6, 728, 1168) ; 48 Geo. III, cc. 29, 33, 34.

vessels on their way to Europe, either to Gibraltar or to Malta or to any port in the British Isles.

In addition to all this, finally, there were pure measures of reprisal, framed according to their French counterparts. Trading vessels were to remain enemy property and to be confiscated as such, even if they were sold to neutrals ; and what was the most unreasonable of all the regulations, the mere possession of a French certificate of origin as to the non-British nationality of the cargo was to involve the confiscation of both ship and cargo. On the other hand, since the lack of such certificates involved capture on the part of the French, a neutral vessel, at least if it did not sail under British convoy, had, according to this last regulation, no alternative between breaking the orders of one power or the other, with the consequent risk of capture from one side or the other, provided, it is well to remark, that they wished to act openly and honestly, which therefore was practically impossible. The only effect of all this was the establishment of a system of double ship's papers, which gradually attained an immense scope ; and thus in reality the consequence was that the laws of both sides were broken.

In this multiplicity of regulations—which, however, have not by any means been fully reproduced here—the most prominent thing of all is the obligation to call at a British port, with the possibilities thereby created of controlling and rendering dearer enemy products, especially enemy colonial goods. In the course of time, too, the British ministers managed to find a comparatively clear expression of their ways of thinking in this respect. This was especially the case in almost identical utterances made in the spring of 1812 by three of the ministers. As formulated by Lord Bathurst, the president of the Board of Trade, that is to say, minister of commerce, it ran as follows : ' France by her decrees had resolved to abolish all trade with England : England said, in return, that France should then have no trade but with England.' [1] This, of course, did away

---

[1] House of Lords, Feb. 28, 1812. Hansard, vol. xxi, p. 1053. Almost to the same effect, cf. Rose, vice president of the Board of Trade, in the House of Commons, Mar. 3, 1812, and Perceval on the same day and Apr. 17, 1812. Hansard, vol. xxi,

with the idea of blockade as such, and the licensing system took its place in the seat of honour, partly through the ' proviso ' regulations of the ordinances themselves and partly through the licences expressly permitted in them.

This, however, was far from clear to everybody ; nor was it approved by all to whom it was clear.  Some of the home critics of the British government, somewhat later including Canning, who was a member of the government when the ordinances were issued but had to leave it in 1809, considered that they ought to be true to their alleged purpose of making the enemy feel the consequences of his own injustice and to that end cut off his supplies.[1]  But more numerous were those attacks of the opposition which blamed the government for its advertised intention, doing so under the unfounded assumption that it was sincere.  These critics dwelt on the impossibility of starving out the Continent, the small extent to which a shortage of certain articles of luxury was felt, the encouragement to new branches of production and the invention of substitutes which such a blockade might introduce into the Continent, and all the consequent injury to British industry and British colonies.  In point of fact, however, all this criticism did not apply to the Orders in Council as they worked and as they were intended to work, but to Napoleon's Continental System.  To that extent, therefore, it implied a recognition of the appositeness of that system, which was certainly not the intention of the critics.  The real character of the government policy did not, however, escape criticism altogether, as when Lord Grenville in one of his first discussions on the Orders in Council, in the House of Lords on February 15, 1808, declared that : ' This principle of forcing trade into our markets would have disgraced the darkest ages of monopoly.'  On the whole, however, it may be said that the criticism, usually very much embittered, missed the true point of the policy of the government.[2]

pp. 1120, 1153; vol. xxii, p. 434.  Cf. also, Lord Wellesley's utterance in 1811 (see below, p. 208).                                                          [1] See *ante*, p. 99.

    [2] The following are a few examples : First standpoint : Canning in the House of Commons, Mar. 3, 1812 (Hansard, vol. xxi, p. 1147) ; Lord Sidmouth, the former and far from eminent prime minister under the name of Addington, in the

## Territorial Expansion of the Continental System (1807)

In order to make the connexion clear, the British counter-measures to the Berlin decree have been followed to the close of the year 1807, and even somewhat beyond. But on the Continent the year 1807 had been rich in tremendous events with far-reaching consequences for the Continental System. At Tilsit Napoleon had prevailed upon Russia to join the great policy of reprisals in the event of her failure to mediate a peace between Great Britain and France; and naturally enough she failed. The bombardment of Copenhagen—Canning's act of violence against Denmark, which, as we know,[1] was quite superfluous—had thrown that country entirely into the hands of Napoleon and made its ruler, the Crown Prince Frederick, who shortly afterwards ascended the throne as Frederick VI, one of his few sincere allies. Meanwhile, Napoleon's own aggression against Portugal had put an end to the independence of that country after the royal family had fled to Brazil. The remaining states of Europe were either more or less purely subsidiary states to France, or at least had been so recently vanquished by Napoleon that they could not contemplate resisting the introduction of the Berlin decree. To the former category belonged the kingdoms of Italy (North Italy), Holland, and Naples, the Confederation of the Rhine, and in the main (for the present) Spain; to the latter, Prussia and Austria. Besides these, the kingdom of Etruria (Tuscany) was reduced to submission by military occupation and the other Italian territories

House of Lords, Feb. 17, 1809, and Feb. 28, 1812 (Hansard, vol. XII, pp. 791-2; vol. XXI, p. 1071). Second standpoint: Lord Auckland, president of the Board of Trade in 'All the Talents' and in his time the eponymous negotiator of the Eden Treaty, in the House of Lords, Feb. 15, 1808 (Hansard, vol. X, p. 468); Lord Henry Petty, chancellor of the exchequer in 'All the Talents' and afterwards Lord Lansdowne, in the House of Commons, Feb. 18, 1808 (Hansard, vol. X, p. 682); Whitbread, one of the principal speakers of the Opposition, in the House of Commons, Mar. 6, 1809 (Hansard, vol. XII, pp. 1167-8). Third standpoint: Lord Grenville, as above (Hansard, vol. X, p. 483). Cf. the more perspicacious criticism of Lord Grey, formerly Lord Howick, in the House of Lords, June 13, 1810 (Hansard, vol. XVII, pp. 545 et seq).

[1] For the Scandinavian investigations the reader is referred to the leading authority on Danish history in the eighteenth and early nineteenth centuries, Professor Edvard Holm, *Danmark-Norges Historie fra 1720 til 1814*, vol. VII.

by suitable pressure. Even Turkey bound herself to exclude British goods. In this connexion it was especially important that the great emporium of Leghorn was closed to the trade of England by the overthrow of the independence of Etruria. At the close of 1807, therefore, there was only one European state that openly refused to become a party to the Continental System; and that state was Sweden, the sole ally of Great Britain. Against her, accordingly, Russia, at the instigation of Napoleon, made the attack which was to end with the conquest of Finland and the deposition of Gustavus IV Adolphus. Thus during its very first year the Continental System attained a territorial range which far transcended even the boldest plans that had been formulated in the minds of its author's predecessors under the Convention and Directory, when they spoke of a blockade from the Tagus to the Elbe or from Gibraltar to Texel.

### First Milan Decree (Nov. 23, 1807)

At the same time Napoleon had laboured further at the internal structure of the system in forms which, in the main, belong to part III. After regulating in greater detail the treatment of British vessels and goods on the especially exposed coast-line of North Germany, he gave to certain provisions which applied to that coast validity for his own empire through the first Milan decree (November 23, 1807). This contained detailed regulations concerning the manner in which it was to be determined that vessels had called at a British port, concerning the confiscation of vessels and cargoes in this case (not merely their expulsion, as was prescribed in the Berlin decree), and concerning the certificates of origin previously mentioned touching the non-British provenience of goods.

### Second Milan Decree (Dec. 17, 1807)

It was during his stay in the kingdom of Italy that Napoleon was informed of the British Orders in Council of November 11; and he seems to have been seized by a violent fit of anger, which found expression in the second of the fundamental laws of the Continental System, namely, the second Milan decree, issued on December 17, 1807. The part of the Orders in Council to which he especially devoted his attention was the in itself not very remarkable examination (the warning) by British war-ships ; but of course he also took notice of the obligatory call in England and the duty on re-exports. He hurled out his decree as a measure of reprisal against the English government, ' which,' he said, ' assimilates its legislation to that of Algiers,' and applied it only against such nations as failed to compel England to respect their flags, and also, as usual, made it valid only so long as England continued to disregard international law (Article 4). Every vessel which submitted to any of the three regulations—examination, call in England, or paying duty there—was declared to be denationalized ; it had forfeited the protection of its own flag and, from the view-point of French legislation, had become English property (Article 1), and had thus become lawful prize both in port and at sea (Article 2). The doubt which had hitherto prevailed concerning the application of the Continental System by sea was thereby removed. The real content of the Milan decree is simply the express and unrestricted extension of the system from the Continent to the sea, in so far as French privateers could make it effective there. This fact finds expression in the curious formula that the British Isles are now declared in blockade both by land and by sea ; and every vessel on its way to or from an English port, or an English colonial port, or even a port occupied by England, are declared to be fair prize (Article 3). Moreover, by attaching these regulations in the first place to the examination, which the neutrals almost entirely lacked the power of preventing, and not only to the call in a British port, where a certain amount of independent will might perchance remain for the masters of neutral vessels, the Continental System had approached the Nivôse law of 1798 more closely than in its previous workings ; that is to say, it had come to apply against neutral shipping as such. This was quite deliberate on the part of Napoleon ; and from this point of time dates his view that there were no longer any neutrals, inasmuch as they were either, and as a rule, Englishmen in disguise, or, at all events, had made themselves the accomplices of the English by accommodating themselves to the Orders in Council. This construction put upon non-French shipping applied almost as a matter of course to vessels, not only from allied, but also from purely vassal powers. On the very same day that the Milan decree was issued, for instance, Napoleon gave orders to Decrès, his minister of the marine, to detain a Russian vessel—that is to say, a vessel belonging to an allied nation—which had arrived in the port of Morlaix in Brittany; and for this order he gave the truly Napoleonic justification that it was either really English—in which case it was condemned as a matter of course—or that it was really Russian, and in that case should be detained to prevent it from being taken by the English. Decrès was also charged to give orders to the same effect to all French ports concerning Danish, Dutch, Spanish, and all other vessels, and to investigate whether the regulations were similarly applied in the vassal states. On this basis Napoleon afterwards systematically built up his treatment of non-French vessels in the ports of France and its subsidiary states, with gradually more and more developed protectionist tendencies as against shipping which was not purely French.[1]

On the same day that the Milan decree was issued, Champagny, the foreign minister at the time, received orders to transmit it by a special courier to Holland, Spain, and Denmark, with the request that these nominally sovereign states should comply with (obtempérer à) it; and the continental powers immediately set to work to bring their legislation into accordance with the new decree of the master.[2] Of greater interest than the details of this development, which becomes important only in connexion with the inquiry into the actual workings of the system, is the attitude assumed by the United States—

[1] First Milan decree: Bulletin des lois, &c., 4th ser., bull. 172, no. 2,912. Second Milan decree: Correspondance, no. 13,391; cf. also, Napoleon to Champagny, Jan. 10, 1810, no. 16,127; also, Napoleon to Decrès, no. 13,398.

[2] Correspondance, no. 13,393; Martens, Nouveau recueil, &c., vol. I, pp. 458 et seq.

at that time almost the only remaining neutral power—toward this blow directed by both the belligerents mainly against neutral trade. The highly instructive development of the American attitude toward the Continental System went on alongside the development of European affairs down to the practical collapse of the system in 1812. It will form the subject of the next chapter.

# CHAPTER IV

## POLICY OF THE UNITED STATES

### AMERICAN POSITION

THE policy of the United States during the period of the Continental System is an example of the type which, in the course of an economic war to the knife, seeks to maintain neutrality to the uttermost and to take all the consequences of that attitude, without, it is true, the support of either external military power or an efficient internal administration.[1] Down to the close of 1807 this policy brought with it a unique development of American shipping and foreign trade, especially the carrying trade. But when the commercial war became more intense in 1807, it made a complete right-about-face and led to the second great self-blockade caused by the Continental System ; and finally, when this became quite untenable, it drove the American Union into the very war which its leading men had done everything in their power to avert.

The desire of the American statesmen for neutrality scarcely calls for any detailed explanation. The sympathies of the population were strongly divided between the combatants. Anglophiles predominated among the Federalists, who later developed into the Republican Party, while Francophiles predominated among the opposite party, the Republicans, later known as Democrats. The Federalists dominated the commercial and sea-faring states of New England, while the main support of their antagonists lay in the agricultural states of the South. The latter party tended to get the upper hand, strongly supported, as it was, by President Jefferson in 1801-9, and

---

[1] The best survey of American developments in this field is to be found in Mahan, *Sea Power in its Relations*, &c., vol. I, ch. IV. Diplomatic correspondence and other relevant matter is to be found in Hansard, as well as in *The Statutes at Large of the United States of America*.

again by President Madison in 1809–17, partly because of political tradition dating from the time when France co-operated in the American War of Independence, and partly because the conflicts of a neutral sea-faring nation must always be keenest with that combatant who commands the sea. The remarkable thing about the situation is that it was precisely those economic interests and those parts of the country for the defence of which the campaign of neutrality was carried to extremes, that were its most zealous opponents and did their utmost to prevent its efficacy. Nor did they hesitate to follow the same tactics even during the war to which the policy of neutrality led, just because the measures of neutrality had necessarily to be directed against the few remnants of inter-national intercourse that the belligerents had left undisturbed. Both in this respect and in other respects the neutrals of our day have had something to learn from American developments.

The increased severity in the British treatment of neutrals, as we know, went back especially to the new interpretation of ' broken voyages ' in the *Essex* case in the summer of 1805, and in April, 1806, it had occasioned the American counter-measure in the form of the Non-importation Act,[1] which prohibited the importation, both from England and from other countries, of most of the main groups of British industrial products, excluding, however, cotton goods. But the American law did not enter into force until November 15, and was suspended at the close of the year, so that it turned out to be nothing more than a threat. The Berlin decree of November 21, 1806, immediately led the American envoy in Paris to address an inquiry to the French minister of the marine, Vice Admiral Decrès, as to the interpretation of the new law at sea. In the absence of the Emperor the answer was favourable,[2] and consequently there was no immediate occasion for uneasiness on the part of America. On the contrary, there were complaints in England that the Americans were making common cause with Napoleon in order to supply France with the industrial products that she was otherwise wont to obtain from England. Nor was any great

---

[1] *United States Statutes at Large*, vol. II, p. 379.    [2] See *ante*, p. 91.

alteration made in this respect by the first British Order in Council of January, 1807, owing to its restricted range. Accordingly, during the greater part of the year 1807 American trade and shipping continued not merely to flourish, but even to grow, as is shown by the table previously printed.[1] In reality, the year 1807 marked the high-water mark of the trade and navigation of the United States for a very long time to come.

But the turning-point was to be reached before the close of the year. The beginning was made with the authentic interpretation of the law which Napoleon, as the sole final authority, gave to his Berlin decree, whereby it came to apply also to the sea. Then followed the new British Orders in Council of November and Napoleon's Milan decree of December.

### EMBARGO ACT (DECEMBER 22, 1807)

All this set going the great American series of counter-measures, which also, so far as they concerned Great Britain, were affected by the latest act of aggression, the so-called ' *Chesapeake* Affair ' of June, 1807. A British man-of-war requested to be allowed to search the American frigate *Chesapeake* with the object of recapturing some alleged deserters from the British navy ; and when the request was refused, as a matter of course, the British vessel opened fire, captured the American man-of-war, and took away four of the crew. To this was added the American annoyance at the British practice of impressing for naval service sailors on American trading vessels on the pretext that, having been born before the American states became independent, they were British subjects ; and this, combined with the *Chesapeake* Affair, gave rise to a very pretty diplomatic conflict.

But what gave the principal impulse to the American commercial, or rather anti-commercial, intervention was not the measures of Great Britain, but rather those of France, that is to say, the new adaptation of the Berlin decree, which brought it about that a stranded American vessel, the *Horizon*, had that

[1] See *ante*, p. 103.

part of its cargo which was of British origin declared fair prize. However, the new Orders in Council were known in the United States (in fact, though not officially) when on December 22, 1807, Congress and the President enacted the Embargo Act,[1] which is one of the most interesting legislative products of the period.  As has already been indicated, it was a self-blockade of the purest water, but, unlike Napoleon's, an open and direct one.  An embargo was laid on all vessels lying in American ports and bound for foreign ports.  The only exceptions were foreign vessels, which were allowed to depart after being informed of the enactment of the law ;  and vessels in the American coasting trade were to give security that the cargo should be discharged in an American port.  Almost at the same time the Non-importation Act, passed in the previous year against British goods, was put into force and excluded importation in foreign bottoms from the only power that was in a position to carry on trade by sea.  Under the pressure of the unreasonable procedure of both the combatants, the American government thus sought to cut off at a blow the abnormally large trade and shipping that the United States had until then enjoyed.  In principle the policy was impartial, inasmuch as it was intended, on the one hand, to deprive Great Britain of American cotton and grain, as well of sales on the American markets, and, on the other hand, to put an end to the colonial trade from which France and Spain and their colonies derived equal advantages, and also to the importation of the industrial products of the European Continent into America.  Although the measure was thus indisputably two-sided, the simultaneous enforcement of the one-sided Non-importation Act gave the policy the appearance of being directed distinctly against Great Britain.  That country, indeed, had touched on a particularly tender point by imposing duties on the goods which compulsorily passed through its territories, inasmuch as both the United States and the British opposition put it on a level with the taxation of American trade which in the preceding generation had given the final

[1] *United States Statutes at Large*, vol. II, p. 451.

impulse to the Declaration of Independence by 'the old thirteen '.[1]

President Jefferson's motive seems to have been partly the bias of the plantation owners, emphasized by his physiocratic tendency toward regarding agriculture as the highest work of man and his grave distrust of everything which departed from agriculture.   To begin with, at least, he undoubtedly considered, as the American historian, Channing, says, ' that to put an end to, let us say, three quarters of the commerce of the United States would be a blessing, albeit somewhat in disguise '.[2]   But evidently this, like most of the measures of the different powers in the commercial war, was also a measure of reprisal, an endeavour to compel the embittered belligerents to be reasonable.   In fact, unlike the majority of their own measures, it was a sincere attempt in that direction. It seems also as if the Embargo Act was a means of saving the great American merchant fleet, the largest next to that of Great Britain, from the extinction which must otherwise have been the almost necessary consequence of the Berlin and Milan decrees and of the Orders in Council.   Thus, for instance, a large ship-owner in Maryland stated that of fifteen vessels which he had dispatched during the bare four months between September 1 and the enactment of the Embargo Act, only three had arrived at their destination, while two had been captured by the French and the Spaniards, one had been seized at Hamburg, and nine had been taken to England.

However, it is rather an academic question what the effect of the Embargo Act would have been had it been obeyed, for nothing was further from reality.   It makes an almost moving impression to see how one supplementary law after another, each more detailed and more draconic than the other, seeks to stop up the holes in the original law, which was very summary ;   but it has seldom been shown more distinctly that a constant succession of new laws on the same subject means

[1] Cf. Lord Grenville in the House of Lords, Feb. 17, 1809.   Hansard, vol. xii, p. 774.
[2] Channing, *op. cit.*, vol. xii, p. 201–2.

a constant disobedience to the provisions of the law. As early as January 9, 1808, special enactments were made as to the security that coasting and fishing vessels would have to give, and it was declared that the exceptions made in the Embargo Act in favour of public armed vessels did not apply to privateers (chapter 8). On March 12, in the same year, foreign vessels also were required to give security to the extent of four times the value of vessel and cargo, or twice as much as for native vessels, that they would not sail to foreign ports ; and for fishing vessels, a declaration was imposed under oath as to whether any of the catch had been sold during the trip. At the same time, however, the President was authorized, very imprudently, to grant vessels the right to go in ballast to foreign ports in order to fetch from there the property of American citizens, on giving a pledge to return with that property, and not to carry on any other trade, etc. (chapter 33). Still more forceful was the intervention a month and a half later by a law of April 25, which both forbade all loading of vessels except under the control of the authorities, and also in general terms forbade any vessel to depart, without the special permission of the President, to any United States port or district which was adjacent to foreign territory ; and the customs staff was charged to take under their care any suspiciously large stocks of goods in such border regions. Further, the law gave to naval and customs vessels the right of search and authorized the customs staff, pending the President's decision, to detain vessels suspected of intending to break the law, and so on (chapter 66). Finally, on January 9, 1809, there was passed an Enforcement Act,[1] which summoned all the weak public powers of the Union to compel obedience to the law. Thus the President was authorized to employ the fighting forces of the United States by land and sea and to hire the imposing number of thirty vessels for the purpose. At the same time all the previous laws were made more severe. Vehicles were also subjected to the embargo, in order to prevent the law from being circumvented by land routes ; permission had to be obtained for the

[1] *United States Statutes at Large*, vol. II, p. 506.

loading of vessels; and the right of the customs officials to refuse permission was extended to the right of ordering the discharge, in suspected cases, of goods already loaded, and also to take goods from vessels into their custody; and the surety deposited was raised to six times the value of the goods. Finally, the right to sail to foreign countries for American property was annulled.

These convulsive regulations give a kind of negative to the actual circumstances, which would seem to have been character- ized by even more systematic transgressions of the law than generally occurred during that exceptionally lawless period. In Passamaquoddy Bay, on the borders of British North America, and on the St. Mary's River, which formed the boundary toward the still Spanish Florida, there were collected whole flotillas of American vessels, which, under the pretence of sea damage, put in with flour and fish at the ports of Nova Scotia and of the West Indian Islands, and gave the skippers' need of money to pay for repairs as an excuse that the cargoes had been sold there. This transfer of trade outside the territories of the Union went to the north, west, and south. Northward seven hundred sledges went back and forth between Montreal in Canada and the boundary of the State of Vermont; and at the same time great quantities of potash were imported into Quebec. That city and Halifax in Nova Scotia had halcyon days, the former having more shipping than the whole of the United States; and the British governor of Nova Scotia declared that the Embargo Act was 'well calculated to promote the true interests of His Majesty's American colonies', which, to say the least, was not its intention. In the West Indies, it is true, there appeared at first a serious shortage of foodstuffs and timber, accompanied by a great rise in prices; and the French islands never regained their former prosperity. But many circumstances contributed to this; and in the British West Indies the prices of grain sank again rapidly, and a number of American vessels went there, as also to Havana, where on one occasion, in 1808, there lay nearly a hundred at one time. On the cotton market at Charleston, where the law had evidently been effective in 1808, an agent stated that it had been broken every week since December of that year and January of 1809. Of course the right to sail for American property abroad was particularly abused, and was therefore finally cancelled. Five hundred and ninety vessels are said to have left under this pretext, and as a rule they stayed away, like the American tonnage which happened to be outside the limits of the United States when the law was passed, and which took very good care not to come again under their jurisdiction. On the other hand, of course, those vessels which remained at home in obedience to the law remained largely without employment. Admiral Mahan supposes that those that remained in the states were in the majority, although, on the other hand, the complaints about the sufferings that the law was alleged to cause gained in volume from the desire to make party capital out of the matter. That part of the trade which, as far as one can judge, was hit hardest was the export of raw materials to Europe, especially the export of raw cotton from the Southern States to England. Thus Liverpool received only 25,426 bags in 1808 as compared with 143,756 bags, or nearly six times as much, in 1807. Even that part of the British importation of raw materials which was not directly dependent on American supplies showed a great decline in 1808. This was presumably due to the general shortage of shipping that was a consequence of the withdrawal from traffic of a fairly large part of the second largest mercantile fleet in the world.[1]

In spite of the immense extent to which the law was disregarded, therefore, it would be an exaggeration to call the Embargo Act ineffective as a means of giving trouble to the belligerents. During the years 1808 and 1809 the British opposition never wearied of holding up to the government the

[1] Cf. also, Mahan, *Sea Power in its Relations*, &c. ; Channing, *op. cit.*, vol. XII, pp. 216 *et seq.* ; Roloff, *op. cit.*, p. 207 ; Lord Grenville in the House of Lords, Feb. 17, 1809, and Whitbread in the House of Commons, Mar. 6, 1809 (Hansard, vol. XII, pp. 780, 1167) ; Tooke, *op. cit.*, vol. II, p. 391 (table) ; Daniels, *American Cotton Trade with Liverpool under the Embargo and Non-intercourse Acts*, in *American Historical Review* (1915–16), vol. XXI, pp. 278, 280 ; Sears, *British Industry and the American Embargo*, in *Quarterly Journal of Economics*, (1919–20), vol. XXXIV, pp. 88 *et seq.* Cf. also, vol. XXXV, 1920–21, pp. 345 *et seq.*).

disastrous consequences that its Orders in Council had had by
giving rise to the Embargo Act, which had cut off both the
supply of raw materials from the United States and, above all,
the possibility of sales there.  In accordance with the good old
British parliamentary custom, they made the government
responsible for all the maladies of the body politic, while the
government, also in the usual stereotyped fashion, pictured the
situation in as favourable a light as possible and ascribed
the undeniable difficulties to other causes.  Any inquiry of
scientific value, however, must consider the course of economic
development as a whole, and for this reason the question of the
effects of the Continental System on the belligerents has been
held over for separate treatment in the fourth part of this work.
In any case, the difficulties accruing to Great Britain in consequence of the Embargo Act were not of such consequence as
to lead its government in 1808 either to rescind the Orders in
Council or even in the least degree to modify their application.
On the contrary, Canning, as foreign secretary, conducted the
almost continuous exchange of notes with an ironic superiority
and a diplomatic skill which were calculated to irritate more
and more the American government with its clumsier methods.[1]

## BAYONNE DECREE (APRIL 17, 1808)

The American law had, if possible, still less effect, in the
direction intended, on Napoleon's measures.  Decrès's original
uncertainty as to the scope of the Berlin decree had inspired
the American government with what it somewhat vaguely
called an assurance that the measures would not be applied
against the United States ;  and this curious position was
maintained by the Americans in the exchange of notes with
Great Britain even after the Milan decree and its application
should have definitely dissipated all such hopes.  Like Great
Britain, France was constantly capturing American vessels ;

[1] The most important debates on this subject were in the House of Lords on
Mar. 8, 1808, and Feb. 17, 1809, and in the House of Commons on Mar. 6, 1809.
For the diplomatic correspondence, cf. Hansard, vol. XII, pp. 241 *et seq.* ; vol. XIII,
app. ; vol. XIV, pp. 881 *et seq.* ; vol. XVII, app.

and in so doing she behaved, if possible, in a still more violent manner than her adversary, especially by confiscating vessels simply and solely because they had been subjected to examination by British cruisers, a thing which they could not possibly have escaped.  This interpretation was carried to such an extent, and with such disregard of actual conditions, that in 1808, for instance, an American brig was declared lawful prize because of the British examination, despite the fact that, immediately after the examination, it had endeavoured to flee from the British cruiser into the port of Bilbao, which belonged to Napoleon's ally, Spain, and had thus done its best to show its desire to stand well with the continental powers.  As a matter of fact, Napoleon was so little inclined to except the United States from his proposition that neutrals did not exist, that with his usual ability to draw unexpected logical conclusions he managed to find in this very Embargo Act a justification for seizing all American vessels that arrived at French or ' allied ' ports.  In a letter addressed to his minister of finance, Gaudin, on April 17, 1808, he declared, in fact, that, as the government of the United States had laid an embargo on its vessels and resolved not to carry on foreign trade during the war, ' it is evident that all the vessels that say they come from America really come from England and that their papers are fictitious ' ; and consequently all American vessels that came to the ports of France, Holland, the Hanse Towns or Italy were to be seized.[1]  This was the Bayonne decree, and was all that the United States got out of France by the Embargo Act.

## Non-intercourse Act (March 1, 1809)

The hopelessness of the struggle against the disregard of the law by the Americans themselves finally led the President and Congress to give it up, and that, too, shortly after the passing of the Enforcement Act in January, 1809.  The fact is that this law gave rise to disturbances and to a still greater feeling of irritation in the shipping states, so much the more so as the

[1] *Correspondance*, no. 13,753.

insurrection in Spain in the late summer of 1808 seemed to open
up new and bright prospects to American trade. The result
was a new and famous law, the Non-intercourse Act, passed on
March 1, 1809.[1] That law repealed the Embargo Act as a complete all-round self-blockade, and limited the embargo so as to
make it apply only to the two sets of belligerents, Great Britain
and France; but by way of compensation it was made, if
possible, still more strict against them. Over and above the
prohibition of American trade and shipping contained in the
Embargo Act, which remained in force with regard to those two
countries, all British and French vessels, all goods shipped from
Great Britain and France, and all goods produced there, were
now forbidden to enter American ports as from May 20, 1809.
The substitution of the two-sided prohibition for the one-sided
Non-importation Act, which was exclusively directed against
Great Britain, gave a really consistent expression to an impartial
policy of reprisals. The intention was to provide an outlet for
American trade which could make the measure feasible without
blunting the edge of its task as a measure of reprisal; and it
was thus, practically speaking, a rationalization of the Embargo
Act. But it was obvious beforehand that any control of its
observance must be more difficult than ever when once American
vessels obtained the right to sail to Europe. The character of
the law as a means of exerting pressure was further marked by
the fact that the President was authorized to announce by proclamation when either of the two belligerents revoked or amended
its laws to such an extent that they no longer violated the
trade of the United States; after which event commercial intercourse with the country of that belligerent was to be renewed.

The natural result was a considerable recovery in American
foreign trade, in the first place with the more or less neutral
places, such as the Hanse Towns, Altona, and especially Tönning
in Schleswig and probably Gothenburg. The trade with England
continued to go chiefly to Canada and Nova Scotia, and also,
especially for cotton, *via* Amelia Island in the St. Mary's River
and thence to Europe in British bottoms, which could not be

---

[1] *United States Statutes at Large*, vol. ii, p. 528.

regarded as attractive from an American standpoint. Cotton went also *via* Lisbon, Cadiz, the Azores or other permitted ports, while persons who had no reputation to lose made shipments direct to Liverpool. But the need of the goods was so small, comparatively, in Great Britain, that the increased prices which were a consequence of the roundabout journey and the difficulties of transportation lowered profits for the American exporters.[1]

But while the economic effects continued to arouse discord, the political effects seemed, though somewhat late, to promise the results expected from a policy of reprisals. Madison, who had succeeded Jefferson as President three days after the passing of the Non-intercourse Act, was rejoiced to receive an English proposal for a settlement, which rapidly attained an apparent result. In reality, to be sure, Canning's conditions for an agreement were entirely unacceptable by the American government. But the British minister at Washington, Erskine, son of the Lord Chancellor in the ' All the Talents ' ministry, went in his zeal for a settlement quite beyond his instructions and promised on behalf of his government the rescinding of the Orders in Council as against the United States from June 10, 1809. On this, Madison, in accordance with the authority given him in the Non-intercourse Act, announced this concession on the part of Great Britain in a proclamation which suspended the American act from the same day. An immense movement immediately began in all American ports, where six hundred vessels lay ready to sail on the appointed day ; and during the week June 16–23, Liverpool received more American cotton than it had received throughout the entire year of 1807. At this point, however, it was found that the British government disavowed its minister, and the President was compelled to revoke his proclamation. The new British envoy who succeeded Erskine came immediately into sharp conflict with the American government and was recalled ; after which all prospects of an immediate settlement in this quarter were again blighted.

---

[1] Vogel, *op. cit.*, p. 36 ; Rubin, *1807–1814, Studier til Københavns og Danmarks Historie* (Copenhagen, 1892), pp. 381–2 ; Bergwall, *Historisk under ättelse om staden Götheborgs betydligaste varu-utskeppningar* (Gothenburg, 1820), p. 9 note ; Daniels, *loc. cit.*, p. 281.

## Freedom of Trade (1810–11)

The Non-intercourse Act now also had to be dropped. Its place was taken on May 1, 1810, by a third law,[1] which was intended to give the belligerents a period of grace within which they might amend their ways, but at the same time to play out the one who did so against his still obdurate antagonist. It was laid down that, if either of the two countries, Great Britain and France, rescinded her regulations before March 3, 1811, but the other country did not follow the example within three months, the President might by proclamation put into force against the latter country the principal provisions of the Non-intercourse Act. For the moment, therefore, trade was free with all countries and consequently grew apace during the year 1810. However, this did not hold good of the colonial carrying trade, which had largely dropped out of American hands, not only, or perhaps not even principally, because of the Continental decrees and the Orders in Council, but also in consequence of the military events themselves, in that at first the insurrection in Spain in 1808 and afterwards the capture of the French colonies in 1809–10, put the British themselves in a position to take over the trade in almost anything that could be called colonial goods. The trade that did grow apace, therefore, was especially imports and also all trade in the products of the United States, chiefly the sale of raw cotton to Great Britain and of grain to the combatants in the Iberian peninsula ; but this is of comparatively little interest from our present point of view.

## Revocation of Continental Decrees (1810–12)

These two American laws of 1809 and 1810 gave Napoleon an opportunity for a diplomatic game of hide and seek, the like of which has seldom been seen, and which completely fogged the Americans and finally led to the attainment of his object by making inevitable a breach between Great Britain and the

[1] *United States Statutes at Large*, vol. II, p. 605.

United States.  At first he took no notice of the Non-intercourse Act and pretended that he did not know of it, although a note to his minister of the interior, dated December 21, 1809, speaks of it in plain terms ; and three weeks later a letter to his foreign secretary, Champagny, shows that he desired a settlement with America.  But about a year after the American law was passed he suddenly proceeded to a measure of reprisal, the Rambouillet decree, dated March 23, 1810, but not published until about the middle of May.  The least remarkable thing about this decree is that, on the ground of the Non-intercourse Act, it was ordered that all American vessels should be seized and sold for the benefit of Napoleon's *caisse d'amortissement*, although this was going a good deal farther than his earlier measures, which had not explicitly involved confiscation.  What made this particular measure especially ruthless, was another feature, that it was given retroactive force as far back as the date on which the American law came into force, May 20, 1809. Thus it made Napoleon master of a number of vessels and cargoes (according to an American estimate, 100 vessels with cargoes representing a value of $10,000,000), which, suspecting no evil, had gone to the ports of France or her allies.  But shortly afterwards, when the Emperor learned of the American law of 1810, he immediately saw in it a possibility for a most bewildering diplomatic action, namely, by means of an apparent concession concerning the Continental decrees, to drive the United States into putting the law into force against Great Britain.  In a more than usually characteristic letter to Champagny (July 31, 1810) he rejects the idea of rescinding the Berlin and Milan decrees—which, he says, ' would cause disturbance and not fulfil my object,'—and simply charges Champagny to inform the American envoy in a diplomatic note that he might feel assured that the decrees would not be enforced after November 1, and that he should regard them as revoked. ' This method,' he says with calm effrontery, ' seems to me to be more in accordance with my dignity and with the seriousness of the case.'  Two days later Napoleon sent a draft for such a note, which Champagny forwarded practically unaltered to the representative of the United States (August 5). The foreign secretary there says that he is authorized to declare that the Berlin and Milan decrees are revoked and that they cease to be enforced after November 1, ' it being understood, of course, that in consequence of this declaration the English must rescind their Orders in Council and renounce the new blockade principles that they had wished to establish, or else that the United States, in accordance with the law of which you have informed me, should make their rights respected by the English '. This note was inserted in *Le Moniteur* a few days later, and toward the end of the year it was followed by a letter from the minister of finance to the director general of customs, written by the Emperor's order, to the effect that the decrees should not be applied to American vessels ; and this, too, was inserted in the official newspaper of France.[1]

One can not be surprised, it is true, that the American statesmen and diplomats were at the first blush highly delighted with the French declaration of August and, on the strength of it, immediately requested a corresponding concession on the part of Great Britain. Nevertheless, the very form in which the ' fundamental principle ' of the French Empire—the laws around which the whole of European politics had revolved for well-nigh four years—was revoked was so far peculiar that it might reasonably be expected to superinduce scepticism. And it proved almost immediately that the Continental decrees were applied just the same as before, not only in general, but also against American vessels. When this was pointed out to him, Napoleon declared that it was really due to the fact that the vessels had disobeyed his port regulations and not the international rules contained in the Berlin and Milan decrees. But in reality the fact of the matter was that the only vessels which were liberated were those which had not disobeyed the Continental decrees ; and with regard

---

[1] *Correspondance*, nos. 16,080, 16,127, 16,384, 16,736, 16,743 ; *Bulletin des lois*, &c., 4th ser., bull. 286, no. 5,402. *Memoirs and Correspondence of Lord Wellesley* (Pearce ed., London, 1846), vol. III, pp. 116–17. 134 (here, too, can be found the correspondence of 1810–11 between Wellesley, in his capacity as British foreign secretary, and the American minister in London) ; *Le Moniteur*, Aug. 9 and Dec. 25, 1810.

to those which had disobeyed them, no change took place
except that they were not, it is true, condemned to confiscation
but were nevertheless detained by the French authorities.
None the less, Napoleon did accord a limited amount of consideration to the trade and shipping of the United States in the
autumn of 1810, inasmuch as he issued a number of licences to
American vessels that wished to import into France certain
American colonial goods, with French consular certificates
written in cipher in order to provide security that the British
should not appear in the guise of Americans. He also reduced
to one quarter the enormous customs dues that the Trianon
tariff of August 5, 1810, had imposed upon colonial goods when
the importation had been directly effected by American vessels.
A contributory motive behind this measure was the necessity
of being able to appeal to the support of the United States in
the pressure which Napoleon was now bringing to bear, though in
vain, on Emperor Alexander of Russia in order to keep that
country within the Continental System. But none of these
things altered the fact that the system itself remained unchanged.[1]

However, the American statesmen had already bound themselves to regard Champagny's August note as a genuine and
already effective revocation and therefore were placed in an
extremely awkward position when compelled to maintain this
standpoint in their negotiations with the British. For they
were at the same time exerting all their powers of persuasion
to induce the French to make the revocation a reality. As the
putting into force of the American law of 1810 was made dependent on the willingness of the one or the other of the
belligerents to rescind his laws, there consequently arose a
difficulty in applying the law against Great Britain, which had
not taken any conciliatory steps; and it was therefore considered necessary, on March 2, 1811, to pass a new law which,

---

[1] Napoleon to Eugene, Viceroy of Italy, Sept. 19, 1810, and to Champagny,
Dec. 13, 1810 (*Correspondance*, nos. 16,930, 17,206); decree of Nov. 1, 1810 (*Bulletin
des lois*, &c., 4th ser., bull. 324, no. 6,067; Martens, *Nouveau recueil*, &c., vol. I,
pp. 527–8).

irrespective of this question of interpretation, put the previously mentioned parts of the Non-intercourse Act into force again as against Great Britain. This was the Non-importation Act of 1811.[1] Curiously enough, this law seems to have been very effective, so that the old methods of evading the prohibition on trade by shipping cargo *via* Amelia Island in Canada were but little used. Cotton accumulated more and more in Charleston in the course of 1811 ; and in the autumn no quotations could be published because there were no buyers. The whole situation was very peculiar from a commercial point of view, inasmuch as the claims of the cotton exporters on England could not be satisfied directly, in the natural manner, by the importation of British goods, since all such imports were now forbidden. Probably the triangular trade through other countries also offered great difficulties, for we find the cotton broker in Charleston whose reports Mr. Daniels has edited complaining of the fact that drafts on England were unsaleable, thanks to the new Non-importation Act ; and similar complaints were registered on the British side in a petition from the cotton importing town of Liverpool.[2]

However, it now became more necessary than ever for the Americans to convince the British of the genuineness of the French revocation ; and this offered greater and greater difficulties, especially in the face of Napoleon's own utterances. In two great speeches delivered in March, 1811, one to deputies from the Hanse Towns and another to deputies from the French Chambers of Commerce (the second of which was not published officially, but was circulated in different versions), he repeated his old phrase about the Berlin and Milan decrees as the fundamental laws of the Empire, whose validity was coextensive with that of the Orders in Council. In the second of the speeches, it is true, he declared himself prepared to receive the Americans in French ports, on condition that they should uphold the same principles as he did ; and if they could not compel England to respect them, that they should declare war on that country.

---

[1] *United States Statutes at Large*, vol. II, p. 651.
[2] House of Commons, Apr. 27, 1812 (Hansard, vol. XXII, p. 1061).

But manifestly this implied something quite different from the idea that the decrees had been abolished as far back as the November of the previous year. Napoleon expressed himself in a still more unqualified manner in an unpublished message to his *Conseil d'administration du commerce* (April 29, 1811), after the passing of the American law of 1811. Inasmuch as that law forbade American vessels to go to England, it followed, he thought, in accordance with his old way of thinking, that a vessel which nevertheless went there was not American at all but English ; and on this hypothesis one could quite well say that the Berlin and Milan decrees were revoked, at least so far as the United States were concerned![1]

### REVOCATION OF ORDERS IN COUNCIL (1812)

Meanwhile, the British government remained undecided and awaited developments. But after Napoleon had caused to be published a report by Maret, Champagny's successor as foreign minister, on March 10, 1812, in which the blessings of the Continental decrees were once more asserted, the British Prince Regent replied by a proclamation, dated April 21, to the effect that, as soon as the Berlin and Milan decrees had been expressly and unreservedly revoked, the Orders in Council should also be regarded, without further ado, as having lapsed. This at last placed in the hands of the American diplomats a weapon against France which bore fruit. Maret allowed himself to be induced by it to bring forward the last of this series of strange documents, namely, a decree of April 28, 1811, which, according to its date, was more than a year old, but which was never published and was quite unknown until that time. This decree declared that the Berlin and Milan decrees had ceased to hold good for American vessels from November 1, 1810, more than six months earlier, in accordance with the original declaration. When this document was laid before the British government, the British statesmen were not a little confounded, for which

[1] *Correspondance*, nos. 17,482 and 17,669. For the speech to the deputies of the Chamber of Commerce, cf. Thiers, *Histoire du Consulat et de l'Empire* (Paris, 1856), vol. XIII, pp. 27 *et seq.*

one can hardly blame them ; but after some delay they considered that they ought to declare that, though the decree did not contain the general revocation that had been stipulated in the Prince Regent's proclamation of April 21, nevertheless the Orders in Council should be rescinded as regards American vessels. Accordingly, with the enthusiastic approval of the British opposition, the Orders in Council were revoked on June 23, 1812, so far as American vessels with American cargoes were concerned. This revocation was to take effect as from August 1, though only under the condition that the American government revoked its prohibition of commercial intercourse with Great Britain. It is evident that many factors contributed to this result : dearth and disturbances in England itself, for which the opposition laid all the blame on the Orders in Council; the desire to disarm the war party, which had grown stronger and stronger in the United States ; and the need of American supplies of grain for the greatly impoverished Iberian peninsula.[1]

When the British government had at last made its decision, however, Napoleon had already attained his object, although neither he nor anybody else had been able to foresee the order in which the events were to take place. On June 19, in fact, that is, four days before the rescinding of the Orders in Council, the United States had declared war on Great Britain, partly because of the disputes which have here been described and partly because of the impressment of seamen and various other things. In Great Britain it was generally expected, especially by the opposition, that the declaration of war would be recalled when the conciliatory decision of Great Britain became known. But this was not the case ; and the war went on for two and a half years, until Christmas Eve 1814. It came too late,

---

[1] For the documents issued by Maret and the British Prince Regent, cf. Martens, *Nouveau recueil*, &c., vol. I, pp. 530 *et seq,*, 542 *et seq.* For the revocation of the Orders in Council, cf. Hansard, vol. XXII, pp. 853 *et seq.* (under an incorrect date), and vol. XXIII, pp. 716 *et seq.* For the debates on the subject in the House of Commons on May 22, 25, 26, and June 16, 19, 23, and in the House of Lords on June 18, 1812, cf. Hansard, vol. XXIII, pp. 286 *et seq.*, 295 *et seq.*, 486 *et seq.*, 496–7, 587 *et seq.*, 600 *et seq.*, 715 *et seq.* See also Mahan, *Sea Power in its Relations*, &c., vol. I, pp. 266–76.

however, to exert any noteworthy influence on the course of events in Europe, which was now entirely determined by Napoleon's Russian campaign ; and so far one may say that Great Britain's great adversary, owing to the delay in the outbreak of the conflict, failed to attain his object. In any case, American events now disappear from the horizon of the Continental System.

### GENERAL SURVEY

A summary—only very partial and sketchy, it is true, but readily comprehensible—of this peculiar development of events as regards America can be found in the following commercial statistics of the United States from 1807 to 1817. These form a continuation to the table printed on page 103 : [1]

FOREIGN TRADE OF THE UNITED STATES (1807-1817)

| Year | Exports | | | Imports | |
|---|---|---|---|---|---|
| | Domestic goods | Foreign goods | Total | For home consumption | Total |
| 1807 | $48,700,000 | $59,640,000 | $108,340,000 | $78,860,000 | $138,500,000 |
| 1808 | 9,430,000 | 13,000,000 | 22,430,000 | 43,990,000 | 56,990,000 |
| 1809 | 31,410,000 | 20,800,000 | 52,200,000 | 38,600,000 | 59,400,000 |
| 1810 | 42,370,000 | 24,390,000 | 66,760,000 | 61,010,000 | 85,400,000 |
| 1811 | 45,290,000 | 16,020,000 | 61,320,000 | 37,380,000 | 53,400,000 |
| 1812 | 30,030,000 | 8,500,000 | 38,530,000 | 68,540,000 | 77,030,000 |
| 1813 | 25,010,000 | 2,850,000 | 27,860,000 | 19,160,000 | 22,010,000 |
| 1814 | 6,780,000 | 150,000 | 6,930,000 | 12,820,000 | 12,970,000 |
| 1815 | 45,970,000 | 6,580,000 | 52,560,000 | 106,460,000 | 113,040,000 |
| 1816 | 64,780,000 | 17,140,000 | 81,920,000 | 129,960,000 | 147,100,000 |
| 1817 | 68,310,000 | 19,360,000 | 87,670,000 | 79,890,000 | 99,250,000 |

It is true that these figures have one great weakness, namely, that they seem not to pay any regard to smuggling. The enormous decline in exports and the very pronounced decline in imports shown in the year 1808, therefore, undoubtedly give an exaggerated notion of the effect of the Embargo Act, but picture quite correctly the almost complete disappearance of legitimate exports. Professor Channing's calculation that, as a whole, the exports diminished by 75 per cent. and the imports by 50 per cent., is probably too high, especially with regard to exports.[1]  For consonant with the facts as it may be, that the figures show a stronger decline for exports than for imports, the decrease of exports can hardly be as great as this hypothetical figure would seem to indicate. True, it was against American exports that both the Continental decrees, the Orders in Council, and the Embargo Act directed their blows with practical unanimity ; but, on the other hand, it is to be observed that smuggling also directed its successful counter-action to the same point.   The subsequent Non-intercourse Act marks a powerful improvement, as appears from the figures for 1809 ; and the law of 1810 makes the imports and exports for that year and the exports for 1811 still higher.   But, for reasons previously given, the export has changed its character from the colonial carrying trade to the sale of the United States' own products.   In 1812 began the war with Great Britain, which gradually led to the almost complete cessation of all American foreign trade, especially of all exports.   Finally, the years 1815–17 show the restoration of peace conditions, and thereby provide a suitable background for the alterations of war time.   Especially noteworthy, in comparison with the situation in 1807, are the low figures for re-exports, which are only a little higher in 1815–17 than under the Embargo Act of 1808.   This brings out very clearly the wartime character of this trade.

It may also be of interest to see the development of one special line of this trade, namely, the imports of American cotton into Liverpool.   The figures were as follows : [2]

IMPORTATION OF AMERICAN COTTON INTO LIVERPOOL

| Year | No. bags | Year | No. bags |
|------|----------|------|----------|
| 1806 | 100,273  | 1811 | 97,626   |
| 1807 | 143,756  | 1812 | 79,528   |
| 1808 | 25,426   | 1813 | 18,640   |
| 1809 | 130,581  | 1814 | 40,448   |
| 1810 | 199,220  |      |          |

[1] Channing, *op. cit.*, p. 228.
[2] Daniels, *op. cit.*, p. 278.

As is only natural, 1808, the year of the Embargo Act, stands lowest of the years before the war year 1813, while the Non-importation Act of 1811 also brings with it a heavy decline. The Non-intercourse Act of 1809, on the other hand, has no very strong repellent effect, although, of course, 1810, the only year with full freedom of trade, stands still higher. These figures, which presumably include smuggled goods, as well as lawful exports, thus confirm the preceding statements in all essentials.

# CHAPTER V

## THE CONTINENTAL SYSTEM IN EUROPE (1808–1812)

### The 'Coast System'

During the years 1808–10 external political events in Europe were characterized by the steadily-continued extension of the ' coast system '. In the very first of these years occurred the formal incorporation of Etruria with the French Empire; and at the same time Rome was occupied by French troops, to be also incorporated in the following year together with the rest of the Papal States. By this means the Italian peninsula was completely subjected to the power of Napoleon; and of all that we now count as Italy, only Sicily and Sardinia succeeded in preserving their independence, thanks to the direct support of Great Britain. During 1809 the occupation of the coasts was followed up on the Balkan peninsula—a movement which had begun as early as the close of 1805 with the acquisition of Dalmatia and part of Istria. By the Peace of Vienna (Schönbrunn) Austria had now to cede, among other things, the rest of her coast, the remainder of Istria and Croatia; and the acquisitions of 1805 and 1809 were incorporated with France, like all the territories previously mentioned, under the name of the Illyrian Provinces. From the point of view of the Continental System, the most important thing about all this was that Napoleon's power was now extended to Trieste, which with some exaggeration might be called, after the incorporation of Leghorn, the Leipzig of South Europe.

### Disappearance of the French Colonial Empire

As is well known, however, the year 1808 was a red-letter year in the history of the Continental System, and, for that matter, in the history of the great trial of strength as a whole. The change was exactly the reverse of that indicated by these new acquisitions, for the insurrection in Spain gave to events in the most western of the peninsulas of southern Europe exactly the opposite course to that in the two other peninsulas. The effect on the Continental System was brought about partly by military conditions, in that the coastal defence on the North Sea was weakened in respect of the forces required for the war in the Iberian peninsula ; but the Spanish insurrection had a much larger bearing on the Continental System, through its consequences for colonial trade and for Napoleon's colonial empire. The German historian of Napoleon's colonial policy, Professor Roloff, has shown how decisively the events in Spain put an end to Napoleon's colonial plans, which had previously been built to a large extent on the Spanish possessions. From having been the basis for privateers against British trade, their passing into the hands of the enemy served as a weapon against the remains of the French colonies, which one after another fell into the hands of the British. In January 1809 French Guiana was taken ; in April, Martinique ; in July, what was originally the Spanish part of Haiti, Santo Domingo (the French part, St. Domingue, had already for seven years been in the hands of the insurrectionary negroes), and at the same time Senegal in Africa ; in 1810 fell first Guadeloupe, the last French possession in America, and then the remaining African colonies, Isle-de-France (Mauritius) and Réunion. In the same year, it is true, Java had nominally passed to France through the annexation of its mother country, Holland ; but this large island, too, fell finally into the hands of the British in September 1811. The doctrine that Napoleon had championed ever since the days of the Milan decree—though not, it is true, without some relapses—namely, that there were no neutrals and that all colonial goods were English, he had thus the doubtful pleasure of seeing stern reality confirming *ex post facto*. But evidently, on the other hand, this in a way increased the chances of the policy of ' conquering England by excess ',[1] and made him not less, but rather more, zealous to press

[1] See p. 57.

ruthlessly through the continental self-blockade with all available means.

In Great Britain, however, in the course of 1809 expression was given to the prevailing belief in the relaxation of the pressure by a new Order in Council of April 26, which limited the blockade so as to include Holland as far as the Ems, France, with her colonies and the possessions dependent thereon, and North Italy as far as Pesaro and Orbitello, approximately including Tuscany, the old Etruria.[1] The Orders in Council of November 11, 1807, were declared to be cancelled; but in reality their policy was continued without any change by the manner in which licences were granted. But a general optimism diffused itself in England during the course of 1809, thanks to the expansion of the colonial trade.

## THE CONVULSIONS OF 1810

The year 1810, on the other hand, was to be a year of heavy ordeals for both the ' mighty opposites ', and that, too, both politically and economically. Sweden, which had resisted the Continental System longer than any other mainland state, was compelled as early as January to bind herself by the Treaty of Paris to exclude British vessels and commodities, except salt—a merely verbal profession of no very great importance, it is true, as Admiral Saumarez with his British squadron maintained friendly intercourse with the country without a break, even after Sweden had been compelled, in November, to declare war on Great Britain. Consequently, a far greater change was effected by events on the North Sea coast, in that Napoleon became more and more convinced of the impossibility of compelling obedience to the self-blockade beyond the limits of his own direct authority. For this reason there followed in rapid succession, first, in March, the acquisition of southern Holland as far as the River Waal, then the incorporation of the whole of Holland in July, after Napoleon's brother Louis had abdicated and fled from the country, and finally, in December, the further

[1] Martens, *Nouveau recueil*, &c., vol. I, p. 483.

annexation of the Hanse Towns, the coast of Hanover, which had formerly been assigned to the kingdom of Westphalia, the Ems department of the Grand Duchy of Berg, Lauenburg, and, after some hesitation, Oldenburg. The result of all this was that, at the turn of the year 1810–11, France extended along the whole of the North Sea coast and the Holstein border up to the Baltic at the mouth of the Trave. At the same time measures were being taken along the south coast of the Baltic by constantly more violent menaces against its three owners, that is, Prussia, helpless but bitterly hostile to Napoleon, Mecklenburg, and Sweden, as the possessor of Swedish Pomerania.

It was precisely in the Baltic, however, that there happened before the close of the year an altogether revolutionary event, the strongest possible external blow against the structure that was geographically almost completed, *viz.*, the apostasy of Russia. This occurrence had many causes, but the opposition between the two Emperors became visible when the Emperor Alexander declined Napoleon's request in the autumn of 1810 to confiscate a large flotilla of commercial vessels trading in the Baltic under different neutral flags ; and the final emancipation was marked by the famous customs ukase which Alexander issued on the last day of the year (December 19/31). In this document a clause about the destruction of prohibited goods was renewed after an interval of thirteen years, undoubtedly in imitation of Napoleon's own measures, to be mentioned presently. Nothing could have been more welcome to the French Emperor, if this had applied only to British goods ; but now the clause worked exactly in the opposite direction. For some important imports, foremost among them wines, had to arrive by sea in order to be legal ; and as French produce could come only by land, the blow struck at France herself. True, British goods were excluded, *ipso facto*, as coming from an enemy country. At the same time, however, American vessels were accorded preferential treatment ; and as they were the disguise principally used by British shipping, the whole measure was rightly regarded by Napoleon as an informal manner of opening a door to the navigation of his enemy. To complete the picture, duties on the wines of France and her allies were increased to twice the amount levied upon those of South-eastern Europe.[1]

The order of Napoleon which received this unwelcome imitation was the Fontainebleau decree of October 1810, which prescribed the destruction of all English goods throughout the Continent. This formed the complement to the Trianon tariff of August of the same year, which, in contrast to this, admitted colonial goods, although only against enormous duties. Precisely at the time of this new turn in the Continental System, moreover, a serious crisis broke out in England and in France, and also in many other places; and the difficulties of Great Britain inspired Napoleon with stronger hopes than ever of attaining the object of his great system, regardless of the fact that the dislocation of French economic life was at least equally deep and far-reaching.

## THE FINAL COLLAPSE

By the apostasy of Russia, however, the Continental System had lost one of its retaining walls; and in the course of 1811 the breach was more and more widened by Alexander's constantly more open favourable treatment of British shipping. Napoleon had to try to raise a new barrier along the western frontier of Russia toward Prussia, the Grand Duchy of Warsaw, and Austria, and to have recourse to still more active measures to bar the south coast of the Baltic, now that British ships had *points d'appui* on its east coast in addition to those they had had all the time among the Swedish skerries. The last step in this direction was taken by the occupation of Swedish Pomerania in January 1812; but the immediate effect of this was to cause Sweden openly to fall away. Meanwhile, the preparations for the great trial of strength with Russia afterwards made heavier

---

[1] I have followed the translation of the ukase in *Le Moniteur*, Jan. 31, 1811. Vandal, in his *Napoléon et Alexandre Ier* (vol. II, pp. 529–30), refers to this paper, but I have been unable to bring his account into accord with the text of the decree. The *Correspondance* is, of course, full of the subject.

and heavier demands on Napoleon's attention ; and with the beginning of the Russian campaign the cordon was relaxed everywhere. After the retreat from Moscow, in the beginning of the year 1813, insurrections took place both on the North Sea coast and in the Ruhr district (the Grand Duchy of Berg), which, like the Hanse Towns, had been very badly treated. It is true that they were ruthlessly suppressed, and Napoleon, sometimes at least, adhered to his old idea that the Continental System had shaken the power of England. But in the rush of more pressing claims that now came upon him, it exceeded even Napoleon's ability to devote to the enforcement of the system the superhuman energy which, even under more favourable auspices, would have been necessary to prevent it from falling asunder. Moreover, the falling away of his compulsory allies cost the system its continental extension, so that even his sincere collaborator, Frederick VI of Denmark, took a cautious step backward ; and with the advance of the allied armies into France there also followed whole swarms of forbidden goods. Finally, the Continental decrees were formally rescinded, immediately after Napoleon's abdication in April 1814. With that the system passed into the realms of history, not without dragging with it in its fall large parts of the new branches of production which were indebted to it for their existence.

But before that disintegration of the system which was visible from without and which was conditioned by external causes had had time to take effect, forces from within had appeared which made it a thing quite different from what had been originally intended. What has now been described, over and above the contents and significance of the foundational decrees, is merely the external political façade behind which the real machinery worked. It is the latter that is to be the subject of part III.

# PART III
## INTERNAL HISTORY AND WORKING OF
## THE CONTINENTAL SYSTEM

# CHAPTER I

## TREATMENT OF CONFISCATED GOODS

THE task that Napoleon made the central point of his policy manifestly imposed the greatest demands on its inventor and his helpers, especially when we take into consideration the administrative powers at the disposal of the governments of the time.

With regard to what was by far the most important point, namely, the exclusion of British and colonial goods, the question of the application of the system at once struck upon a peculiar difficulty, namely, the problem of what to do with the confiscated merchandise. To Napoleon himself, strange as it may seem, this problem was a matter of minor importance, inasmuch as from first to last he adhered to the view taken over from the politicians of the Convention, that all goods were sold on the credit of Englishmen and thus were not yet paid for when they were seized, and that, accordingly, the loss in any case hit the enemy. With a persistence that never wavered he preached to his allies and helpers the doctrines that, ' inasmuch as the (continental) merchants never buy except on credit, it is a fact that no goods are ever paid for,' and that, ' all goods being the property of the English,' their confiscation means ' a back-handed blow for England which is terrific '.[1] On this assumption, moreover, the whole difficulty would pretty soon have been overcome ; for after a sufficiently large number of such losses had been inflicted on the English they might reasonably

---

[1] Quotations from two letters addressed to his brother Jerome, King of Westphalia, on Jan. 23, 1807, and to the Emperor Alexander of Russia on Oct. 23, 1810. *Correspondance de Napoléon Ier*, nos. 11,682 and 17,071. In consonance with this the representative of Napoleon in Switzerland, Rouyer, declared in 1810 that the Swiss commercial houses were generally only ' *commanditaires et expéditionnaires* ' of the English. Letter reproduced in de Cérenville, *Le système continental*, &c., p. 337. See also Schmidt, *Le Grand-duché de Berg*, p. 374, note 2.

be expected to grow weary of sacrificing their goods and thus abandon the attempt to force them on the Continent. It is true that not even under Napoleon's assumption did it do to allow goods, at least the industrial products of England, to make their way into France itself, where they competed with the French products. But for the industries of the rest of the Continent Napoleon had no such interest, wishing solely to prevent their competition with the continental exports of France; and, lastly, it is manifest that neither of these points could create uneasiness in respect of colonial goods of British origin.

From the very outset this caused an expedient which could not fail to lead the whole system into a wrong track, namely, that the towns and other places where the goods were seized received the right to repurchase them, usually at an extremely high figure. Consequently, the goods were not excluded. On the contrary, the different continental markets were able, to a very large extent, to provide themselves by means of such repurchases (*rachats*), and the control of illicit imports was thus rendered exceedingly difficult—a result which was also furthered by the great auctions that Napoleon caused to be held for the sale of captured and confiscated, though not repurchased, goods.[1] The only device which might have completely eradicated the difficulty would have been the absolute destruction of the illicit goods in accordance with earlier methods ; and for several years it does not appear to have occurred to Napoleon to go so far. But the injury done by the repurchase tactics was not limited to this, but went much deeper, inasmuch as from the very beginning it robbed the policy of its ideal attributes and its stamp of grandeur, as being a means for the emancipation of the Continent. It gave rise to intrigues, which in an incessant crescendo strengthened the notion that the intention of the whole affair was merely to levy blackmail, to find a means of squeezing money out of the continental peoples for the benefit of the Emperor and French funds, as well as of French marshals, generals and soldiers, ministers and consuls. Already in connexion with the events of 1808 an unusually

[1] König, *Die Sächsische Baumwollenindustrie*, &c., pp. 204 *et seq.*, 215–6.

competent observer, Johann Georg Rist, the German-born representative in Hamburg of France's intimate ally, Denmark, writes in his memoirs, compiled in the years 1816 to 1821, that no one among the merchants, peasants or officials, or even among the scholars, believed in any plans for the good of Europe, but only in the desire to line French pockets.   It was commonly held that no justice was to be expected, but merely arbitrariness and the basest motives, all marked by high words, threats, and deception.   And with regard to the last phase of the system (from 1810 onward) almost exactly the same words fall from Mollien, who was Napoleon's good and faithful servant, though a man of strong and independent judgment.   He says that ' this pretended system . . . deprived of every vestige of political prestige, has only proved itself in the eyes of everybody to be the most pernicious and false of fiscal inventions '.[1]   It was precisely fiscalism, the bane of so many systems of commercial policy, which thereby got a footing from the very beginning in the imposing and soaring plan and threw radical difficulties in the way of its execution.

This was all the more the case for the reason that Napoleon's assumption that everything was sold on credit was so far from being correct that it was the very reverse of the truth.   Apparently the demand that prevailed on the Continent for British and colonial goods made it possible for them to be sold practically always for cash ; consequently it was the continental buyers who were the chief sufferers.   And even when that was not the case, one finds the continental buyers, e. g., not only Hamburg merchants, but importers all over Germany and Holland generally—according to the evidence in 1807 of their British creditors themselves—displaying an extraordinary zeal in the regular payment of their debts.[2]

[1] J. G. Rist, *Lebenserinnerungen* (Poel ed., Gotha, 1880), vol. II, pp. 29–30 ; Mollien, *Mémoires*, &c., vol. II, p. 462.   Cf. Louis Bonaparte to his brother Jerome, Oct. 15, 1808, in Duboscq, *Louis Bonaparte en Hollande, d'après ses lettres* (Paris, 1911), no. 185.

[2] Mollien, *op. cit.*, vol. II, p. 461 ; König, *op. cit.*, pp. 180–1 ; Mahan, *Influence of Sea Power*, &c., vol. II, p. 305 ; Tarle, *Kontinental'naja blokada*, vol. I, pp. 287, 351, 384 ; Tarle, *Deutsch-französische Wirtschaftsbeziehungen, loc. cit.*, pp. 679–80, 718.

Consequently there was little or no likelihood that the British would tire of supplying the Continent with goods. On the contrary, the inner history of the Continental System came to consist essentially in the embittered and uninterrupted struggles against the endless stream of British goods.

This difficulty with which Napoleon was confronted with regard to the very structure of the blockade was further complicated by the difficulty of getting honest and zealous persons to assist him in putting it into execution. It was almost impossible to obtain such assistants among his allies and their organs ; and consequently one of the most amply justified views in the historical literature of the present time is the explanation that the incessant extension of the empire along the coast of Europe was due to the Emperor's need of direct control, with a view to the observance of the Continental System. Of the innumerable examples of this we may mention two, one Swedish and one Prussian. In August 1811, when Sweden was nominally at war with Great Britain, Axel Pontus von Rosen, the Governor of Gothenburg, informed the minister of state, von Engeström, that for once in a way he had caused to be confiscated ten oxen intended for Admiral Saumarez's English fleet, which lay off Vinga, and added : ' I entreat that this be put in the papers, so that I, wretched that I am, may for once wear the nimbus of Continental zeal in the annals of Europe. Saumarez was informed beforehand, so that he will not be annoyed.' During the winter of 1811–12 a systematic import of forbidden colonial goods by the state itself went on in Prussia through a special commissioner for the minister of finance, Privy Councillor von Heydebreck; and at the same time Hardenberg, the leading minister, wrote to that very man and requested the strictest inquiry into the smuggling.[1]

But the fact that the situation was untenable when the application of the system lay in such hands must by no means be interpreted to mean that the difficulties were overcome so

[1] Von Rosen to von Engeström, Aug. 7, 1811, in Ahnfelt, *Ur Svenska hofvets och aristokratiens lif* (Stockholm, 1882), vol. v, p. 259 ; Peez and Dehn, *Englands Vorherrschaft. Aus der Zeit der Kontinentalsperre* (Leipzig, 1912), p. 258.

soon as Napoleon was able to set his own administrators to the task. The general weakness of authority in those days, in comparison with the present day, was perhaps best expressed in the lack of will and capacity on the part of subordinate organs to follow out the intentions of the heads of the state, and that, too, even under such an almost superhumanly equipped ruler as Napoleon. The fiscal methods—to use a fine-sounding expression—which Napoleon employed in his own interest were often turned by his subordinates against him, or at least against his policy; and his altogether unabashed endeavour to turn these abuses to his own account never failed to divert the Continental System still further from its task. In these respects the difference is inconsiderable between the various organs which were more or less completely employed for the purposes of the blockade policy, viz., the large detachments of troops along the coast and their naval coadjutors in ports and estuaries, the customs staff and border police, and finally the local administration in the territories belonging to the Empire and the French legation staffs and consuls in vassal states and occupied territories.

# CHAPTER II

## RESULTS OF THE SELF-BLOCKADE (1806–1809)

### EXECUTION OF THE SELF-BLOCKADE

In order to form a concrete notion of the manner in which the Continental System worked, one may properly begin by following the general lines of its development, even though the constant efforts and hindrances exhibit a certain monotony, which, however, is broken in 1810 by what constitutes a change in principle. Our account in the first place concerns the coasts of the North Sea and the Baltic and the parts of the mainland that lie behind them, Germany and Holland, which played the principal parts in the policy, and in which, moreover, that policy is best known.

The Continental System, being an almost unbroken continuation of the previous policy, led to the peculiar effect that the seizures of British goods began before the actual issue of the Berlin decree—in Leipzig, Frankfurt-am-Main, Meppen, which was important for trade up the Ems, Holland, Switzerland, &c. But it was in the Hanse Towns that the centre of gravity lay, and the military cordon in particular was during this first phase (the close of 1806) mainly limited to the North Sea coast from Emden, in East Friesland, which was just at that time ceded to Holland, to Hamburg, with the salient along the boundary of Holstein, at that time belonging to Denmark, as far as Travemünde, the outport of Lübeck on the Baltic.

### NAPOLEON'S ORDERS IN DECEMBER 1806

The best idea of the apparatus which was set going can be obtained from the letters which Napoleon wrote on December 2 and 3 to Marshal Mortier in Hamburg, to the police and navy ministers, and to his brother, King Louis of Holland,

and from the simultaneously issued proclamation (December 2) as to the blockade in the northeast.  In the first of the letters Mortier received orders to occupy Vegesack on the Weser, north of Bremen, in order to complete the blockade of that river.  King Louis was to place batteries on the left bank of the river, in order to have a cross fire from corresponding batteries at Bremerlehe on the eastern shore.  In the mouth of the Elbe a redoubt and a battery were to be erected on an island in the river immediately opposite Stade, so that no vessel could pass without being examined, and no English goods could come in through Altona, Hamburg, or any other place ; and in all three Hanse Towns French troops were to be stationed to stop English letters.  A brigadier general was to be stationed in Stade, and another in the outport, Cuxhaven ; and in addition to this, two cordons—one from Hamburg to Travemünde along the frontier of Holstein, and another along the left bank of the Elbe as far as a point just opposite Hamburg—were to be placed under the command of yet a third brigadier general.  As regards troops, the greater part of General Dumonceau's division, two Italian regiments and a third of the Dutch cavalry, were to be used for these purposes ; and at the same time the minister of the marine received orders to send a post captain with two ensigns and forty sailors to equip some sloops in Stade.  The customs authorities received orders to send five hundred (according to the proclamation, three hundred) customs officials under a director of customs and two inspectors of customs. These were the ' green coats ', and in point of fact they arrived before the close of the year and soon drew upon themselves the bitter enmity of the population.  Finally, Marshal Moncey was to have at his disposal one hundred gendarmes for distribution along the barrier.  On that very same day (December 2) Napoleon wrote a second letter to Mortier with a renewed exhortation to set up a good battery at Stade ; and above all things he was to prevent all communication between Hamburg and Altona, to confiscate on the Elbe all vessels with potash, coal, and all other goods coming from England, and to detain all letters from England. In these very first orders, however, the difficulty emerged of obtaining honest executors of the measures. The naval minister received a special reminder to send ' unbribable ' officers ; and from the very beginning an effort was made to interest the soldiers themselves in the effectivity of the blockade by the regulation that they should have the benefit of all confiscations of goods which should try to pass. But in several of the letters, especially that to Fouché, the minister of police, Napoleon says that he has received complaints—in reality only too well founded—about his consul in Hamburg, Lachevardière, who ' seems to steal with impunity '.[1]

In Hamburg there still survived the continental establishment of the Merchant Adventurers' Company, the most notable English trading company of an older type (the ' Regulated Company '), though it no longer played any considerable part. In order to save this for the English, the Senate of Hamburg purchased the whole establishment, called ' The Merchant Adventurers' Court ', and presented it to the members, who became citizens of Hamburg besides and in this way escaped imprisonment, so far as they did not escape by flight. The main thing, however, was the seizure of the English stocks of goods, which Napoleon, after various negotiations, fixed at the somewhat high figure of 17,000,000 francs for Hamburg and 2,000,000 francs for Lübeck ; meanwhile Bremen, by delaying the operation for a whole year, managed to smuggle away the greater part of the goods there and had to account for only 377,000 francs. In Leipzig, whose Fair still constituted by far the most important market in Central Europe, especially for manufactured goods to and from all points of the compass, the stocktaking gave a value of 9,150,000 francs, which was redeemed for 6,000,000 francs. Things went in the same way elsewhere.

In Great Britain the publication of the Berlin decree caused, according to evidence given before a parliamentary committee, a cessation of exports to the Continent during the

---

[1] *Correspondance*, nos. 11,355 ; 11,356 ; 11,363 ; 11,378 ; 11,383 ; Proclamation of Dec. 2, 1806, printed in König, *op. cit.*, Anlage 2.

months of December 1806, and of January and February 1807, with a rise in the marine insurance premiums. But the absence of captures on the basis of the decree, which, as we have seen before, was at first regarded as not applying to the sea, after that put new life into commercial intercourse; and an Order in Council of February 18, with instructions for the commanders of vessels, granted unrestricted traffic for the vessels and goods of the Hanse Towns and the rest of that part of North Germany which was occupied by the French; and this safeguarded intercourse with them.[1]

During the whole of the first six months of 1807, indeed, the Continental self-blockade may be said to have been practically ineffective, at least in North Germany. The systematic dishonesty of Napoleon's tools gave rise to regular orgies during this time, especially with the help of the new commander-in-chief in Hamburg, Marshal Brune, whom Napoleon, with unusually good reason, branded as an 'undaunted robber'. According to the report of de Tournon, who was sent there especially to investigate, Brune's instructions themselves to the customs staff were calculated to encourage smuggling; but that was the case to a very much greater extent with the application of the instructions. When vessels came up the Elbe, they were allowed, in absolute defiance of the instructions quoted above, to continue their journey past Stade, with only one single person from the barrier control on board, usually an ignorant seaman, while the customs officials themselves were consistently kept at a distance. The bill of lading was examined by a sub-officer of the navy; and the inspection which it was the duty of Consul Lachevardière to carry out, was handed over by him to a Hamburg broker, who had the greatest possible interest in letting everything pass. On the basis of the entirely uncontrolled investigation of this person,

---

[1] For this and what follows concerning the Hanse Towns, cf. Wohlwill, *Neuere Geschichte*, &c., pp. 339 *et seq.*; Servières, *L'Allemagne française*, &c., pp. 98 *et seq.*; Vogel, *Die Hansestädte*, &c., *loc. cit.*, pp. 18 *et seq.*; Schäfer, *Bremen und die Kontinentalsperre, loc. cit.*, pp. 416 *et seq.* Also König, *op. cit.*, pp. 179 *et seq.*, 355 *et seq.*; Stephen in the House of Commons, Mar. 6, 1800 (Hansard, vol. XIII, app. pp. xxxiii *et seq.*); Order in Council of Feb. 18, 1807 (Hansard, vol. X, pp. 129 *et seq.*).

the consul afterwards issued a certificate as to the non-English origin of the goods; and fabricated Holstein certificates of origin were always available to bolster up the certificate. At the close of May 1807, Brune went a step farther and removed the always relatively zealous customs officials from the Hamburg–Travemünde frontier line and the Elbe line from Harburg (immediately opposite Hamburg) to Stade, replacing them by gendarmes. Consequently, during the five and a half months down to the beginning of August there arrived in Hamburg, without impediment, 1,475 vessels with cargoes estimated at 590,000 tons, including the most notoriously English goods, such as coal. According to the investigator just mentioned, Hamburg was chock full of English and colonial goods, which were sold as openly as in London, and not a single seizure had occurred. This would also seem to have been the time at which Bourrienne, Napoleon's envoy in Hamburg—according to his own story, which is in this case confirmed from English sources—obtained cloth and leather from England in order to be in a position to supply Napoleon's own army with the uniform coats, vests, caps, and shoes which he had to procure.[1]

The farce of Brune's conduct in Hamburg, however, was too much for Napoleon, who removed him in the latter half of July and appointed Bernadotte as his successor. This appointment manifestly brought with it a stricter enforcement of the law, although the new and well-meaning despot that the Hamburgers thereby got proved rather costly to the town; nor did he entirely escape more or less unproven accusations of corruptibility, both from Napoleon and also, later on, from the Senate of Hamburg.[2] Above all, however, after the removal of Brune, Napoleon regulated the blockade by means of two new decrees of August 6 and November 13, 1807. These placed the right of seizing English goods into the hands of the customs staff, which was strengthened at the same time, while the troops were placed at the disposal of the customs officials

[1] Bourrienne, *Mémoires sur Napoléon*, &c. (Paris, 1829), vol. VII, pp. 291 *et seq.*

[2] *Lettres inédites de Napoléon Ier* (Lecestre ed.), nos. 523 (Sept. 12, 1809), 823 (June 13, 1811), 826 (June 22, 1811); Servières, *op. cit.*, p. 124; Wohlwill, *Neuere Geschichte*, &c., p. 300.

and increased guaranties were provided in various ways that unlawful goods should not be permitted to escape examination. In doing this Napoleon fell back on the old and very clumsy expedient of declaring large main groups of goods to be *eo ipso* British when they did not come from France, that is to say, the majority of textile goods, (except certain ones imported by the Danish East Asiatic Company), cutlery and hardware, glass, pottery, and lump sugar ; and for the colonial goods detailed certificates of origin were required from the French commercial agents in the exporting port. As regards the question as to whether a vessel had put in at an English port, a searching examination was prescribed of the captain and the sailors separately, and the arrest of such of them as should give false information, after which they should be set free only after the payment of a heavy fine (6,000 francs for the captain and 500 francs for each sailor). All such vessels were to be confiscated, while the Berlin decree merely prescribed their expulsion. The latter of these two decrees, that concerning certificates of origin, the examination of the crews, and the confiscation of the vessels, was given practically unaltered validity for the whole Empire through what is called the first Milan decree, issued ten days later (November 23). Within barely a month, as we have seen,[1] there followed the answer to the Orders in Council, the great second Milan decree, which marks the end of Napoleon's measures bearing on the Continental System in 1807. On the heels of all this, immediately after the beginning of the new year (January 11, 1808) there came the so-called Tuileries decree, which sought to induce the crews and passengers of vessels to reveal any call in an English port by promising one-third of the value of the vessel and cargo as a reward. In September 1807, Napoleon, with his customary ruthlessness, had intervened in Holland and, to the despair of his brother Louis, had calmly caused his gendarmes to convey to France from that nominally independent kingdom a citizen of Breda and a citizen of Bergen-op-Zoom on the suspicion of smuggling.

[1] See *ante*, p. 123.

At the same time, thanks to Canning's almost Napoleonic contempt for the independence of neutrals, Napoleon received valuable assistance in the blockade of the North Sea coast in consequence of the bombardment of Copenhagen in the beginning of September and the breach between Denmark and Great Britain. As a matter of fact, Schleswig-Holstein, during the whole of the preceding period, had been a serious obstacle in the way of Napoleon's measures south of the Elbe. When the Elbe and the Weser were barred, Tönning in particular, but also Husum on the west coast of Schleswig, had largely replaced the Hanse Towns during the years 1803–6 as importers of English and colonial goods; and their trade had flourished like plants in a forcing-house. All attempts to prevent the passing of goods to the south from Holstein territory through the town of Altona, which was practically continuous with Hamburg (*all zu nah*), met with almost insuperable difficulties, all the more as the local Holstein authorities never failed to certify the neutral origin of the goods. It was, therefore, of very great importance that the ruler of Denmark, the Crown Prince Frederick, embittered through the conduct of Great Britain, placed himself at the service of the Continental System, with almost unique loyalty, and as early as September 1807 ordered the seizure of all forbidden goods in Holstein. Almost alone among the allies of Napoleon, he repudiated the idea of feigning adherence to the system while the real intention was to allow intercourse with Great Britain. His was not the principle *suaviter in re, fortiter in modo*, to quote a modern historian. It is true that the British, on their side, made a counter-move which was to have far-reaching consequences in the opposite direction, in that, simultaneously with the attack on Copenhagen, they occupied the Danish possession of Heligoland; but the effects of this did not immediately show themselves.[1]

---

[1] For the decrees of Aug. 6 and Nov. 13, 1807, cf. König, *op. cit.*, Anlage 2. For the first Milan decree, cf. *Bulletin des lois*, &c., 4th ser., bull. 172, no. 2,912. For the Tuileries decree, cf. Martens, *Nouveau recueil*, &c., vol. I, p. 457; Duboscq, *op. cit.*, no. 95 and p. 14; Holm, *Danmark-Norges Historie*, &c., vol. VII, pt. I, pp. 123–4, 180, 197; Linvald, *Bidrag til Oplysning*, &c., vol. VI, pp. 448 *et seq.* The following may also be consulted: France: Levasseur, *Histoire des classes ouvrières*, &c., de

## RESULTS IN 1807

It remains to be seen, accordingly, to what extent Napoleon, at the close of the year 1807, had attained his immediate object, the self-blockade of the Continent, not only in form but also in substance. As regards France herself, this had clearly been the case to a very high degree, as we can see from a very good barometer, namely, that a shortage of raw cotton was already threatening. As early as September the cotton manufacturers were speaking of having to close their mills if a breach with the Portuguese and Americans occurred; and the price of Brazilian cotton (Pernambuco) in Paris rose from 6·80–7·30 francs to 8·10–15 francs per kg., while the price in London of 1s. 10d.–1s. 11d. per pound corresponded to only 5–5½ francs. As the British prohibition on the exports of raw cotton was not issued until the year 1808, and the imports of raw cotton into Great Britain were uncommonly large in the year 1807 (74,900,000 lb. as against only 58,200,000 lb. in the previous year), it is apparent from the very first how the difficulties of importation into the Continent expressed the strength of the self-blockade and not of the British measures of reprisal.

The position in Central Europe can usually be best followed from the great meeting-point for continental trade, the Leipzig Fair, which was sensitive to every change; and the position there is illustrated by the unusually impartial and detailed Saxon 'reports of the fair' (*Messrelationes*), in the form in which they have been worked up by the German historians Hasse and, more particularly, König. In these reports there appears throughout a lively movement of both British industrial

*1789 à 1870*, vol. I, pp. 409–10, 422 note 4; Ballot, *Les prêts*, &c., vol. II, pp. 48–9, 54–5; Mollien, *op. cit.*, vol. II, p. 120. Central Europe: König, *op. cit.*, sec. III; Hasse, *Geschichte der Leipziger Messen* (Leipzig, 1885), pp. 409 *et seq.*; Tarle, *Kontinental'naja blokada*, vol. I, p. 397; Schäfer, *op. cit.*, pp. 434 *et seq.*, tables I–III. Great Britain: Hansard, vol. XIII, app., pp. xxxvii *et seq.*, xliii *et seq.* (House of Commons, Mar. 6, 1809); trade statistics in Hansard, vols. XIV, XX, XXII, app.; Tooke, *A History of Prices*, &c., vol. II (tables of imports and prices), vol. I, pp. 273 *et seq.*; Baines, *History of the Cotton Manufacture in Great Britain* (1835), p. 350 (table); Mahan, *Influence of Sea Power*, &c., vol. II, pp. 304 *et seq.*

products and colonial goods during the earlier part of 1807, including among other things the parcels confiscated in Hamburg and redeemed. These commanded a ready sale, despite the fact that the manufactured goods included in them were largely out of date. But the autumn measures in the Hanse Towns and Holstein led to a great scarcity of British textiles and an enormous rise in price (over 150 per cent.) on British cotton yarn, so that Napoleon could here be assured of an immediate result from his own measures and those of his new Russian ally. For the Hanse Towns this result extended also to colonial goods, so that the price of coffee, for instance, stood 20 per cent. higher in the old coffee-importing town of Hamburg than in Leipzig; and contrary to anything that had ever before been beheld, it was conveyed to the former place from the latter. Accordingly, the decline of shipping in Bremen stands out very clearly even in the statistics of 1807. A similar transformation occurred in Holstein, but with regard to the rest of Central Europe the effects did not yet extend to the colonial goods. This was chiefly due to the fact that the trade through Holland, in spite of everything, was still comparatively undisturbed, especially with American vessels, as the Embargo Act was not passed until the latter part of December 1807. Moreover, Rotterdam was alleged to have daily communication with England, just as in time of peace. British yarn was also shipped to Leipzig and Holland, and in September, 1807, the Belgian manufacturers complained that The Hague was so crowded with British cottons that a man might fancy himself in Manchester. With regard to colonial goods, it was also stated that the great Amsterdam firm of Hope & Co. had huge stores of sugar and coffee. This firm, which during the whole of this period played a leading part in almost all great international transactions of a commercial and financial nature, and also intervened in matters of public policy, was, incidentally, a living monument of the close commercial relations between the enemies, as it had a French head, Labouchère, who stood in close connexion with the world-famous British commercial house of Baring Brothers. Nor does there appear to have been any great scarcity of raw cotton, especially owing to imports through the Mediterranean ports of Lisbon, Leghorn, and Trieste.   The first of these, however, disappeared through the conquest of Portugal in the autumn of 1807, and the second through the occupation of Etruria at the close of the year. But Holland remained as an important gap, which became the more serious from Napoleon's point of view after he had, in the second Milan decree of December 1807, passed to the view that there were no such things as neutrals ; and consequently he could no longer tolerate the American shipping in Dutch ports.   At the turn of the year 1807–8, it is true, British industrial products did not seem to enter as easily as before ; but it was soon to prove that Napoleon had underestimated the strength of two forces which were constantly to rise up against his plans, *viz.*, smuggling and the opening-up of new commercial routes.

Finally, if we regard the process of development from a British standpoint, we have the evidence, already cited,[1] of the witnesses before a parliamentary committee that Napoleon's many counter-measures in the late summer and autumn caused a sudden stagnation in trade with the Continent.   The marine insurance premiums, which at the time of the issue of the Berlin decree had risen from 6 to 10 per cent., but had then declined to 4 per cent., were stated to have reached such amounts as 15, 20, and 30 per cent. before the middle of October 1807. In sixty-five cases during September and October vessels that had taken in cargo for the Continent had requested permission to discharge them again.   If we look at the statistical material available to throw light on the matter, we can establish in a comparatively exact way the effects of the Continental blockade during 1807.   It is especially noteworthy that the great exports of cotton goods show almost absolutely unaltered figures (£9,708,000, as against £9,754,000 in 1806 and an average of only £7,340,000 in the years 1801–5, all according to the ' official values ', which are based upon unchanged unit prices from year to year) ; nor do the far less important exports

[1] See *ante*, p. 164.

of yarn show any great decline (£602,000 in 1807, as against £736,000 in 1806 and an average of £666,000 in the years 1801–5). The probably less reliable figures for total exports show a somewhat more marked but nevertheless insignificant decline, namely, in relation to the year 1806 (8.1 per cent. according to the 'official values' and only 6.4 per cent. according to 'real values', which are also affected by changes in price). On the other hand, we can see from these statistics that the sales on the Continent were much more limited, namely, by nearly 33 per cent., according to 'real values' in 'the north of Europe, including France'; and probably the exports of manufactured goods to those markets declined more than exports as a whole. This result agrees very well with what might have been expected under the restrictive measures of the last quarter of the year.[1]

Next we have to consider colonial goods, which were intended to 'conquer England by excess'.[2] The trade statistics do not show any decrease of exports at all, but rather a slight increase; and not even the sales to the Continent are notably diminished. But one can see from the tables in Tooke's *History of Prices* that the price of coffee and sugar declined slightly in the autumn of 1807. Possibly one may point to a slightly greater dislocation in one single department, namely, in the imports of Baltic goods; and the fact is that this applies to the Baltic trade in general, evidently in consequence of the breach with Russia and Prussia, rather than through the Continental System proper. Hemp and more especially tallow, both from Russia, show a rise in prices in the course of the year, and timber from Memel exhibits violent fluctuations from the middle of 1806. But all this is a trifle; and during 1807 there are, broadly speaking, no traces of any substantial result of the policy as regards Great Britain's foreign trade as a whole.

---

[1] It should be remarked once for all that the British commercial statistics are not only highly uncertain in themselves, but also show inexplicable variations in different sources. But the relative changes, as a rule, exhibit a considerably better agreement than the absolute numbers, and may therefore be assumed to deserve greater confidence than the latter. For the absolute figures, see *post*, p. 245.

[2] See *ante*, p. 57.

In fact, there are considerably less than one would have expected from the diminished importation of British industrial products to the German market.

## Transmarine Markets (1808)

It was important for Napoleon, accordingly, to attain during 1808 a more effective application of the measures of the preceding year. Great Britain also now encountered various new difficulties ; but the peculiar thing about them is that they had no direct connexion with Napoleon's proceedings, but at the most with the British Orders in Council—a fact which the British opposition, as in duty bound, did not fail to point out. The truth is that they were chiefly caused by the American Embargo Act, partly through the diminished importation of American goods, and partly through the great diminution of tonnage, as explained in part II, chapter IV. Accordingly, the result for Great Britain was a diminished importation of, and raised prices on, raw materials, which in reality did not at all correspond to Napoleon's wishes that prices should be low in England and high on the Continent. The imports of raw cotton sank by 42 per cent., of American cotton to Liverpool by no less than 82 per cent., of wool by 80 per cent., of flax by 39 per cent., of hemp by 66 per cent., of tallow by 60 per cent., &c. Naturally enough, under these circumstances, the price of the most important kinds of raw cotton, for instance, increased in the course of the spring and summer 100 per cent. or more. Especially striking, too, was the rise in prices on goods from Scandinavia and from the Baltic countries in general : timber, hemp, flax, tallow, bristles, tar, but above all linseed, the price of which, at least according to Lord Grenville's statement in the House of Lords, rose more than tenfold. The shortage of raw cotton reacted on the spinning industry, which did not fail to complain of its distress by a whole series of petitions to Parliament, wherein special emphasis was laid on the consequences of the breach with America. According to undisputed statements made by the opposition speakers in the beginning of the following year, for instance, the poor-law burdens in Manchester doubled in the course of 1808; only nine mills were running full time, thirty-one had been running half time, and forty-four had entirely suspended operations.[1]

Many of these complaints, however, referred to the first months of the year. The rise in prices, on the contrary, was partly due to speculation, which began in the latter part of the year and in many respects quite revolutionized the situation. The year 1808, as it went on, came to be dominated in fact by one of the great events in the history of the Continental System—the Spanish uprising. But the direct economic significance of this movement was not primarily what Napoleon once stated, namely, that it gave to England a ' considerable amount of sales on the Iberian peninsula '.[2] What a limited part this matter played can be most easily perceived from the following export figures taken from the British trade statistics ('real values').

| | United Kingdom Produce | | | Foreign and Colonial Produce | | |
|---|---|---|---|---|---|---|
| Year | Exports to Spain | Exports to Portugal | Total exports | Exports to Spain | Exports to Portugal | Total exports |
| 1807 | £30,000 | £970,000 | £40,480,000 | £80,000 | £200,000 | £10,000,000 |
| 1808 | 860,000 | 430,000 | 40,880,000 | 260,000 | 170,000 | 9,090,000 |
| 1809 | 2,380,000 | 800,000 | 50,240,000 | 660,000 | 320,000 | 15,770,000 |

As appears from this table, the Pyrenean states after 1807 do not figure very largely in the total exports of Great Britain, despite the fact that the increase for Spain is very large in itself; and a good deal, even, of the amount which is included is the direct opposite of new sales, being really supplies for the maintenance of the British troops and the insurgents. More-

[1] Petitions and speeches in the House of Commons, Feb. 22 and 23, Mar. 10 and 18, 1808 (Hansard, vol. x, pp. 692–3, 708–9, 1056 et seq., 1182–83); Speeches of Whitbread and Alexander Baring in the House of Commons, Mar. 6, 1809 (Hansard, vol. xii, pp. 1169, 1194); Worm-Müller, Norge gjennem nødsaarene 1807–1810 (Christiania, 1917–18), p. 123.

[2] Note pour le ministre des relations extérieures, Oct. 7, 1810 (Correspondance, no. 17,014).

over, it is inseparable from the geographical position of the country that the Iberian peninsula could not be suited for what Great Britain chiefly needed on the Continent, namely, an entrance gate for its goods. The smuggling which now began across the Pyrenees into France cannot have weighed very heavily, as is shown by the figures in the tables themselves.[1] The establishment of the new relations with Spain in 1808, like the flight of the Portuguese royal family to Brazil in the preceding year, was principally important in quite another way, namely, in that it placed Great Britain in very close connexion with the transmarine markets. The West Indian possessions of Spain, especially Cuba and Porto Rico, thus transferred the trade in colonial goods to England, while the mainland colonies in South America and Mexico created a large new market for British industrial products. It is easy to understand that in British eyes this new position seemed to open up the possibility of circumventing the whole of Napoleon's laboriously constructed rampart against British trade ; and this was all the more welcome because at the same time the United States had shut herself off from the rest of the world. The very peculiar British export figures to America for these years show the following fluctuations ('real values') :

| Year | United Kingdom Produce | | Foreign and Colonial Produce | |
|---|---|---|---|---|
| | Exports to United States | Exports to rest of America (incl. West Indies) | Exports to United States | Exports to rest of Amerida (incl. West Indies) |
| 1807 | £11,850,000 | £10,440,000 | £250,000 | £910,000 |
| 1808 | 5,240,000 | 16,590,000 | 60,000 | 1,580,000 |
| 1809 | 7,260,000 | 18,010,000 | 200,000 | 1,820,000 |

The whole of this striking transformation, which caused the exports to Central and South America to become a more than abundant compensation for the very great reduction in exports to the United States, was wont to be cited by the

[1] Darmstädter, *Studien zur napoleonischen Wirtschaftspolitik, loc. cit.* (1904), vol. II, pp. 596–7. The decline in the exports of France to Spain in 1808, which is there given as amounting to 32,400,000 francs (£1,300,000), cannot possibly have been compensated by British exports, if the table given above is reliable. Probably it largely corresponds to the imports of grain from the United States.

British government speakers as evidence that the Orders in Council had not injured the exports of the country, but had only caused a transition to direct trade with the former markets instead of sales to the North Americans as intermediaries. The mouthpieces of the opposition, however, maintained, and with more reason, that this new trade was really a new conquest brought about by the Spanish uprising and consequently no result of the destruction of trade with the United States by the Orders in Council.

## British Speculation in South America

The new outlet for sales which thus seemed to offer itself gave rise to a violent speculation with all the distinctive characteristics of a boom—general optimism, great sales, industrial activity, and rising prices in the articles of speculation. As early as 1806 Sir Home Popham, the second in command of a naval expedition, had made of his own accord an attack on the mouth of the Plata and had taken Buenos Aires, upon which he sent home eight wagon-loads of silver accompanied by a boastful circular addressed to the manufacturing towns of England together with a list of all the goods that could find a ready sale in his conquest; but as ill luck would have it, Buenos Aires had to be evacuated before the goods had yet arrived. Now that access to those markets was secured, merchants were attracted, by the memory of the hope aroused by Popham's circulars and the loads of silver, into incredibly bold ventures in the way of exports. McCulloch, the political economist, describes the frenzy, after a contemporary source, as follows :

We are informed by Mr. Mawe, an intelligent traveller resident at Rio Janeiro, at the period in question, that more Manchester goods were sent out in the course of a few weeks than had been consumed in the twenty years preceding ; and the quantity of English goods of all sorts poured into the city was so very great, that warehouses could not be provided sufficient to contain them, and that the most valuable merchandise was actually exposed for whole weeks on the beach to the weather, and to every sort of depredation. But the folly and ignorance of those who had crowded into this speculation was still more strikingly evinced in the selection of the articles sent to South America. . . . Some speculators actually went so far as to send *skates* to Rio Janeiro.[1]

The final consequences of these speculations could not be advantageous, but for the time being the situation seemed flourishing. The total exports during 1808 exhibit approximately unaltered figures, but the exports of cotton goods rose by 29 per cent., irrespective of the change in price. But this did not hold good of Central and Northern Europe, where the British trade statistics indicate a very heavy decline for both British goods (from £5,090,000 to £2,160,000) and colonial goods (from £5,730,000 to £3,270,000). This, however, is largely counterbalanced by a corresponding rise in exports to the Mediterranean countries; and other information points to considerably larger exports to the north of Europe, as shall be shown shortly.[2]

If we examine the position on the mainland and especially in Germany somewhat more closely, we find the greatest change in 1808 to be a unique rise in the price of raw cotton and a shortage in the supplies, which were obtained mainly from the sale of captured cargoes. At the Michaelmas Fair in Leipzig the price of Brazilian cotton (Pernambuco) rose 223 per cent. above the normal; and, as before, this was especially felt in France, where the textile industry in Nantes was enabled by government loans to go over from cotton to wool. As Great Britain herself suffered from a shortage of raw cotton, this can only in part be ascribed to the Continental self-blockade. With regard to its efficaciousness, Napoleon was able to record an advance in one quarter, namely, in Switzerland, where the smuggling of British goods ceased after 1808; but Holland, which was far more important from this point of view, was still a tender spot. It is true that King Louis, as early as January,

---

[1] McCulloch, *Principles of Political Economy* (London, 1830), 2d. ed. p. 330; Smart, *Economic Annals*, &c., vol. I, pp. 122–3, 184. Cf. speech in the House of Commons, June 16, 1812 (Hansard, vol. XXIII, p. 503); Louis Simond, *Journal of a Tour and Residence in Great Britain during the years 1810 and 1811, by a French Traveller* (New York, 1815), vol. I, p. 242 (under date of Aug. 1, 1810).

[2] See *post*, p. 179.

did something to bring about an effective barring of the coast; but the smuggling went on so openly that, according to the evidence of Louis himself, the shops of Leyden displayed without disguise quantities of British manufactures. By decree of September 16, 1808, Napoleon, who a little earlier had asserted that there were people who had pocketed 20,000,000 francs through smuggling in Holland, had recourse in violent indignation to the measure of closing the frontier of France to all colonial goods from Holland. This seems to have had a certain effect, as one can see from the fact that the imports of British yarn and British manufactures, which last had already been insignificant, to Leipzig through Holland ceased entirely at this time. A month later (October 23, 1808) there was issued an extremely draconic Dutch decree as to the closing of the ports. This decree was so *outré* that it bears every mark of applying the principle *suaviter in re, fortiter in modo* : all exports were prohibited until further notice ; no commercial vessels, domestic or foreign, might put in at any Dutch ports, under any pretext, on pain of being fired at ; fishing vessels were to return to their port of departure, but were to be confiscated on the least sign of intercourse with the enemy, &c.[1]

## New Trade Routes via Heligoland and Sweden (1808)

The effect of this, however, was a new change in the channels followed by trade. To begin with, Heligoland now showed its immense importance as an emporium or base for the smuggling of British goods into north Germany. In 1808, according to Rist's dispatches, Great Britain expended £500,000 in building a port, fortifications and warehouses on the little island covering about 150 acres. A number (stated to be 200) of British merchants and representatives of commercial houses settled there and formed a special chamber of commerce ; and this peculiar centre of trade was jestingly called ' Little London '.

[1] De Cérenville, *op. cit.*, p. 309 ; Duboscq, *op. cit.*, nos. 117, 118, 126, 146, 158, 159, 160, 167, 178, 189, 190 ; and pp. 47 *et seq.* ; *Correspondance*, no. 13,781. Dutch Ordinances : Martens, *Nouveau recueil*, &c., vol. I, pp. 458-9, 474-5.

According to the statements of the British merchants themselves, during three and a half months (August–November 1808) nearly 120 vessels discharged their cargoes there, and the yearly imports were estimated—though, to judge by the commercial statistics, this estimate was almost certainly too high—at £8,000,000, or nearly a sixth of the total exports of Great Britain for 1808 (£50,000,000).  It is not surprising, therefore, that great quantities of goods had to lie exposed to wind and weather, and that there was scarcely standing room on the island.  The difficulty consisted, of course, in smuggling the goods into the mainland afterwards;  but the Continental blockade had again been weakened by the fact that in the beginning of the year Napoleon had been obliged to evacuate Oldenburg out of regard to his Russian ally, who was related to the Duke of Oldenburg.  It is difficult to determine from accessible sources what routes the goods afterwards followed. From Bremen a certain amount reached Leipzig for the Easter Fair, but after that nothing;  and both the shipping of Hamburg and the trade of Bremen had, according to their own sources, almost ceased to exist.  But there were many possibilities left, especially through Holstein, where the population and the officials alike did their best to neutralize the loyalty of the Danish government to the system.  They succeeded admirably, and it is certain that there are no symptoms at all of decline in the traffic *via* Heligoland.

During 1808, moreover, Sweden had begun to serve as a storing place for British goods.  The Swedish trade statistics had previously shown an excess of exports during the century, especially as regards Great Britain ;  but during 1808 there was a complete reversal, so much so that the imports from there amounted to 6,650,000 riksdaler, as against exports amounting to 2,610,000 riksdaler.  It was colonial goods that went this way, for the most part through Gothenburg, the position of which as one of the *foci* of the commerce of the world had, to judge by its export statistics, been coming into view even in the previous year.  Imports more than doubled in one year. What were for the circumstances of the time very considerable quantities of sugar and coffee (2,900,000 lb. and 1,300,000 lb., respectively) were exported from there in 1808 ; and when Admiral Saumarez was in the town, in May, he wrote to his son : ' Gothenburg is a place of great trade at this time ; at least 1,200 sail of vessels of different nations are in the port.' From there the goods tried to find their way into Germany through the South Baltic ports.[1]

Thus Napoleon was still far from his goal, and the Spanish rising in particular was to carry him farther and farther away. As early as October 1, 1808, his brother Louis—who was always pessimistic, it is true—wrote to the eldest of the brothers, Joseph Bonaparte, the newly created King of Spain : ' Far from settling down, matters get more and more tangled, and— perhaps I speak too much as a Dutchman, but I find something revolutionary in the way in which war is made on commerce— it seems to me that they never will attain the object that they have set before them '. At the same time as Spain and Portugal, he thinks, South America and Mexico have thrown themselves open to the English ; ' and for a chimerical system the whole Continent is losing its trade and shipping, while that of England grows prodigiously '.[2]

### DIMINISHED VIGILANCE DURING THE AUSTRIAN CAMPAIGN
### (1809)

This line of development was especially marked in 1809 when Napoleon's campaign against Austria and the Spanish uprising also made heavy demands on him and his troops, while trade under a neutral, that is to say, American flag, again became possible through the Non-intercourse Act, bringing it about that the importation of raw materials into Great Britain

---

[1] Fisher, *Studies in Napoleonic Statesmanship : Germany* (Oxford, 1903), pp. 338 *et seq.* ; Rubin, *1807–1814*, &c., pp. 383–4 ; Clason, *Sveriges Historia intill tjugonde seklet* (Stockholm, 1910), vol. IX : A, pp. 26–7 ; Bergwall, *Historisk underrättelse*, &c., p. 48 (table) ; *Memoirs and Correspondence of Admiral Lord de Saumarez* (Ross ed., London, 1838), vol. II, p. 105 ; Ahnfelt, *op. cit.*, vol. V, p. 225 ; Ramm, *När Göteborg var frihamn* (Gothenburg, 1900), p. 3.

[2] Duboscq, *op. cit.*, no. 182.

again became normal and the possibilities of smuggling into the Continent grew greatly. Great Britain could also now rejoice in the highest prosperity in the new trade she acquired through the Spanish uprising, as is most plainly shown by the tables given above.[1] The British exports of cotton goods show a unique rise : manufactured goods from £12,500,000 to £18,400,000 and yarn from £470,000 to £1,020,000 (' official values ', that is to say, irrespective of changes in prices). The former thus underwent an increase of nearly 50 per cent., and the latter of more than 100 per cent., as compared with the in themselves high figures of 1808.

This was not solely an effect of the possession of new markets. On the contrary, all our sources are agreed in attributing it to the diminished watchfulness on the North Sea, where the self-blockade was alleged—with some exaggeration, it is true—to have in reality ceased ; and it was considered that trade was being carried on almost as in time of peace. This is made visible, indeed, by a rise in the figures for British exports to North Europe from £2,160,000 to £5,700,000 for British goods, and from £3,270,000 to no less than £8,870,000 for colonial goods. With a zeal that infallibly reminds us of the saying, ' When the cat's away the mice will play,' all Napoleon's tools on the North Sea coast took advantage of his absence in Austria to relax the bonds and to let in vessels, especially those under the American flag. As early as the middle of March 1809, King Louis of Holland declared to the Emperor that his country was ' physically unable to endure the closing of the ports ' in combination with the closing of the Franco-Dutch frontier ordered by Napoleon in the previous September ; and accordingly he made certain relaxations in the blockade by sea at the close of the month. When Napoleon, at the beginning of June, rescinded his September decree, his brother embraced the opportunity to rescind the order prohibiting American vessels to put in at Dutch ports. This caused Napoleon to put the barring of the frontier in force again in the middle of July ; but not only the showers of abuse which Napoleon poured over

[1] See *ante*, p. 174.

his unhappy brother, but also his brother's correspondence with the Dutch ministers, show distinctly enough how smuggling was going on in Holland itself throughout the entire year.

Farther to the north smuggling through Oldenburg continued into the following year. A sudden fall in the price of cotton yarn in northern Germany was caused in February 1809, by the large stocks that the Manchester manufacturers had laid up in Heligoland ; and as an example of the scope of the traffic which was carried on from that island, it may be mentioned, on the authority of the statements of the Heligoland merchants, that sixty-six vessels and seventy smaller boats were able, during nineteen days in June 1809, to land on the coast goods to the value of several hundred thousand pounds. According to French reports, the guards along the Elbe and the Weser, too, were now reduced to a few untrustworthy Dutch soldiers and gendarmes under the command of a drunken officer. If we cross to Schleswig-Holstein territory, we find there the same phenomenon, namely, a huge expansion of the colonial trade. What is called the second Tönning period, which is marked by these American visits, began in June 1809, and lasted to the end of the year. The traffic all along the line was formally facilitated by the British government by means of the new Order in Council of April 26, which restricted the declaration of blockade in the north to the River Ems, at least in so far as the German North Sea coast was not reckoned as a dependency of France, which, of course, is just what it actually was. In reality, however, this meant comparatively little, inasmuch as the old regulations were in practice applied by the issue of the British government licences, which shipping was scarcely able to do without.

At the same time English trade was being transferred to Gothenburg and the Baltic ports. In Gothenburg the British set up, in 1809, special warehouses and stores on Fotö immediately opposite the entrance to the harbour. The re-exports of raw sugar almost trebled, while the exports of coffee, like the shipping of the port in general, more than doubled. The Prussian and the Pomeranian ports now became regular gates of entry for the importation of goods; and the Baltic coast came to be the centre of trade to such an extent that the *fierante*, the Jewish traders of Eastern Europe, went to Königsberg and Riga, instead of Leipzig, in order to cover their requirements of British manufactures. Finally, great quantities of British yarn came to Trieste and Fiume before the Austro-French war, and even after its close, from the repurchased parcels.[1]

### REES-BREMEN BARRIER (SCHÖNBRUNN DECREE OF JULY 18, 1809)

Obviously this development did not escape the notice of Napoleon. On the contrary, he was kept informed by a veritable army of spies as to what was happening both within and without his empire, and it is clear that he did not wish to let it go on without taking steps to stop it. He did not even delay his counter-measures until the close of the Austrian campaign, but limited them in the main to the attempt to isolate Holland, which in his eyes was the most serious breach of all in the system. At the same time as he renewed, as has been mentioned above, the closing of the frontier against France,[2] he suddenly ordered, by the decree of Schönbrunn on July 18, 1809, a corresponding closing of the frontier on the side of Germany and caused this to become operative at once without even informing the ' protected ' princes in the Confederation of the Rhine who were affected by the blockade, *viz.*, his brother Jerome, King of Westphalia, and the Grand Duke of Berg. The smuggled goods were considered by the French director-general of customs, Collin de Sussy, to go direct up the Rhine and the Ems, and then to go by land through the Grand Duchy of Berg, practically corresponding to the Ruhr district, to the whole Confederation

---

[1] *Lettres inédites*, nos. 476, 477, 527, 555; Duboscq, *op. cit.*, nos. 209, 220, 277; Schmidt, *Le Grand-duché de Berg*, pp. 348 *et seq.*; Wellesley, *Memoirs and Correspondence*, vol. III, p. 196; Prytz, *Kronologiska anteckningar rörande Göteborg* (Gothenburg, 1898), p. 95; Bergwall, *op. cit.*, table 3; Channing, *op. cit.*, vol. XII, p. 253; Tarle, *Kontinental'naja blokada*, vol. I, p. 486.

[2] See *ante*, p. 181.

of the Rhine. At the close of July, French customs officers were moved into the country, forming a chain from Bremen through Osnabrück down to the Rhine at Rees close to the Dutch frontier, which was thereby cut off from connexions eastward. This cordon was made threefold, consisting of troops, gendarmes and customs officers. According to one statement, one of the lines went along the Dutch frontier from Varel, near the beach of Jade, to Emmerich on the Rhine immediately north of Rees. The violence with which the whole thing was carried out, however, caused great confusion. The local authorities refused to assist the customs officers and protested against their movements; the gendarmes were at times positively hostile to them; and to crown all, the customs officials were sometimes corrupt, so that the blockade of the non-French part of the Continent still continued to be practically a failure on well-nigh all points. The unbroken severity of the action that Napoleon followed in Holland, especially by the incorporation of the region south of the Waal in March 1810, seems not to have borne any great fruit either. At any rate, as late as May of the same year King Louis wrote sourly to Marshal Oudinot, Duke of Reggio : ' I have received the letter in which you inform me that smuggling is going on to a great extent on the coast of my kingdom. Like you, I believe that it goes on wherever there are coasts, in Germany as in Holland, and even in France.' The complete annexation of Holland in July created a new situation here, but at the same time it made the barrier between Holland and Germany somewhat purposeless.

During the first half of the year 1810, therefore, the situation was not greatly changed. Frankfurt, in particular, could rejoice in an entirely undiminished trade in colonial goods, which came in through the ports of the North Sea and the Baltic, and were conveyed thence to northern Italy, southern France, and even to Holland and eastern France. The then minister of Prussia in this capital of the Confederation of the Rhine actually declared at the beginning of the year that the town had never before played such a part in the trade of

Europe nor been so full of colonial goods; and the trade seems further to have increased in the course of the summer. As regards Leipzig, to be sure, it was stated before and during the Easter Fair in 1810 that the imports through the North Sea ports, especially of English yarn, had practically ceased. But to make up for this, the transfer of the trade to the Baltic ports was now definitive, helped with the best of good-will by Prussia, and also by Sweden and Mecklenburg, to circumvent the Continental System in every conceivable way, and, for that matter, with useful help from the corrupt French consuls in the ports. Königsberg above all, but to a great extent the other towns on the south coast of the Baltic—Rostock, Stralsund, Stettin, Memel, and even Riga—now took the place of the Hanse Towns and the Dutch ports; and there began a unique importation of American cotton, which attained its highest level during the summer. The whole of the Confederation of the Rhine, Austria, Switzerland, and even France, were provided from there at a time when spinning mills were springing up on the Continent like mushrooms from the ground. At the Michaelmas Fair in 1810 the value of the supplies of colonial goods in Leipzig was estimated at 65,500,000 francs; and although only a sixth part remained in the town, all cellars, vaults, and storehouses were full to overflowing, chiefly with cotton, but also with coffee, sugar, and indigo.[1]

## D'IVERNOIS'S EPIGRAM

Naturally enough, people in England, especially in government circles, took a very optimistic view of the situation. The new Order in Council of April 1809, however modest was its modification of the paper blockade, is an evidence of this fact. Reasons are found for it in ' different events and changes which have occurred in the relations between Great Britain and the territories of other powers ', which meant, of course, the Iberian

---

[1] *Correspondance*, nos. 16,476, 16,713; Duboscq, *op. cit.*, no. 290; Schmidt, *op. cit.*, pp. 350–3; König, *op. cit.*, pp. 225 *et seq.*, 230–1, 238 *et seq.*, 241–2; Darmstädter, *Das Grossherzogtum Frankfurt* (Frankfurt-am-Main, 1901), pp. 311–12.

peninsula. In February 1809, Lord Liverpool, formerly Lord Hawkesbury, who was home secretary at the time, spoke in the House of Lords about ' the flourishing state of commerce ' ; and as late as May 1810, the British budget debate was marked entirely by a feeling of booming trade and prosperity, so that even on the side of the opposition Huskisson considered that the country was in a happy state of development. Especially seductive was the roseate description given by Perceval as chancellor of the exchequer ; and Rose, the vice-president of the Board of Trade, said that he was unable, to be sure, to explain how it could be so, ' but somehow it appeared, that from the industry and ingenuity of our merchants every pro-hibitory measure of Bonaparte's had utterly failed of its object. In fact, our trade, instead of being limited by it, had rather been extended, in spite of the hostile proceedings of the enemy.' The same idea was expressed with a touch of $ὕβρις$ in a contemporary epigram placed on the title-page of a pamphlet by Sir Francis d'Ivernois, a Swiss naturalized in England, entitled *Effets du blocus continental* :

> Votre blocus ne bloque point,
> et grâce à votre heureuse adresse
> ceux que vous affamez sans cesse
> ne périront que d'embonpoint.[1]

[1] Hansard, vol. XII, pp. 801 ; vol. XVI, p. 1043 *et seq* ; d'Ivernois, *Effets du blocus continental sur le commerce, les finances et la prospérité des Isles Britanniques* (London, 1809 : dated July 24) ; Servières, *op. cit.*, p. 131 note.

# CHAPTER III

## SMUGGLING AND CORRUPTION; FISCALISM AND LICENSING

THE tendencies described in the last chapter made it increasingly clear to Napoleon during the year 1810 that he must find new expedients if he was ever to succeed in making the Continental self-blockade effective; and he also had another reason for reshaping his policy, in the great inconveniences which had revealed themselves both in his finances and in French economic life. In order to form a clear idea of this second phase of the history of the Continental System, however, we must consider in a little more detail the smuggling and the system of bribery.[1]

### SMUGGLING

Concerning the prevalence of smuggling under the Continental System lengthy books might be written, for it flourished throughout Europe to an extent of which the world since then, and perhaps even before then, has rarely seen the like. Coercive measures in the sphere of commercial policy have at all times found a palliative in smuggling. But that palliative was used to an infinitely larger extent now that coercion acquired a range previously undreamt of; and at the same time it was felt to be unendurable in a quite different way than

[1] For the smuggling and corruption there are almost unlimited materials in the extensive literature bearing upon this subject, particularly in the works of König, Schmidt, Servières, Fisher, de Cérenville, Rambaud, Rubin, Peez and Dehn, and also in the treatises of Tarle and Schäfer. To these, moreover, should be added the work of Chapuisat, *Le commerce et l'industrie à Genève*, &c., pp. 29 *et seq.*, 44. The quotation from Bourrienne refers to his *Mémoires*, vol. VIII, ch. XI, pp. 195–6. The quotation from Rist refers to his *Lebenserinnerungen*, vol. II, pp. 106 *et seq.* The reference to Simond's *Journal* will be found in vol. I, p. 242; vol. II, p. 77. As to the trustworthiness of Bourrienne and Rist, cf. Wohlwill, *Neuere Geschichte*, &c., especially pp. 295 note, 397 note; also his review of Servières, in *Hansische Geschichtsblätter* for 1906.

formerly, owing both to the increased importance of international intercourse and to the fact that outside the limits of France proper it represented a foreign dominion and lacked moral support in all classes of the community. The purely external forms of the smuggling are of relatively subordinate importance in this connexion. The examples that have been mentioned in the preceding pages, and that will be mentioned in the following pages, may here be supplemented by a couple of contemporary descriptions. One of these by Bourrienne refers to the year 1809 and has a more or less anecdotal character.

### Bourrienne's Anecdote

To the left of the short road leading from Altona to Hamburg there lies a field that had been excavated in order to get gravel for building houses and roads. The intention was to repair the broad and long street in Hamburg running to the Altona gate. During the night the hole from which the gravel had been taken was filled up ; and the same carts which as a rule conveyed the gravel to Hamburg were filled with raw sugar, the colour of which resembles sand. They contented themselves with covering the sugar with a layer of sand an inch thick. The pikes of the customs officials easily penetrated this thin layer of sand and the sugar underneath it. This comedy went on for a long time, but the work on the street made no progress. Before I knew the cause of this slowness I complained about it, because the street led out to a little country place which I owned near Altona, and where I used to go daily. Like myself, the customs officials at last found out that the work of road-making took rather a long time, and one fine day the sugar carts were stopped and seized. The smugglers then had to devise some other expedients.

In the region between Hamburg and Altona, on the right bank of the Elbe, there is a little suburb inhabited by sailors, dock-labourers, and a very large number of house-owners, whose burial ground is in the churchyard of Hamburg. One now saw more often than usual hearses with their adornments and decorations, processions, burial hymns and the usual ceremonies. Amazed at the enormous and sudden mortality among the inhabitants of Hamburgerberg, the customs house officials at length ventured to examine one of the deceased at close quarters and discovered sugar, coffee, vanilla, indigo, &c. This, accordingly, was another expedient which had to be abandoned ; but others remained.

## Rist's Description of Hamburg Smuggling

With this may be compared the more informative and certainly quite trustworthy account given by Rist, the representative of Denmark, of the position at Hamburg a year after the period with which we are chiefly concerned here, namely, at the beginning of 1811.[1]

For some time there had developed a peculiar and flourishing contraband traffic which was carried on from Hamburgerberg with varying success in full daylight and under the eyes of the customs officers. About this I wish to speak, because it was not only peculiar in its kind, but also not without influence upon the manners of the people and later events, and even became the subject of a genuinely humorous popular poetry.

The abundance of cheap colonial goods in Altona, which could not be prevented by any prohibitions or other measures from this side of the frontier, and the similarly unpreventable connection with Hamburgerberg, made this last-named place a regular emporium for contraband goods. Speculators in that line of business had at that time hit upon the idea of entrusting to all kinds of low-class people, chiefly women, boys and girls of the rabble, the task of carrying the forbidden goods in small quantities through the customs guard stationed at the town gates. The attempt had been successful and was soon continued on a large scale. The city gate was thronged with all kinds of *canaille* coming in and going out in a steady stream. Behind some wooden sheds near the city gate one saw the arsenal of this curious army and its equipment, which was at once disgusting and laughable. There women turned up their dresses in order to shake coffee beans down in their stockings and to fasten little bags of coffee everywhere under their clothes ; there boys filled their ragged trousers with pepper in the sight of everybody ; others poured syrup in their broad boots ; some even claimed to have seen women conceal powdered sugar under their caps in their black tangled hair. With these burdens they at once started off, and afterward delivered over their goods in certain warehouses located near the city gate and received their pay. In this way immense quantities of goods were brought in ; and agreements with these petty dealers, based solely on good faith, seem seldom to have been broken on either side.

This trickery could not long remain concealed from the customs officers ; and there is no doubt but that they could soon have checked it. But this does not seem to have been the intention at all. This ' filtration '

[1] We know from a letter of Bourrienne to Napoleon in October 1809 that the same situation existed at that time. Lingelbach, *Historical Investigation and the Commercial History of the Napoleonic Era*, in the *American Historical Review* (vol. XIX (1913-14), p. 276.

—that was the technical term—was regarded as a happy hunting-ground, which was preserved as a means of enabling officers always to cover their requirements from it. If the officials seized every third or fourth ' bearer ' (*Träger*)—that was the people's technical term—and kept his or her load, they derived a fine income from it ; but the traffic was not at all disturbed by this, for losses were part of the business, and the customs officials had simply to hold out their hands to get all that they needed. Many of them were also well bribed by the principal participators in the traffic. If an unknown face appeared on duty, recourse was had to strategical measures : a dense column was formed, some heavily armed persons in the van were sacrificed, and the others burst through like a whirlwind, to the great joy of the spectators. The manifold incidents and perils which surrounded this *Schuckeln* or *Tragen*, the spirit of good-fellowship with which the trade was carried on, and the gallows humour that it created, inspired a poet, and by no means contemptible poet of his kind, from this or some neighbouring depart-ment to indite some '*Schuckeln* ditties ', which for some time were in everybody's mouth and were highly characteristic. It is certain that this business was for several years in succession a source of good earnings for the poorest elements of the population and considerably diminished mendicity. When the poor law officials asked parents receiving support about their children's means of livelihood, their answer as a rule was : ' Hee [or see] drigt ' (he—or she—bears). This offscum of society had suddenly appeared as if sprung out of the soil, and in the same way it afterwards vanished.

All this was by no means peculiar to Hamburg, although the fact that Hamburgerberg and country residences and places of amusement lay on the Holstein side rendered control very difficult and led to the rudest and most repulsive corporeal searchings of both women and men in the middle of the open road. Rist says that it was an especially difficult time for the corpulent, just as seems to have been the case during the recent World War on the shores on the Sound. On the North Sea coast the smuggling was still more systematic in Bremen, which, according to Max Schäfer, the latest describer of its fortunes under the Continental System, was a ' smuggling metropolis '. It derived special advantage from what Vandal has called the amphibious nature of the coast, in that, thanks to *Die Watten* (the numerous islands lying flush with the water), goods could be smuggled in direct from the British. From English sources we learn how raw sugar was sent when refined sugar was prohibited, and *eau sucrée* when raw sugar was prohibited; how coffee went in as horse-beans, sugar as starch; and how the names of pepper were legion. The same system flourished, however, from Gothenburg in the northwest around all the coasts of Europe to Saloniki in the southeast, without any great variation in the methods. Probably the most primitive expedients were resorted to on the Balkan peninsula. Here sugar was packed in small boxes weighing at the most 200 kilograms, so that they could be transported on horses and asses; in this way it was conveyed by armed bands through Bosnia, Serbia and Hungary to Vienna. France proper was undoubtedly the most closely guarded country, but even there, according to both English and French witnesses, smuggling flourished to a very large extent. At the very same time when the Berlin decree was flung out, when the new prohibitive customs ordinance was enforced for France herself, the English *Monthly Magazine*, following the statements of experts, described how British goods of different kinds were exported on French orders to France everywhere along the frontiers and could easily be insured up to the place of their destination, and how immediately after their arrival they were stamped as of French manufacture and made to serve as evidence of the high level attained by French industry. A well-informed and intelligent French-American traveller, Louis Simond, who visited Great Britain in 1810–11, relates how the English goods ' are packed in small packages, fit to be carried by hand, and made to imitate the manufactures of the country to which they are sent, even to the very paper and outward wrapper, and the names of the foreign manufacturers marked on the goods.' On pieces of broadcloth in Leeds, for instance, he observed the mark of Journaux Frères of Sedan.

On the sea the smuggling is said to have started principally from Cowes, in the Isle of Wight. Here the goods were packed into hermetically sealed chests, which were afterward thrown into the water, chained to little buoys, like fishing nets, and safely hauled ashore on the French side by the inhabitants under the very eyes of the patrolling vessels. If we may credit an active French customs officer at the time, Boucher de Perthes, the use of British textile goods came very close to the Emperor's person. According to him, Napoleon learned, in the course of a journey with Josephine, that her trunks were crammed with the forbidden goods, and made the customs authorities mercilessly seize them all.

## Normality of Smuggling

Through this all-pervading system smuggling acquired a stamp of normality, which was of great importance, especially for Napoleon's subsequent policy, and which forms yet another significant example of the general contrast between appearance and reality by which the policies were dominated. On both sides the smugglers were used as ordinary means of commercial intercourse in cases where it was not desired to recognize a traffic which could not be done away with. In this case the French made use of the English word in the slightly corrupted form of ' smoggler '. Boucher de Perthes, who was sub-inspector of customs at Boulogne in 1811 and 1812, in a letter from there defines them as ' contrabandists of their (the British) nation, who are attached to our police and who at the same time carry on a traffic in prisoners of war and guineas, people of the sack and the rope, capable of everything except what is good '. In another letter he relates how they smuggled French brandy into Great Britain, as well as guineas out of that country, besides acting as spies for both sides. Two or three letters from Napoleon are particularly striking as to the normality of these transactions. In a warning that has already been mentioned,[1] one of the many received by King Louis of Holland, the Emperor writes (April 3, 1808) : ' If you need to sell your gin, the English need to buy it. Settle the points where the English smugglers are to come and fetch it, and make them pay in money but never in commodities.' In a letter two years later (May 29, 1810) to Gaudin, his minister of finance, he develops in the following way the trade which is carried on with the help of the ' smogglers ': ' My intention is to favour the export of foodstuffs from France and the import of money from abroad.

[1] See ante, p. 71.

At the same time it should be possible to impose a pretty stiff fee, which should be fairly profitable . . . For that matter I should be very much inclined to let the smugglers in only at Dunkirk, unless current practice required that they should also be received at Flushing.' Thus the whole line of thought as it appears in this letter is almost grotesque; the influx of money is to be effected by smugglers, who are to be treated with such consideration that even their habits are respected. This last is especially striking when compared with Chaptal's account of Napoleon's behaviour toward the legitimate trade, how he wished to command it like a battalion and ruthlessly directed it now here, now there. But the smugglers were necessary for the prosperity of Dunkirk and made that town exempt from the general crippling of economic life in the ports; it was therefore a serious matter for the town to see the smugglers moved from there, as Napoleon threatened to do in 1811.[1]

Naturally enough, this good-will toward the smugglers was displayed only when they served the interests of the government policy; apart from this there prevailed a war to the knife. On the other hand, the normality was not limited to these cases, but held good over the whole line; and the governments maintained an unequal struggle against the smugglers. In one passage Mollien speaks of the futility of the efforts of 20,000 customs officials, whose posts were known, to guard a frontier threatened by more than 100,000 smugglers, who were supposed to have good connexions in Paris and were favoured by the population besides.[2] According to Bourrienne's statement, there were no fewer than 6,000 smugglers in Hamburg

---

[1] De Watteville, *Souvenirs d'un douanier*, &c., *loc. cit.*, vol. ii (1908), p. 113 note 2; vol. iii (1909), pp. 78, 82–3. Although the anecdote about Josephine's British goods does not appear in the contemporary letters, but in the much later memoirs, it gains credibility from the assertion of Boucher de Perthes that the ex-Empress often reminded him of the incident during her last years. For the smuggling from Cowes, cf. Kiesselbach, *Die Continentalsperre*, &c., p. 122. For the rest of the text, cf. *Correspondance*, nos. 13,718, 16,508; *Lettres inédites*, nos. 874, 877; Chaptal, *Souvenirs*, &c., pp. 274–8; Tarle, *Kontinental'naja blokada*, vol. i, pp. 306–7, 615–6. The authenticity of the letter of 1808 is not altogether above suspicion, but it is in complete consonance with Napoleon's correspondence as a whole.

[2] Mollien, *Mémoires*, &c., vol. iii, p. 10.

alone, a figure, of course, which can make no higher claims than
those of Mollien to express anything more than a general notion
of the enormous scope of the smuggling.

### Commercial Organization of Smuggling

Of special importance is the organized, or, to express it
better, the commercial, character of the smuggling. In Naples
an economic writer, Galanti, spoke of it as ' a useful trade,
inasmuch as it prevents the ruin of the state ' ;   and in various
places Napoleon's organs complain that it is regarded as a quite
honourable occupation.  Smuggling had also quite lost the character of managing by chance to break through the customs
barrier on the chance of profit.  It was based on definite business practices, with fixed commissions that varied with the
degree of certainty surrounding a successful result or the difficulties in the way of getting through to different places or with
different goods.  In Strassburg there were ' insurers ' of different
grades, the chief of which charged a commission of from 40 to
50 per cent. ;   in 1809 it was considered that the expenses of
passing the frontier of France were, as a rule, 30 per cent., while
the above-mentioned new customs line between Rees and
Bremen could be broken through for 6 or 8 per cent. ;   and at
about the same rate it was possible to smuggle any commodity
whatever from Holstein into Hamburg.  A convincing impression of the business-like character of the smuggling is
also given by Napoleon's Fontainebleau decree (October 18,
1810), where a careful distinction is drawn between leaders or
undertakers—in Adam Smith's sense—(*entrepreneurs*), insurers
(*assureurs*), shareholders (*intéressés*), managers of the practical
work (*chefs de bande, directeurs et conducteurs de réunions de
fraudeurs*), and finally ' ordinary bearers ' (*simples porteurs*),
in which we find a complete hierarchy ranging downwards
from the directors of the smuggling enterprises through the
capitalists and officials to the unskilled workers.

But there was a marked difference with regard to the ease
with which the different kinds of goods could be smuggled.

British industrial products, it is true, came in on a large scale, though, to judge by a statement from Leipzig, principally yarn ; but their entrance was resisted by the different governments even in most of the vassal states of France, because they wished to exclude British manufactures on protectionist grounds.    The situation was quite different with regard to colonial goods.    In this respect all people, from the crowned ruler down to the day labourer, were of one mind and thought in their desire to break the iron band of the Continental System ;   and the smuggling of these goods accordingly met with nothing but assistance and support.

### Official Corruption

But the unevenness of the struggle with the great organization at the disposition of the smugglers was enormously increased by the thorough-going corruption which was also distinctive of all branches of administration at the time, especially those branches which had to deal with the blockade.

In part the system of bribery in earlier times undeniably formed simply a kind of pay for the servants of the state, although of the most objectionable kind possible ; and the line between perquisites and bribes was often as fine as a hair. With regard to Bremen, for instance, we are told how the constant exactions of money for commandants, war commissaries and consuls—for non-dutiable goods, certificates of origin, and all kinds of lawful intercourse—took the form of fixed fees with definite names ;   thus the fees for certificates of origin, for instance, increased tenfold during the first six quarters after the issue of the Berlin decree.   There was scarcely a place in the territories occupied by France or under French control where similar tactics were not employed.   In the autumn of 1810 Napoleon wrote to Marshal Davout instructing him not to let the commander at Danzig, General Rapp, tolerate any corruption, although ' everybody takes bribes '.   Hamburg seems to have been especially exposed to people of this type.   Marshal Brune, Consul Lachevardière, and almost more than anybody else, Bourrienne, were perfect *virtuosi* in this respect.   As regards Bourrienne, Napoleon is alleged to have said that he (Bourrienne) would have been able to find a silver mine in the garden of the Tuileries if he had been left alone there ; and at the beginning of 1811 the Emperor calculated that his former secretary had made seven or eight million francs at Hamburg. The Emperor's letters are full of embittered outbursts against his corruption, which seems to have been carried on quite systematically with the connivance of sub-agents of different sorts, and which finally led, first to his being prohibited to sign certificates of origin, and then to his being removed from office. But these are only isolated examples of things that occurred everywhere.[1]

Rist, who, like the purely Hamburgian writers, fully confirms the French statements as to the corruptibility of Bourrienne and his associates, does not represent the conduct of his Holstein compatriots in any better light. Moreover, passing to another country, we are informed that in Geneva eighty customs officials had to be dismissed in seven months for complicity in malversation ; and from the Rhine frontier we have further information that the director of customs and his relations directly helped the illicit trade in the smuggling centre of Strassburg, and that the customs lieutenants on the Rhine lived on bribes when they had no British pension.

However oppressive a corrupt administration may be to the population, yet the bribery system would scarcely have led Napoleon to change his policy, if the whole thing had been limited to exactions above those allowed by laws and ordinances. From the standpoint of the Continental System, however, the unfortunate thing was that at least as much, and probably more, could be gained by facilitating or actually encouraging—always for a consideration—precisely the traffic which the Continental System aimed to annihilate by every possible means. For such illegalities on the part of the officials the people were willing to pay munificently, and they were, if

---

[1] Besides the above-cited passages, cf. especially Napoleon's letters of Sept. 2, 11, and Dec. 18, 1810, and of Jan. 1 and Sept. 3, 1811. *Correspondance*, nos. 16,859, 16,891, 17,225, 17,257, 18,111.

anything, somewhat more amiably disposed than before toward their foreign rulers.  One of the very few persons who from the beginning to the end really made the resolute execution of the Continental System the lodestar of all his conduct, namely, Marshal Davout, Prince of Eckmühl, the last French Governor-General of Hamburg—an ever reliable sword in the Emperor's hand, and, as far as one can see, a man of the same type as the German generals who during the recent war governed occupied territories—for that very reason brought upon himself perhaps a stronger hate than any of Napoleon's other tools; and among the inhabitants of Hamburg he passed under the name of Marshal ' Wuth ' (Fury).

## FISCALISM

But it was not enough that the Continental System was rendered illusory by the ever-present smuggling, which was constantly assisted *sub rosa* by the corruptibility of the officials. That smuggling involved another disadvantage in that Napoleon at the same time lost for himself and for France the benefits which an openly conducted traffic of the same scope would have brought with it.  This was primarily a matter which concerned the finances of the state ;  and such a development could not fail to irritate the Emperor, who, of course, always had difficulties in obtaining sufficient revenue, especially as he would not openly have recourse to loans.  The customs receipts which a system of imports that were allowed, but made subject to duties, would have yielded, and even, under the former and milder régime, had actually yielded, now fell into the hands of the smugglers and dishonest officials.  The customs receipts of France herself, which in 1806 had been 51,200,000 francs and in 1807 had even risen to 60,600,000 francs, declined in 1808 to less than one-third of that amount, or 18,600,000 francs ;  and in 1809 they declined still further to the insignificant sum of 11,600,000 francs.  The powerful head of the French customs system, Collin de Sussy, and also Montalivet, who was somewhat later home secretary, then conceived the characteristic idea that the state might be able to enter into what was literally a competition with the smugglers. This was to be arranged in such a way that in some form or other the importation of the hitherto forbidden goods was to be permitted, but only on payment of a duty that exactly corresponded to an amount which, as we have seen, the smuggling business had previously cost. In that case no more goods would come into the country than had been the case beforehand, but the profit would fall to the state instead of to the smugglers.[1]

Such a device could not fail to appeal to Napoleon with his cynical sense of reality for everything that had to do with means; but what he shut his eyes to till the last was the great extent to which this means damaged his great end. As a matter of fact, this meant that fiscalism had definitively gotten the upper hand over the Continental System, at least in one-half of its range. The object was no longer to exclude goods, but to make an income by receiving them instead; and no sophistry in the world could make the latter compatible with the former. But we cannot maintain that Napoleon in this respect consciously acted in opposition to his objects. His line of thought was as inconsistent as that which is still constantly found outside the circle of professional economists, in which the fact is ignored that the more prohibitive or protectionistic a customs tariff, the less it brings in, and consequently that that part of a customs duty which keeps goods out brings in no money to the treasury. This duality of conception in Napoleon finds a very typical expression in a letter addressed to his brother Jerome, King of Westphalia, on October 3, 1810, in which he first points out how advantageous the new system would be for this young prodigal by bringing him in a larger income; and after that he goes on to say: 'It will also be a great advantage in other respects, since the continental customers of the English merchants will not be able to pay for them (the goods), and the consumption of colonial goods, which will be rendered dear in this way, will be diminished. They will thus be exposed to

---

[1] Darmstädter, *Das Grossherzogtum Frankfurt*, p. 308 note 3. Cf. Perceval in the House of Commons in the Debate on the Budget, 1810. Hansard, vol. xvi, p. 1056. See also Schmidt, *Le Grand-duché de Berg*, pp. 358-9.

attack and at the same time driven out of the continent.' The
representatives of Napoleon used the same language in dependent countries.[1] So far, therefore, the reshaping of the
Continental System aimed at no real increase in its efficacy,
but rather at the reverse, inasmuch as Napoleon acquired
a direct interest in the admission of goods into the country.

On paper, however, no departure from the principles of the
Continental System was ever acknowledged, inasmuch as the
Berlin and Milan decrees were retained unchanged to the last ;
and Napoleon zealously impressed on his stepson Eugene, the
Viceroy of Italy, the necessity of not letting the goods in ' to
the detriment of the blockade '. But in his inexhaustible supply
of expedients Napoleon found a simple means of circumventing
his own system in fact, namely, by granting exceptions from
the prohibition on import in the matter of captured goods.

## Prize Decree (January 12, 1810)

By a law issued at the very beginning of the year 1810 (January 12), it was laid down that goods the importation of which
was forbidden (with the exception of certain kinds of cotton
fabrics and hosiery) might be introduced into the country on
payment of a customs duty of 40 per cent. when they came
from prizes captured from the enemy by war vessels or licensed
privateers. This was called ' permitted origin ' (origines per-
mises). But the exception here established with regard to
cotton goods was developed still further in the course of the
year ; and in this process Napoleon skilfully took advantage
of the different feeling that prevailed on the Continent with
regard to colonial goods and English industrial products. In
accordance with this, the new system involved a relentless
prohibition of British goods, but made concessions with regard
to colonial goods, which were admitted on payment of huge
duties. So far as the system in this form could be enforced,
Napoleon contrived at least not to favour British industry,
but only British trade. That the exception was in form

_____
[1] Correspondance, no. 16,983 ; de Cérenville, op. cit., pp. 331-2.

restricted to prize goods was in reality of no importance. It is true that Napoleon declared, in a letter to Eugene, that all colonial goods which had not been captured or seized should remain excluded; but according to Thiers, express orders were given in the correspondence of the Customs Department that this should not be strictly observed—and there can be no doubt about the practical extension of the concession to all colonial goods.[1]

As regards the customs rates, the principle, as has been said already, was that they should correspond to the costs of smuggling. When Holland was incorporated with France on July 9, 1810, it was laid down, in approximate conformity with the above-mentioned law of January, that the large stocks of colonial goods in that country should be admitted to the empire on payment of a duty which in the decree of incorporation was fixed at 50 per cent. of the value, but which, according to a somewhat later declaration, was to be 40 or 50 per cent., according to the time of the declaration. This principle was applied not only to France, but also to all the vassal states, which now became the object of the same merciless pressure with regard to the new system as they had formerly been with regard to the Continental decrees and which, as a rule, formally submitted at least as obediently as then. But to make assurance doubly sure, every stock of colonial goods which was as much as four days' journey from the French frontier was to be regarded as intended to injure France, and was therefore to be subjected to examination by French troops; in fact, French troops were actually employed for the purpose. In order that the right degree of pressure should be attained, it was the intention that the new order should be carried through simultaneously over the whole Continent, so that there would be no country to which the goods could fly in order to escape these heavy burdens; consequently Eugene at least received orders to keep the new instructions secret for the present. Principally

---

[1] Law of Jan. 12, 1912 (*Bulletin des lois*, &c., 4th ser., bull. 260, no. 5,122); Letters to Eugene of Aug. 6 and Sept. 19, 1810 (*Correspondance*, nos. 16,767, 16,930); Thiers, *Histoire du consulat*, &c., bk. XXXVIII, vol. XII, p. 186 note.

out of regard for the captors, but not exclusively in their favour, it was conceded that the duty might be paid in kind, that is to say, by means of a corresponding part of the goods which were to come in, and also in promissory notes; and without this concession it is certain that in many cases such large amounts could not have been gathered in. Every holder of colonial goods was bound to declare them, so that, as Thiers expresses it, the whole was taken in any attempt at barratry and half in case of honest declaration.

## Trianon Tariff (August 5, 1810)

The whole of this arrangement has taken its name from the Trianon tariff of August 5, 1810, which is one of the fundamental laws of the new system. This does not provide for customs duties based on a percentage of the values, but laid down specific duties by weight (per 100 kilograms) on the different kinds of colonial goods. Duties of 40 and 50 per cent. still seem to have been applied, however, for prize goods and goods imported by licence, respectively. How high these rates were may perhaps be more clearly set forth by comparing with the highest rates of duty, namely, those on goods from non-French colonies, in the tariff of 1806, to which reference has already been made; and yet the 1806 duties had already formed the corner-stone of a whole series of rises in customs duties. The duties at different dates are tabulated in appendix ii, which will perhaps afford the clearest view of the amount of the increase. The most violent was the rate on raw cotton, which as late as 1804 was assessed at only one franc per 100 kilograms. In 1806 this rate was raised to not less than sixty francs, notwithstanding that raw cotton had become the foundation of a main department in the new industrial development which began under the Empire. These rates, however, dwindle into insignificance when compared with what was now enacted. According to the Trianon tariff, South American and long-stapled Georgia cotton had to pay 800 francs; Levantine cotton, if imported by sea, 400 francs, and if passing through the custom-houses on the Rhine, 200 francs; other cotton, except Neapolitan, 600 francs. This classification was evidently intended to hit hardest the goods which were most dependent on English imports. We have already mentioned the fact that all goods from French (Dutch) colonies, with the corresponding vessels, were free, and that the direct imports by American vessels only paid one quarter of the amount, a matter which in reality meant nothing, as the British blockade prevented all such direct imports. Indigo was raised from 15 francs (1803) to 900 francs, after which (in January, 1813) there followed a new rise to 1,100 francs; cloves from 3 francs (1806) to 600 francs; tea from 3 francs (besides, in certain cases, 10 per cent. of the value) to 600 francs for green tea and 150 francs for other kinds; coffee and cocoa from 150 francs and 200 francs, respectively (1806), to 400 francs and 1,000 francs; while fine cinnamon, cochineal and nutmeg, which had not been specified in the older tariffs, all paid 2,000 francs per 100 kilograms. Some thirty new headings were added to the tariff by a supplementary schedule of September 27 of the same year.

### Fontainebleau Decree (October 18, 1810)

But as a new road was now in reality opened for the legitimate importation of colonial goods, it was important for Napoleon not only to strike still harder at the illicit importation of those goods, but also to make the sale of British industrial products impossible. It is this idea which lies at the bottom of the immense increase in the rigour of the customs laws which is marked by the Fontainebleau decree of October 18, 1810, the last of the great laws in this department. Both the penalties now introduced and the treatment of the goods themselves involved a reversion to the most violent methods of the prohibitive system. First as regards the prohibited goods, that is to say, manufactured products, the smuggling leaders of different grades were punished with ten years' penal servitude and branding, while the lower-grade tools might under extenuating circumstances get off with a milder kind of punishment (*peines correctionnelles*) and 5 to 10 years' police supervision. The smuggling of the goods specified on the tariff, that is to say, colonial goods, involved as much as four years' penal servitude, while ' simple smuggling,' that is, smuggling ' without any agreement or obligation of a kind to form an undertaking or insurance,' did not lead to penal servitude.

The regulations as regards the treatment of the goods were carried to still greater lengths than the punishment for smugglers. As regards colonial goods the penalty was limited, as before, to confiscation, the goods to be sold by auction every six months; but with regard to prohibited goods Napoleon now went to the extreme and ordered that they should be publicly burned or otherwise destroyed after a list had been made of them with prices attached. Here Napoleon was following precedents which were to be found in English legislation of the seventeenth century, and which was repeated as late as the beginning of the reign of George III.[1] For the whole of this draconic legislation there were erected special customs courts (*cours prévôtales des douanes*), the operations of which have stood out to later generations as the culmination of the oppression involved in the Continental System.[2]

## Napoleon's Complicity

The system of corruption created by Napoleon's tools under the old order of things could not, however, be abolished simply by the fact that the Emperor himself introduced fiscalism

---

[1] 3 Geo. III, c. 21. It may be questioned, however, whether the truculence of this statute was seriously meant. The later British measures were, however, made the subject of a very effective article in *Le Moniteur* of Dec. 9, 1810.

[2] Decree of July 9 regarding the incorporation of Holland, sec. 10; decree of Aug. 5 (Trianon tariff); decree of Sept. 27; decree of Oct. 18—according to the archives, Oct. 19—(Fontainebleau decree); decree of Nov. 1 (*Bulletin des lois*, &c., 4th ser., bull. 299, no. 5,724; bull. 304, no. 5,778; bull. 315, no. 5,958; bull. 321, no. 6,040; bull. 324, no. 6,067); Kiesselbach (*op. cit.*, pp. 133–4) gives a translation of the enlarged Trianon tariff of Sept. 27 which is not in the *Bulletin des lois*. See also Thiers, *op. cit.*; Levasseur, *Histoire des classes ouvrières*, &c., *de 1789 à 1870*, vol. I, pp. 481 *et seq.*; Zeyss, *Die Entstehung der Handelskammern*, &c., pp. 140 note, 149 *et seq.*; Schäfer, *op. cit.*, p. 444; Bourrienne, *op. cit.*, vol. VII, p. 233.

instead of the complete blockade. On the contrary, we find proportionally a still larger number of examples of bribery and embezzlement after the Trianon and Fontainebleau decrees than before. But Napoleon, on his side, had to a great extent changed his treatment of them, in accordance with his new fiscalist tendencies. His method became simply to demand a share of the bribes of the dishonest officials, and in that way convert them into sponges with which to soak up revenue from the illicit trade. The resemblance to the Trianon system is thus striking. Two or three cases from the beginning of 1811 are particularly characteristic in this connexion. One of the most fully compromised officials was the French consul at Königsberg, Clérembault, who released fourteen British ships in the Baltic, belonging to a large flotilla which Napoleon had pursued the whole autumn—of which more anon—with a cargo worth 2,800,000 francs, and was stated to have obtained the magnificent sum of 800,000 francs on this affair alone and 1,500,000–1,600,000 francs altogether. At the same time the malversations of Bourrienne and Consul Lachevardière still went on in Hamburg. With reference to this Napoleon wrote to his foreign minister, Champagny, a highly characteristic New Year's letter to the effect that Clérembault was to hand over to the Foreign Office all that he had received; and he also declared his intention to compel Bourrienne to pay in 2,000,000 francs in the same fashion, while Lachevardière was to pay 500,000 francs to the sinking-fund of the French government. His intention was that the first two amounts should be employed for the erection of a residence for the foreign minister; and the letter ends : ' You will see that I shall get the money for a really handsome palace which will cost me nothing.'[1] This was not a mere idle fancy; on the contrary, it turned out that Clérembault had already anticipated matters by paying of his own accord 500,000 francs to the Emperor's privy purse (*caisse de l'extraordinaire*), and that he had still earlier paid

[1] Letters to Champagny (Jan. 1) and Savary, minister of police (Jan. 7). *Lettres inédites*, nos. 733, 748. Cf. letter to Davout (Jan. 1). *Correspondance*, no. 17,257. See also König, *op. cit.*, p. 237.

200,000 francs into the cash box of the Foreign Office. In this manner the Continental System was perverted into a gigantic system of extortion, for naturally this was no way to cut off the Continent from the supply of goods.

## LICENSING SYSTEM

The Trianon policy is supplemented by the second great novelty which was introduced during the noteworthy year 1810 in the sphere of the Continental System, namely, the licences. It is true that these in themselves did not form any novelty, even on the part of Napoleon, and, as we know, still less on the part of Great Britain; but on the Continent their importance had been slight, as is shown by the fact that, according to Thiers, the total value of the trade which had been carried on by licences before the Trianon tariff had amounted only to 20,000,000 francs. It was only now that they became a normal and integral part of the Continental System, in close conjunction with the general tendency of the new policy, and thereby contributed, just as much as the new customs regulations, to lead away from the original aim which was still officially maintained. The difference with respect to the Trianon policy in reality lies only in the fact that Napoleon here considered himself to be faithfully copying his adversary.

### Great Britain

In Great Britain, in fact, the licensing system had acquired an immense range, culminating in 1810 with the granting of over 18,000 licences in a twelvemonth; and, according to almost unanimous information, it was carried through to such an extent that the greater part, not only of British foreign trade, but also of the maritime trade of the whole world, was carried on with British licences. But this did not prevent the Heligoland merchants, for instance, from feeling their operations restricted by not getting so many licences as they wished. The licence system placed practically the whole power over foreign trade in the hands of the British government, more particularly in the hands of the president of the Board of Trade. This very fact was enough to provoke incessant attacks on the whole system on the part of the opposition; and it also aroused great dislike on the part of the business world, which had already begun to regard as almost an axiom the incapacity of the state to judge commercial questions. It is true that on two different occasions, in 1805 and 1807, certain general exceptions had been granted from the current regulations, especially for importing foodstuffs and raw materials into Great Britain. But evidently the merchants considered—probably on the ground of dearly bought experience—that the commanding officers of the warships and privateers did not refrain from seizing other vessels than those which had licences in due form, and therefore continued to take out such licences even when, from a strictly legal point of view, that was superfluous.

In the opinion of the opposition, this state of affairs could not cease until the laws had been repealed from which the licences granted freedom in individual cases. Thus the opposition regarded the licensing system as a further inconvenience of the Orders in Council and as subject to the same condemnation as they. In the House of Commons the chief speakers of the opposition in economic questions, especially Alexander Baring, the junior partner in the famous firm of Baring Brothers & Co., Henry Brougham, the barrister, and Francis Horner, the originator and chairman of the famous Bullion Committee of 1810, were therefore indefatigable in their attacks on the licensing system. The first two named, together with the lawyer J. Phillimore, author of a pamphlet entitled *Reflections on the Nature and Extent of the License Trade* (1811), carried on the campaign outside Parliament too—Baring especially, by his pamphlet entitled *An Inquiry into the Causes and Consequences of the Orders in Council* (1808). The attacks of the opposition, however, were met by the government with the assertion that licences would be quite as necessary, even if the Orders in Council and the blockade were entirely revoked, to serve as a form of dispensation from the prohibition of trading with the enemy.  In 1812, for instance, Lord Castlereagh, then foreign secretary, declared that not a fifth of the licences were due to the Orders in Council; and as it was generally considered to be equally self-evident that this trade with the enemy should be forbidden by law and encouraged in reality, the government so far had the better of the argument.

But the opposition to the licences was nourished by the looseness with which the whole thing was managed by the incompetent administrators who were at that time guiding the destinies of Great Britain.  In one case, for instance, two licences granting an otherwise refused right to import spirits were given out, according to the statement of the minister concerned, Rose, owing to a purely clerical error on the part of the official in the Board of Trade who made out the papers.  One of these licences by itself was said to have brought in to the fortunate owner no less than £4,000; and Baring, 'perhaps the first merchant in the Kingdom, or perhaps in the world ', declared that he would gladly pay £15,000 for such a licence.  On another occasion it was alleged without contradiction in Parliament that 2,000 guineas had been paid for two licences to trade with the Isle-de-France (Mauritius) and Guadeloupe, and that bribes were openly given for the purpose, though not to the Board of Trade itself.  That British licences were openly bought and sold, not only in Great Britain, but also all over the Continent, was a fact known to all the world ;  they were a mere trade commodity not only in Gothenburg and Norway but even in French maritime towns, such as Bordeaux and Amsterdam.  The opposition, which naturally insisted upon the rights of Parliament as against the government, also objected—in the same way as was the case in Sweden during the recent war—that the licensing system gave the government revenue outside the control of Parliament and was therefore unconstitutional.

On the other side, the licences formed a manifest advantage, not merely for the British government but also for British external policy in general, by permitting a regulation of foreign trade according to circumstances, without the proclamation of more or less disputable principles of international law ; and so far they accorded pretty well with the general attitude of horror displayed in British public life toward all doctrines and declarations of principle.  It was really the licensing system that rendered possible the formal concession with regard to the original Orders in Council which was effected by the new Order in Council of April 26, 1809, in that the old regulations could in reality be maintained without being put on paper, simply by being made the condition for the granting of licences.  This found quite open expression, for instance, in the letter which the Marquis of Wellesley, as foreign secretary, wrote to the new British Minister at Washington, Foster, in 1811, and in which, among other things, he says : ' You will perceive that the object of our system was not to crush the trade with the Continent, but to counteract an attempt to crush the British trade.  Thus we have endeavoured to permit the Continent to receive as large a portion of commerce as might be practicable through Great Britain '—of which there is not a word in the only Order in Council of 1809 then in force—' and that all our subsequent regulations, and every modification of the system by new orders or modes of granting or withholding licences, have been calculated for the purpose of encouraging the trade of neutrals through Great Britain.'

The licences were thus, in the first place, a flexible means of carrying through the policy that had been marked out once for all.  It is true that this did not prevent them, as we have seen, from coming to serve quite other purposes through the inefficiency and laxity of the officials ; but these abuses did not imply that the British government had altogether lost its control over the licensing system.  Thus, for instance, the ease with which the Norwegians obtained licences in 1809–11, despite the fact that the Dano-Norwegian monarchy was at war with Great Britain, was due to the British need of Norwegian timber.  Later on, when pressure was regarded as desirable for political reasons—it was just at the time when Norway was suffering immensely from shortage of foodstuffs—the granting of licences in effect ceased entirely, although under the form of a claim for security to amounts which it was not possible to achieve (£3,000–4,000 per licence).

Even in its consistent form, however, the licence system led to embittered resistance in many quarters of Great Britain, especially in the seaports.   In 1812 Hull, Sunderland, South Shields, Scarborough, Aberdeen, &c., overwhelmed Parliament with petitions against the licensing system, largely for reasons opposite to those usually alleged by the opposition.   Here the attitude adopted was that the neutrals, with the object of maintaining connexion with the self-blockaded ports of the mainland, were admitted to too large a share in trade and shipping, and further that British subjects, contrary to the Navigation Act, were allowed to ship cargoes in neutral vessels. In this way these, petitions alleged, it was unintentionally made possible for Napoleon himself and his allies, under a neutral flag and with British licences, to take part in trade with impunity. Thus one example was cited when thirty-seven vessels were allowed, in 1810, to go without hindrance from Archangel to Holland ;  but this was due evidently to the usual carelessness in the application of the system.   With regard to admitting foreign vessels and sailors, on the other hand, the government could point to the insufficiency of the British shipping for all purposes and to the advantage of penetrating to the markets of the Continent under a neutral flag when it could not be done under a British flag.   This last was an idea which was strongly confirmed by Napoleon's view of the matter.   On the whole, the British licences, despite their luxuriance of growth, re- mained, at least in principle, what they had been from the beginning, namely, a means of combining the formal British blockade of the Continent with the real mercantilist aims of the policy, as has been described in part I of this book.   This found expression, among other things, in regulations which really placed a premium on exports, namely, in the form that the granting of a licence to import was made dependent on making exports to the same value, either in general or for certain goods ; e.g., the granting of licence for the importation of wine in return for an engagement to export colonial goods.   And although licences were often sold for high sums on the Continent (700 Rigsdaler in Norway, it is said, and 500 florins in Amsterdam) and in Great Britain itself were supplied by the state at such a considerable price as £13 or £14 apiece for individual licences, with the addition of a guinea for each licence when a large number were in question—on some occasions, however, higher charges did occur—yet the opposition, so far as I know, despite its repudiation of the whole system on constitutional grounds, never insinuated that the state was influenced by fiscal points of view, but only alleged abuses in favour of individuals. Even if one accepts the highest number of licences for a twelvemonth, about 18,000 for the year 1810, and the highest conceivable average amount per licence (*i.e.*, £14, which is assuredly too high an estimate), the highest annual amount would only be about £250,000 or 6,250,000 francs.

### FALSE SHIPS' PAPERS (BROUGHAM'S DESCRIPTION)

But the licences in Great Britain had also another object which, from the standpoint of the Continental System, was more important than all the matters we have just dealt with— namely, that of providing trade and shipping with an oppor- tunity of circumventing Napoleon's commercial prohibitions without thereby being exposed to capture by British ships, which undoubtedly would have been the consequence if the formal British regulations had been applied. What had to be done was to avoid both Scylla and Charybdis; and on both sides the regulations had been brought to such a pitch that this was absolutely impossible without a dispensation. What the licences rendered possible, in this particular, was a completely systematic and commercially organized traffic with false ships' papers designed to show the continental authorities both the non-British origin of the goods and the departure of the vessels from non-British ports—a parallel to the case of smuggling. The best and most graphic description of the whole business is perhaps contained in a speech made by Brougham in the House of Commons on March 3, 1812, the relevant part of which may

therefore be quoted *in extenso*.  It will hardly be thought
necessary to draw special attention to the priceless business
letter in the forgery line which concludes this account.[1]

But the last and most deplorable consequence of this licensing
system, is the effect which it is producing on the morals of the trading
part of the community of this country.  Here I implore the attention
of the House, and the attention of the hon. gentlemen opposite (would
to God I could appeal to them in a more effectual manner), and intreat
them to consider the consequences of giving continuance to a traffic
which has so often been described as ' a system of simulation and
dissimulation from beginning to end '.  These are the words of the
respectable Judge who presides in our Courts of Admiralty [Sir William
Scott], who as he owes in that capacity allegiance to no particular
sovereign, is bound to mete out justice equally to the subjects of all
nations who come before him.  This is the language of the right hon.
and learned gentleman alluded to, but in my opinion, it would be still
more accurate to say that it is a system which begins with forgery, is
continued by perjury, and ends in enormous frauds.  I will read a
clause from the first license that comes to my hand—for it is in them all
—in 18,000 licenses a year—and it is a clause which demands the most
serious attention of the House.  What are we to say when we find that
the government of the country lends the sanction of its authority to
such expressions as the following, in the licenses from port to port :
' The vessel shall be allowed to proceed, notwithstanding all the documents which accompany the ship and cargo may represent the same
to be destined to any neutral or hostile port, or to whomsoever such
property may appear to belong.'  Notwithstanding, says his Majesty in
Council— at least his Majesty is made to use such language—notwith-

---

[1] Brougham's speech will be found in Hansard, vol. xxi, pp. 1110 *et seq.*  Other
parliamentary matter, including petitions bearing upon the British licence system,
will be found under the following dates : Jan. 29, Mar. 7, 1808 ;  Feb. 17, 1809 ;
May 23, 1810 ;  Feb. 18, 27, 28, Mar. 3, Apr. 16, 17, 27, 29, May 4, 20, June 16, 1812.
Hansard, vol. x, pp. 185 *et seq.*, 923 *et seq.* ;  vol. xii, pp. 791–2 ;  vol. xvii, pp. 168–9 ;
vol. xxi, pp. 842 *et seq.*, 979 *et seq.*, 1041 *et seq.*, 1092 *et seq.* ;  vol. xxii, pp. 411 *et seq.*,
424 *et seq.*, 1057–8, 1118–9, 1152 *et seq.* ;  vol. xxiii, pp. 237, 540.  Miss Cunningham,
*British Credit*, &c., pp. 62–3 ;  Mahan, *Influence of Sea Power*, &c., vol. ii, pp. 228
*et seq.*, 308 ;  also, *Sea Power in its Relations*, &c., vol. i, p. 246 ;  Wellesley, *Memoirs*,
&c., vol. iii, pp. 195–6 ;  *Quarterly Review* (May, 1811), vol. v, pp. 457 *et seq.* ;  Grade,
*Sverige och Tilsit-Alliansen, 1807–1810* (Lund, 1913), pp. 424, 428–9, 431 ;  Worm-
Müller, *op. cit.*, *passim* ;  Jacob Aall, *Erindringer som Bidrag til Norges Historie
fra 1800–1815* (Christiania, 1844), vol. ii, p. 197 ;  Holm, *Danmark-Norges Historie*,
&c., vol. vii : 2, pp. 351–2, 385–6 ;  Servières, *op. cit.*, p. 286.  Some very drastic
Norwegian instructions to ships' masters may be found in Worm-Müller, *op. cit.*, pp.
501 *et seq.*

standing, says this paper, which is countersigned by his Majesty's Secretary of State 18,000 times in a year, this trade is carried on by fraud and perjury, we will sanction that foulness, and we will give orders that these ships shall be enabled to pass through the British fleets. Perhaps the full import of this clause is not known to the House. It is proper they should be informed that papers are put on board stating the actual place from which the ship cleared out, signed in the proper and usual manner, with letters from the ship-owner to the proper persons ; and that these real documents form what is called the ship's papers. By this license the captain is enabled to take on board another set of papers, which are a forgery from beginning to end, and in case his vessel happens to be overhauled by our cruizers, he escapes detention. If the ship happen to clear from London, it is perhaps said to clear from Rotterdam, and the proper description is made out, as nearly as possible, in the hand-writing of the Custom-house officer at Rotterdam, and if it be necessary that the paper should be signed by a minister of state, as is the case in Holland, his handwriting must be forged, frequently that of the duke of Cadore [Champagny], or perhaps, as I happened to see the other day, that of Napoleon himself. Not only are the names forged, but the seal is also forged, and the wax imitated. But this is not enough. A regular set of letters is also forged, containing a good deal of fictitious private anecdote, and a good deal of such news from Rotterdam as might be supposed to be interesting to mercantile people, and a letter from a merchant in Rotterdam to the ship-owner. Thus provided, the vessel sails, and the object of the clause in the license which I have just read, is to prevent her from being seized by any of our cruizers who may intercept her. This is what is meant by the general expression of— ' Notwithstanding all the documents which accompany the ship and cargo may represent the same, &c. &c.' So much for the system of forgery on which this license trade rests ; but all this is not enough. All this must be done with the privity of the merchant here, and of his clerks. That most respectable branch of society, and these young men, whom they are initiating into trade, are no longer at liberty to follow the system, by which our Childs and our Barings have risen to such respectability and eminence ; but from their very outset in life, are now to be initiated in the humiliating mysteries of this fraudulent commerce. All these forgeries, too, are confirmed by the solemn oaths of the captain and crew when they arrive at their destined port. They are obliged to swear in words, as awful as it is possible to conceive, that all these documents and letters are genuine. Every sort of interrogatory is put to the captain and the whole crew, which is calculated to discover what is the real port from which the vessel sailed, and to the truth of the answers to all these interrogatories the captain and the whole crew are obliged to swear. They are obliged to declare from what quarter the wind blew when they left Rotterdam (although they were never near the place) when they took a pilot on board, and a number of other particulars, which they are obliged to asseverate on the most solemn oath which it is possible to conceive ; knowing at the same time that they sailed from London and not from Rotterdam, that they took no pilot on board, and that their other statements are utterly false. So that, under this system, the whole crew and captain are under the necessity of perjuring themselves, if they wish to act up to their instructions. In confirmation of these statements, I will read to the House a letter of a most curious description which has been put into my hands, written to an American merchant, of the highest respectability, the contents of which would be extremely ludicrous, if the contemplation of them were not accompanied by a feeling of disgust at the moral depravity it displays. It is written by a professional man, not that he is either a lawyer, a physician, or a divine, for he would be a disgrace to any of these honourable occupations ; but he is a man who has made the forgery of ships' papers a regular and organized profession. I shall omit the names of any of the parties, because I should be sorry to injure individuals, whose only connection with the writer has been, that he has dared to send them this most atrocious circular. It is as follows :

Liverpool, — —.

GENTLEMEN—We take the liberty herewith to inform you, that we have established ourselves in this town, for the sole purpose of making simulated papers [Hear, Hear !] which we are enabled to do in a way which will give ample satisfaction to our employers, not only being in possession of the original documents of the ships' papers, and clearances to various ports, a list of which we annex, but our Mr. G——B—— having worked with his brother, Mr. J——B——, in the same line, for the last two years, and understanding all the necessary languages.

Of any changes that may occur in the different places on the continent, in the various custom house and other offices, which may render a change of signatures necessary, we are careful to have the earliest information, not only from our own connections but from Mr. J——B——, who has proffered his assistance in every way, and who has for some time past made simulated papers for Messrs. B—— and P——, of this town, to whom we beg leave to refer you for further information. We remain, &c.

Then follows a long list of about twenty places from and to which they can forge papers (having all the clearances ready by them, from the different public agents) the moment they receive intelligence that any merchant may need their assistance in this scheme of fabrication.

## France

That part of this which made an impression upon Napoleon must above all have been the last-mentioned side of the licence system, for it evidently enabled the British to evade his blockading decrees with success.  But the whole fashion of saying one thing, and meaning and doing another, accorded exquisitely with his general bent and created a possibility, which was particularly welcome under the then prevailing circumstances, of altering his régime in fact without formally repealing ' the fundamental law of the Empire ' before the English had given way.  It was only natural, therefore, that the licensing system on the British side should encourage imitation on the side of Napoleon.  Accordingly, the Continental System during its last years developed into a huge system of jugglery on both sides, when neither side honestly applied its own regulations, but both broke them with a capriciousness that to some extent increased the sufferings of the already more than sufficiently harassed peoples.

But this external resemblance between the tactics of Great Britain and Napoleon concealed a fundamental internal dissimilarity.  In this case there is an unusual amount of truth in the old dictum *quum duo faciunt idem, non est idem*.  The licences created, or at least had the power to create, a perfectly consistent application of the policy that Great Britain wished to pursue, namely, the promotion of trade with the Continent.  For Napoleon, on the other hand, every licence, his own no less than his opponent's, meant a breach in the self-blockade of the Continent and in the isolation of Great Britain, and thus drove one more nail into the coffin of the Continental System.  For Napoleon the licences were an integral part of the new order of things, the other half of which was the Trianon régime ; and like that, the licences on his side contributed greatly to the more and more dominant fiscalism, which was not the case, to any notable extent, in Great Britain.  In this way the licensing system in Great Britain acquired its real importance for the Continental System by inveigling Napoleon into an imitation which removed him still further from his great aim.

Sometimes this fact finds very open expression in Napoleon's copious explanations of the licensing system, alternating with highly confusing and obscure accounts of its significance.  ' In this place it is necessary to tell you again what you already understand,' runs an unusually explicatory letter to Eugene, Viceroy of Italy (September 19, 1810), ' namely, what is meant by a licence.  A licence is a permission, accorded to a vessel that fulfils the conditions exacted by the said licence, to import or export a certain kind of merchandise specified in that licence. For those vessels the Berlin and Milan decrees are null and void.'

### LICENCE DECREE JULY (25, 1810)

What an almost all-embracing range this suspension of the Continental decrees attained is shown by an express order, the so-called ' Licence decree,' of July 25, 1810, and also by a number of confirmatory measures adopted by Napoleon during the subsequent period.  Thus it was laid down in the licence decree that beginning on August 1, 1810, no vessel bound for a foreign port might leave French ports without a licence signed by Napoleon's own hand.  If the vessel was bound for any of the ports of the Empire, or was engaged in coasting traffic in the Mediterranean, a more general permit (*acquit-à-caution*) was required, but also a written bond which was not annulled until evidence could be furnished of the vessel's arrival at the French port.  All vessels that were devoted to *le grand commerce* or *la grande navigation* were therefore obliged to have a licence ; and for this procedure there was given the highly significant justification that no such traffic was possible without calling at a British port or at least being examined by the British—which, according to the Milan decree, involved ' denationalization ' and confiscation.  Despite the fact that both the Berlin and Milan decrees strictly forbade all intercourse with England and all calling at English ports, Napoleon now went so far as to make it a point of honour that French vessels should visit English waters, and go to London, even though they were under a neutral flag.  ' Under this disguise England receives them, and I make laws for her owing to her pressing need of commercial intercourse.'  It was not surprising that such a change of front, which in 1812, for instance, led to a licence for the importation of rice from London, befogged many people completely.

It goes without saying, however, that licences were not given for nothing, either for visits to England or for any other purpose. At first they had to be paid for, as a rule at very high prices. At an early period we hear of 30 or 40 napoleons (600 or 800 francs); at a later period 40 napoleons (800 francs) plus 30 francs per ton of wheat, and 15 francs per ton of rye, was regarded as cheap for exports from the Hanse Towns. Import licences for colonial goods from England fetched as much as 300 napoleons or 6,000 francs, that is to say, much higher amounts than the British licences. Nor did Napoleon make any secret of the fact that they were intended to yield him *un revenu considérable*.

## OBLIGATION TO EXPORT

But further the licences were intended to serve Napoleon's aims in the sphere of trade policy. In this connexion the main thing was to encourage the exportation of French, and to some extent also Italian, industrial products and, in good years, foodstuffs from both countries, as well as from Danzig and other granaries. In exchange for this there was granted, as a rule, the importation of colonial goods, which was simultaneously regulated by the Trianon policy, either generally or with special reference to Levantine and American products. But there were also stricter rules where nothing was to be brought back to France except ship-building materials or precious metals, and specie, which were in constant request, and which Napoleon, in consonance with his well-known views, was always seeking to draw from England. Thus from 1809 on there was a long series of varying types of licence, which differed widely in detail, but do not offer many points of interest. One of the most significant types is the combined one which permitted vessels to take corn from German ports in Napoleon's empire to Dunkirk and thence to England, provided the corn was discharged in England and naval stores were taken as return freight to Dunkirk, where French wine, silks, and manufactures had to be taken on board and conveyed to Hamburg.  One of the most stringent conditions for licences was that imports into France, and to some extent also into Italy, of whatever kind they might be—apart from foodstuffs during years of famine, as in 1812—required from the importing vessel a return cargo of French goods from France or Italian goods from Italy of at least the same value.  Such return freight was particularly silk and other French textiles, but also wine and brandy, and, in good years, natural produce, especially from Italy.  All this was to be in proportions which varied a great deal from time to time, but were usually determined in great detail.  This very far-reaching system, which also had something, though on a smaller scale, corresponding to it on the British side, as has already been mentioned,[1] had developed from a regulation introduced into the French customs ordinance of 1803 as a kind of punishment for vessels whose papers were not above suspicion in respect of the innocent origin of their cargo.  This even applied to incorporated territories, such as the Hanse Towns, when importing to ' the old departments '.

It may be said at once that this attempt on the part of Napoleon to transform the Continental System from a gigantic plan of blockade against Great Britain to an in itself less noteworthy method of augmenting the exports of France, led to an almost complete fiasco.  The goods were taken on board, of course, but as their importation was prohibited in England, and as, moreover, they were not in a position to compete with British manufactures, there could be no sale.  And it is in the very nature of things that the method of circumventing such export ordinances must be still more varied than in regard to obstacles in the way of imports, and the dodges invented were all the more numerous.  On the whole, it may be regarded as a general rule that purely coercive laws in the sphere of economics have far fewer possibilities of being made effective in a positive direction than in a negative one.  In most cases, in fact, it is almost impossible that the positive law can effect anything more than the external forms of economic transaction, while the negative regulation or prohibition can much sooner

[1] See *ante*, p. 84.

make the transaction impossible both in substance and in form. Of course, goods were exported when their exportation was ordered; but as it was difficult to fix the quality of the goods in the law, the consequence was that people bought up every conceivable kind of rubbish—articles long since out of fashion or useless from the very start—in the French idiom ' nightin- gales ' (*rossignols*), which sing only by night,—which could be purchased for a song and then priced at any figure whatever. Under these circumstances, of course, there was less chance than ever of effecting any real imports of goods into England, and it was stated openly, for instance, in the French Council of Commerce and Industry in 1812, and was for that matter generally known, that the goods were simply thrown into the sea. All this held good of that part of Napoleon's policy which to some degree stood in connexion with the Continental System, namely, the trade with England. With regard to the countries incorporated or allied with the empire, the possibilities were probably greater, inasmuch as the vessels could be controlled on their arrival with the French goods; but obviously all this was valueless as a weapon in the struggle with the enemy.

### FRENCH SHIPPING MONOPOLY

Finally, also, the licensing system was elaborated into a purely protectionist measure with regard to French shipping. In his letter to Decrès, the naval minister, written on the same day as the issue of the Milan decree, Napoleon had already prescribed that all non-French vessels should be detained in his ports; and now the licensing system was adopted to the end of creating a practically complete monopoly for the French mer- cantile marine. Especially openhearted in this matter is the Emperor's commentary on the licence decree of July 25, con- tained in a letter to his lieutenant in Holland after the in- corporation of that country, the arch-treasurer Prince Lebrun (August 20, 1810). After observing that no vessel, according to the first article of the decree, could depart to a foreign port without licence, he goes on to say: ' The article ' applies to all kinds of vessels, French, neutral or foreign ; that is to say, with the exception [sic] that I do not grant licences to other than French vessels. In two words, I will not hear of any neutral vessel, and as a matter of fact there is in reality no such thing ; for they are all vessels which violate the blockade and pay tribute to England. As to the word foreign, that means foreign to France. Thus foreign vessels cannot trade with France or leave our ports, because there are no neutrals.' According to a previously cited letter to Eugene, of September 19,[1] Napoleon develops still further the idea, in that, with the sole exception of naturalized captured vessels, he requires that the vessels shall even be built in France. It is true that all this did not apply without exception, for in some individual cases licences were granted to vessels of allied or neutral states. Likewise the Hanse Towns, which belonged to Napoleon, Danzig, and towns in Italy, received licences, though only upon payment of unusually high fees ; as a rule, however, allies were excluded as rigorously as neutrals. Especially hard did the system strike against France's most faithful ally, Denmark, who saw all her vessels in the ports of Napoleon seized and detained, despite endless negotiations and the support of Davout ; and when the vessels were finally released, in the spring of 1812, at which time there were still eighty left, their release was conditioned upon exportation of huge quantities of French silks, which was an absolute impossibility. We obtain the right background for these tactics when we take into consideration the fact that Denmark had also to submit to supplying other vessels for the transport of corn to Holland and at the same time to place officers and sailors at Napoleon's disposal for the naval expedition that he was then equipping on the Scheldt against England.[2]

[1] See ante, p. 215.
[2] Licensing decree of July 25, 1810, printed in Martens, *Nouveau recueil*, &c., vol. I, p. 512 ; *Correspondance*, nos. 16,224, 16,767, 16,810, 16,930 ; *Lettres inédites*, *loc. cit.*, nos. 652, 874, 927, 928, 929, 972, 1082 ; Servières, *op. cit.*, pp. 134–9, 265 *et seq.* ; Schäfer, *op. cit.*, pp. 436–7 ; Tarle, *Kontinental'naja blokada*, vol. I, pp. 310–11, 560 ; Holm, *Danmark-Norges Historie*, vol. VII : 2, pp. 54–5, 188–9, 207–8, 271–2. The work of Melvin, *Napoleon's Navigation System* (New York, 1919), has reached me too late to be taken into account.

Thus there can be no doubt that the Continental System had missed its mark in several decisive respects.   Instead of hitting the enemy, it had partly shot past him and become a means of promoting the interests of France—correctly or incorrectly conceived—at the expense of her own helpers in the struggle against Great Britain.   The customs policy proper had had this tendency from the very beginning; and its later development, which continued along the same lines, will be described in connexion with the effects of the system on the Continent, in part IV of this book.   To what extent all this had driven Napoleon into the very course that the British in reality aimed at from start to finish, is shown with unusual clearness by a statement made in the autumn of 1811 by General Walter-storff, the Danish minister in Paris at the time, to the effect that France had no other trade except with England and, of course, wished to keep that for herself.   Here we find the position described in words almost the same as those employed by the British ministers with regard to the object of their policy.[1]   So far the success of the system was almost incontestable—for Great Britain.

[1] See *ante*, p. 120.

# CHAPTER IV

## THE TRIANON AND FONTAINEBLEAU POLICY IN OPERATION (1810–12)

### ADMINISTRATION OF NEW POLICY

FROM what has been said in the foregoing chapter it is by no means to be inferred that the Continental System had failed altogether. The Fontainebleau policy was directed primarily against the exports of British manufactures; and here Napoleon was in deadly earnest.

But there was no sharp line of demarcation between the prohibitory measures directed against Great Britain and the orders relating to the importation of colonial goods, which were, in Napoleon's view, half repressive and half fiscal; nor could any such line be found owing to the lack of clearness in men's grasp of the matter. It is quite impossible, therefore, to keep them distinct in this account. The administrative organs were largely the same for both, and both were violent and detested by the people; but there can be no doubt that the fiscal measures formed beyond comparison the most effective half of the new system, because the desire for the goods always made the people comparatively willing to pay, if only they could get the goods by so doing. It is true that the competition with the smugglers came far from putting an end to their traffic, that is to say, to continue the same terminology, far from giving the state the monopoly of importing prohibited colonial goods; but in any case it brought substantial sums into the public treasuries. Napoleon's customs revenues alone rose to 105,900,000 francs in the period from the Trianon tariff to the close of 1811, this as compared with only 11,600,000 francs in 1809; and the auctions of confiscated goods, together with the licence fees, brought in far more, to say nothing of what the vassal states contrived to make. We have at present no complete survey of the total yield of the new policy to the government treasuries, but a general idea of the whole situation is given by the fact that, according to Thiers, the auctions alone during the remaining months of 1810 yielded a cash return of almost 150,000,000 francs. In the contemplation of such figures it is not difficult to understand the magnitude that the fiscal side of the policy was destined to attain; and, indeed, it was to become more and more marked during each of the remaining years.

The corner-stone of the new building, visible to all the world, was formed by the incorporation with France of the Hanse Towns and Oldenburg and the rest of the North Sea coast. This took place about the turn of the year 1810–11, and brought it about that the new measures, both administrative and military, struck by far the hardest on the North Sea. It is true that from the beginning this involved a great limitation in effectiveness, inasmuch as the centre of gravity of the British continental traffic had already been moved definitely from there to the Baltic coasts and Gothenburg.

The special regulations that were issued in the early part of October concerning the payment of customs duties for goods between the coast and the old Rees-Travemünde line are of less interest; and their relations to the Trianon tariff are not clear in all details. Of the greatest importance, rather, are the new judicial system—if such a fair-sounding word can be used—and the new military barrier.

## Customs Courts and the Military Cordon

It was on the North Sea coast that the new customs courts were of the most importance, and it was there that they proceeded with all the cruelty and contempt for private rights that invariably characterize an unscrupulous police. The new customs staff, which is represented as a rabble scraped together from different countries, penetrated by day and night into dwelling houses, and espionage flourished more than ever.

With grim irony Eudel, the former head of the customs system in Hamburg who was tolerably well hated by everybody, was able, according to Bourrienne, to prophesy that he and his greencoats would be positively missed : ' Hitherto,' he said, ' they have seen only roses.'   Rist, on whose evidence what has been just said is partly based, furnishes the following information of greater value :

A tribunal of blood, the prevostal court, the most frightful tool of fiscal despotism, was soon domiciled in Hamburg.   In defiance of common law, the unfortunate accused here became a victim to the unlimited caprice of his merciless tyrants.   *Le Grand Prévôt*, half customs official and half judge, here settled matters of life and death ; and as a kind of mockery against every notion of honour, this bastard offspring of civil and military authority had received the same rank as the prefect and the president of the supreme court of justice.   Everybody shunned his presence ; and, for my own part, I have never been able to meet without a sense of loathing this, as far as one can judge, quite worthy holder of such an office.

During one fortnight in 1812 *Le Grand Prévôt* in Hamburg pronounced one hundred and twenty sentences of six months' imprisonment, all for offences against the blockade decree. The result was that in Hamburg the prison became so crowded that a hundred prisoners had to be conveyed to the galleys of Antwerp, while at Bremen the prison conditions were so bad that $22\frac{1}{2}$ per cent. of the prisoners died.   Death sentences were also passed and executed, as Rist correctly states in the passage just cited, although no justification for this was to be found in the Fontainebleau decree.   The whole system became still more detestable for the reason that the licensing system was its background.   Bourrienne states that the father of a family came near being shot in 1811 for having imported a small sugar-loaf in the Elbe Department, possibly at the very moment when Napoleon was signing licences for the importation of a million sugar-loaves.   Moreover, in Hamburg the system gave rise to perfectly meaningless intrigues in conjunction with the usual lawless robbery on the part of the functionaries ; all of which was especially troublesome owing to the fact that Holstein was indissolubly united with Hamburg, and after the annexation of the Hanse Towns people suddenly found the border of the Empire running between Altona and Hamburg. Consequently, the most elementary economic functions had to come to a standstill owing to the prohibitive legislation. This was carried to such an extent that the Holstein peasants were at first not permitted to take back over the frontier the money they had received in payment for the foodstuffs that they had sold, because it was against the law to take money out of the country.

Alongside this new system of justice on the basis of the Fontainebleau decree, Napoleon now fell back on his military resources to a greater extent than ever before. Masséna's army corps, now under the command of Oudinot, was stationed on a line from Boulogne along the coasts of Brabant and Holland, with its strongest division at Emden to maintain the connexion with the Hanse Towns. Next came Davout's corps, which, according to Thiers, was ' the finest, most reliable, and best organized ' in the army, ' the invincible third corps,' the only corps in the whole of Napoleon's army which now, during the short interval of peace upon the mainland, was kept upon a war footing. It consisted of three divisions, each composed of five regiments of infantry divided into four battalions (sixty battalions of infantry in all), with eighty cannons ; and in addition to these there was one division of cuirassiers and one division of light cavalry, a great siege train, and finally a flotilla of gunboats stationed in the mouths of the rivers. The extreme outpost of this line was General Rapp's force at Danzig. In a letter of September 28, 1810, to Davout, the mainstay of this organization, Napoleon gave detailed instructions as to how the different generals with their forces were to be distributed, and he expressly declared that the two divisions stationed along the German North Sea coast had as their sole task the prevention of smuggling. Moreover, considerable fortifications were made along the coast with the same purpose in the last months of 1810, after a plan to capture Heligoland without maritime forces had had to be abandoned.

### Confiscations

As was to be expected, the execution of the new decrees encountered far greater obstacles in the vassal states than in the incorporated territories. According to French opinion, the Trianon decree, in the beginning at least, remained a dead letter in all the states of the Confederation of the Rhine, except Baden. Prussia, like Saxony, made an attempt to except raw materials from the tariff; and the somewhat more independent states, such as Russia, Austria, and Sweden, never, so far as is known, introduced the tariff as a whole. It seems as if it was just this passive resistance in August and September 1810 that contributed to bring about the issue of the Fontainebleau decree in October. The great decree (for France) that usually bears this name, dated October 18 or possibly 19, was preceded a few days before (October 14) by a decree for the Grand Duchy of Frankfurt and followed by corresponding laws promulgated by the other states of the Confederation of the Rhine, as well as by Denmark and Switzerland. The most notorious and dramatic was Napoleon's intervention in Frankfurt. Although that town, and the Grand Duchy created for the last electoral prince of Mainz that bore the name of the town, was nominally a sovereign state, on October 17 and 18 it was suddenly entered by two French regiments of infantry without the Grand Duke being so much as informed of the event. All the gates were occupied and artillery was stationed on the great square, after which the decree was posted up and an order was given that a declaration should be made of all colonial and English goods. French customs officials searched all warehouses, sealed all vaults and seized all books and letters; in fact, the whole of the great trade movement was stopped. For several days there was a violent agitation, as the general belief was that all the goods were going to be confiscated; but the excitement abated somewhat when the colonial goods were released, by a new decree of November 8, on payment of duty according to the Trianon tariff. As usual, malversation occurred on a large scale; but none the less Darmstädter, the German historian, reckons the yield to the French treasury at 9,000,000 francs.

The fact that the direct intervention of France thus caused the other states to lose the profit served to stimulate the measures of those states themselves; and externally, at least, they began to show great zeal in obeying the new decrees, so that colonial goods were seized everywhere. In Leipzig, which corresponded in eastern Germany to Frankfurt in the west, there was an unusual amount of colonial goods in the autumn of 1810, as has previously been mentioned; [1] but the great interest of the Saxon government in maintaining the fairs evidently prevented very forcible measures there against goods that were always in such great request. Among the most striking measures are those taken in Holstein, which had become one of the principal regions for the storage of colonial goods. In order to get them into his hands, Napoleon now conceded that for a limited time they might be imported into Hamburg on payment of the duties corresponding to the Trianon tariff; and at the same time he caused the Danish government to impose corresponding duties within his territory, in order that the owners should not be tempted to retain their goods. From Napoleon's point of view this move turned out better than most of the others. The final date had time after time to be moved forward until the spring of 1811, so that the enormous stores could be completely exported; and the French treasury made 19,700,000 francs on the payments in kind alone, and 42,500,000 francs altogether. Rist describes how during the last weeks the highways from Tönning were never free of loaded carts, inasmuch as half the peasants of Holstein had deserted their fields. Thousands were lost, many thousands were stolen, and hundreds of cart-loads waited all night at Hamburgerberg for the gates of the town to be opened. Cotton lay all about the fields like snow.

For the states of the interior there was a special difficulty in the treatment of colonial goods that had already passed through another state in Napoleon's sphere of power and had there paid duty according to the Trianon tariff. The method adopted at first, namely, the exaction of the duty in every

[1] See *ante*, p. 185.

country, was evidently fatal for intermediary states such as Frankfurt ; and gradually an arrangement was made whereby the tariff was generally applied as a tax on consumption, not as a transit duty, but with freedom for goods that had once paid the duty. In this connexion, however, there was the usual difficulty created by the systematic measures of Prussia and Sweden (Swedish Pomerania) calculated to make the Continental System illusory, despite the most abject terms in the ordinances issued. Prussia allowed payment at par in government securities, which stood at 50·5 per cent. ; and when the goods afterwards went through to other quarters with Prussian certificates of payment, the measures once again missed their aim. This went on until in the spring and summer of 1811 the Prussian certificates were disapproved and a fresh violent raid was made on what had been let through in the meantime. In consequence of this, the results of the new policy in Central Europe proper could not emerge clearly until the middle of 1811.

Owing to the confiscations which took place when non-declared colonial goods were discovered, great auctions were arranged—preferably in towns which lay at some distance from the great smuggling places, because the prices were highest there. Foremost among these was Antwerp, but of considerable importance also were Frankfurt, Cologne, Mainz, Strassburg, Milan, Venice and other towns near the old frontier of France. At these auctions the colonial trade was provided with goods and thus given a constant source of supply alongside the smuggled goods and the duty-paid imports ; and by this means there was created a possibility, besides smuggling, of purchasing the goods at a rate lower than the foreign price plus the customs duty.

### Autos–da–fé

What we have here dealt with are the colonial goods pure and simple. British industrial products, of course, according to the Fontainebleau decree were under all circumstances condemned to destruction ; and from this rule Napoleon never, so far as is known, made an exception. But it would be a great mistake to conclude from this that the blockade was more effective in this point than in the other. On the contrary, quite the reverse is true, and the reason is the total absence of pecuniary interest, public and private, in obedience to the latter regulations. The public burning of goods, as ordered by the decree, was a genuine *auto-da-fé* (act of faith), which was performed publicly to the accompaniment of military music and in the presence of all the high dignitaries of the place. But the ceremony was just as great whatever was the real value of the goods burnt at the stake ; and against the possibilities of malversation that this offered the virtue of Napoleon's officials could naturally make no resistance. It is improbable, indeed, that the *autos-da-fé* were ' comedies ', as Darmstädter calls them, everywhere ; but the fact that they were so in a large number of cases is shown by the accessible material, and was also admitted in cautious terms even by Napoleon himself. This was especially the case in Frankfurt, where at the first inventory, in November 1810, there was set to work an imperial commission consisting, among others, of French officers. When rolls of gold coins were placed in a drawer especially set apart for the purpose, the goods became Swiss or Saxon instead of British ; and the goods which actually came to the stake were regarded as having a value of only 200,000 francs, although they were officially valued at 1,200,000 francs. At the renewed purgation at Frankfurt, after the Prussian certificates of origin had been condemned in the spring of 1811, one firm had a whole warehouse full of British goods ; but here again the same story was repeated. A Jew from Friedberg by the name of Cassella was made a scapegoat, and only his British cottons were burnt. On this occasion the mayor wrote with refreshing candour : ' When they were spread out, there seemed to be a lot of cloth, and they could give the impression of a great quantity at the burning '—which, in his opinion, was all that was required, as the object must be ' to ward off unpleasantness from France, not to ruin our own population '. For other places we have less detailed statements, although a number of figures are available. It is, however, impossible to check these figures with reference to their authenticity for

the *autos-da-fé* in North Germany.   A number of them, which
are given in Servières' account for the Hanse Towns and in
M. Schäfer's account for Bremen, show the total value of goods
burnt to be about 4,500,000 francs.   But in addition to these
many burnings took place for which we have no figures ;   and
besides it is very difficult to determine the truth behind the
official statements.

Nevertheless, these burnings of British goods formed the
most striking and amazing feature of all in the new system, as
the conflagrations, especially during the last months of 1810
and the beginning of 1811, blazed in hundreds of towns from
one end to the other of the territory of Napoleon and his allies,
with the sole exception of Denmark.   Undoubtedly these
blighting scenes produced a tremendous though altogether
exaggerated impression of the Emperor's dogged determination
to follow out his plans for the economic overthrow of England,
regardless of anything else ;   and consequently they were a very
cunning display of power.   Even now it is impossible to read
the *Moniteur* without being impressed by the incessantly recurring inventories and details concerning British goods com-
mitted to the flames, sometimes in a dozen different places on
a single day.   The French Chambers of Commerce and Industry
naturally struck up what one of them appositely calls ' a
concert of blessings ' that the Emperor in this unusually direct
way had freed them from an overwhelming competitor, although
it is true, as the German historian Zeyss has shown, that some
of these blessings were conferred in consequence of orders from
high places.[1]

---

[1] *Lettres inédites*, nos. 803, 830, 837, 845, &c.   Prussian ordinances in Martens,
*Nouveau recueil*, &c., vol. I, pp. 514 *et seq.* ;   Rist, *op. cit.*, vol. II, pp. 78, 87, 105–6 ;
Bourrienne, *op. cit.*, vol. VII, p. 233 ;   vol. IX, pp. 50–1 ;   Rubin, *op. cit.*, pp. 393
*et seq.* ;   Darmstädter, *Das Grossherzogtum Frankfurt*, pp. 312 *et seq.*   The decree for
Frankfurt in *Le Moniteur*, Nov. 11, 1811 ;   Kiesselbach, *op. cit.*, pp. 135 *et seq.* ;
Schmidt, *Le Grand-duché de Berg*, pp. 375 *et seq.*, 380, 386 ;   Servières, *op. cit.*,
pp. 148–9, 273 *et seq.* ;   Schäfer, *op. cit.*, pp. 429–30 ;   König, *op. cit.*, pp. 195, 231–2,
&c. ;   Thiers, *op. cit.*, vol. XII, pp. 28 *et seq.*, 191–2 ;   Tarle, *Kontinental'naja blokada*,
vol. I, p. 294 ;   de Cérenville, *op. cit.*, pp. 57 *et seq.* ;   Zeyss, *op. cit.*, pp. 140 *et seq.*,
Anhang IX ;   Levasseur, *Histoire des classes ouvrières*, &c., de *1789 à 1870*, vol. I,
pp. 485 *et seq.*

## New Commercial Routes (1810–12)

The most remarkable consequence of the new system was a new arrangement of the trade routes, which took place in two directions. In the first place, the sea route was again brought officially into favour by the licence system, as it had not been since the Berlin decree. This change evidently was mainly important for France herself, where smuggling had always encountered the greatest difficulties; and it put an end, for instance, to the prosperity which Strassburg had enjoyed as a staple for French imports, both legitimate and illegitimate.[1] In the second place, and this was the most important, the whole of this trade in colonial goods and British manufactures shifted from Central Europe proper—the regions of the Rhine, Weser, Elbe and Oder—to Eastern Europe and the Danube basin. Beginning with the summer of 1811, there was a practical cessation in the supply of British goods to the Leipzig fairs, and even colonial goods declined there to an insignificant proportion of what they had been. Curiously enough, Frankfurt suffered less, comparatively speaking. This was evidently due to the fact that a genuine good-will to obey the system existed to a considerably greater extent in Saxony than in the other states of the Confederation of the Rhine; and this, in turn, is partly explained by the fact that the great and flourishing textile industries of Saxony profited by the measures against British competition, while Frankfurt in particular had nothing similar to gain by those measures. But at all events, this development shows an increasing efficacy of the blockade in great parts of Germany. The question naturally arises, however, why Leipzig did not take advantage of the licence system with regard to colonial goods; but the answer seems to be that imports through the Baltic ports could not penetrate to Leipzig after the Prussian certificates of payment had been disapproved. But this does not imply any general success for the new policy

[1] Darmstädter, *Die Verwaltung des Unter-Elsass* (*Bas-Rhin*) *unter Napoleon I,* in *Zeitschrift für die Geschichte des Oberrheins* (N. F., XIX, 1904), pp. 662 *et seq.*; Tarle, *Kontinental'naja blokada*, vol. I, pp. 274–5, 280.

in Germany, so long as the Baltic coast could only be barred ineffectively.   Consequently, the chief effect, in fact, still was to cut off Western Europe itself, while making Germany the purveyor of smuggled goods.

## Bacher's Account

The main thing, however, is the changed trade route which Napoleon thus brought about.   With unusual insight and openness the course of developments was predicted as early as October 2, 1810, in a report (printed by Schmidt in his work on the Grand Duchy of Berg) by Bacher, Napoleon's minister to the Confederation of the Rhine.   This seems to give such an excellent picture of the situation that it may be reproduced, as regards its main part, instead of a special account.   If the reader will go to the trouble of placing a map of Central Europe before him, Bacher's reasoning will prove extremely instructive.

The new direction which colonial goods take, now that the coasts of Holland and the Hanse Towns as far as the Oder are no longer accessible, is stated to have created such activity on all roads leading from different places in Russia to Prussia on one side and through Poland and Moravia to Vienna on the other, as also from the Turkish provinces to the Austrian empire with regard to British goods discharged in the Levantine ports, that the Danube will now take the place of the Rhine as the channel through which the states of the Confederation of the Rhine will in future be able to provide themselves.   The German merchants consider that this sweeping change in trade that has reduced Holland and Lower Germany to commercial nonentity will lead to active new connexions between Russia, Austria, and Bavaria, and consequently serve to create secure routes, which will convey not only colonial goods, but also British products, as far as the states of the Confederation of the Rhine, and from there to the Rhine and even to Switzerland, as soon as the price there covers the costs of transport.   Even if one should admit that the connexion between the Rhine and the Elbe has been really cut by the threefold cordon created by the measures taken in Lower Saxony and Westphalia, which is far from being the case, still the effect would be nothing but the increase of the supply of colonial goods from Russia through Königsberg and Leipzig.
Even supposing that the King of Saxony, who has spent very considerable sums in encouraging the muslin, calico, and cotton factories

and printing works that are now so flourishing in his territories, might be willing to extend the customs cordon from Wittenberg to the frontier of Bohemia, and at the same time be induced to place a tax on raw cotton, which is in conflict with his interest in procuring the best conditions and qualities for his mills, nevertheless this painful sacrifice, which would reduce the whole of the mountainous part of Saxony [Erzgebirge, the chief seat of the calico industry] to the deepest misery, would be no profit to France. It would only enrich the government and merchants of Austria, who would derive benefit from the customs duties on imports and exports and a substantial profit on the transit of colonial goods, which one could never prevent from penetrating as contraband.

Through Bohemia into Voigtland, Bayreuth, and the Upper Palatinate, and through Upper Austria and Styria into Salzburg [which at that time belonged to Bavaria] and Berchtesgaden. For these have always been corridors through which French and other prohibited goods have passed into the empire of Austria [that is to say, in the opposite direction], despite all vigilance on the part of the customs officials of that empire.

The cotton trade workers would be compelled to emigrate from Saxony and Voigtland, and even from Bavaria, Baden, and Switzerland, in order to seek their livelihood in the Austrian factories erected and managed by Englishmen, who by this means would again overwhelm the states of the Confederation of the Rhine with their products. In this way France during and since the Revolution has lost a valuable part of the masters and workmen who in their time contributed to make famous the manufactures of Lyons, St. Étienne, Sedan, and Verviers, and the departments of Ourthe and Roer, but who afterwards enriched Austria, Moravia, and also Saxony.

In other words, the fact was that trade had moved outside Napoleon's jurisdiction. Vienna, in particular, now obtained a great part of the central position in the trade of the Continent that had previously belonged to Leipzig. At an even earlier stage the Jewish *fierante* of East Europe had sought on the coast of the Baltic, at Königsberg and Riga, the British goods which they or their customers would not do without, and had not been satisfied with the substitutes in the way of Saxon and Swiss manufactures that Leipzig had to offer. They now found a staple in Vienna. To that place the goods went by two routes, a northern one through the Prussian and Russian Baltic ports round the Grand Duchy of Warsaw to Brody in Galicia (on Austrian territory, quite close to the Russian frontier); and a southern one to the same point (Brody), at first from Odessa, that is to say, across the Black Sea, and after the outbreak of the Franco-Russian war, *via* Constantinople and Saloniki to Lemberg. But this connexion was by no means limited to supplying Eastern Europe. On the contrary, it also became, just as Bacher had predicted, the starting-point of a transport of goods through Bavaria, which permitted the duty-free transit of colonial goods and even passed British manufactures, to the rest of South Germany and Switzerland, and making possible their smuggling into France.

But it is obvious that these roundabout routes and licensing fees or smuggling expenses and bribes were bound to increase the cost of transport enormously ; and so far this new policy also threw serious obstacles in the way of British trade, although these were relative and not absolute hindrances, as the Continental System in its original form was intended to create. Tooke gives a number of interesting examples of the immense cost of freight during the years 1809–12 in comparison with the year 1837, when his book was written.[1] For instance, wheat freights were 50 shillings per quarter, as against 4*s*. 6*d*. ; hemp freights were £30 per ton, as against £2 10*s*. ; timber freights were £10 per load, as against £1, &c. Silk had to go roundabout ways from Italy, *e.g.*, from Bergamo in one case *via* Smyrna, and in another case *via* Archangel (*sic*), so that the transport took one year and two years, respectively ; and when it went through France, the expense was £100 per bale, besides the freight from Havre to England. Tooke particularly states that the freights to and from France were enormous. For a vessel of little more than one hundred tons the freight and the French licence might amount to no less than £50,000 for a trip from Calais to London and back to Calais, which for indigo meant a freight of 4*s*. 6*d*. per English pound, as compared with 1*d*. (that is to say one fifty-fourth) in 1837 ; and the gross freight for a ship whose total value was £4,000 was £80,000 for a trip from Bordeaux to London and back.

---

[1] Tooke, *History of Prices*, &c., vol. I, pp. 309–10 note.

## BALTIC TRADE

All this shows clearly how important the Baltic trade, side by side with the Mediterranean trade, had become since the North Sea blockade had increased in efficiency. British shipping passed more and more to the Baltic ; and it was there, accordingly, that Napoleon had to exert his greatest pressure—a fact, indeed, which found expression in repeated warnings issued to the Baltic powers in the course of the summer. But it was not until the autumn of 1810 that matters became really critical ; and the events that then occurred had far-reaching consequences. A British commercial flotilla of six hundred vessels under different neutral flags, with a cargo worth £8,000,000 or, £9,000,000 had been delayed at Gothenburg by unfavourable weather until August (according to Lord Bathurst's statement in the House of Lords in 1812, it was only until June) and had then passed into the Baltic in September in order to proceed to Swedish, Russian, and Prussian ports. Napoleon now saw in this a possibility of striking a great blow against this important part of English trade, and in October he overwhelmed the different governments, partly through Champagny, his foreign minister, and partly by direct appeals, with the most urgent reminders to confiscate all these vessels, which, in the words of Champagny, were ' wandering about like the fragments of a scattered army '. Threats that Napoleon himself would send people to confiscate the cargoes, if the governments failed to do so on their own account, alternated with highly-coloured pictures of the economic crisis in England and of the certainty of her submission within a year as a consequence of complete confiscation ; and also, finally, inducements were offered by reference to the profits which would be reaped by confiscation.

In Mecklenburg Napoleon considered that he had effected his will by this means, namely, in the shape of the expulsion of the vessels ; and Prussia also gave way, although Clérembault, the Emperor's own consul at Königsberg, largely made seizures illusory, as we know. The question now was about Russia ; but here Napoleon met with resistance. Emperor

Alexander obstinately refused to have all nominally neutral vessels confiscated, and, besides, denied that more than about sixty vessels (the French ambassador at St. Petersburg, Caulaincourt, gave the figure for loaded vessels since the middle of September, according to Russian allegations, as only fifteen) had arrived at his ports ; and this fact he tried to explain by stating that some of them had returned and others had discharged at Gothenburg and other Swedish ports. This latter statement may indeed be nearly correct. In consequence of all this, it is apparent that Napoleon's action had failed in the main, although evidently a good deal had been seized in Russia. A memorandum from British merchants in 1816 gave such a high amount (as far as we can judge, much too high) as 140 cargoes with a value of £1,500,000. In Sweden, where smaller practical results than ever were to be attained—so unreservedly was Swedish policy based on the support of the British fleet under Saumarez—there was effected in the spring of 1811 at Karlshamn, by accident, a great seizure of over a hundred vessels under the flags not only of Denmark and Prussia, but also of Hamburg, Papenburg, &c., in the belief that they really were cargoes of the first two nationalities. But when they proved to be British property, of an estimated value of £500,000, a settlement was effected whereby the goods were treated as Swedish and then by fictitious purchase returned to their former owners, so that the British here lost nothing. The heat with which Napoleon had pursued his course of action against Russia with regard to the British vessels—among other things, the demands laid down in a personal letter addressed to the Emperor Alexander—largely contributed to widen the gulf between the two allies, and was a contributory cause to the breach in the sphere of trade war which was practically brought about on the last day of 1810 by the famous Russian customs ukase, which, as has been mentioned before,[1] was directed against French goods. In the course of 1811 the split was steadily increased by Alexander's more and more openly displayed good-will towards British vessels, which now came in

[1] See *ante*, p. 152.

without hindrance in large flotillas and discharged their goods on the Russian coast. According to a letter written by Napoleon at the end of August 1811, 150 vessels had in this way been received in Russian ports under the American flag.

## Gothenburg

The importance of Gothenburg for the trade of Europe has neither before nor since been so great as during the two years 1810 and 1813. The fact that the two intervening years showed less commercial activity was due partly to French and Danish captures, and partly also to the general decline in the Baltic trade under the pressure of a scarcity of corn and Napoleon's Russian campaign ; and, moreover, the more and more open connexions between Great Britain and Russia manifestly diminished the need for Swedish intermediacy. In September 1810, Axel Pontus von Rosen, the Governor of Gothenburg, and the most original, humorous and energetic Swedish actor on the stage of the Continental System in this exciting time, describes how the roadstead presented an appearance such as it had never had since the Creation, with 19 British men-of-war and 1,124 merchantmen lying at anchor ; and in the course of one single day, when the wind veered round to the east, several hundred vessels sailed away at the same time. The instructions given to von Rosen in the following November explained that in the case of vessels with cargoes belonging to Swedish subjects, and flying the American or other acceptable flag, ' His Majesty does not require you to recur to extremities of diligence, but on the contrary to suppress facts and facilitate traffic as far as you may do so in consonance with necessary precautions and without compromising your position.' Imports which had quadrupled between 1807 and 1809, quintupled in 1810. Especially flourishing, of course, was the *entrepôt* trade in colonial goods. Thus the exports of raw sugar were 14,500,000 pounds (about twice as much as the year before), and of coffee 4,500,000 pounds, not reckoning what was conveyed to other places in Sweden and from there to foreign countries. A native of the town who returned in 1811, after an absence of fifteen years, declared that he looked in vain for traces of the past and that he moved in an unknown world. But Gothenburg under the Continental System has as yet no historian. In the Baltic itself it was Hanö and the little loading-place of Matvik on the Swedish south coast, in the province of Blekinge (by some writers erroneously located in Finland), which, like Gothenburg on the west coast, was made, by the instructions of the Swedish government, both a base for the British squadron and an emporium for colonial goods and manufactures. But, for that matter, Sweden as a whole formed a great point of transit for British and American trade, partly to Russia and partly to the southern ports of the Baltic, because that route was regarded as more secure from French and Danish privateers than the direct route.[1]

[1] *Correspondance*, nos. 16,476 ; 16,713 ; 17,040 ; 17,041 ; 17,062 ; 17,071 ; 17,098 ; 17,099 ; 17,179 ; 17,395 ; 17,517 ; 18,082 ; Vandal, *Napoléon et Alexandre Ier* (Paris, 1893), vol. II, pp. 487 *et seq.*, 508 *et seq.*, 557 ; vol. III (1896), pp. 208–9, 215–6. The Memorial of 1816 printed in the *English Historical Review* (1903), vol. XVIII, pp. 122 *et seq.* ; Hansard, vol. XXI, p. 1056 ; Schinkel Bergman, *Minnen ur Sveriges nyare historia* (Stockholm, 1855), vol. VI, pp. 69–70, and app. 10 (letters from Governor Rosen to Bernadotte, the Crown Prince, Karl Johan) ; Lars von Engeström, *Minnen och Anteckningar*, vol. II, pp. 182–3, and app. 5 c (letters from von Rosen to von Engeström) ; *Memoirs, &c., of Lord de Saumarez*, vol. II, pp. 229 *et seq.* ; Clason, *op. cit.*, vol. IX : A, pp. 26–7, 149–50, 156 *et seq.*, 213. Governor von Rosen's letter of Sept. 8, 1810, is printed in Ahnfelt, *op. cit.*, vol. V, p. 239. See also Bergwall, *Historisk underrättelse*, &c., table 5 ; Fröding, *Det forna Göteborg* (Stockholm, 1903), pp. 115 *et seq.* ; also, *Göteborgs Köp- och Handels-gille . . . 1661–1911* (Gothenburg, 1911), pp. 124 *et seq.* ; Ramm, *op. cit.*, pp. 3, 8–9 ; Grade, *op. cit.*, p. 429.

# CHAPTER V

## THE BRITISH CRISIS OF 1810–12

How did the trade of Great Britain fare under the pressure of the events on the Continent described in the last chapter? With regard to the exports of manufactures, one might surmise a decline beforehand, for sales *via* the North Sea coast were made distinctly more difficult, and the roundabout route *via* the Baltic coast could not fail either to make the goods dearer for the consumer, and thus diminish sales, or, alternatively, to lower the price for the producer. As regards the trade in colonial goods, on the other hand, it was not clear, *a priori*, that the conditions would be greatly altered, inasmuch as the increased control and the new duties were counterbalanced by the extensive imports involved by the Trianon policy and the licences.

Nor, if one looks at the actual course of events, does that give any certain *points d'appui* for the connexion between cause and effect, a thing which must always to a great extent have to be solved by theoretical reasoning. At the first glance, it is true, that connexion might seem fairly obvious. For the fact is that the economic boom in England was brought to an end by a severe crisis in July and August 1810. The purely commercial difficulties, with bankruptcies occurring to an extraordinary extent among merchants, formed the beginning of this; but they abated in some degree later on in the summer of 1811 and still more from February 1812. On the other hand, the great lack of employment and the profound distress which somewhat later made its appearance, especially in the cotton industry and among workers, still continued during the greater part of 1812 and in their turn brought about serious disturbances— in particular, the ' Luddite riots ', with the wholesale destruction of looms from November 1811. It was, therefore, only natural that in these events, combined with the heavy depreciation of British currency, Napoleon should see the long-desired fruit of his protracted struggle against the foundations of the enemy's economic existence. But the very fact that the crisis broke out not solely in England, but quite as much in France, and not solely in those countries, but also in Amsterdam, the Hanse Towns, Prussia, and Switzerland, and above all in New York, shows how complicated the whole connexion was. From the standpoint of the general effects of the Continental System on the economic life of the different countries, this question belongs to part IV ; but the most palpable side of the question must be anticipated here.[1]

Undoubtedly it was a peculiar combination of circumstances that worked together. In comparison with the systematic policy of economic blockade and the comparatively limited military results of the recent war, the Napoleonic wars exhibited a considerably greater uncertainty both in the execution of the blockade and in its range. The licensing system and the uncertainty of the customs policy against which complaints were so often raised in France, on the one side, and Napoleon's lightning conquests on the Continent and Great Britain's colonial acquisitions, on the other, could not fail to give rise to dislocations and consequently to speculative enterprises which, within the department of economic life affected by it, namely, foreign trade, transcended anything we know in our own time. So far the existence of a very general crisis during the years 1810-11 is fully explicable ; and so far it has no direct connexion with the Continental System, but only the indirect connexion that follows from the influence of the Continental System in bringing about general unrest in the world. At all events, it is very obvious that we here have to do with effects that did not strike Great Britain alone or even specially.

Next, as regards the purely British crisis, what stands

---

[1] For the United Kingdom (and in part other countries) : *Report of the Select Committee on the State of Commercial Credit*, Mar. 7, 1811 (Hansard, vol. XIX, pp. 249 *et seq.*) ; also the debates and petitions on the subject (Hansard, vol. XIX, pp. 123, 327, 416, 493, 529, 613, 662 ; vol. XX, pp. 339, 431, 608, 744) ; Simond, *Journal of a Tour*, &c., vol. II, pp. 48-9, 265 ; Tooke, *op. cit.* (extracts from the *Monthly Magazine*), vol. I, pp. 300 *et seq.* ; vol. II, pp. 391, 393 *et seq.* (tables) ; Smart, *op. cit.*, vol. I, pp. 203-4, 226-7, 263 *et seq.*

out as a principal cause is the all but inevitable rebound from the huge speculation, especially in South America, but also in the West Indies and the Iberian peninsula, which has been described previously ; [1] that is to say, it is still a phenomenon having no direct connexion with the Continental System. In all probability it was further accelerated, as the British opposition always maintained, by an exaggerated granting of credit, caused by too extensive an issue of notes (inflation). The course of events appears to have been somewhat as follows : First of all, exporters could not get payment from their South American buyers. As early as August 1, 1810, we hear of five business houses in Manchester, with aggregate liabilities amounting to what was for that time the stupendous sum of £2,000,000, that had come to grief in this way ; and at the end of the year we hear of bankruptcies in Manchester occurring not merely daily but even hourly. The inability of exporters to honour bills drawn upon them by manufacturers involved the latter also, particularly the Scotch ones, in the crisis ; and later the confusion spread to the credit-giving banking houses and through them, in ever-widening circles, not only to the cotton trade but also to the hardware trade. Excessive speculations on the South American market also affected prospects of the future, inasmuch as not only was there no payment for goods already sold, but also new sales were largely rendered impossible. So far a completely adequate explanation of the dislocation is given by the South American trade. But to this there was added, as from March 1811, a new factor, which likewise lacked any direct connexion with the Continental System, namely, the unusually successful strangling of Anglo-American trade which the United States set going through the passage of the Non-importation Act. Finally, it is a self-evident matter that the sufferings caused by the crisis, and the deep traces it left among the working population of Great Britain, were largely due to the fact that the country was in the midst of the sweeping transformation to which Arnold Toynbee gave the name of ' Industrial Revolution '.

[1] See *ante*, p. 176.

But if it is clear that many factors independent of the Continental System were at work, it would nevertheless be a great mistake to regard the crisis as entirely uninfluenced by the policy of Napoleon. Externally the situation was, almost to the extent that the Emperor himself might have desired, one that must inevitably have led to ' the conquering of England by excess '. The year 1810 was characterized by unprecedented imports of raw materials and colonial products. This appears from the following table, which gives a convenient summary of the gross imports of those goods from the outbreak of war in 1803 to the final peace in 1815. (See next page.)

This table shows that the figures for 1810, with only two exceptions, are in general much higher than the even high figures for 1809 ; and in the two most important items, cotton and sugar, they are higher than in any other year during the whole period. The explanation of this fact is stated to be, first, that the payment for exports to South America, so far as there was any payment, was made in colonial goods ; and, secondly, that the great warehouses at the London docks had led to a great storing of all the products of the world and consequently to extensive speculation in them by middlemen. It is self-evident, too, that a great and expressly acknowledged part in this development was played by the trade with the United States, which was quite unimpeded in 1810, as well as by the conquest of the French and Spanish colonies, and also, so far as wool is concerned, by the British successes on the Iberian peninsula. When a stoppage of sales took place, therefore, the situation had unusually large chances of becoming serious.

Accordingly, there followed in rapid succession during the summer and autumn of 1810 the events we all know about. As early as the spring (April and May) the signs of a crisis had really shown themselves in France, a crisis which might possibly have reacted on Great Britain ; but far more important was the incorporation of Holland, in the beginning of July, by which, according to British evidence, there was, at least for the moment, a complete interruption of the trade between the two

GROSS IMPORTS TO ENGLAND FROM 1803 TO 1815

| Year | Coffee | Sugar | Raw cotton | Wool | Flax | Hemp | Raw silk | Thrown silk | Tallow |
|---|---|---|---|---|---|---|---|---|---|
|  | (cwt.) | (cwt.) | (lb.) | (lb.) | (cwt.) | (lb.) | (lb.) | (lb.) | (cwt.) |
| 1803 | 219,000 | 3,186,000 | 53,812,000 | 6,021,000 | 295,000 | 730,000 | 804,000 | 385,000 | 537,000 |
| 1804 | 507,000 | 3,248,000 | 61,867,000 | 8,157,000 | 353,000 | 727,000 | 1,032,000 | 449,000 | 534,000 |
| 1805 | 354,000 | 3,179,000 | 59,682,000 | 8,546,000 | 467,000 | 611,000 | 1,190,000 | 433,000 | 394,000 |
| 1806 | 529,000 | 3,815,000 | 58,176,000 | 7,334,000 | 355,000 | 730,000 | 803,000 | 515,000 | 537,000 |
| 1807 | 418,000 | 3,641,000 | 74,925,000 | 11,769,000 | 421,000 | 757,000 | 778,000 | 346,000 | 367,000 |
| 1808 | 727,000 | 3,753,000 | 43,606,000 | 2,354,000 | 258,000 | 260,000 | 637,000 | 139,000 | 148,000 |
| 1809 | 708,000 | 4,001,000 | 92,812,000 | 6,846,000 | 533,000 | 859,000 | 698,000 | 502,000 | 353,000 |
| 1810 | 829,000 | 4,809,000 | 132,489,000 a | 10,936,000 | 512,000 | 9⁻6,000 | 1,341,000 | 451,000 | 479,000 |
| 1811 | 560,000 | 3,918,000 | 91,662,000 | 4,740,000 | 244,000 | 4 9,000 | 602,000 | 20,000 | 293,000 |
| 1812 | 406,000 | 3,762,000 | 63,026,000 | 7,015,000 | 405,000 | 8 2,000 | 1,330,000 | 618,000 | 309,000 |
| 1813 b | .... | .... | .... | .... | .... | .... | .... | .... | .... |
| 1814 | 1,030,000 | 4,035,000 | 60,060,000 | 15,713,000 | 525,000 | 545,000 | 1,635,000 | 646,000 | 589,000 |
| 1815 | 815,000 | 3,985,000 | 99,306,000 | 14,982,000 | 351,000 | 732,000 | 1,443,000 | 358,000 | 642,000 |

a This figure is corrected in accordance with the table in Baines, *History of Cotton Manufacture in Great Britain* (Lond. 1835) p. 347, which agrees with the table in Porter, *Progress of the Nation*, p. 178. The remaining figures follow Tooke.

b Missing, the customs accounts being lost in the fire.

countries which had been going on throughout the reign of
King Louis. At the beginning of August there followed the
Trianon tariff; in October, the intensified blockade of the
German North Sea coast, the Fontainebleau decree, and the persecution of British and colonial goods in all Napoleon's vassal
states; and at the same time six hundred trading vessels were
wandering around the Baltic. It was also in the sphere of
colonial trade that the first blow occurred, in that one of the
foremost dealers in West Indian products became insolvent and
dragged down with him his bankers, who in their turn dragged
after them the provincial banks with which they were associated.
A meeting of London merchants and representatives of the
Scottish manufacturing districts in February 1811, summed up
in proud and somewhat exaggerated terms the situation in its
connexion with the Continental System by saying that Great
Britain had become ' the emporium of the trade, not only of the
Peninsular but also of the Brazils, of Spanish settlements in
South America, of Santo Domingo, the conquered colonies of
Guadaloupe, Martinique, &c., but even of countries under the
direct influence of the enemy ', inasmuch as the latter had
wished to take advantage of the protection of British justice
and the honesty of British merchants. ' The measures of the
enemy having been especially directed toward preventing the
exportation of the immense quantities of merchandize of all
descriptions thus accumulated, the consequences are that the
goods became a burthen.' The following remarks of the French-
American, Simond, upon his visit to the West Indian docks in
August 1811, are in full accord with this : ' At present . . . the
giant receives, but sends nothing away. The warehouses are
so full that it has been necessary to hire temporary ones out
of the docks. The export district is literally deserted.'

The connexion with the Continental System thus seems to
be manifest ; and to judge by all English sources, the difficulties
connected with the disposal of colonial goods were at first
even greater than in the case of exports of manufactures. During
1810, for instance, the trade statistics give practically unaltered figures for the exports of British goods, though, of course,

it is possible that in the first half year there was a rise which made up for the decline in the second half year; on the other hand, they show a decline of 19¼ per cent. for foreign and colonial goods, and it was not until 1811 that the exports declined more or less parallel for both groups. From this one may safely conclude that the Trianon and Fontainebleau policy practically had the effect, at least for the moment, of making things more difficult by the stricter control than of making them easier by the fiscal customs and licensing system. As regards the effect of the different markets on the development, we may possibly make cautious use of the trade statistics, although their reliability is undoubtedly limited even with regard to the legitimate trade, and of course much more dubious with regard to smuggling into the Continent. We are here concerned with 'real', that is to say, declared, values; but the decline is no less marked as regards the 'official' values, in which changes of price have been eliminated.[1]    (See opposite page.)

We note immediately the pronounced decline in 1811—for colonial goods partly even in 1810—for the northern part of the Continent, which, together with the almost complete disappearance of exports to the United States and the substantial diminution in the figures for South America explains the great decline in the totals.  On the other hand, it is remarkable how little the Mediterranean trade was disturbed, which indicates the importance of the Balkan peninsula as a port of penetration for the new trade route through Vienna.  The relatively strong rise for Portugal in 1811 indicates a transformation at this point, which was favoured by Wellington's military successes. This increase in the trade with Portugal, which is confirmed from other sources, constituted the first sign of the limitation of the crisis in the sphere of foreign trade as early as the spring and early summer of 1811.

It is also of interest to follow the development at closer range, so to speak, with regard to the most important domestic

[1] Hansard, vol. XXII, app. 1, cols. lxi–lxii (the total figure for 1806 being corrected). As usual, the figures are for Great Britain only, not for Ireland.

Exports of United Kingdom Produce ('Real' Values)

| Year | North of Europe, including France | Spain | Portugal | Gibraltar, Malta, Sicily, the Levant, &c. | Ireland, Guernsey, &c. | Asia | Africa | United States | Rest of America | Total |
|---|---|---|---|---|---|---|---|---|---|---|
| 1805 | £10,320,000 | £50,000 | £1,850,000 | £1,410,000 | £5,000,000 | £2,900,000 | £760,000 | £11,010,000 | £7,770,000 | £41,070,000 |
| 1806 | 7,570,000 | 30,000 | 1,700,000 | 2,960,000 | 4,510,000 | 2,940,000 | 1,160,000 | 12,390,000 | 10,880,000 | 44,140,000 |
| 1807 | 5,090,000 | 30,000 | 970,000 | 2,920,000 | 5,070,000 | 3,360,000 | 770,000 | 11,850,000 | 10,440,000 | 40,480,000 |
| 1808 | 2,160,000 | 860,000 | 430,000 | 5,570,000 | 5,870,000 | 3,520,000 | 630,000 | 5,240,000 | 16,590,000 | 40,880,000 |
| 1809 | 5,700,000 | 2,380,000 | 800,000 | 6,960,000 | 5,450,000 | 2,870,000 | 800,000 | 7,260,000 | 18,010,000 | 50,240,000 |
| 1810 | 7,700,000 | 1,400,000 | 1,310,000 | 5,210,000 | 4,210,000 | 2,980,000 | 600,000 | 10,920,000 | 15,640,000 | 49,980,000 |
| 1811 | 1,500,000 | 1,230,000 | 4,650,000 | 5,450,000 | 5,020,000 | 2,940,000 | 340,000 | 1,840,000 | 11,940,000 | 34,920,000 |

Exports of Foreign and Colonial Produce ('Real' Values)

| Year | North of Europe, including France | Spain | Portugal | Gibraltar, Malta, Sicily, the Levant, &c. | Ireland, Guernsey, &c. | Asia | Africa | United States | Rest of America | Total |
|---|---|---|---|---|---|---|---|---|---|---|
| 1805 | £6,330,000 | £140,000 | £180,000 | £160,000 | £1,400,000 | £210,000 | £400,000 | £440,000 | £790,000 | £10,040,000 |
| 1806 | 5,860,000 | 30,000 | 80,000 | 220,000 | 1,300,000 | 320,000 | 490,000 | 480,000 | 1,010,000 | 9,790,000 |
| 1807 | 5,730,000 | 80,000 | 200,000 | 410,000 | 1,970,000 | 200,000 | 260,000 | 250,000 | 910,000 | 10,000,000 |
| 1808 | 3,270,000 | 260,000 | 170,000 | 1,270,000 | 2,100,000 | 190,000 | 190,000 | 60,000 | 1,580,000 | 9,090,000 |
| 1809 | 8,870,000 | 660,000 | 320,000 | 1,490,000 | 2,120,000 | 120,000 | 170,000 | 200,000 | 1,820,000 | 15,770,000 |
| 1810 | 6,160,000 | 340,000 | 920,000 | 1,180,000 | 1,550,000 | 140,000 | 100,000 | 300,000 | 2,040,000 | 12,730,000 |
| 1811 | 1,980,000 | 270,000 | 1,510,000 | 1,940,000 | 2,190,000 | 120,000 | 70,000 | 30,000 | 900,000 | 9,020,000 |

articles of export, namely, the products of the cotton industry. On this point only ' official ' values are available : [1]

COTTON

| Year | Manufactures | Yarn |
|------|-------------|------|
| 1803 | £6,442,037 | £639,404 |
| 1804 | 7,834,564 | 902,208 |
| 1805 | 8,619,990 | 914,475 |
| 1806 | 9,753,824 | 736,225 |
| 1807 | 9,708,046 | 601,719 |
| 1808 | 12,503,918 | 472,078 |
| 1809 | 18,425,614 | 1,020,352 |
| 1810 | 17,898,519 | 1,053,475 |
| 1811 | 11,529,551 | 483,598 |
| 1812 | 15,723,225 | 794,465 |
| 1814 | 16,535,528 | 1,119,858 |
| 1815 | 21,480,792 | 808,850 |

In full accordance with the preceding table we here find almost the same position in 1810 as in 1809 contrasting with a huge decline in 1811—quite independent of the change in prices, be it noted—a decline which for woven goods amounts to $35\frac{1}{2}$ per cent., and for yarn to no less than 54 per cent.

Practically all pronouncements on the question of the causes of the crisis, especially in 1811, are also agreed in attributing it to the scarcity of sales and the closing of the continental ports. The main factors are very well summarized in a letter from Liverpool, dated November 22, 1810, reprinted by Tooke, from which we may quote the following paragraph :

The effects of a vast import of colonial and American produce, far above the scale of our consumption at the most prosperous periods of our commerce and attaining a magnitude hitherto unknown to us, have, in the present cramped state of our intercourse with the Continent, developed themselves in numerous bankruptcies, widely spreading in their influence, and unprecedented in extent of embarrassment. It is but fair, however, to ascribe a portion of these evils to the consequences of a sanguine indulgence of enterprise, in extensive shipments of our manufactures to South America, which so confidently followed the

---

[1] After a table in Baines, *op. cit.*, p. 350. To avoid mistakes, it might be well to utter a warning against the natural conclusion that it is possible to read from the figures the relation between manufactures and yarn in the exports ; to judge by the years when there are ' real values ' available, a doubling of the figures for yarn would give an approximately correct notion of this.

expedition to La Plata, and the removal of the government of Portugal to Brazil.  They are further aided by the speculations which prevailed during the various stages of the American non-intercourse, and which, unfortunately, were not confined to the duration of the circumstances which excited them.

The effect of all this was a fall in prices in England, especially for colonial goods ; and this, in consideration of the high prices for the same goods on the Continent, served Napoleon as a decisive proof of the success of his policy.  Thus, for instance, the prices of coffee, according to Tooke's price statistics for four different points of time in each year, showed a downward tendency as early as July and November 1810, and fell with a crash in March 1811 ; e. g. the price of ' St. Domingo, for exportation ' fell from 96–105s. per cwt. in January 1810 to 36–42s. per cwt. in March 1811 ; and for ' British Plantation, in bond, inferior ' the fall was from 70–112s. to 25–52s. per cwt. in the same period.  For sugar the decline was somewhat less pronounced, but the price had reached its lowest level somewhat earlier, namely, for most grades, as far back as November 1810. Thus for ' Havannah White, for exportation ' there was a fall from 60–75s. per cwt. in July 1810 to 38–51s. in November ; and for ' East India, Brown, in bond ', from 50–60s. in April to 37–45s. in November.  As regards cotton, of course, there were numerous quotations for the many different qualities, and the general effect is somewhat varied during 1810 ; but the spring of 1811 shows, almost without exception, figures that are about half of those that held good a year previously. Thus, ' West India, Surinam ' fell from 22–27d. to 9–15d. per pound ;  South American (Pernambuco) from 25–27d. to 14–15d. ; and the most important kind of all, North American cotton (intermediate quality, Bowed Georgia), fell, according to Daniels' Liverpool figures, from 21–22d. in January 1810 to $10\frac{1}{2}$–$12\frac{1}{4}d$. in June 1811 ; while Tooke's figures here reveal a still heavier fall—from 17–19d. in April 1810, to 7–9d. in April 1811, respectively.  The same was the case with Spanish wool, which between the same two points of time sank from 13–14s. to 7–8s. per pound.

# CHAPTER VI

## SELF-DESTRUCTION OF THE SYSTEM

NAPOLEON completely misinterpreted the significance of British difficulties; and how much the dislocation of British colonial trade was an effect of the general insecurity of the world, that is to say, not solely of Napoleon's measures, is shown by the fact that the French crisis, too, had its origin in huge speculations with regard to colonial goods.[1] It is also doubtful to what extent Napoloen's torrent of words concerning the impending ruin of England fully convinced even himself. At any rate, a remarkable document dating from as far back as the beginning of 1812 shows how far he had come to doubt the expediency of maintaining the Continental System in its original form and purpose. The document referred to, which is printed from an official copy in the great edition of Napoleon I's correspondence which came out under Napoleon III, is there called *Note sur le blocus continental*. It was dictated in the Council of Merchants and Manufacturers on January 13, and, like many of Napoleon's other dictated utterances, it has the character of a kind of imperial monologue. In the case before us, however, it gives us the unusual impression of half-formed thoughts in the mind of a man who does not see his way clearly before him; and if it did not end in charging the home secretary to work out plans in accordance with the lines laid down, one might easily conceive the whole as a mere experiment in thought. The pre-history and consequences of the plan have never been examined, so far as I know, and consequently much of it is obscure; but, notwithstanding this fact, it is of uncommonly great interest as an indication of the general trend of Napoleon's thoughts.

[1] Darmstädter, *Studien zur napoleonischen Wirtschaftspolitik, loc. cit.*, vol. II,

In his introductory words Napoleon lays it down that there are two alternatives : ' either to remain where we are, or to march with great steps toward a different order of things '. As an illustration of the established order he makes a comparison between the prices of sugar in the different countries under his rule in relation to the customs rates, and on the basis of this comparison he concludes that the laws are enforced loyally in France, the Kingdom of Italy, and Naples, but less diligently in the states of the Confederation of the Rhine ; after this a calculation is made of the requirements in those three countries, on the supposition that the consumption has been reduced to a third. So far as one can understand, it is on the basis of this that the second alternative is to be founded, namely, an altogether unimpeded granting of licences for the whole requirements of all transmarine goods, on payment of heavy duties, and also on condition of the export of French goods. The requirements of sugar imports, estimated at 450,000 *quintaux*, will thus bring into the coffers of the state no less than 70,000,000 francs ; and this importation will be allowed against an export of money to the amount of 10,000,000 francs and of goods to the value of 30,000,000 francs. The same system is afterwards to be applied to coffee, hides, indigo, tea, raw cotton, and dyewoods. ' This will produce,' he says, ' a great activity in industry, encouragement for navigation, the navy and the brokerage business, a customs income of 200,000,000 francs a year, and a germ of prosperity and life in all our ports.'

So far there was nothing more than a consistent following-out of the established licensing system, even though the last expression cited hints how heavily the policy had fallen on French economic life. But the reasons alleged and the immediate execution show how far Napoleon had travelled from the original plan of the Continental System. It is true that he does not make the slightest admission of this. ' For France,' he says, ' the result will be a dream '— a dream which could not have been attained without the Continental System. ' His Majesty does not regard this as a change in the system, but as a consequence of it.' He maintains, in fact—in the most palpable conflict with his own decrees, though without the slightest sign of embarrassment—that he has never said that France should not receive sugar, coffee, and indigo, but alleges that he has been content with customs duties thereon. What he now pretends to have said is merely that the goods were not to be received except in exchange for French goods on French vessels and dependent upon the licences. Of all this, needless to say, the Berlin and Milan decrees gave not the slightest hint. 'Accordingly, it is the thus improved system that has achieved this result, which had not been counted upon for several years.'

However, the question arises how such a general granting of licences, with the object of bringing in money to the treasury and forcing up exports, would affect England, the crushing of whom, of course, was the primary object of the original policy. 'This will not benefit England with regard to industry, brokery, or freights; it will profit England solely as a sale for her [colonial] goods, and a part of those goods are really Dutch and French [as originating in their colonies]. Without doubt this is very advantageous for England, but it will cause an upheaval there; and is the profit less or greater for France?' 'That profit,' continues Napoleon, 'is for France like three to one, while the profit of the Treaty of Versailles (the Eden Treaty) was more like one to seven,' and therefore we have now to deal with 'a lasting system that may well be eternal'.

For the present, however, in the opinion of the Emperor, it is unnecessary to discuss whether the system can be introduced, for it should at all events be attempted; if it fails, the whole thing may well remain in the minutes of the Council. The execution is to take the form of a normalization of the licensing system, in that two kinds of licences are to be granted, the one unconditional for the import of foodstuffs, the other for the import of colonial goods on condition of the export of wine and brandy from Nantes and Bordeaux and of textiles from the north of France. For the non-French territories of Napoleon there are to be arranged fourteen 'series' of importing places with corresponding export obligations, which will partly include the products of these countries themselves, but should take place through French licences. Of the duties, an amount between one-third and two-thirds shall fall to the princes concerned and the remainder shall fall to the French treasury, provided they follow the routes indicated. Danzig may possibly be allowed to export not only building timber but also corn to England, on condition of sending twice as much to France, and on payment of a special export duty, which should be considered in detail.[1]

We thus see on what courses Napoleon had now started out. We are here concerned with a balancing of the purely commercial advantages of France against those of Great Britain, that is to say, the points of view of the kind that are usually put forward, for instance, in negotiating a commercial treaty; and in full analogy with this, the system is thought of as a permanent measure, not as a war measure, designed to destroy England. The concession, deliberately shoved aside by Napoleon and treated by him as a trifle in form, that the new order of things would be advantageous for England in respect of the trade in colonial goods, stands in the strongest possible contrast to the proud announcement of 1807 [2] that England sees her vessels laden with superfluous wealth, wandering around the seas and seeking in vain a port to open and receive them. Now Napoleon himself considers opening all his ports for the purpose, if only he can get these vessels to take French goods in exchange. This means that the principle of the Continental System has been abandoned. To use an expression of Professor Hjärne, in his book *Revolutionen och Napoleon*, in connexion with other sides of the policy of the empire, one may call this the ' self-destruction of the system '.

During the period of barely four months that remained before Napoleon's departure for the Russian campaign we find

---

[1] *Correspondance*, no. 18,431. There is a kind of germ of all this in the Memorandum of July 25, 1810, which forms the basis of the licence and Trianon decrees, extracts from which are given in Schmidt, *op. cit.*, p. 358.

[2] See *ante*, p. 74.

no traces in his correspondence of any formal measures on the lines of the January memorandum. Even his superhuman powers were more and more completely absorbed by his military preparations; and in the sphere of economics the threatening shortage of corn formed a peril which occupied his thoughts to the exclusion of all plans with more remote objects in view. From what is so far known, therefore, it does not appear that the new order of things was ever formally accepted, even though the actual policy, so far as one can judge, came nearer and nearer thereto. Besides, already during 1812 the economic situation slowly improved in Great Britain, especially after the South American trade had got into a healthy state as early as February, although, it is true, there were still disturbances in the textile districts. The Continental System was deprived of a main pillar quite early in 1812 (March) through the fact that Davout, whom Sorel calls the ' archi-douanier ' of the empire, left for the front, which meant the removal of the inflexible determination to prevent smuggling into the country *via* the North Sea coast. After the retreat from Moscow and the advance of the Russian troops along the Baltic coast in the beginning of 1813, it became manifestly impossible to maintain the barrier. Thus the prefect of the Weser department reports that ' smuggling was raising its head all along the line '; the warehouses were filled with contraband, and smuggling vessels went openly across the seas to the enemy. Rist gives a vigorous description of the rising against the French customs officials in Hamburg at the close of February 1813, when a whole army of trouserless smugglers hurled their hereditary enemies into the dried-up canals and good-humouredly stormed their premises. ' Thus,' he goes on, ' there disappeared within a few hours all those barriers, those dens of imperial avarice, and the forbidden goods streamed unimpeded along the forbidden ways.' In the same way smuggling broke out openly in Switzerland, after having been kept down as much as possible during the preceding period.

This, however, did not mean that Napoleon had abandoned the Continental System. In Hamburg Davout resumed his power and exacted a frightful vengeance ; and as late as May and June 1813, the Emperor caused quantities of colonial goods to be confiscated in the Grand Duchy of Berg, Hamburg, &c., even such as had paid the proper dues or had been sold by the French customs officials, and had them conveyed to the usual places for the collection of such goods. On the other hand, this does not settle the question whether, and to what extent, the object pursued was the great aim of the Continental System, or whether Napoleon, after the retreat from Moscow, still believed in the possibility of success in his struggle against the economic fabric of England. At times this last was undoubtedly the case, as is stated by so credible an observer as Mollien, who lays particular stress on the hopes of an impending ruin for the credit of England with which the unfavourable rates of exchange inspired the Emperor at that time. Still, this question must be separated from that of gaining the end in view through the particular means called the Continental System ; and on this subject, which concerns us here, it must be said that fiscal considerations had now become so pressing that it was necessary to brush aside the idea of carrying out the war against the trade of Great Britain. Napoleon's utterances at this period become more and more frankly mercenary ; and we may regard as the epitaph of the system a new memorandum by the Emperor immediately after his return from Moscow (December 22, 1812), a significant counterpart to the long memorandum of January in the same year that we have summarized at length above. In that document the Emperor charges his minister of finance to inform the ministry of commerce that he needs 150,000,000 francs in ordinary and extraordinary customs revenues during 1813, giving the following reasons :

In order to arrive at this result, you must consider what remains to be received for licences already granted ; and for those additional ones which must be granted to obtain this result, which is necessary for the first of all considerations, namely, that of having what is indispensable for the present service of the state. Undoubtedly it is necessary to harm our foes, but above all we must live.[1]

[1] *Correspondance*, no. 19,391 ; *Lettres inédites*, nos. 1,002, 1,013, 1,018, 1,082 ; Mollien, *op. cit.*, vol. III, p. 237 ; Rist, *op. cit.*, vol. II, pp. 142–3, 159–60 ; Smart,

This necessity to live, that is to say, fiscalism, in combination with the hopelessness of a consistent application of the self-blockade, was what had led to the self-destruction of the Continental System; and we have good reasons to doubt the possibility of its continuance in spirit and in truth, even if the Russian campaign and the wars of liberation had not intervened. As it is, the gigantic experiment had been followed to such a point that the end seemed to be in sight, though it was not obtained. It is therefore inevitable that opinions as to its feasibility must remain divided. Nevertheless, a good deal more light falls on this question if one investigates the effects of the Continental System on the economic life of the different countries. This is to be the subject and the object of part iv.

*op. cit.*, vol. i, pp. 335 *et seq.*; de Cérenville, *op. cit.*, pp. 113, 310; Tarle, *Deutsch-französische Wirtschaftsbeziehungen*, pp. 686–7; Schmidt, *op. cit.*, pp. 408 *et seq.*

# PART IV

# EFFECTS OF THE CONTINENTAL SYSTEM ON THE ECONOMIC LIFE OF GREAT BRITAIN AND THE MAINLAND

# CHAPTER I

## DIFFERENT TYPES OF EFFECT

THE Napoleonic wars occurred during a period of far-reaching importance for the material development of Europe. That implies that during this period the economic life of Europe must have undergone a great transformation which can be ascribed only in part to the system under discussion. The problem will therefore be not only too widely extended, but also—which is of more consequence—altogether erroneously stated from the very outset, if we regard it as identical with the task of showing the general changes in the economic life of Western Europe during the first decade and a half of the nineteenth century. Instead of that, what we have to do is to isolate those aspects of the development which can be connected in any way with the Continental System. This is a problem of a more or less theoretical nature, which presupposes a knowledge of the general connexion that exists between cause and effect in the sphere of economics, and which can therefore not be solved by purely historical methods.

The point which offers the greatest interest in such a problem is the working of the blockade policy in so far as it became effective. Consequently, we now lay aside the weakness (proved in detail in the preceding part) of the Continental System as a measure of blockade, and turn to the results of the policy.

On the Continent proper the Continental System necessarily came to work as a gigantic protectionist policy pursued to the limit. By excluding foreign goods it stimulated the domestic production of all kinds of goods which found any general use within the country or even within the Continent. To this extent, the Continental System, like the system that prevailed during the recent war, affords an occasion of studying the effects of a high protectionism enforced with the greatest violence and with all the resources of the state for a short period. The difference between this and the régime which characterized the blockaded states of the Continent during the recent war lies solely in the fact that such a system of protection was then freely chosen, while in our own day it was imposed from without. On the other hand, the Continental System, like the state of affairs prevailing during the recent war, exhibits one significant and very fatal dissimilarity from the ordinary kind of protection that prevails in peace time, namely, that under the latter régime the obstacles in the way of imports usually embrace only the products of industry and agriculture, not the raw materials of industry, whereas the nature of the Continental System as a general self-blockade compelled, or at least should have compelled, equally rigorous embargo against all kinds of commodities imported by sea. The efforts of the all-important individual who dominated the Continent had consequently to be directed toward procuring of raw materials within his own territories, a task which always encounters more insuperable limits than that of working up materials which are to be found within one's own borders. And so far as such an effort failed, there was an irremediable self-contradiction within the policy itself. Either, in fact, it was necessary to sacrifice the industrial development by which the position of Great Britain as the workshop of the world was intended to be crushed, or it was necessary to accept raw materials through the co-operation of the ruler of the seas and thereby fail in the object of destroying the commercial and maritime power of Great Britain and consequently fail also in the object of ' conquering her by excess '. When Mollien speaks of the inexplicable ' contradiction ' between the obstacles in the way of the supply of raw materials and the prohibition of British manufactures, because the former benefited British industry more than the latter damaged it, consequently he puts his finger on this irremediable doubleness of the very principle of the Continental System.[1]

On the Continent, however, there existed a further contrast,

[1] Mollien, *Mémoires*, &c., vol. II, p. 462 ; vol. III, pp. 32–3.

which was not at all implicit in the idea of the Continental System, but was a consequence of the fact that the overthrow of Great Britain was not the all-dominating thought of Napoleon or his system to the extent that he usually pretended. As has already been shown in several places in the preceding account, in fact, the purely protectionistic aims of the system for France herself practically took the same rank as the object of conquering the enemy. It was for that reason that Napoleon not only neglected what otherwise ought to have been done, in the interest of the first object, to form an economic combine of continental Europe, but even directed his policy against the countries of his own continental vassals and allies.

## FRANCE

It follows that the effects of the Continental System in the country of Napoleon's heart, that is, in France itself, were all that a protectionist policy pursued with absolute ruthlessness can involve for a country that adopts it. When we say ' France ' here we use it as an abbreviation for the old French monarchy and the French acquisitions of the revolutionary period, *i. e.*, including Belgium and the left bank of the Rhine but not, in the main, the conquests of the consulate and the empire, which were otherwise treated. The effects here were bound to be the typical consequences of an embargo policy ; and, as appears from what has just been said, such a policy directed not only against the supply of goods by sea and from lands beyond the seas, but also to a large extent against the supply of goods by land and from the other continental states. We might here foresee that the situation must be characterized as that of economic self-sufficiency and of a hothouse development of industrial production.

## THE REST OF THE CONTINENT

As regards the other continental states within Napoleon's more or less undisputed realm of power, on the other hand, the effects were bound to be far more varied, differing not only according to the degree of their political independence and to their actual observance of the Continental decrees within their territories, but also according to the relative importance of the two opposite tendencies of which they were the object. A moment's consideration will show that their position had features in common both with that of France and with that of Great Britain. It resembled the former in so far as they, like France, had to abstain from supply by sea ; it resembled the latter inasmuch as they, like Great Britain, were shut out from sales in the markets which were under the direct sway of Napoleon. Consequently, the effects in the non-French parts of Central and Southern Europe cannot be expected to have the same self-evident, consistent appearance as in France; but they have a practical and historical interest of their own.

Moreover, the effects on the Napoleonic mainland were bound to vary with the position of foreign trade and of the production of goods intended for foreign sale. In this connexion, however, we must emphasize at the outset the limitation in the effects which follow from the fact that in scarcely any of the continental states was economic life centred on international exchange. The great commercial cities of Hamburg, Bremen, Amsterdam, Rotterdam, Antwerp, and, in France, Bordeaux, Marseilles, Nantes, Havre, and La Rochelle, were, it is true, entirely dependent on foreign trade and suffered proportionately from the blockade in so far as it became effective ; but this point has been already so fully illustrated in the preceding part that it is not necessary to dwell further upon it here. Among the non-French states, countries which, like Saxony, Switzerland, the Grand Duchy of Berg, Bohemia, and Silesia, had already reached the industrial stage and were therefore very dependent on international intercourse, were those most affected by the Continental System; however, they too were affected very differently, according to their political position.

The difference between industrial countries and countries especially given over to agriculture and the yielding of raw materials, namely, North Germany and especially the Baltic States, Prussia, Mecklenburg, Russia, Austria, and Hungary,

did not primarily consist in the fact that the latter were
independent of foreign trade, since they also had exports.
It consisted, rather, in the fact that, from the standpoint of
the Continental System, the industrial life of the two groups
of countries was affected quite differently by the blockade.
The industrial countries, on the one side, found obstacles
placed in the way of their supply of raw materials ; but, on
the other hand, owing to the strangling of British supply, they
increased the possibilities of sale for their own manufactures
outside of France and Italy.  It was as regards sales that the
agrarian countries were more or less hard hit, partly through
the general obstacles in the way of navigation, which offered
almost the only possibility for the conveyance of their bulky
goods, and partly also through the prohibition of intercourse
with Great Britain, who was their chief buyer.[1]  Owing to the
tendency of the Continental System to render difficult only
imports into the Continent, however, the effect of this factor
was considerably diminished for the countries producing raw
materials and corn.  For instance, it practically did not make
itself felt in Mecklenburg during this first period.  But, as will
be explained more fully later on in this book, Napoleon's attitude toward the supplying of England with foodstuffs was so
opportunistic, that it is not worth while to attempt to draw any
conclusions in principle as to the results that might have
ensued.  So much may be asserted, however : the difficulties
of the agrarian countries were due, not to Napoleon's deliberate
intention to cut off England from the supply of foodstuffs or
raw materials, but to his very well-grounded apprehension that
an export to England from countries which were not directly
under his sway would give rise to the importation of colonial
goods and English manufactures.  In this way, primarily,

---

[1] The great advantages accruing to the northern countries in their intercourse
with Great Britain constitute the main contention upheld in J. Jepson Oddy's
valuable book, *European Commerce* (London, 1805), and his figures bear out his
statements.  As regards Russia, he ' cannot help observing how amazingly advantageous its trade is with the British dominions.  Not only is the amount of the
sales nearly equal to those of all other nations, but it is from Great Britain only
that Russia receives a balance in cash ' (p. 209).

the situation for both Prussia and Russia is explained. During the second period of the Continental System, it is true, the difficulties for the agrarian countries were increased; but that was because all maritime trade within Napoleon's sphere of power was now made dependent on French licences, that is to say, on the Emperor's need of money or his favour. The particular ill-will with which the Continental System was manifestly regarded in the agrarian countries is explained less by the actual damage it did to the economic life of those countries than by the fact that the policy did not contain any protectionist elements, and consequently did not offer the popular imagination any compensation whatever for the incessant and intensely irritating intervention that it caused.

As regards all the continental states within Napoleon's realm of power, the Continental System had a restrictive effect on exports by throwing difficulties in the way of imports, which it is the sole business of exports to pay for. One may also express the matter in this way : increased self-sufficiency must diminish the need of exports by diminishing imports. The only reasonably conceivable exception from this might be if in any case imports by land increased more than imports by sea diminished ; and it is not impossible that the greatly extended intercourse of Saxony with Eastern Europe led to such a result.

### Great Britain

Such, from the standpoint of general principles, must have been the position of the continental states. In regard to Great Britain, on the other hand, one may express oneself more briefly at this stage. The prime object of Napoleon's policy, of course, was to bring about a dislocation, to prevent the sale both of manufactured products and of the colonial goods imported with a view to re-export, and consequently to ruin the credit system and create unemployment in industry. So long as it was a question only of such ephemeral phenomena, the contrast between Great Britain and the Continent must have been very great, with excess of goods prevailing on the island kingdom and scarcity of goods prevailing on the Continent. On the other hand, in so far as the exclusion of goods from the Continent proved to be lasting and was not made unimportant through increased sales in other parts of the world, the economic life of Great Britain necessarily aimed in the same direction as that of the Continent, namely, toward increased self-sufficiency. The losses incurred in foreign trade, shipping and export industry, indeed, must have made production for sale at home more profitable and thus have given a backward wrench to the unprecedented development which Great Britain was just then undergoing. There is nothing to indicate that Napoleon thought so far ahead ; on the contrary, any such speculations would undoubtedly have been answered by one of his usual candid expressions about ' ideologues '. But that would not have prevented the results from being what we have indicated.

Manifestly, this would have damaged the economic position of Great Britain immensely, quite apart from the great dislocations that occurred during the period of transition. It would have reduced her national income far below what it had been before, inasmuch as such a development would have involved passing over from industries which were excellently suited to her in her then position to other industries which were far less suitable. For this reason, too, the losses consequent upon a lasting mutual embargo between Great Britain and the rest of the world would have been far greater for Great Britain than for the Continent. For the international division of labour, specialization in industry and commerce—to confine ourselves now to what was most typical at the time—formed the fundamental condition for the possibility of Britain to derive benefit from her position as the almost sole possessor of the great new inventions. The position of the continental states, on the other hand, was already, at the outbreak of the great struggle, so much less widely separated from economic self-sufficiency that a return thereto would have involved far more limited sacrifices. They would thereby, it is true, have largely lost the advantages of enjoying, by means of purchase from England, the fruits of the great inventions and of covering their requirements in transmarine goods ; and at the same time they would have had, with increased sacrifice and diminished results, to find substitutes for both by a kind of production which was in itself, from an economic point of view, misdirected. But the extent of all this must nevertheless have remained insignificant in comparison with the corresponding reshaping of Great Britain. Evidently this result by no means implies that the position of Great Britain would have been absolutely worse than that of the Continent, but only that Great Britain would thereby have lost far more considerable advantages which she had already gained. The turning back of the clock could only have had its worse effects on the situation in the country where the greatest advances in material development had just previously taken place. Whether Great Britain in the long run, under the suppositions just given, would have been able to preserve her relative precedence, is quite another question, and one which it is difficult to answer. Nevertheless, in this case the answer may quite well be conceived to be in the affirmative, and for the reason that the blockade itself rendered difficult, and would have continued to do so, the spread of the industrial revolution from Great Britain to the Continent. In reality, of course, the development did not at all follow this course; but, nevertheless, the theoretical results following from a given position are being examined in this place, not only to illustrate what the Continental self-blockade, thought out to its logical conclusion, would have involved, but also in order to be able to confront with it the actual course of development in due time.

### Countries having Intercourse with Great Britain

Finally, what must be made clear is the position of the countries which had unhampered supply from Great Britain, that is, chiefly Sweden and, before the complete carrying through of the American self-blockade, the United States. The position of these countries was necessarily marked by an abnormally facilitated supply, inasmuch as Great Britain was obliged to seek there the greatest possible compensation for the markets from which she was debarred. While the countries of the self-blockade were forced into the greatest possible many-sidedness of production, therefore, the countries now in question fell into a kind of hypertrophy of imports. This means that they were brought to buy industrial products and colonial goods in return for a relatively slight output of their own products—a development in itself very advantageous, in so far as it gives a great indirect result of the productive forces of the country. In contrast with these advantages, however, stand the dislocations in the economic organization of the country which would have been a consequence of the necessary discontinuance of previously existing branches of industry. But this was scarcely the case as regards either Sweden or America. Moreover, it is not really necessary in principle, because, as has been said, the development in itself merely implies that one gets more than usual in exchange for one's own goods. It is therefore of greater importance, from the standpoint of the temporary nature of the whole situation, that the industrial development of those countries was somewhat delayed by the exceptional facility of importing British goods, a matter which was of no little consequence for the United States. To this the workings of the Continental System in those countries would have been confined if the Napoleonic self-blockade of the Continent had been complete and effective. But as this was very far from the case, and as the breaking of the blockade was especially done by countries of the type now in question, there was a huge increase of re-exports, that is to say, of intermediary trade, and this became beyond all comparison the most important factor in the actual situation. Nevertheless, the importance of the former factor was not cancelled by this; there was also a great increase in the imports which remained within the country. Again, with the immense increase of prices for British and colonial goods on the Continent, the occupation of the middleman must obviously have been extremely profitable when successful, but, of course, proportionately speculative and uncertain.

Having set forth the position of the different countries in principle, we may now pass on to a consideration of the concrete development, which offers an abundance of instructive features to illustrate and compare with those of our own day.

# CHAPTER II

## EFFECTS ON FRANCE

The development of the industrial life of France under the influence of the Continental System, like the development of all the industrial countries under that system, took place especially in the sphere of textile industries; and nowhere did the conflicting tendencies appear so marked as there. Nevertheless, a great deal of the development of the French textile industry was not only devoid of connexion with the blockade policy itself, but, on the contrary, an evidence of its restricted range.[1]

### Luxury Industries

This applied especially to everything which falls under the heading of luxury industries, including the most brilliant and historic textile industry of France, the manufacture of silk. We, who only recently felt the pressure of a rigorous blockade and shortage of supplies, can best appreciate the fact that in

[1] Chaptal, *De l'industrie françoise*, vols. i–ii; Levasseur, *Histoire des classes ouvrières*, &c., *de 1789 à 1870*, vol. i, especially bk. ii, chs. v–vi, and bk. iii, chs. ii–iii; Darmstädter, *Studien zur napoleonischen Wirtschaftspolitik, loc. cit.*, vol. ii; Tarle, *Kontinental'naja blokada*, vol. i (devoted almost exclusively to the trade and industry of France); Ballot, *Les prêts aux manufactures, loc. cit.*, vol. ii; Schmidt, *Jean-Baptiste Say et le blocus continental*, in *Revue d'histoire des doctrines économiques et sociales* (1911), vol. iv, pp. 148 *et seq.*; also, *Les débuts de l'industrie cotonnière en France, 1760–1806, ibid.* (1914–19), vol. vii, pp. 26 *et seq.*; Ballot, *Philippe de Girard et l'invention de la filature mécanique du lin, ibid.* (1914–19), vol. vii, pp. 135 *et seq.*; also, *La révolution technique et les débuts de la grande exploitation dans la métallurgie française, ibid.* (1912), vol. v, pp. 29 *et seq.* For the incorporated territories, cf. Varlez, *Les salaires dans l'industrie gantoise* (Brussels, 1901), vol. i, pp. 9–36, and apps. iii and iv; vol. ii (1904), pp. 24–32; Herkner, *Die oberelsässische Baumwollindustrie und ihre Arbeiter* (Strassburg, 1887), pp. 35–93; T. Geering, *Die Entwicklung des Zeugdrucks im Abendland seit dem XVII. Jahrhundert*, in *Vierteljahrschrift für Social- und Wirtschaftsgeschichte* (1903), vol. i (founded principally upon the great work of A. Jenny-Trümpy, *Handel und Industrie des Kantons Glarus, und in Parallele dazu: Skizze der allgemeinen Geschichte der Textilindustrien mit besonderer Berücksichtigung der schweizerischen Zeugdruckerei*; Glarus, 1899–1902); Darmstädter, *Die Verwaltung des Unter-Elsass*, &c., *loc. cit.*, vol. xix (1904), pp. 631–72; Zeyss, *Die Entstehung der Handelskammern*, &c., pp. 62–90, 103–29. For comparison with England, cf. especially Mantoux, *La révolution industrielle au XVIIIᵉ siècle. Essai sur les commencements de la grande industrie moderne en Angleterre* (Paris, 1906), and Baines, *History of the Cotton Manufacture of Great Britain*.

such a situation the production of luxuries would hardly expand and take more and more varied forms, and perhaps still more the fact that governments, however great their lack of intelligence in the sphere of economics, would be foolhardy indeed to go so far as to encourage, not to say enforce, such production. As this was the case during the first French empire, therefore, it is in the very nature of things that the cause can not be sought in the Continental System regarded as a measure of blockade against Great Britain. On the other hand, it is intimately connected with the general protectionist tendency that completely dominated Napoleon and forms the explanation of the peculiar nature of the Continental System as contrasted with the corresponding system of the present day. It was precisely the historic luxury industries of France that the inheritor of the administrative traditions of the Bourbons most unhesitatingly and enthusiastically supported; and it was mainly in the interest of the silk industry that, on the one side, a licensing system was carried out with its obligation to export French industrial products, and, on the other side, the commercial measures against the allies of France, which comprised a monopolization of Italian raw silk for the requirements of the French silk industry and every conceivable measure against the foreign rivals of that industry.

The vaunting luxury in both word and deed, which in Napoleon's view was a principal means of raising the prestige of the empire both internally and externally, also worked particularly well with the tendency to create sales for industries of the kind in which the French had excelled for centuries; and a great deal of the encouragement of industry therefore consisted, quite naturally, in orders of all kinds on behalf of the court and imperial palace. Probably the fact that such a policy diverted productive forces from turning out what was necessary for the support of the people as well as for the prosecution of the war, did not greatly occupy Napoleon's thoughts. To him, in fact, the function of economics presented itself more in the light of the popular notion of the necessity of ' providing employment ' than as a need to bring about the greatest possible result from the efforts of limited powers. But in this respect a far more correct perception has forced its way into the minds of the governments of nearly all countries during the recent war—the German *Vaterländischer Hilfsdienst* (vulgo, *Zivildienstpflicht*), the British National Service, and various other names, form the best evidence of this—despite almost equally great economic ignorance in the beginning; and this shows how comparatively gentle, after all, was the pressure of the Continental System in comparison with that of the recent war. As the object of our investigation is to determine the actual effects of the blockade policy, therefore, there is no reason to pursue any further the industrial development on its luxury side.

## WOOLLEN AND LINEN INDUSTRIES

On the other hand, the situation is quite different in the case of the other branches of the textile industry. Of these, the cloth manufacture had quite as deep roots in the history of France as the silk industry; and it had, like that, and in fact like the whole of French industrial life, suffered greatly from the storms of the revolution, both through the general insecurity of life and limb and through the hopeless state of the currency in consequence of the *assignat* system. It now raised itself out of its decay and had a brilliant period, which, —for instance, in Rheims—surpassed the last years of the *ancien régime*, which was now justly remembered as having marked the summit level of old French material culture. Undoubtedly, the development of the woollen industry was promoted by Napoleon's policy, especially by careful work in the way of production of wool and the procurement of wool from Spain, and also with regard to the coarser clothing in consequence of the military requirements, which always and everywhere in our climes make special demands on this branch of the textile trade. Remarkably enough, so far as one can judge, the greatest progress was made in one of the incorporated territories, namely, the Roer department, meaning that particular part of the present Rhine province which is situated on the left bank of the Rhine (Nieder-Rhein). In the now world-famous textile centres, Aix-la-Chapelle, Cologne, &c., there were almost the only industrial centres which the old French manufacturers recognized as equal rivals in the finer branches of the clothing trade.[1] It is true that the blockade against Great Britain also played its part here, and still more, perhaps, the blockade against the continental rivals of France. But we cannot speak here of any at all decisive effect of the Continental System itself, as the woollen industry was long established in France and was not brought to any distinctly higher state of prosperity than it had attained before the Revolution, despite the fact that various new specialities were taken up and also various technical advances were made, of which more anon. Thus it was principally for the regions which had previously been outside France, or had been treated by the customs authorities as foreign countries, that the policy became important, inasmuch as it gave them a share of the sales on what was at least intended to be the hermetically-sealed French market. According to Chaptal's calculation, exports had indeed absolutely declined, if one takes into consideration only the old French territory, although internal sales and the total production had increased since 1789. The situation was less favourable as regards the linen industry, where even in the incorporated territories it was only the Belgian district of Ghent that showed any marked development.

## COTTON INDUSTRY

Especially with regard to the linen and woollen industries, however, it is true that the comparatively slow development was caused by the expansion of the cotton industry, an expansion which was unique, and, in the eyes of contemporaries, quite phenomenal. Here there is no doubt that we are brought

[1] Cf. a pronouncement of the leading man in the clothing industry, Ternaux, sen., in *Conseil général des manufactures,* immediately after the Restoration ; printed in Levasseur, *Histoire des classes ouvrières,* &c., *de 1789 à 1870,* vol. I, p. 732, app. A.

face to face with an effect of the Continental System ; for, on one side, the whole of this branch of industry was comparatively undeveloped before the Revolution, while, on the other side, the competition of Great Britain was more overwhelming here than anywhere else in the industrial life of France. The French people had already accustomed themselves to cotton goods to such an extent that the prohibition on imports in 1806 was all that was required to speed up the domestic production amazingly, especially as the foundation had been largely laid by the many prohibitions and embargoes during the whole of the preceding decade.

Here again it was two incorporated territories that exhibited the most violent growth, namely, Mülhausen in Upper Alsace, with old traditions in that line, and Ghent, which under the leadership of one man, Liévin Bauwens, the great captain of industry, stands out as a striking example of one of the two kinds of development due to the Continental System. Ghent, it is true, had old and boasted textile traditions, dating from the Middle Ages ; but long before the Revolution almost all manufacture had disappeared there, and as the revolutionary wars put an end to the little that remained, this old manufacturing centre had come to be looked upon as a dead town. In 1801, however, Liévin Bauwens started there a machine cotton-spinning mill and also a hand weaving establishment. To begin with, he was almost alone in the matter, being helped merely by his brothers, but as early as 1803 he had no less than 227 workmen. It was not long before his example began to be followed by a number of other persons, especially relatives, who entered into violent competition with him, particularly for the altogether inadequate supply of labour. An enormous expansion thereupon began; the whole of Flanders and northern France were covered with spinning-mills and home weavers, the new enterprises extending, in fact, as far as Paris and its environs. But Ghent remained the main centre, and for a fairly long time it was the only place in the empire where cotton goods were manufactured on a large scale, especially for military requirements ; and it also obtained as markets, not only France and Belgium, but also Holland, Italy, Spain and the larger part of Germany. At the summit level of this prosperity the former ' dead town ' was stated to have fifty factories and ten thousand workers in the cotton trade; and the shortage of labour was so great that wages jumped up to what was then the amazing amount of 5–8 francs *per diem*.

In contrast with this production for sale on a large scale there existed in Mülhausen, and in southern Alsace in general— and had long existed—a flourishing manufacture of the finest qualities of calicoes and printed cotton goods. The real impetus, however, came with the annexation of the town by the French republic in 1798; and the Continental System made it the leading centre for calicoes and prints upon the Continent, at the expense both of Basel and of British sales in Europe. The importance of the development at Mülhausen appears best, perhaps, from the population statistics, which show an increase from 6,628 in the year 1800 to 8,021 in 1805 and 9,353 in 1810, a growth of 41 per cent. in ten years. Alongside this, however, there were also very important and comparatively new centres for the cotton trade within the limits of old France, especially in the old textile districts of northern France and in Paris and its suburbs. One of the most celebrated French leaders of industry, Richard Lenoir, was stated by a German observer who is generally regarded as reliable (Fahnenberg) to have had in his factories such for that time incredible numbers of workmen as 10,600 in 1808 and 14,000 in 1810. According to the statements of Chaptal, who is throughout obviously a partisan of the new industry, it is true, but who in spite of this is in many ways our most reliable source of information, the production of cotton yarn was already sufficient for home requirements almost up to the highest number (finest grades)—in reality, however, up to number 100 only. Even as regards woven cotton goods, in his opinion, the imports had declined to about 6 per cent. of the figure for the last year of the *ancien régime*; but in this estimate a considerable amount of smuggling, for which an overwhelming evidence exists, was assuredly left out of account. It is also worthy of note that what was at times a very considerable export of piece goods had begun.

Evidently this development was calculated to give Napoleon himself and his helpers a great certainty of victory, both as an evidence of the profitableness of the Continental System to France and as a blow against the economic supremacy of Great Britain. To what a great extent the whole thing was regarded as an important item in the struggle against Great Britain is shown by many facts. When Napoleon visited Oberkampf, the most famous of the leaders of the cotton industry, who as early as 1760 had laid the foundation of calico printing in old France by the establishment of his famous works at Jouy, outside Versailles, he decorated him and added the explanation : ' We are both carrying on war against the British, but your war is the best.' And Liévin Bauwens produced a wonderful judgment on the part of the British Court of King's Bench, by which, on the accusation of Lord Erskine, he had been condemned to death *in contumaciam*, because, ' not content with having stolen the secrets of England in the art of tanning, he had also robbed her of the most important branch of her trade, the cotton manufacture, which was the apple of her eye.'

In reality, however, there was no point where the two opposing tendencies of the Continental System were so much in conflict with one another as here ; and the reason was, of course, that the industry was based on a raw material which was for the most part unobtainable by other means than by the forbidden route across the seas. From the very first moment, therefore, the shortage of raw materials hung like the sword of Damocles over the head of the flourishing new development, causing continual fluctuations and constant changes. During the year 1808, for instance, Liévin Bauwens, according to his own statement, employed 1,269 workmen on May 1, but only 230 on November 1 ; and the same state of affairs was said to prevail among his competitors. Moreover, according to the same authority, the price of raw cotton rose at the same time from 5.25 to 11 or 12 francs per half a kilo and then sank to

6 or 7. As early as 1807 the shortage of raw cotton had begun to make itself felt in France, and in the course of 1808 it produced a genuine crisis in the cotton industry, which found expression in many forms. Thus, for instance, the prefect of the Aube department declared that the closing of the spinning-mills in Troyes caused by the ' equally sudden and unique rise in the price of raw cotton ' had reduced 10,000 people to misery ; and on this account he submitted a placard which was apparently insurrectionary.[1]  According to another statement, the difficulties of the French weaving mills were further increased by the fact that the weaving mills in Germany and Switzerland, owing to the scarcity of yarn prevailing there, had gotten hold of French cotton yarn and thus rendered that dearer. The difficulty was partly overcome this time, and the state of prosperity continued into the year 1810, which as a rule marks the summit level of the industrial prosperity of France, as also of England and the non-French parts of the Continent. But then, as we know, came the great crisis, of which the shortage of raw cotton formed one of the most obvious causes; and this shortage was made worse by Napoleon's Rambouillet decree, issued in the spring of 1810, which dealt a severe blow at American shipping. During the following years of the empire the shortage became more and more acute, and in 1813 it led to a complete stoppage of operations.

The whole of this position is not in the least degree difficult to explain, but its importance is worthy of illustration with figures. The available statistics especially show how practically impossible any real competition with the British industry—or, to be more explicit, the impossibility of creating an industry that could provide the whole population of the Continent with cotton goods on approximately the same terms as were offered to British and American consumers—must have been made by the mere fact that raw material was scarce or unobtainable. (See next page.)

On examining the columns for North and South American

[1] Report to the home secretary, June 15, 1808, printed in Tarle, *Kontinental'-naja blokada*, vol. I, 720–1.

PRICES OF RAW COTTON IN GREAT BRITAIN AND ON THE CONTINENT (FRANCS PER KILOGRAM)[1]

| Year | South American (Pernambuco) | | | North American (Bowed Georgia) | | Levantine (Smyrna) | |
| | London | Leipzig | Paris, Ghent | London | Leipzig | Leipzig | Paris, Ghent |
| --- | --- | --- | --- | --- | --- | --- | --- |
| Easter 1806 . . . | 4·64-4·87 | 6·80-7·04 | 6·80-7·30 | 2·78-3·02 | — | 4·40-4·48 | — |
| 1807 . . . | 4·87-5·10 | 7·60 | 8·10-15·00 | 2·78-3·25 | 6·00 | 4·32 | — |
| 1808 . . . | 4·87-5·33 | 19·20 | 24·00 | 5·57-6·96 | 12·80 | 7·68 | 15·00 |
| 1809 . . . | 4·64-5·10 | 20·00 | — | 2·32-2·78 | 10·40 | 6·08-6·16 | — |
| 1810 . . . | 5·80-6·26 | 16·80 | 12·00-14·00 | 3·94-4·41 | 7·60 | 6·56-6·80 | 8·00-10·00 |
| 1811 . . . | 3·25-3·48 | 8·00-8·48 | 16·00-16·40 | 1·52-2·09 | 5·60-6·40 | 4·48 | 9·00-9·20 |
| 1812 . . . | 3·94-4·64 | 11·20 | 13·00-13·50 | 2·55-3·02 | 4·16 | 4·16 | 8·50-10·00 |
| 1813 . . . | 5·33-5·57 | 10·40 | — | 3·71-4·41 | 6·08 | 4·48 | — |
| 1814 . . . | 6·03-6·73 | 7·68 | — | 6·50-6·96 | 6·08 | 4·80-5·04 | — |

[1] Sources: London: Tooke, A History of Prices, &c., tables of prices; Leipzig: König, Die Sächsische Baumwollenindustrie, &c. (table, p. 219); Paris: (1806-8, 1811), Levasseur, Histoire des classes ouvrières, &c., de 1789 à 1870, vol. I, p. 422 note 4 (his figures on p. 488 note 3, on the other hand, are quite untrustworthy); Tarle, Kontinental'naja blokada, vol. I, pp. 510, 512 (in the latter passage the text has funt = lb.—evidently a mistake for kg.); Ghent: (1810, 1812), Varlez, op. cit., vol. I, p. 32 and app. IV. All these figures have been reduced to a common basis at par. For the years 1808 and 1811 there are figures (reproduced on p. 276 post) for other places on the Continent, according to Tarle, loc. cit. The time of the year is for Leipzig that specified in the table, and for London approximately the same (about Mar. 22-Apr. 7). The only exception is that, in the absence of figures for the Easter fair, the Michaelmas prices have been used for North American cotton at Leipzig in 1808 and for Levantine cotton there in 1811; and for the sake of consistency herewith, the London prices for 1808 refer to the period Nov. 8-15. For Paris and Ghent the time of the year varies more, or else is undetermined; and in consequence of this the figures are both less comparable with the others and less safe to build upon.

cotton we note the enormous distance between British and continental prices. During the years 1808–13 the prices, even in Leipzig, the centre of the European cotton trade, are almost without exception twice as high as in London, and in certain years (1808–9) they are four times as high. To a far greater extent than one would have expected beforehand, the figures follow one another at similar distances—a fact which appears with particular clearness in the increase of price on Georgia cotton in 1808 (autumn) and in the fall of prices corresponding to both qualities in 1811. This illustrates what has been previously said concerning the almost uniform increase of prices caused by smuggling. It is quite true, indeed, that we have no security here for agreement in quality between the different quotations; but the conclusions here put forward may be said to hold good *a fortiori*, as at least one factor is excluded which would increase, and not diminish, the distance, namely, the heavy depreciation of British currency, which makes the British prices too high when, as here, they are converted to francs at par. A levelling-down tendency first appeared in 1813, in connexion with the Anglo-American war, which raised the British prices, and the fall of the Continental System on the European mainland, which lowered the continental prices; and the year 1814, owing to the continuance of the former factor and the peace on the Continent, led to a unique situation, in that Georgia cotton was cheaper in Leipzig than in London.

However, the table shows something more, namely, that the French prices without exception stood higher than the Leipzig prices. Nor is this surprising, in view of the stricter customs watch in France; but it is none the less a fact which made still more difficult the position of the French cotton industry. Unfortunately, it is precisely these figures that least bear comparison in the table; but light can be thrown on the matter by other figures, based on French consular reports, for a number of different places at the same two points of time, namely, the two crises of May 1808 and June 1811. If we arrange these places as nearly as possible in accordance with the magnitude of the prices, the figures assume the following shape (francs per kilogram):

| City | May 1808 | | | City | June 1811 | |
| | Pernambuco | Louisiana | Smyrna | | Brazil | Levantine |
|---|---|---|---|---|---|---|
| Marseilles | — | — | 6·50 | London | 2·30 | 1·28 |
| Antwerp | 10·81 | 8·40 | 6·92 | Naples | — | 4·38 |
| Paris | 12·00 | 9·50 | 7·50 | Trieste | — | 5·08–7·55 |
| Rouen | 12·90 | 10·00 | 7·92 | Leipzig | 8·28 | 5·78 |
| | | | | Frankfurt | — | 6·55–7·20 |
| | | | | Basel | — | 6·96 |
| | | | | Milan | — | 7·55 |
| | | | | Paris | 16·00–16·40 | 9·00–9·20 |
| | | | | Bremen | — | 9·61 |

As we see from this table, the French industrial centres come last, with the sole exception, at the later time, of Bremen.

As all this necessarily followed from the nature of the self-blockade, it could not take Napoleon by surprise; and in point of fact he was prepared for it, although his counter-measures were somewhat hesitating. At times the only expedient he saw was to replace the colonial cotton by some other cotton which did not have to be obtained by sea. The most obvious kind was Levantine, but here, too, there were great difficulties, arising partly from its short staple and generally inferior quality and partly from the great delays and inconveniences of transportation, as it could not be conveyed across the Mediterranean and as a very expensive transport in wheeled vehicles had consequently to be arranged through Bosnia *via* Genoa and Marseilles. The figures given above also show how the French prices for Levantine cotton ran up, even in comparison with the British prices for the far more valuable American cotton. The situation was all the more unsatisfactory because Napoleon would by no means be satisfied with the coarse goods that alone could be produced from Levantine cotton. Thus there arose the idea of starting the cultivation of cotton nearer home, preferably within the borders of the empire; and in this connexion the most obvious choice was Naples. Naples, to use the expression of the French envoy

there, was to be ' France's richest colony ', or, to borrow a
phrase from a French historian,[1] ' the tropical element ' in the
Continental System ; it was this fact that caused Neapolitan
cotton alone to be excepted from the enormously increased
customs duties imposed by the Trianon tariff. But the cotton
that could be obtained from Naples (Castellamare), even in combination with that which was admitted in later years from Spain
(Motril) and with what could be otherwise scraped together
from places nearer home (from Romagna, &c.), supplied but
a small fraction of the total requirements ; on the basis of
Chaptal's figures for the output of the spinning-mills in 1812,
one may perhaps calculate this supply at 12 per cent. of the
whole.[2]

All this was so obvious that Napoleon could never feel
unmixed joy at the prodigious development of the cotton
industry, but, on the contrary, time after time occupied his
thoughts with the idea of rooting out cotton goods and replacing
them by other textiles, such as had long been manufactured
in France and were based on domestic raw materials. Even
as early as 1809 he declared that ' it would be better to use only
wool, flax, and silk, the products of our own soil, and to proscribe
cotton forever on the Continent, because we have no colonies ;
but as we cannot control the fashions, of course, . . . '[3]

The same thought lay behind his resolution, effected in
the following year, to offer a prize of no less than a million
francs for the invention of a flax-spinning machine; but
after the outbreak of the crisis of 1810–11, he took such a strong
step against what was after all largely his own work as, in
January 1811, to banish cotton goods from the imperial palaces.
But for the very reason that Napoleon had given two years
previously, the extirpation of cotton goods—at which he
assuredly did not even aim at this stage—was a hopeless

[1] Rambaud, *Naples sous Joseph Bonaparte*, p. 437.
[2] The weight of spun yarn in 1812 was 13,470,000 kgs., which with the addition of
one-twelfth for loss of weight corresponds to 14,590,000 kgs. of cotton. In comparison
with this the supply of Italian and Spanish cotton was 3,000,000–4,000,000 livres
(French pounds), or an average of 1,750,000 kgs. Chaptal, *op. cit.*, vol. II, pp. 7, 15.
[3] Quoted by Tarle, *Kontinental'nuja blokada*, vol. I, p. 513.

undertaking ; and he, like his people, had to take the consequences of a situation from which there was no escape.

The development of the cotton industry is characteristic
of the effects of the Continental System, not only through the
dualism that existed between the exclusion of raw materials
and the forcing of manufacture, but to an equal extent through
the violently enforced stimulation of a production that had not
grown up out of increasing natural requirements for an article
but out of a sudden embargo in combination with state measures
of all kinds.   There is no doubt that great over-speculation had
occurred in the industry and had had its share in the French
crisis of 1810–11, just as a similar over-speculation in the colonial
trade gave the impulse to the crisis in Great Britain.   Mollien,
an observer who formed unusually cool judgments, pointed
this out in a letter to Napoleon, and especially called his
attention to the insufficient supply of capital possessed by the
industry and its consequent dependence on loans and bills
of exchange.   In his memoirs he is, on the whole, very critical
not only of the heads of factories, especially Richard Lenoir,
whose untenable business position and reckless way of living
he says that he explained to the Emperor, but also of the
industry itself, where, in his opinion, many millions had been
invested in what could have been made equally serviceable
at half the expense.[1]

When, after some months, the crisis of 1810 reached the
cotton industry, it hit it very hard and effectively, especially
the spinning-mills, which as a rule seem to have seen their
number of workmen decline by a third in the course of 1811.
There was a general improvement in the course of 1812 which
continued in places during most of the following year, at least
if we may credit the deliberately roseate reports of the home
secretary to Napoleon in the latter half of 1813.   But the Ghent
industry declined steadily early in 1813, and later on in the same
year, that is to say, before the fall of Napoleon, the decline
spread in ever-widening circles.   Probably with great exaggeration, but certainly not without grounds, the Executive Committee

[1] Mollien, *Mémoires*, &c., vol. III, pp. 12, 22 *et seq.*

for Cotton of the Council of Manufactures expressed the view in the following year, immediately after the Restoration, that the whole of this branch of industry was ruined in 1813 to such an extent that 600,000 individuals had to choose between begging or putting an end to their misery on a battlefield. Capital to the amount of 300,000,000 francs was paralysed and working power to the value of 230,000,000 francs was lost. The most comprehensible picture of the decline from the summit year of 1810 to the autumn of 1813 is offered by the official figures for the Ghent industries, reproduced on the next page.[1]

We note in these figures the powerful effect of the crisis of 1811 as regards the spinning-mills, but, in contrast with this, no effect at all as regards the weaving-mills or printing works, while the decline in 1813, with a quite different kind of uniformity, extends over all branches of the industry; and, if we judge by the number of spindles, it implies a reduction of almost a half.

The strongest evidence of the enforced stimulation of the industry, however, is shown in the events occurring at the fall of Napoleon. When the frontiers were opened in connexion with the march of the allied armies, and later, in April 1814, formally opened by a series of decrees issued by the Provisional Government, the cotton industry collapsed altogether, and almost all the leading manufacturers were ruined. The majority of them—chiefly Richard Lenoir, but also Liévin Bauwens—had received liberal support in the form of loans from Napoleon during the crisis of 1810–11, which they had not been able to repay; and with the fall of the empire all prospect of their ever repaying them disappeared. Bauwens, who had been lauded in every conceivable fashion as the benefactor of his town and as a pillar of the prosperity of France, saw his property sold by distraint, and he himself had to flee to Paris to escape imprisonment. Chaptal particularly regrets the ruin of the

---

[1] Varlez, *op. cit.*, vol. I, app. III. The reports of the home secretary are printed in Tarle, *op. cit.*, vol. I, pp. 735 *et seq. The Report of the Committee of the Council of Manufactures* in 1814 is printed in Levasseur, *Histoire des classes ouvrières*, &c., *de 1789 à 1870*, vol. I, pp. 726–7, app. A.

COTTON INDUSTRY OF GHENT

| Period | Spindles at work | Raw cotton (Kgs.) | Spinners employed | Looms at work | Weavers employed | Goods (pieces) | Printers employed | Printed goods (pieces) |
|---|---|---|---|---|---|---|---|---|
| 1st half-year 1810 | 110,716 | 288,570 | 1,228 | 2,908 | 3,065 | 53,059 | 615 | 35,786 |
| 2d ,, ,, 1810 | 115,810 | 276,866 | 1,280 | 2,703 | 2,728 | 48,378 | 637 | 39,842 |
| 1st ,, ,, 1811 | 77,266 | 169,193 | 1,076 | 2,800 | 2,960 | 49,572 | 624 | 29,665 |
| 2d ,, ,, 1811 | 74,632 | 187,075 | 1,062 | 2,956 | 3,366 | 58,241 | 641 | 31,135 |
| 1st ,, ,, 1812 | 103,020 | 264,260 | 1,183 | 3,611 | 4,027 | 69,725 | 747 | 35,943 |
| 3d quarter 1812 | 103,020 | 132,100 | 1,183 | 3,611 | 4,015 | 34,805 | 756 | 18,250 |
| 4th ,, 1812 | 103,644 | 141,061 | 1,185 | 2,996 | 3,608 | 34,089 | 699 | 34,024 |
| 1st ,, 1813 | 70,042 | 118,413 | 624 | 2,119 | 2,329 | 19,873 | 408 | 18,573 |
| 2d ,, 1813 | 60,798 | 75,197 | 506 | 1,979 | 2,329 | 20,600 | 490 | 21,165 |
| 3d ,, 1813 | 64,056 | 84,944 | 306 | 1,367 | 1,510 | 15,990 | 213 | 28,852 |

great nankeen manufacture owing to the overwhelming competition of Indian and British goods, which were allowed to enter on payment of duty ; and the amount of the duty was in reality, according to circumstances, 45–50 centimes per metre, which can not have been less than 20–25 per cent. of the value of the goods and consequently no mean protection in itself.[1]  But, of course, this was a very considerable step from complete embargo, despite the smuggling.

Whatever construction one may put on the matter, the fate of the French cotton industry on the fall of Napoleon shows that it had by no means become capable, during the time of the blockade, of holding its own against foreign competition.  Nor is the great prosperity which, after a quite short interval, occurred under the Restoration any real evidence of its competitive efficiency, inasmuch as a prohibition of the imports of foreign textiles was almost immediately re-introduced; and the protection of the industry was thereby even considerably increased, as raw cotton now came in free.  Indeed, as will be shown throughout this chapter, the technical advances in French industry were not, on the whole, very great under the Continental System, and they still fell far behind Great Britain in almost every respect.  Without the help of Englishmen very little progress could as yet be made in anything which had to do with engineering or metal working industries ; and Liévin Bauwens, for instance, started his machine spinning-mills with the help of five foremen whom he had virtually kidnapped from England, and whom he detained half with their consent and half by violence.  As has been indicated before, however, it was almost inevitable that the blows of the Continental decrees against everything living or dead which bore the name of English should have a restraining effect on the spread of English ideas and the removal of English mechanics or inventors to the Continent ; and, indeed, Mollien said somewhat bitingly, in connexion with his

----

[1] *Loi relative aux douanes*, Dec. 17, 1814.  *Bulletin des lois*, &c., 5th ser., bull. 62, no. 529.  Cf. Levasseur, *Histoire des classes ouvrières*, &c., *de 1789 à 1870*, vol. i, pp. 562 *et seq.*

general criticism of the new industry, that the machinery was built by ' roving Englishmen who were not the best mechanics of their country '. Chaptal's complacent account of how, through his far-sightedness, machines were procured which were the best in Europe and were continually being developed by improvements from without and by native invention, must also be taken *cum grano salis*.

This appears best from what, in the main, is distinctive of the two great branches of industry that were revolutionized by the inventions of the immediately preceding generation (the textile and iron industries), namely, that France and the Continent in general were even at the time of Napoleon's fall far from being in a position to take up the new fundamental processes on which the industrial life of England had been based for quite a long time.

### Fundamental Processes

In the sphere of the textile industry this holds good both of the power to spin high numbers of yarn (fine grades), the use of the steam-engine in the spinning industry, and the power-loom. Regarding the first of these, as has already been mentioned, they had not gotten beyond number 100 in cotton yarn in 1815; it was reserved for the Restoration to move forward in a few years to number 200 or (as a rarity) even 291. With regard to the steam-engine, we have already mentioned that one single French spinning-mill had passed, as early as 1787 (the year after the Eden Treaty) to the use of steam power, which was at that date a complete novelty even in England. It would be difficult to find anything more indicative of the technical stagnation which then occurred than the fact that the next time a French steam spinning-mill is mentioned is no less than twenty-five years later. It was not until 1812 that the pioneering firm of Dollfus, Mieg & Cie., which is still famous all over the world, set up such a mill in Mülhausen— that is to say, in an incorporated territory. Power-loom works, which, it is true, came far later than the revolution in spinning in England also, but which nevertheless began to be set up there as early as 1801, are scarcely mentioned on the Continent during the whole of this period. The only examples known to the writer from the territory of the empire—where, for that matter, there is a total lack of detail—belong, like steam spinning-mills, to the incorporated territories, namely, Ghent and Sennheim (in Upper Alsace); and neither of them can have been of any great consequence, as the information about them is so sporadic. In the department of mechanical printing, it is true, greater advances were made on the Continent, in that the great invention in this department, cylinder printing, appears to have come into use at Oberkampf's factory at Jouy, as the first place on the Continent, in 1800, and in Mülhausen and other places in 1805–6; but even this was just twenty years after the institution of similar technical processes in England. In the department of engineering technics it was only outside the cotton industry that the Continent during this period ever took the lead in any decisive respect, namely, as regards both the Jacquard loom, which at first really served the silk industry alone, and Girard's invention of a flax-spinning machine. This last, which was patented in 1810 and thus realized one of Napoleon's hopes, significantly enough, left France before anything had been achieved; the inventor had to flee from his creditors to Austria, and an Englishman got hold of his invention. This gave rise to a flourishing English industry, which did not return to the native country of the inventor until twenty-five years after the invention. The continental textile industry reached the same level as the British textile industry in only one single department, namely, in dyeing and other branches where chemistry could be employed, of which more anon.

## IRON INDUSTRY

Still more striking is the stagnation and backwardness of French economic life in the sphere of the iron industry; and it is highly significant that Chaptal, in his detailed and enthusiastic description of the progress of industry, here confines himself exclusively to the department of manufacturing—especially the making of scythes, pins and needles, files, awls, hammers, and other tools—and says nothing about the production of iron, although it was just that which in England had undergone a complete revolution in all its stages during the preceding period. The explanation must be found in an almost incredible backwardness attributable to the French iron industry, which is all the more remarkable in view of the fact that that branch of industry was manifestly of the greatest importance in the incessant wars, and, to judge by accessible figures, had also undergone a very great quantitative development. Nevertheless, the fact itself seems to be quite evident, as shall now be shown.

Although coking and the making of pig-iron by means of coke—that is to say, the smelting of iron-ore with the help of fossil fuel—date back to about 1735, and at least twenty years later had begun to be widespread in English iron-working, French smelting-furnaces continued to be operated almost entirely with charcoal, even after 1808, in spite of the shortage of wood which made its appearance in that year. The only known example of coke smelting-furnaces was offered by the now world-famous Creusot works, which had started the new methods in 1785; but the entire process went steadily backward during the revolutionary era. In 1796 the iron was so bad that it could be used only for ballast; in 1806 the orders of cannon for the Navy were taken away; and the annual production during the years 1809 to 1812 rose to no more than 2,300 to 3,000 tons. Quite parallel was the case with the revolutionary change in the production of malleable iron—smelting in Cort's reverberatory furnace or the puddling process—which freed this second stage of iron-working from dependence on charcoal. This invention was considerably younger, it is true, as it dates from 1783; but even during the eighties it had come into use in England and was at the time of the Continental System widely employed in English iron-working. During the years 1802 and 1803 it had been searchingly studied by the Swede, Svedenstjerna, and the Frenchman, Bonnard, working together. Here, too, the Creusot works seem to have been the only ones of any importance, inasmuch as a reverberatory furnace was started there in 1810, though it is not clear whether this involved any use of coal fuel ; other experiments with puddling were failures from the very start.

As regards the production of steel, that is to say, iron with a large content of carbon, Huntsman—also in England— had found a solution of the problem of producing cast-steel (crucible steel) about 1750, a solution which was rapidly noised abroad and twenty years later was pretty generally adopted in England. On the Continent this method seems to have been introduced in 1808 by the Swiss manufacturer, J. C. Fischer, whose establishment outside Schaffhausen became the object of great attention ; and in 1812 the firm of Krupp was founded for the same purpose. But in the territories of the French empire only one isolated example of such manufacture is known, and that was introduced by two Belgians in Liège, incorporated territory. Finally, the level attained was also remarkably low in the engineering trade, which in England was already enormously developed as compared with the pre-ceding period. The real pioneers in this respect within the French empire seem to have been two Scotsmen, father and son, of the afterwards famous name of Cockerill, who—also in Liège, in 1807—laid the foundation of the Belgian engineer-ing trade.[1]

Thus France proper and the most important parts of the empire, as regards the iron and iron-working industries, prac-tically remained unaffected by the advances of the preceding generation ; this fact stands out in comparison, not only with England, but also with Germany, as well as Sweden, a country which held fast to old processes, but which even with them had attained great eminence. Consequently, the economist Blanqui was quite justified in saying toward the close of the Restoration that the advances in the iron industry in France were made almost entirely after 1814. In consequence of this the French iron industry in 1814 was quite defenceless in face of foreign

[1] Besides the above-named works, cf. a petition presented by Cort's son in 1812 (Hansard, vol. xxi, pp. 329 et seq.) ; Beck, *Geschichte des Eisens* (Braunschweig, 1897), vol. III, pp. 692 et seq., 1089 et seq. ; vol. IV (1899), pp. 165 et seq. Cf. also *Allgemeine Deutsche Biographie*, s.v. J. C. Fischer.

competitors, who were stated to sell at 30–40 per cent. under French prices; the blockade had had no more stimulating effect than that a 50 per cent. customs duty was necessary to keep the industry going.

The total impression we get in these essential industries, therefore, may be summarized somewhat as follows: The effect of the Continental System was primarily to exclude at least the industry of the French empire from British influences; and under the conditions then prevailing these influences were indispensable for every country desirous of participating in the fruits of the great economic revolution.

### CHEMICAL INDUSTRY

There was one department, however, in which the superiority and pioneering work of French industry were plainly to be seen; and that department is at the same time one where we have an opportunity to study the positive side of the Continental System, the side that promoted progress. This is the chemical industry, or, to put it better, all processes where the results of chemical studies could benefit production.[1]

The fact that the course of development took this direction in France rather than elsewhere, it is true, was fundamentally due to something quite different from politics, namely, the fact that Lavoisier, through his work during the two decades immediately preceding the French Revolution, had laid the foundation of the whole of modern chemistry and had made it immediately applicable to a number of practical tasks. Moreover, he had had a number of eminent pupils whose work, to a still higher degree, was directly beneficial to industry; their results, too, were to a large extent apparent before or about the outbreak of the Revolution, when the external pressure had not yet begun to make itself felt. In certain cases, also, they had become economically usable before the Con-

---

[1] Cf. the brilliant sketch by Professor Arthur Binz, *Ursprung und Entwickelung der chemischen Industrie* (a lecture delivered at the *Berliner Handelshochschule* in 1910). His statement as to the development of artificial soda (p. 7 note 2) cannot, however, be brought into accord with the facts; and the use of chlorine bleaching is older than one might infer from his words (p. 10 note 7).

tinental System and consequently had great importance for industrial development during its sway.   In this connexion the first place should be given to Berthollet's theory, based on the discovery of the Swede, Scheele, for the production of chlorine, which became of very great importance for the whole of the weaving industry owing to the fact that as early as 1785 chlorine bleaching took the place of sun bleaching.   James Watt almost immediately brought about the transference of the new method to England, which undoubtedly here followed in the wake of French progress instead of taking the lead.   Another chemical method of still more central importance—which also had come into use during the years before the outbreak of the Revolution—was the production of sulphuric acid, which became the starting-point for a whole series of other branches of production.

In this connexion, however, it is evidently not the chemical advances of this kind that possess the greatest interest, but rather such as were first helped on their way by the great self-blockade, the importance of which for the process of development was—if the expression may be allowed—maieutic. It may be laid down as a general rule, indeed, that the economic service rendered by a war or by a blockade consists mainly in breaking down the barriers which impede the use of new inventions rather than in evoking those new inventions or discoveries themselves.   So far the dictum to the effect that ' necessity is the mother of invention ' would hit the point better if it were rephrased ' necessity is the nurse of invention '. In a war situation, indeed, public feeling is so unnerved, as a rule, that there is seldom sufficient calm for profound scientific work ;  and even if there were calm, time is lacking, for everything has to be done on the spur of the moment, and science seldom allows herself to be commandeered.   What is done in war and in case of blockade, therefore, is rather to seize violently upon inventions which have been already or almost completed —that is, in a purely technical sense—but which have previously been devoid of economic importance.   When a country is suddenly cut off from the old sources of supply, processes that previously lacked economic importance may become the best or even the only expedient.  This is largely the explanation of the ' development of the great industrial marvels ', of which Chaptal and others of that period speak.  Afterwards, when the exceptional situation disappeared, the marvels also vanished, for they had done their work.  They fell back under the threshold of consciousness, so to speak, and became once more potential instead of actual ; and this is the only proper thing, if we wish to keep the economic position of the people at its highest level.  In this way is explained without difficulty the general *débâcle* which overwhelmed the industrial creations of the Napoleonic age at the dawn of peace.  In certain happy cases, however, the blockade has given rise to a new production that has only needed such a help to strike root ; and in those cases it has really carried economic development onward and proved itself a genuine protectress.

In the sphere of chemical industry proper the great example here is the production of soda from sea salt.  This discovery had been made by Leblanc as early as some time about 1789— statements as to the year vary somewhat, as is usually, and quite naturally, the case in the matter of inventions and discoveries.  The efforts of the great French chemist during the whole of the revolutionary age to make his work bear fruit had come completely to grief, however, and he was ruined several years before his death in 1806.  Then came the severance of intercourse with Spain, whence soda had previously been obtained, and this gave a hitherto undreamt of importance to the production of soda, which now proved itself to be, even economically, thoroughly justified, inasmuch as it was developed to such an extent that the price could be reduced from 80–100 francs to 10 francs per 100 kgs.  A similar development attended the manufacture of another product, which in the fullness of time was one day to become the basic material for a substitute of Leblanc soda, namely, ammonia ; and the production of alum and camphor by chemical methods may perhaps be mentioned here, and possibly, too, the advances made in the important production of nitric acid.

These fundamental discoveries led afterwards to a great many others, as has always been the case in the sphere of chemistry, owing to the many different products that are obtained by a synthesis. But it would fall far beyond the writer's competence to give a detailed account of all this. Yet one might venture the assertion that the French chemical industry during this period, on the basis of the first great advances of modern chemistry, went through, and caused the world to go through, a development of somewhat the same kind as did the chemical industry of Germany after 1870, chiefly on the basis of the derivatives of coal-tar. To mention only one or two more examples, the supply of soda formed the foundation for the manufacture of soap, while the hydrochloric acid obtained as a by-product of sea salt in recovering soda became, in its turn, the basis for the manufacture of chlorine. Of special importance also in the development of the textile industry were the new possibilities in the manufacture of dyes and the printing of them on different kinds of material, which were brought about by the increased knowledge of chemistry. Most famous in the former respect was the manufacture of ' Berlin blue '—also called ' Raymond blue ', after its inventor—and the use of ' Adrianople red ' in calico-printing, where a member of the famous textile firm of Koechlin (Mülhausen) made advances in 1810 and 1811 which far exceeded what had been achieved in England.

## SUBSTITUTES FOR COLONIAL GOODS

The question of the dye industry led one naturally to the problem of finding substitutes for the more or less inaccessible, and always condemned, colonial goods. It was quite natural that the work of the French government and its organs, perhaps Chaptal above all, should be directed primarily to this point.

That measures were urgently needed here with regard to dyeing substances can be deduced from the great rise in prices, which, at least at Leipzig, was sometimes more marked than for raw cotton : for indigo the price was ordinarily twice as high, but sometimes even three, four, or five times as high, while for cochineal, dyewood and other dyes the price was usually doubled.[1] By far the most important dyeing substances were the two first-named : indigo and cochineal. As a matter of fact, this was no great novelty in either case, for people had long used two native dyeing plants, woad (Isatis tinctoria) and madder (Rubia tinctorum), for the production of blue and red, respectively, but it was now regarded as a great advance that the chemists had been able to establish the presence of the same dyeing substance, indigo, in woad as existed in Indian and American indigofera. Expectations, particularly as to the domestic production of indigo, were raised extremely high. People expected to be forever independent of the colonial product, and even as late as 1818, that is to say, after the Restoration, Chaptal cherished the hope that France, by means of her domestic production of indigo, would even get an export article that might compensate her for the profitable trade in colonial goods that she had lost when in 1814 and 1815 she had had to sacrifice the greater part of her colonial empire. In reality, however, the results were very small, and they had no importance whatever for the future. The cultivation of 32,000 hectares with woad had been prescribed ; Indian indigo had been declared an English product and its importation had consequently been forbidden ; three imperial indigo factories had been founded and prizes had been awarded to private individuals ; but even as late as 1813 the output came to only 6,000 kgs., apart from 500 kgs, of Indian indigo (called 'anil indigo') from an Italian plantation. Only one single factory survived 1814 ; and the whole episode vanished without leaving any traces behind. As is well known, it is by synthetic methods that substitutes have been found in our own day for the natural dyeing substances, indigo and alisarin (the dyeing substance contained in madder) ; and during the recent war the reverse state of things prevailed to such an extent that Great Britain had sometimes to fall back on natural indigo to take the place of the unobtainable synthetic indigo from Germany.

With regard to the other colonial goods, the substitutes

---

[1] Figures given in König, *op. cit.*, p. 224.

for coffee and tobacco offer us no interest other than that which lies in ' looking into one's own windows '. Among coffee substitutes were included chicory, dried carrots, acorns, sunflower seeds, and sugar beets ; as substitutes for tobacco were used leaves of gooseberries and chestnuts and milfoil (Achillea millefolium) ; and the scope of the production of Europe as a whole is illustrated by the fact that Denmark alone had seventeen factories for making coffee substitutes.[1]

## BEET SUGAR INDUSTRY

But the great example indicating the importance of the Continental System for industrial development that is usually cited is the manufacture of beet sugar ; and there certainly is a kernel of truth in this, if one only recalls what was said above regarding the character of the effects distinctive of such times.

The fact is that it is far from true that the possibility of obtaining sugar from beets was a novelty dating from the time of the Continental System. As early as the year 1747, the German chemist Marggraf, of Berlin, had discovered that sugar beets contained the same substance as sugar cane ; and from the close of the eighteenth century another German chemist, Achard, had worked incessantly on experiments in the production of beet sugar. In a raw-sugar factory located on his Silesian estate, Kunern, Achard had even succeeded in producing sugar and had published his results in 1809 ; but no manufacture of importance had arisen in consequence of all this. Achard's fate exhibits a great resemblance to that of Leblanc some ten years earlier, in spite of the fact that a domestic production of sugar had also been the subject of investigation in France, through a committee appointed by the *Institut de France* in 1800. Thus the matter was technically in a fairly advanced state, though it served no economic purpose as long as it was possible to procure colonial sugar under something like the old conditions. When those conditions were changed,

[1] Besides the works mentioned at the beginning of this chapter, cf. also de Cérenville, *Le système continental*, &c., pp. 306 *et seq.* ; Vogel, *Die Hansestädte*, &c., *loc. cit.*, p. 35 ; Rubin, *1807–1814*, &c., p. 436.

therefore, it is not at all surprising that advantage was taken of the theoretical results already attained; on the contrary, there is more reason to be astonished that there was so long a delay before it was determined to replace colonial sugar in this way. Before that the shortage of sugar had had time to make itself very perceptible. At Leipzig the price of sugar rose almost uninterruptedly until 1813, when it was approximately three and one-half times the amount it had been seven years earlier; and in Paris the price rose first (1810) to four francs per livre, and later (1812) to six francs, or approximately eight and twelve francs, respectively, per kg. Meanwhile, the London quotations for even the best qualities of sugar during 1812 corresponded to between 1·35 and 2 francs per kg., that is to say, from one-fourth to one-ninth of the French price.[1]

Naturally enough, therefore, people had at a much earlier date begun to search the Continent for a substitute, and there was scarcely any substance containing sugar that was not employed before they came to the beet. Honey, whey, chestnuts, pears, apples, maize, maple, potatoes, figs, cherries, plums, sea-weed, and finally grapes were tried. Grape sugar was the first stage, and as much as 2,000,000 kgs. were manufactured in the years 1810–11 and given a bounty; but this syrup, which was black and did not crystallize, was repulsive and had an unpleasant odour.

At this time, however, the cultivation of sugar beets had already been started, and the manufacture of beet sugar had begun at several places, especially at Passy by the firm of Delessert. It is only natural that enthusiasm was great when the result appeared; and it was alleged, assuredly for that time with great exaggeration, that the product could not be distinguished from cane sugar. There followed a visit (dramatically described by Chaptal in his *Memoirs*) by Napoleon to Delessert, who was decorated by the Emperor and regarded as a pioneer. The imperial administration took the matter in

---

[1] Calculated from figures given in König, *op. cit.*, p. 225. See also Levasseur, *Histoire des classes ouvrières*, &c., *de 1789 à 1870*, vol. I, p. 475; Tooke, *op. cit.*, vol. II, p. 414.

hand, in accordance with its usual methods, by means of measures which ran exactly parallel with the treatment of the manufacture of indigo, and which followed one another in rapid succession. A prohibition was established on the importation of colonial sugar, and it was ordered that beets should be cultivated first on 32,000 hectares and afterwards on 100,000 hectares, which order, it is true, was never carried out. It was ordered further that there should be four imperial sugar factories, and a special one in Rambouillet. There is no question that this gave rise to a lively development of both the culture of sugar beets and the manufacture of sugar, not least among the German-speaking people residing within and without the borders of the empire, and experimentally as far north as Denmark. And Napoleon's organs made all that could be made of this success in the work of becoming independent of the supply by sea. Thus the home secretary, in his survey of the condition of the empire submitted to the *Corps législatif* in February 1813, stated how it had seemed an impossibility to find anything to replace sugar, indigo, cochineal, soda, and cotton ; but ' we have exercised a strong will, and the impossible has been accomplished through our efforts '. From the year 1813 onward, he held out prospects of a manufacture of 7,000,000 livres (nearly 3,500,000 kgs.) of sugar in 334 factories, which were stated to be ' almost all ' at work ; and this he considered to correspond to at least half of the demand, which had diminished greatly owing to the rise of price.

As usual, the reality was somewhat less brilliant. According to the home secretary's own report to Napoleon later in the year, it turned out that, owing to ignorance and unfavourable weather, they had only got 1,100,000 kgs. of sugar and that of the 334 licences issued only 158 had been actually used ; and if one may believe a statement made by the director-general of manufactures and trades immediately after the Restoration, the quality of the sugar placed on the market was so bad that it had created a prejudice against the home product. As a matter of fact, the retrograde tendency began as early as that same year (1813), and afterwards the fall of the empire drew with it the decline of the industry, so that not a single one of the sugar factories held its own. But after only two years two new factories were started, one of them by Chaptal on his estate at Chanteloup. A high duty on colonial sugar set the manufacture of beet sugar on its feet toward the close of the 'twenties, so that the contribution of the Continental System on this point turned out to bear fruit after the lapse of a decade and a half. Thus the sugar beet industry stands, by the side of the Leblanc soda, as an evidence that a blockade may, in certain cases, remove some of the obstacles that stand in the way of an important economic development.

# CHAPTER III

## EFFECTS ON THE REST OF THE CONTINENT

### FRENCH POLICY OF INTERESTS

THE strain of egoism in Napoleon's policy is a well-known and abundantly proved side of the Continental System, which naturally weakens the sympathy usually shown by German writers for the fundamental idea of the plan to exclude England from the Continent.[1] The pretended object [2] of combining the Continent of Europe into an economic unit against Great Britain did not, it is true, altogether lack champions. The fairly obvious and undeniably important idea of developing the Confederation of the Rhine (which embraced the whole of Germany, with the exception of the possessions of Austria, Prussia, Sweden, and Denmark, and whose creator and powerful protector Napoleon was) into a customs union, which, incidentally, would have been an antecedent of the German *Zollverein* of 1833, was put forward by Beugnot, the ' imperial commissary ' or supreme head of the local administration in the Grand-Duchy of Berg, on two or three different occasions ; it also

---

[1] The best general survey is contained in Darmstädter, *Studien zur napoleonischen Wirtschaftspolitik, loc. cit.* (1905), vol. III, pp. 113 *et seq.* French commercial statistics are given in the earlier section, vol. II, p. 566 note 1. Cf. also Schmidt, *Le Grand-duché de Berg*, pp. 342, 413 *et seq.*, 420, app. C (Champagny's report of Aug. 5, 1807) ; Tarle, *Deutsch-französische Wirtschaftsbeziehungen, loc. cit.*, pp. 699 *et seq.*, 725 ; Tarle, *Kontinental'naja blokada*, vol. I, 119, 570, app. XIV (reports of French spies), app. XIX (petition from Leyden) ; de Cérenville, *op. cit.*, pp. 141–2, 155, 174 *et seq.*, 255 *et seq.* ; Rambaud, *op. cit.*, p. 440 note 3 ; König, *op. cit.*, pp. 267, 289 ; Kiewning, *Lippe und Napoleons Kontinentalsperre gegen den britischen Handel*, in *Mitteilungen aus der Lippischen Geschichte und Landeskunde* (Detmold, 1908), vol. VI, pp. 161 *et seq.* ; Letters to Fouché and Eugene (*Correspondance de Napoléon Ier*, nos. 15,874, 16,824). The North Sea coast from a customs point of view : *Bulletin des lois*, &c., 4th ser., bull. 299, no. 5724 ; bull. 397, no. 7340 ; Zeyss, *op. cit.*, pp. 129–30, 261 *et seq.* (Report of the Krefeld Chamber of Commerce) ; Vogel, *op. cit.*, pp. 47–8 ; Schäfer, *Bremen und die Kontinentalsperre, loc. cit.*, vol. XX (1914), p. 428.

[2] See *ante*, p. 53.

had a spokesman in Bacher, Napoleon's minister to the Confederation of the Rhine at Frankfurt ; but it was not in the least degree this spirit that prevailed in Paris.  In the late summer of 1807 Napoleon charged Champagny, who was just then passing from the Home Office to the Foreign Office, with the task of determining what the princes of the Confederation of the Rhine wished for their trade, and what measures should be taken to secure a market for French industrial products in their territories.  It was assuredly in accordance with the Emperor's intention that the second question was the one that Champagny in reality answered, and in doing so he followed the significant line that it was necessary to prevent the now consolidated German states from throwing obstacles in the way of French sales and particularly the transport of French goods across Germany, obstacles which had been impossible at the time when the states were small and divided.  In accordance with this idea, Napoleon maintained a whole swarm of commercial spies all over Germany, and these made reports on the smuggling of English and continental goods and on the capacity of French manufacturers to beat foreign competitors ; and to a large extent it was on the strength of such information that Napoleon later directed his measures against sales in other countries.

A celebrated illustration of the way in which Napoleon in reality regarded his political mission in this department is contained in a letter which he dispatched from Schönbrunn to Fouché (acting home secretary at the time) after his victory over Austria in 1809 (September 27).  In that letter the master empties the vials of his wrath over the commercial department of the French Home Office :

If the department had done its duty, it would have taken advantage of my march into Vienna to encourage merchants and manufacturers to export their cloth, pottery, and other goods which pay considerable duties in Austria, cloth alone paying 60 per cent.  I should, as a matter of course, have released them from these dues and filled the warehouses of Vienna chock-full of French goods.  But that department thinks of nothing and does nothing.

Accordingly, it was not to exclude England, but to make a breach in the customs wall against French goods, that he here wished to make use of his victories ; and in full accordance with this the French manufacturers just a week later tried to bring about an export of fine French cloth to Vienna on payment of a very insignificant duty, without any reciprocity for Austrian goods in France.

But Napoleon's egoistic policy was most clearly framed with regard to the Kingdom of Italy (North Italy), which he was anxious to transform entirely into an economic dependency of France. Hermetically sealed to the sales of the industrial products of all other countries, it was open to receive French goods and to provide France with needed raw materials (chiefly silk), but without any corresponding right to derive advantages from the French market ; finally, it was designed as a barrier to prevent goods from the competitors of France from penetrating into Naples, Sardinia, and South Europe in general. Owing to the fact that Italy for hundreds and even thousands of years had been economically connected with Switzerland and Germany by close commercial ties, this policy involved a severe dislocation of the industrial life of these last two countries and compelled them to have recourse to other markets or to other branches of activity. Napoleon has never given his general principles relating to the treatment of allies and subordinate non-French territories a more intensive expression than in another famous letter which he addressed on August 23, 1810, to his faithful and reliable step-son, Eugène Beauharnais, who governed Italy in his name as Viceroy. The fundamental idea of this letter appears in the following extract, with Napoleon's own highly significant italics :

My fundamental principle is, France first and foremost (*la France avant tout*). You must never lose sight of the fact that if English trade triumphs on the seas it is because the English are the strongest there. It is reasonable, therefore, that as France is the strongest on land, French trade should also triumph there. Otherwise all is lost. . . . Italy has France to thank for so much that she really should not mind if France acquired some commercial advantages there. Therefore, take as your motto : *La France avant tout.*

The beginning of this policy in Italy has already been described,[1] and the continuation followed along the same lines. The decree of the year 1806 was directed against Bohemian, Saxon, Swiss, Bavarian, and Berg textile goods, and seems to have hit hardest the Grand-Duchy of Berg. That country, which was at that time nominally ruled by Napoleon's brother-in-law, Joachim Murat, but in reality by the Emperor's own organs, managed to obtain an exemption for itself in January 1807; but as early as December of the same year this exemption was cancelled. Beginning with the following year its goods were definitely excluded from the Italian market, while the exports of Switzerland were hit particularly hard by an intensification, introduced about the same time, of the decree of 1806, which forbade all imports of cotton goods except from France. The position of French goods in the Italian market was further strengthened in 1808 by a curious Franco-Italian ' commercial treaty ' which Napoleon, in his capacity as autocratic ruler of both countries, concluded with himself. Finally, this policy culminated in 1810 in a triple regulation which in the first place extended the prohibition of imports from cotton goods to woollen goods, when they came from other countries than France, in the second place supplemented the prohibition on imports by a prohibition of transit, and in the third place forbade the export of Italian raw silk except to Lyons, the export of silk from Piedmont, which was incorporated with France, having been forbidden as early as 1805. The explanation given for this (in the letter to Eugene just cited) was that it would otherwise go to England, because Germany did not manufacture silk; but this explanation ignored the fact, well known to Napoleon, that Switzerland both carried on a trade in Italian raw silk and also had a flourishing silk manufacture. In the Kingdom of Naples, which was ruled first by Joseph Bonaparte and afterwards by Murat, there was applied, under the hard pressure of Napoleon, a similar policy, first with preferential duties on French goods and afterwards with a prohibition on the import of foreign goods.

[1] See *ante*, p. 86.

As regards the states of the Confederation of the Rhine, Napoleon observed considerably greater restraint; and comparatively little is known as to violations of their right of self-determination, despite Champagny's proposals just mentioned. On the other hand, it is highly significant that not even the territories incorporated with the empire in Napoleon's own time were thereby automatically placed on the same footing as 'the old departments'. This was a weakness which had, as a rule, characterized the loosely combined states of the old régime, not least France herself; but in Napoleon's strictly centralized realm it did not mean any such looseness of structure, but something quite different. There, indeed, it is an expression of the fact that the territories were worked into the empire in order to be shut out from British supplies, and at the same time were not to be more than proselytes of the gate; that is to say, they were to be left without participation in the advantages of the French market. This policy, which has not yet been made the subject of special investigation, was applied, for instance, as against Holland and ' the Hanseatic departments,' in such a way that French goods could be conveyed to the incorporated territories without let or hindrance in the same way as to the other parts of the empire; but goods from there, on the other hand, were regarded as foreign when they were conveyed to France. For Holland, it is true, it was laid down in the decree of incorporation that the customs frontier with France should disappear as early as the beginning of 1811, but this disappearance was repeatedly put off and seems never to have been realized. It makes a peculiar impression, for instance, to hear of people from Leyden, in 1811, and from Osnabrück, in 1812, praying for free intercourse with the empire, although both places belonged to the territories incorporated in 1810; and the same was the case with the Hanse Towns.

The whole of this egoistical system probably had an even more irritating than economically injurious effect on the other countries because it ran counter to the most cherished economic sentiments of the natural man as to the advantages of exports and the disadvantages of imports. Moreover, it did not even have the redeeming feature of providing the export goods of France with the dominant position that was its sole object and *raison d'être*. To a considerable extent this was due to the fundamental character of the Continental System, with its tendency to make the supply of raw materials enormously dear and difficult ; for, as the figures already given show very clearly, this hit France the hardest, because smuggling by sea was checked more effectually there than farther to the north, while goods smuggled by land had to be filtered through many customs frontiers before they reached France. But it was further aided by the fact that French industry was marked by the production of luxuries, which rendered sales extremely difficult, especially toward the close of the period, when the burden of the endless wars, both bloody and bloodless, on the whole of Europe was pressing with increasing weight. Finally, there was the fact that France could not by any violent measures overcome the circumstance that her industries had not made so much progress as those of certain other countries. In Italy, it is true, these factors made themselves felt to a less extent, for the industries of that country did not really appear as competitors ; and the blockade towards the north would seem to have had a certain degree of efficacy. At any rate, the available figures for the Kingdom of Italy show that Franco-Italian commerce increased many times over, so that about half the foreign trade, including both imports and exports, fell to the exchange of commodities with France ; and from Naples also there could be ascertained a rise in imports from France. On the other hand, this implies no increase in the exports of France on the whole. Only one year during the period of the empire (1806), according to the official returns, could show figures as high as those of the last years of the *ancien régime*, despite the huge annexations of important industrial regions that had taken place since then ; and, as has already been mentioned, the export of woollens had declined. It is particularly striking how poor a showing France made in competition with her continental rivals in the German market. It is fairly obvious, and also confirmed by the sources, that the obstacles which Napoleon placed in the way of the exports of those countries to the south of Europe must have helped to further their penetration into other markets, where they entered into competition with France. Thus the Swiss showed themselves at a Leipzig fair for the first time at Easter, 1808, after the closing of the frontier toward Italy had been made more strict at the end of 1807 ; and their sales of muslins were forced anew on that market after the still stricter embargo of 1810. In that case it is evident that little had been gained from a French point of view, even though injury was inflicted on the trade of the other countries as a result of its being diverted from its natural course.

The reports of the French commercial spies completely agree with the statements found in German and Swiss sources as to the difficulty for France to compete with the other countries. Thus from Switzerland we learn that French competition was unimportant in Germany, except for silk ; from Bohemia, that French goods could not compete ; and from Frankfurt, that French goods were the least important of all. The French reports usually sought an explanation of the fact that German and Swiss goods had the upper hand in various accidental circumstances, such as greater proximity to the place of production, simpler qualities, greater ease in obtaining raw materials, &c. But some, on the other hand, are more frank. Thus the report from Darmstadt runs : ' The cashmere and cotton factories of Saxony and Switzerland injure our trade in Germany, where they find great sales and are much in request under the name of English wares, the appearance of which they imitate.' And in the autumn of 1810 one of the French commercial spies made a statement which, from the standpoint of Napoleon's egoistic policy, must be regarded as a condemnation of the entire Continental System : Their competition ' is perhaps at the present moment more dangerous for France and Italy than that of the English manufacturers, because they dispute the Continent with us '. Thus, despite the best will in the world and despite unlimited powers to reserve for France what had become free through the blockade against England, Napoleon had scarcely succeeded in obtaining any increased sales for French export industries. As a measure to promote exports in the interest of France, therefore, the Continental System cannot be regarded as having achieved any great results.

We must now examine somewhat more closely how the economic life of certain other continental countries, and particularly their manufactures, was affected by the Continental System ; and in this matter, especially with regard to the general effect, it seems proper to limit ourselves to a few typical examples.

## SAXONY

Of all manufacturing countries on the Continent there is scarcely one which developed so powerfully under the Continental System as Saxony. Various factors contributed to this. To begin with, Saxony lay at some distance from France and was governed by a native prince in whom Napoleon had confidence. A powerful French interest further demanded that its economic life should be spared from violent dislocations and galling restrictions, because the Leipzig Fair, which has seldom had in its long history so much importance as during the Napoleonic wars, demanded a certain liberty of movement for its existence, and that existence was of great importance to French exports, the direct connexions of which seldom extended farther to the east than Leipzig. Under these circumstances it was natural that Napoleon should take care not to exercise there the continual intervention that fell to the lot of his vassal states that bordered on France. On the other hand, Saxony had an excellent situation for connexions both with the North Sea and with the Baltic, and also, before the incorporation of Trieste, with the Mediterranean, and it was therefore less affected than most countries by the changed directions of maritime trade. Even though the Leipzig Fair, owing to this change, diminished in importance during the last years of the Continental System, yet the supply of cotton for the country's own requirements was even then, as far as one can judge, sufficient ; and in any case it was incomparably better than in France, as is very clearly shown by the foregoing tables illustrating the prices of cotton.[1]

Saxony was already at this time a manufacturing country with a many-sided development, both as regards the majority of textile industries—cotton, wool, linen—and iron-working. But so far as I know, it is the history of the cotton industry under the Continental System that has been subjected to the most thorough investigation.    This has been done especially in the work that has so often been cited in these pages, namely, König's *Die Sächsische Baumwollenindustrie am Ende des vorigen Jahrhunderts und während der Kontinentalsperre* (1899), which on the whole would seem to be the most useful of the existing monographs on the industrial conditions of this period. In general, this one-sidedness in the literature very well corresponds to the reality, for it is in the sphere of the cotton industry that one really has to expect the workings of the Continental System in Saxony.

The Saxon cotton industry, which had a long history behind it, had not become the object of British competition until the seventeen-seventies, after the inventions in the spinning industry, principally as regards the fine goods (muslins) that were manufactured in Voigtland in the south of Saxony, mainly in Plauen. The competition had been met by the imitation of the British goods, but for this purpose the Saxon yarn was too coarse ; and this brought about the admission of British yarn for the muslin factories shortly after 1790. But even then there was no more than a short breathing space, for before the close of the century the British competition was regarded as overwhelming, even in the matter of muslins. The second main division of Saxon cottons, the coarser calicoes intended for printing, which were produced on the northern slope of the Erzgebirge, centering in Chemnitz, held out somewhat longer. That too was based on British yarn as warp, but it also went under immediately before the introduction of the Continental System.

[1] See *ante*, pp. 274, 276.

What made it possible to check this development under the Continental System, however, was not only the fact that Saxony was an old home of the cotton industry, which was only gradually disturbed in its position, but also two other important facts. One was that what had been revolutionized in the British cotton trade at this time was really only spinning, while the power-loom was still only in its infancy. The beginning of the Continental System was simultaneous with the well-known and peculiar phase of the British industrial revolution when the hand-weavers, who were later reduced to abysmal misery, had brilliant incomes owing to the scarcity of workers to weave the increased quantities of yarn produced by spinning-machines. No doubt the economic organization of British weaving also had been changed under the pressure of the great spinning-mills, and the technique of weaving had also been improved in Great Britain. But for a country which was able to bring its own spinning industry into approximate equality with the British spinning industry, there was still some possibility of holding out against British competition ; and we here come to the second fact that made possible a restoration of the Saxon cotton industry when the Continental System placed difficulties in the way of the importation of British cotton. This second fact was that the spinning-machinery had already obtained a firm footing in the country before the blockade rendered difficult the importation of British machines and British operators. Hargreaves's spinning-jenny, which was only a multiple spinning-wheel and therefore did not put an end to, but rather supported, home industry, had already reached Saxony in the seventeen-eighties, and there were thousands of machines there before the Continental System. But of far greater significance was the fact that in the year 1801, in consequence of the importations of British operators, two great spinning-mills were started in Chemnitz, one with Crompton's mule and the other with Arkwright's water-frame. This created the possibility of producing both long and fine thread, though not by any means so fine as the British thread (mule-twist up to no. 70 and water-twist up to no. 36), and, in general, of keeping pace with the development of British technique. It was really only the mule-spindles that obtained a firm footing during the period of the Continental System; while water-frames never came into common use, and jennies almost completely disappeared, the number of mule-spindles increasing steadily from 13,200 in 1806 to 255,900 in 1813 (of which in the half-year between Michaelmas 1811 and Easter 1812, there was a rise from 132,000 to 210,150, an increase of 59 per cent.). The development of machine spinning suffered a slight check at the collapse of the Continental System in 1813–14; but on the whole the results attained in this matter seem to have held their ground. Alongside this, moreover, there arose a special and comprehensive industry for the manufacture of spinning-machinery, distributed over some dozen workshops, of which the most technically advanced, though not the largest, was under the management of the British mechanic who had fitted up the first mule spinning-mill in 1801.

Thus it is fairly clear what causes made it possible for the Continental System to check the decline in the Saxon textile industries. Despite their importance, the period did not bring any general quantitative increase in production. According to König's calculations, which are based on the year 1805 when the effects of British competition had already appeared all along the line, there was only one year (1810) that exhibited higher figures (an increase of 25 per cent.) than the year taken as the basis, while the figures of the other years and average were lower. The course of development showed a decline for the muslin industry, which was dependent on the almost unobtainable high numbers of yarn. That industry partly passed to Switzerland, and partly lost through British competition its most important remaining market, Turkey. On the other hand, there was an increase of nearly 40 per cent. for unprinted calicoes, so that the cotton industry of Voigtland, and consequently of Saxony as a whole, passed more and more to the production of calicoes. In a somewhat similar way calico-printing grew, and the results were so satisfactory that the British could sell nothing whatever when, after Napoleon's fall, they first showed themselves openly at the Michaelmas Fair at Leipzig in 1814.

In spite of all this—and here is perhaps the point that presents the greatest interest—the Saxon cotton industry, like the correspondent French one, had not been in a position to keep pace with the technical development of Great Britain during the period of the blockade. There were practically no steam spinning-mills, but somewhat more than half of the spinning-mills were driven by water-power and the rest by animal-power or hand-power. Far more important, however— for the former was evidently mainly due to a good supply of natural power—is the fact that cylinder-printing did not come into use during the period, but calico-printing was still performed by the extremely slow hand method. Consequently, it took the British only three or four years (1817) to get the better of the Saxon calico industry; and under the influence of this competition the transition to machine-printing, which it had not been possible, or, more correctly, necessary, to adopt during the long period of blockade, took place in 1820. Although the Continental System had a very strong stimulating effect on industrial development in many directions, therefore, yet it had not built up industry so firmly as to prevent a relapse for some years after the close of the blockade; and this was due to the incapacity of protection to provide for the adoption of the technical advances that had not been introduced before the beginning of the blockade.

### SWITZERLAND

While the industrial development of Saxony, on the whole, was stimulated by the Continental System, in certain regions in Switzerland the result was quite the opposite, the situation there being far more complicated. And what is now to be said about Switzerland applies also in large measure to the Black Forest and, peculiarly enough, to Geneva as well, though the latter was incorporated with France.[1] In the Swiss and Baden

[1] De Cérenville, *Le système continental*, &c.; Chapuisat, *Le commerce et l'industrie à Genève*, &c.; Geering, *op. cit.*; Gothein, *Wirtschaftsgeschichte des Schwarzwaldes*

regions (with the exception of one single branch of production) there was a violent decline in the previously well-marked industrial development and a distress which was widespread, and, in certain districts, frightful. Nevertheless, it is a great mistake to regard the blockade as the sole cause of this devastating backward movement. The character of Swiss industry made it peculiarly susceptible both to the revolutionary influence of the great inventions and to the changes undergone by the general economic position of Europe toward the close of the Napoleonic wars.

About 1770 Switzerland was the pioneer country in the European cotton industry, with both spinning and weaving highly developed under the forms of home industry, for which the country was uniquely adapted. Shortly afterwards the machine-spun British yarn began to penetrate into the country, but this development was checked by the obstacles which the course of the French Revolution placed in the way of intercourse with England. Also, when Napoleon began to close the land frontiers more and more tightly a new change took place in the situation. The importation of raw materials for all the Swiss textile industries—cotton, flax, hemp, raw silk—was rendered difficult, while the calico-printing works of Geneva, on the contrary, suffered through being placed within the French customs frontier and thereby being shut off from the supply of unprinted cotton from Switzerland. The severance of the many ties that connected Switzerland with all the bordering countries was thus primarily responsible for the confusion that prevailed during the first five years of the nineteenth century. The earlier years of the Continental System brought about, as we already know, the closing of the Italian market, but, on the other hand, they led to what were sometimes great sales in Germany. We are told that at the Easter Fair at Frankfurt, in 1809, the Swiss completely dominated the market. They left the town after having sold their stocks, but furnished themselves anew and had an equally sweeping success with

*und der angrenzenden Landschaften* (Strassburg, 1892), vol. I, pp. 767 *et seq.*, 800, 866.

their new supplies and at equally good prices.   Until this time Switzerland had had no very great difficulty in providing herself with raw cotton or even with British yarn, especially because the important port of Trieste was still open.   It is true that a shortage of Brazilian cotton had made itself felt, but this had been partly replaced by North American cotton.

What really caused suffering during this period was not the general state of the trade, but the hopeless struggle that hand-spinning was carrying on against machine-spinning, hastened, as it was, by the importation of yarn and also by the increasing necessity to fall back on the short-stapled Levantine cotton ; for this quality did not admit of the spinning of fine numbers of yarn, which otherwise constituted the only chance left to hand-spinning.   The misery of the Swiss hand-spinners would seem, as regards the range of the injury, to surpass considerably what we know of the corresponding effects of the industrial revolution in Great Britain.   But it is in the very nature of the case that we here have to deal with sacrifices for what cannot possibly be looked upon as anything but lasting material progress.   The definitive introduction of machine-spinning went on in Switzerland, as in Saxony, under the protection of the Continental System, but on a foundation which had been laid beforehand in both countries—in the year 1801.   In Switzerland, in much the same way as in Saxony, the new branch of production had been in the way of falling a victim to British competition ; but it was saved and now developed itself, partly under Saxon influence, by means of a spinning-machine industry.   The last-named industry gradually became independent, and acquired a great reputation, like machine-spinning itself.   It maintained its prosperity, not only under the Continental System, but also after its fall, though it suffered a momentary dislocation. Probably the manufacture of spinning-machinery in its turn is connected with the manufacture of cast or crucible steel at Schaffhausen, and possibly also with the general development of the engineering industry in Switzerland that has played an important part in the economic history of the country during the nineteenth century.

However, Napoleon, the ' mediator ' of the Swiss Confederation, undeniably had an eye on its industry ; and there was
no comparison between his ruthless and continuous intervention
in Switzerland and his relatively mild treatment of Saxony.
This fact explains many of the dissimilarities in the consequent
evolution of the two countries.  The Emperor never neglected
an opportunity to make Switzerland, a dangerous competitor
that was politically powerless, feel the whole weight of the
measures both of the Italian and of the French governments ;
and the states of the Confederation of the Rhine, especially
Bavaria, were not slow to follow suit.  In 1809 occurred the
incorporation of Trieste, which was a hard blow for both the
imports and the sales of Switzerland ; but it was the years
1810–11 which, so far as external policy is concerned, gave the
decisive turn to events.  It was then that the last measures were
taken in Italy which definitively shut off the south of Europe.
At the same time the Trianon tariff led both to repeated and
violent ransackings of Switzerland for British goods and to
prohibitions on the transport of colonial goods (cotton) from
the states of the Confederation of the Rhine, and finally also
to the decline both of the Frankfurt and the Leipzig Fairs,
so that sales for the north were rendered difficult at the same
time that sales to the south were strangled.  Nevertheless, we
do not form the impression that these external events were the
main cause of the almost all-embracing crisis which now broke
over the whole of Swiss economic life.  Of the seriousness of
this set-back there does not appear to be any doubt.  The
Landammann (President) summed up the situation in April
1812, in the distressful proposition that ' the industries of
Switzerland are now nearing their end ' ; and a considerable
emigration took place, among other places, to the left bank of
the Rhine.

The fundamental cause of this hard blow seems rather to
have been the general distress which now spread over Europe,
and which struck Swiss industry with particular severity
because most of its branches were concerned with the production
of luxuries.  In the cotton industry this especially held good of

the manufacture of muslins and embroidered goods, in which Switzerland and Baden had been beyond the reach of competition on the Continent and had suffered no inconvenience worth mentioning from the Continental System. But it was just here that a devastating crisis broke out which put an end forever to these branches of production in certain districts, and for the moment practically everywhere. To a somewhat smaller extent the position was the same for calicoes and coarser unprinted cottons. Outside the sphere of the cotton industry, both the silk manufacture and the making of watches and jewellery obviously satisfied what was in the main a demand for luxuries. The most highly developed watch industry, that of Geneva, is stated to have declined to a tenth of its former magnitude. Evidently it will not do to see in this an effect of the Continental System ; and the fact that Switzerland during the recent war, despite far greater difficulties in the supply of raw materials and foodstuffs, was yet able to avoid such great dislocations as in 1811–13 is evidently connected with the fact that it has now, not only industries that supply the luxury demand but also, and perhaps to a still greater extent, other kinds of industries.

To outward appearances, consequently, the difference between Switzerland and Saxony is very great. If one tries to get to the bottom of the significance of the Continental System for Switzerland, the dissimilarity, however, will diminish considerably. In both countries machine-spinning secured a firm foothold, while the weaving industry could not maintain itself in either country. But things were undeniably far worse in Switzerland for three reasons ; because of the much greater ruthlessness of the Napoleonic policy there ; because of its more intimate connexion with surrounding countries ; and, above all, because of the fact that Swiss industries were far more concerned with the production of luxuries.

## GRAND DUCHY OF BERG

Of all the regions of the Continent beyond the borders of France there is scarcely one whose fortunes under the Continental System are so indicative of the dualism of the policy as those parts of the right bank of the Rhine that Napoleon combined into the Grand-Duchy of Berg. What this territory at the present moment means to the industry of Europe is well understood when its most important part is mentioned, namely, the Ruhr district ; to this was added the closely allied Siegerland, which forms a continuation of the district farther to the south. To that region belong such centres of trade and Rhine navigation as Duisburg and Ruhrort, textile centres such as Elberfeld, Barmen, and Mülheim, some of the foremost coal and iron mines in the world, and iron-working and metal-manufacturing centres, such as Essen, Gelsenkirchen, Dortmund, Bochum, Siegen, Dillenburg, Remscheid, and Solingen. In a word, it is one of the most eminent and highly concentrated industrial districts in the world. Even though the development of the Rhenish-Westphalian territory into its present position has progressed with giant strides, especially since 1870, yet, even at the beginning of the last century, Berg was one of the most advanced industrial countries of the Continent, particularly in the departments of metal manufacture and of textiles, both woollen and cotton. It was, as a rule, superior to the corresponding French industrial areas and was called, not without reason, ' a miniature England '.

It is evident that a region of this kind would have served better than almost any other to form the central point in a combination of the Continent against the industry of Great Britain ; and few regions would, at least for the moment, have gained more by such a position. But evidently this would have presupposed a willingness to subordinate French manufacturing interests to the demands of the uniform continental policy ; and it was precisely this willingness that was lacking. The very industrial superiority of Berg thereby became its misfortune under the Continental System ; it fell between two stools, being inexorably excluded from the French market, but no less inexorably bound to French policy.

Situated quite close to the French frontier, which at that time, as everybody knows, was formed by the Rhine itself, its mere geographical position threw obstacles in the way of its retaining the relative independence enjoyed by the majority of the other states of the Confederation of the Rhine. But this was all the more impossible because the country in reality was governed throughout on Napoleon's own account, at first in the name of Joachim Murat, but from 1808 even nominally under the rule of the Emperor in his capacity as guardian of the new Grand-Duke, the minor son of Louis Bonaparte. Its position, in combination with the measures described above [1] for the blockade against Holland by means of a customs cordon between Rees and Bremen in 1809 and the incorporation of Holland in 1810, placed difficulties in the way of the supply of colonial goods both from the Baltic and from the North Sea to quite a different extent than was the case in Saxony. This was especially the case after the Trianon tariff, which particularly during its earlier phases involved dues in all the states through which the goods had to pass ; and there was still less possibility of any supply through the Mediterranean than there was in the case of Switzerland. The native minister of the Grand-Duchy, Nesselrode, said with bitterness that Berg was the only country that had ever conscientiously applied the Trianon tariff. Every reason conspired to force her to the French side in the great struggle.

Under such circumstances it constituted an excess of punishment to place the country outside the French customs frontier, so much the more so because a very extensive mutual exchange of commodities with France had commenced before the Revolution, consisting, on the one hand, of the exportation of metal wares, cloth, and ribbons, and, on the other hand, of the importation of wine, oil, and colonial goods. The more unavoidable the sufferings that the new situation caused to Berg, the more persistent and ardent became the desire of its

[1] See *ante*, p. 183.

inhabitants to be incorporated with the empire, like their more fortunately situated countrymen on the left bank of the Rhine; and if that were impossible, at least they asked to enjoy some modification in the prohibitive French regulations regarding customs duties and prohibitions on imports, which, as has been previously stated,[1] did most effectually prevent competition from the right bank of the Rhine. The unbroken stream of prayers from the population in this direction was also actively supported by both Beugnot, the local French governor at Düsseldorf, and Roederer, the secretary of state for Berg in Paris. But all was in vain. Sometimes Napoleon's heart softened, as in January 1807, when he admitted the goods of Berg into Italy; but the old tendencies always regained the upper hand, and, as has already been mentioned, the specific concession referred to was revoked before the end of the year. Particularly violent was the resistance to the incorporation of Berg that was raised from the Roer department on the left bank of the Rhine, where a new and flourishing textile industry in Aix-la-Chapelle, Cologne, and Krefeld was greatly profiting by sales on the closed French market and feared nothing so much as competition from the superior industry of Berg. In this matter there was unusual truth in the saying, 'Preserve me from my relatives'. It makes an impression which is half-amusing and half-repulsive when one reads the addresses, reeking with French patriotism, to Napoleon or to the prefect of the department, in which the Chambers of Commerce of Cologne, Aix-la-Chapelle, and Krefeld, and also the cotton manufacturers of the Roer department, tried, with every conceivable sophism, to prevent any listening to the prayers of Berg, owing to its industrial superiority, its unfair methods of business, and its already sufficient sales in the north of Europe. When we read all this, we are forcibly reminded of a very apt remark made by Professor Morgenstierne to the effect that even a purely temporary frontier calls forth claims to protection against competition, while the same sort of competition is regarded as a healthy and natural development

---

[1] See *ante*, p. 84.

when it takes place within the boundaries of a country. The summit level of cynicism was probably attained in an address to the Emperor from the Cologne Chamber of Commerce in the autumn of 1811, where a plea was coolly put forward to move the population from the unfertile right bank of the Rhine to its fertile left bank :

But it may be said that the great majority of the inhabitants of the French empire cannot but gain by the incorporation of so industrious a region as Berg. We reply to this that the object can be attained without the incorporation of the Grand-Duchy. As soon as Your Majesty has declared that no such incorporation should take place, the manufacturers of the Grand-Duchy, excluded from the markets of France, Italy, and North Germany, will find themselves reduced to the pressing necessity of moving their works to the left bank of the Rhine. All the cotton, wool, and silk factories of Berg will be restored to their mother country, and Berg will have left only the factories that belong to its soil, namely, the iron and steel industry, which will continue to exist.[1]

Instead of growing milder, the French attitude toward Berg rather became more rigorous, especially under the influence of the severe crisis of 1810–11 in France, which naturally made competition from a superior industry still more objectionable than ever ; and as was so often the case during this period, the difficulties were increased by almost meaningless annoyances, as, for instance, when Remscheid's steel manufactures were not allowed to be conveyed through France for exportation to America.

Under such circumstances Berg, on the whole, suffered nothing but injury from the Continental System ; and after 1810, when conditions everywhere began to get worse, the situation in the Grand-Duchy was represented as heart-rending, with unemployment and the increasing emigration of skilled workers across the Rhine (as the Cologne Chamber of Commerce had hoped) and a general discontent which Beugnot, immediately before the Russian Campaign, tried to exorcise by a reduc-

---

[1] Zeyss, op. cit., p. 367; The different petitions are printed in Schmidt, Le Grand-duché de Berg, app. E, and Zeyss, ibid., Anhang VIII. The actual material for the account in the text is taken substantially from Schmidt's model work.

tion of the duties of the Trianon tariff, but which broke out
into open revolts in the beginning of 1813. It is true that the
complaints may be reduced to some extent, as is indeed always
the case ; for nothing would be more misleading than to write
history, and particularly economic history, on the basis of
complaints alone, for ' every torment hath its cry, while health
doth hold its peace '. The loss of the French, Italian, and northwest German markets, and also the scarcity of raw cotton,
certainly brought about great suffering ; but, on the other side,
the smuggling of cotton went on to the last, and at the German
fairs, where Napoleon's measures had no effect, the sales were
good ; in particular, the woollens of Berg were regarded as
keeping all others out in Frankfurt. The diminution in the
exports of manufactures by a bare 30 per cent. (from 55,000,000
to 39,000,000 francs), which Roederer ascertained at the close
of 1810, cannot in itself be regarded as overwhelming ; but,
of course, it meant a great deal for a country that was indus-
trialized to such an extent as Berg and was especially well
equipped for foreign sales. Above all, there was here, in sharp
contrast with the state of things in Saxony and Switzerland,
practically no single point in which the rigid and detested
system afforded any compensation for its inconveniences.
When the effects of the war on Europe in general began to
make themselves felt more and more strongly, therefore, it
was only natural that the situation should become unendurable
in a country which was pressed so hard between two antagonists
—almost literally between the devil and the deep sea—especially when it quite naturally seemed to the population as if the
officially announced aim of the policy might have led to a very
different treatment and rendered possible a favourable development of the country. Just as the left bank of the Rhine was
grateful, and with reason, for the orderly administration and the
economic prosperity brought about there by the French rule,
and just as the time of Napoleon was also important for various
autonomous German states of the Confederation of the Rhine,
e. g., Bavaria, through the indirect French influence, so did the
pressure of the Continental System make itself detestable in

this unique industrial region which was shut out from all quarters through the egoism of French policy.

## INDUSTRIES IN OTHER COUNTRIES

The development of industry in the other states of the mainland offers comparatively few new features; and there is no reason to essay a monographic treatment of the several countries. Conditions in Bohemia seem to have accorded more or less completely with the developments in Saxony, while not only Baden, as has already been mentioned, but to a very large extent Italy, like Switzerland, came to suffer from the closing of the frontier of South Europe to all quarters. In the north the famous linen manufactures of Silesia especially suffered through the closing of the Italian frontier, so that the well-known misery of the Silesian linen-weavers—so dramatically treated by Gerhart Hauptmann, among others—began during this period. Thus we have here a very close parallel to the Swiss development. The industries of Denmark were of so little importance that they could not suffer much harm; but what the Continental System did to them was of a typical forcing-house character; the number of looms in the Copenhagen cloth manufacture increased from 22 in 1807 to 213 in 1814, only to fall back to 74 in 1825.[1]

It is characteristic that the regions which worked for maritime trade were hard hit, not only by the stagnation of trade and shipping, but also by the fact that the blockade removed the very ground from under the feet of their industries, a thing which quite naturally could most easily happen in such countries because their industries are usually based to a very great degree on trade relations with other countries, either for raw materials or for sales or for both. In accordance with this, the industries of Hamburg were seriously crippled in every respect, because its sugar factories suffered from the scarcity of raw sugar and English coal, and its calico-printing works (to a small degree, it is true) from a shortage of unprinted calicoes; in the same way Holland suffered not only through

[1] Rubin, op. cit., pp. 436–7, 510.

the entire annihilation of its carrying trade, but also through the scarcity of salt for its fisheries and an absence of markets for its spirit manufacture.

### COUNTRIES PRODUCING RAW MATERIALS

The account of the development under the Continental System of the countries that provided raw materials must necessarily be very brief, as the sources are strikingly scanty, and as the blockade on the Baltic and in Austria was so intermittent.

In Russia the dislike of the nobility and of persons of political influence for the alliance with Napoleon and the Continental System was extremely strong from the very start, as has been set forth with typical French animation and wealth of colour in Vandal's famous work *Napoléon et Alexandre Ier* (1891–6); and without doubt economic factors also played their part. But one has nevertheless a kind of impression that their importance has been exaggerated. What especially gives occasion for doubt is the fact that the evidence for the stagnation of trade which is always met with is the great decline of the Russian rate of exchange (a loss of 72 per cent.). This cannot be explained by an ' unfavourable balance of trade ', for this cause is never sufficient in any case that occurs in practice to bring about a result of that magnitude. The true cause was and is the depreciation of the currency in Russia and Austria, both then and now caused by an excessive issue of paper money.[1] But this, of course, does not make it impossible that the stagnation in Russian timber exports may have been great, as is indeed stated from French quarters which had some interest in maintaining the opposite ; and the fact is partly and quite irrefutably confirmed by the great increase in the price of timber, to which we have already called attention,[2] in both Great Britain and France. This stagnation was brought about, however, not only by the increased difficulty of maritime intercourse, but also by a rather

---

[1] Oddy, in his contemporary description of the commercial conditions of the time, unhesitatingly explains the state of the Russian exchange in this way. Cf. Oddy, *European Commerce* (London, 1805), p. 197.     [2] See *ante*, p. 173.

unique consequence of the blockade, which has had analogies
during the recent war, namely, the great part that Englishmen
played in the economic life of Russia before the Peace of Tilsit.
This is illustrated by the vast amount of information from
official Russian sources that can be found in Oddy's work.
For instance, in 1804, 35 per cent. of the imports and no less
than 63 per cent. of the exports of St. Petersburg were in the
hands of British merchants ; and the three greatest commercial
houses, all of them British, taken by themselves, carried on
more than one-fourth of the export trade of the Russian capital.
French evidence testifies to the same conditions. General
Savary, who reached St. Petersburg in July 1807, on behalf
of Napoleon, gave a detailed description in his report of the
all-dominating position of the British trade, telling how half
of all the vessels were British and how Englishmen took over
all the timber from the nobility and thereby provided them
with their safest source of income ; and he also remarked
that they themselves founded industrial concerns in Russia
when the importation of British manufactures was too
much hampered by customs duties. When so important
a part of the economic activity of Russia ceased to exist
without warning, it was naturally impossible to obtain substitutes either in Russia itself or from France ; and the natural
consequence was a stagnation in Russian exports. Napoleon
was quite conscious of this position, and in November 1807,
he ordered his ambassador, Caulaincourt, to lay before Emperor
Alexander a proposition whereby the French government
should buy several million francs' worth of mast wood and other
naval stores for its shipyards. It is uncertain, however,
whether this plan was ever carried out.[1]

The Continental System seems to have had a much more
marked restraining effect on the exports of raw materials and
foodstuffs from Prussia, that is to say, chiefly from the districts

[1] Vandal, *Napoléon et Alexandre Ier*, vol. I, pp. 140, 324, 513 (Napoleon's instructions to Caulaincourt, Nov. 12, 1807) ; Oddy, *European Commerce*, bk. I,
especially pp. 130 *et seq.*, pp. 197–8 (computations by the present writer) ; Tarle,
*Kontinental'naja blokada*, vol. I, pp. 477, 482, 486 ; Darmstädter, *Studien*, &c., vol. II,
p. 610 ; Rose, in the *English Historical Review*, vol. XVIII, pp. 122 *et seq.*

east of the Elbe, probably because Napoleon had still greater
reason to distrust the loyalty of the Prussian government than
that of the Russian government toward the system, and
because, moreover, he had considerably greater means of
exercising pressure against the former than against the latter.
According to an account by Hoeniger, great stocks of timber
rotted away at Memel, while the price of corn fell by 60–80
per cent. between 1806 and 1810 owing to the absence of
markets.    The same phenomena appeared in northwest
Germany, which had been wont to dispose of its surplus corn
to England *via* Bremen and now saw its means of export barred,
with the consequence that, while the price of colonial goods at
Bremen increased many times, the price of wheat there declined
by 62 per cent. between 1806 and 1811, and the price of rye
correspondingly.    On the other hand, the shipping and corn
exports of Mecklenburg were allowed to remain practically
undisturbed until the latter half of 1810.    In fact, according to
accessible figures, the year between August 1809 and July
1810 marks the summit-level of development, which, it is true,
was largely caused by the trade with Sweden which was
resumed after the conclusion of the Finnish war.    From
Rostock there sailed during that twelvemonth no fewer than
439 vessels, as compared with 55 in the year 1808–9 and 31
in the year 1810–11 ; and the exports of corn exhibit equal
figures.    Here, as has been previously mentioned,[1] it was the
licence system that put an end to the export of corn.[2]

## Entrepôt Countries

Finally, as regards countries carrying on an intermediary
trade, Sweden and—before the passing of the Embargo Act—
the United States, it appears from what has already been said
that the effects of the Continental System were necessarily

[1] See *ante*, p. 262.
[2] Hoeniger, *Die Kontinentalsperre und ihre Einwirkungen auf Deutschland*, in
*Volkswirtschaftliche Zeitfragen* (Berlin, 1905), no. 211, p. 26 ; Schäfer, *op. cit.*, table
IX ; Stuhr, *Die napoleonische Kontinentalsperre in Mecklenburg, 1806–1813*, in
*Jahrbuch des Vereins fur Mecklenburgische Geschichte und Altertumskunde*, 1906,
vol. LXXI, tables on pp. 361 *et seq.*

limited substantially to the sphere of trade; and in the preceding pages materials have been supplied for the illustration of this development. The United States is of particular interest in this connexion in that it shows a quite different development before and after the enforcement of the self-blockade. At one single blow this transformed the country to the type of France and gave a huge stimulus to the development of industry, especially the cotton industry, which, according to an inquiry of Secretary of the Treasury Gallatin, seems to have sextupled during the four years preceding 1809.

### GENERAL SITUATION ON THE CONTINENT

When, after this discussion of the development of different countries, one undertakes to form a general picture of the situation on the Continent of Europe, it cannot escape the observation of anyone who is at all free from prejudice that the effects of the Continental System on the actual material foundation of the life of the people—what economists call the satisfaction of the wants of the people—were far less than those which accompanied the recent blockade. What was lacking with regard to pure articles of consumption was little else than coffee and sugar, and, to some extent, tobacco; and however severely the scarcity of coffee may have been felt during the recent war, surely no one will deny that the material effects of the war would have been quite insignificant in comparison with what they actually were if they had not extended beyond that. For the rest, the scarcity under the Continental System applied to industrial raw materials, mainly cotton and dye-stuffs, but in many countries also other textile raw materials, such as wool, flax, hemp, and silk. So far, therefore, the situation seems to correspond to our recent experience; but in reality this is not the case. For while the shortage in our own time seriously reduced the supply of woven goods themselves, that is to say, articles actually required for consumption, during the time of the Continental System complaints were always, at least as far as I know, limited to the inconveniences suffered by production in consequence of the lack of raw materials and the resulting unemployment.  Unemployment, in particular, with its consequences in the way of mendicancy and vagrancy, is a consistently recurring theme in the descriptions of the effects of the Continental System—during the whole period in the ports, and in times of war and under the influence of shortage of raw materials in the industrial districts.  Parallel with this run the accounts of the death-like silence in the great coast towns, grass growing in the streets of La Rochelle, the ruin of shipping, and the like.  In order to conceive the importance of these phenomena aright, one must necessarily have a firm grip of the fact that trade, shipping, and industrial activity are means for covering the wants of the people, not ends in themselves ; and what settles the matter in the last resort is to what extent those wants could be satisfied more or less as usual.  So far as we can judge, that was far more the case a hundred years ago than it has been in our own day.

We might perhaps summarize this contrast by saying that the effect of the Continental System on the European mainland was continuous dislocation, while the dislocation of the recent war was, in the main, overcome during the first year of hostilities.  On the other hand, during the recent war, in contrast with the great war of a century ago, the lowering of the standards of life and the decrease in supplies necessary for the general wants continued uninterruptedly and probably at an accelerated pace, but without dislocations, in the proper sense of the term, and with an immense decline in unemployment, as compared with peace conditions.  The fact that the course of development took two such opposite directions then and now and that there was no dislocating effect in our own day shows, on the one hand, how much more flexible and adaptable economic organization has become during the last century.  But, on the other hand, the difference is due to the dissimilarity of the two blockades, which is the reason why the satisfaction of general wants remained comparatively undisturbed a hundred years ago.  At a time when Great Britain asked for nothing more than an opportunity to flood the Continent with colonial goods and industrial products, the supply must, despite all self-blockade, have been quite different from what it was when the normal producers proceed to hinder all supply.

Finally, another contributory cause was the relative self-sufficiency (αὐταρχεία), which evidently greatly limited the effects of the Continental System as regards the satisfaction of general wants of the population of the continental states. The most important fact is that difficulties regarding food did not possess anything like the importance that they had during the recent war ; indeed they practically played no part whatever on the Continent before the winter of 1811–12.   The one exception was in Norway.[1]  This self-sufficiency as regards food was far greater than can be found in our own time, even in countries that produce the necessary amount of food for their own population, because they are dependent upon imports of manure and fodder, while such a situation was practically unknown a hundred years ago.   Moreover, the self-sufficiency within the continental countries, the relative economic independence of the particular household, went far to prevent the hardships occasioned by a blockade in the twentieth century. The fact that, as a consequence of this, the corn problem was really a problem only for England, makes it proper to postpone its treatment to the section in the following chapter dealing with the effects of the Continental System in that country, and makes a mere reference to it sufficient in this place.   In that connexion, too, Norway will be considered.   The explanation of the seeming paradox that the scarcity of raw materials principally hit production and left consumption almost unchanged, also lies in the consumers' comparatively great independence of market conditions as well as in the great reserves of linen, cloth, and wearing apparel kept in every self-respecting household.

In spite of the limitation in the general effects of the Continental System that follows from all this, one cannot shut one's eyes to the fact that the years 1811–13, after the crisis in France, Great Britain, and most of the other countries, are characterized by a serious deterioration of the economic

---

[1] Worm-Müller, *Norge gjennem nødsaarene*, &c., pp. 82 *et seq.*

conditions prevailing everywhere on the Napoleonic mainland. It is true that the character of this deterioration is anything but clear and would deserve a really searching examination; but the fact stands out clearly in many different quarters. As early as the autumn of 1810 one of the French commercial spies speaks openly and very pointedly of the ' pretty general condition of ill-being (*malaise*) ' in Germany; and afterwards the situation finds particular expression in the difficulties, already indicated, that the luxury industries experienced in finding a market. Moreover, the same thing is shown by the difficulty in overcoming the crisis of 1810–11 and its more or less latent continuation down to the great transformation brought about by Napoleon's fall. It was just at that time, too, that food difficulties showed themselves to some extent all over Europe and hit the most vital of the general needs. There is no justification, it is true, for laying the blame for this position entirely on the Continental System, which was merely one side of a state of war that had then existed for twenty years; but undoubtedly the trade blockade had its share in the result. It is possible that conditions would have come to develop in a direction more like our recent experiences if the fall of Napoleon had been delayed a few more years. As things turned out, however, people got scarcely more than a preliminary taste of what would have been involved in such a situation.

# CHAPTER IV

## EFFECTS ON THE UNITED KINGDOM

THERE remains the question of the effects of the Continental System on the United Kingdom, which is in a way the most important of all, inasmuch as it must show the importance of the policy in relation to its special purpose.

### LIMITATIONS OF OBSTACLES TO EXPORTS

In order to be able to judge this matter aright, we must realize clearly the serious weakness that existed in Napoleon's position from the standpoint of the Continental System, a weakness that lay in the fact that the very most that he could be expected to attain by his own resources was the closing of the mainland of Europe. The importance of this for his object of smothering the exports of Great Britain probably appears with sufficient exactitude if we reduce the value figures corresponding to her exports to percentages and then divide them into three groups according to countries of destination. The position is then revealed as follows : [1]

#### A. DOMESTIC GOODS

| Year | | | Europe | United States | Rest of world |
|------|---|---|--------|--------------|---------------|
| 1805 | . | . | 37·8 per cent. | 30·5 per cent. | 31·7 per cent. |
| 1806 | . | . | 30·9 ,, | 31·3 ,, | 37·8 ,, |
| 1807 | . | . | 25·5 ,, | 33·4 ,, | 41·1 ,, |
| 1808 | . | . | 25·7 ,, | 15·0 ,, | 59·3 ,, |
| 1809 | . | . | 35·4 ,, | 16·2 ,, | 48·4 ,, |
| 1810 | . | . | 34·1 ,, | 23·9 ,, | 42·0 ,, |
| 1811 | . | . | 42·9 ,, | 6·2 ,, | 50·9 ,, |

[1] The calculation has been made on the basis of the figures given on p. 245, and like those figures, it applies to Great Britain alone (excluding Ireland). But a change has been made in the fact that the trade with Ireland, the Channel Islands, and the Isle of Man has not here been taken into account.

B. FOREIGN AND COLONIAL GOODS

| Year | Europe | United States | Rest of world |
|---|---|---|---|
| 1805 . . . | 78·7 per cent. | 5·1 per cent. | 16·2 per cent. |
| 1806 . . . | 72·9 ,, | 5·7 ,, | 21·4 ,, |
| 1807 . . . | 80·0 ,, | 3·1 ,, | 16·9 ,, |
| 1808 . . . | 71·1 ,, | 0·9 ,, | 28·0 ,, |
| 1809 . . . | 83·1 ,, | 1·4 ,, | 15·5 ,, |
| 1810 . . . | 76·9 ,, | 2·7 ,, | 20·4 ,, |
| 1811 . . . | 83·6 ,, | 0·4 ,, | 16·0 ,, |

This summary shows, to judge by the position immediately before the organization of the Continental System, that at the very highest about one-third of the exports of domestic goods could be affected by the self-blockade of the Continent, although, it is true, there must be added to this three-fourths of the re-exports. It was, therefore, a factor of fundamental importance for Napoleon's success that the United States should also be driven to the establishment of a self-blockade, inasmuch as that would put an end to another third of the exports of British goods. It is impossible to deny that in this matter he received excellent help from the British government itself, when it allowed things to come to an almost unbroken series of conflicts with America, mainly because of the Orders in Council, which as a matter of fact were never more than quite a secondary weapon in the great struggle. This meant that, strictly speaking, everything had been done which was really possible in the direction of preventing British exports; and so far Napoleon had achieved even more than he could have achieved with the resources of his own empire alone.

But precisely the development thereby created, as it is illustrated in the above figures, shows a limitation in the range even in a course of action which was so surprisingly successful, namely, that it always left trade with the rest of the world undisturbed. We see from the third column of the table how the share of this department of exports with regard to British goods increases in relative importance under the Continental System in comparison with the preceding years; and this tendency will be clear whether the situation is regarded from an English or from a continental point of view. British industry would seek transmarine markets as substitutes for lost European ones ; and it would likewise find them, as the increased self-sufficiency of the European Continent would make the rest of the world more dependent upon British supply than before. Of interest in this connexion is the fact that the Continental System gave the impulse for British transmarine exports of calicoes and prints, which had been unheard of before.[1] And in this respect Napoleon was almost hopelessly impotent, for it must have been inconceivable to prevent for any long time the power that commanded all the seas of the world from exporting goods to other continents.   Even if the self-blockade of the Continent of Europe had been complete, which was, of course, far from the case, the immediate effect would probably have been to hasten the economic orientation of Great Britain both from Europe and also, to a large extent, from the United States, to the rest of the world ; and this orientation, as a matter of fact, has taken place gradually during the last hundred years and has formed one of the most significant changes in the position of Great Britain in the economy of the world. In one of his famous and most overweening utterances (1826), Canning justified British co-operation in the liberation of the South American colonies on the ground that ' he called the New World into existence to redress the balance of the Old '. In the sphere of economics this British tendency already had century-old roots, and indeed it was precisely what was attempted under the Continental System by the speculative exports to Brazil.   When one follows the later development of transmarine exports, one scarcely doubts that this speculative touch would soon have vanished if the blockade of the Continent had become permanently effective.   How important the change has been since the time immediately before the Continental System is shown by the following comparison with the situation immediately before the outbreak of the World War.[2]

---

[1] ' Erst die Kontinentalsperre zwang England, zum Ersatz für den Entgang des kontinentalen Marktes andere überseeische Absatzgebiete aufzusuchen.   Das waren die Levanteländer.'   Jenny-Trümpy, op. cit., vol. II, pp. 370–71, quoted in Geering, Entwickelung des Zeugdrucks, &c., p. 422.

[2] The figures for 1913 are calculated on the basis of the Statistical Abstract for the United Kingdom.

A. DOMESTIC GOODS

| Year | Europe | United States | Rest of world |
|---|---|---|---|
| 1805 . . . | 37·8 per cent | 30·5 per cent. | 31·7 per cent. |
| 1913 . . . | 35·6 ,, | 5·6 ,, | 58·8 ,, |

B. FOREIGN AND COLONIAL GOODS

| Year | Europe | United States | Rest of world |
|---|---|---|---|
| 1805 . . . | 78·7 per cent. | 5·1 per cent. | 16·2 per cent. |
| 1913 . . . | 56·1 ,, | 27·5 ,, | 16·4 ,, |

The same thing can also be illustrated by the quantity figures, namely, the tons actually shipped to the same groups of countries; but in this case we can deal only with the first half of the nineteenth century, because statistics are no longer compiled in this way.

| Year | Europe | United States | Rest of world |
|---|---|---|---|
| 1802 . . . | 66·97 per cent. | 7·53 per cent. | 25·50 per cent. |
| 1849 . . . | 56·00 ,, | 16·90 ,, | 27·10 ,, |

More or less parenthetically it should be observed that at the present time Great Britain, as a consequence of this, would be considerably less susceptible to being barred from exports to Europe than she was a hundred years ago.

The limitation of Napoleon's possibilities of affecting British exports was thus obvious even during the comparatively few years that his continental empire lasted; and, as far as one can judge, it would have become still more so, in ever-increasing degree, if the Continent of Europe had passed through a long period of isolation. We must now try to form a notion of British economic life under the pressure of the blockade as far as it actually became a reality.

Unfortunately it must be regarded as impossible, in the main, to separate these effects in any kind of inductive way from the general tangle of economic development. Not even in the peculiar department of war measures does the Continental System stand in isolation; that is to say, the effects of the war and the effects of the Continental System do not coincide. Here the self-blockade of the Continent has by its side the Orders in Council and the many other subjects of dispute with the United States, which brought about the closing of that great market to British exports; and they were accompanied also by the burdens peculiar to the war itself, which could not possibly have been without importance even if there had been a complete lack of measures and counter-measures in the sphere of commercial policy.  But in addition to all this there was the circumstance that not even this complex of factors could take effect as a whole in anything which could be called, even approximately, a community in a state of economic equilibrium.  On the contrary, the economic life of Great Britain would have been in a state of violent trans-formation quite irrespective of the Napoleonic wars, owing to all the different movements included in the industrial revolution, the effects of which were made still worse by a poor law system which was entirely devoid of guiding principles and was there-fore extremely pauperizing.  Finally, moreover, the confusion of the British currency caused dislocations which must be referred to yet a third cause, which was in the main independent of the others.  It is manifestly impossible, under such circum-stances, to arrive at more than rather general conclusions as to the effect of the Continental System on the economic life of Great Britain as a whole.

### RATE OF INDUSTRIAL DEVELOPMENT

The main thing is to determine to what extent the industry of the country was hit in the way that Napoleon intended. We ask ourselves, therefore, whether the six years during which the Continental System may be regarded as having been in force (1807–12) exhibited any stagnation or decline with respect to the preceding and succeeding development; if there was, we may possibly see in this an effect of this special cause.

The question is not easy to answer, as the period was so short and so full of ups and downs.  But one starting-point might possibly be obtained in the figures for the supply of coal, if such were available; for during the age of coal, coal has usually formed the best common standard of industrial development.  As it is, however, we have no figures for the total amount of coal produced, but only for the quantities of coal shipped from Newcastle and Sunderland; while probably the greater part, and the part that underwent the greatest increase, was consumed within the huge cotton, wool, and iron areas that lay on or behind the coal-fields. But in any case the figures (yearly averages) are of interest.[1]

| Period | Tons | Per cent. increase over preceding period |
|---|---|---|
| First quinquennial period of the century (1801–5) . | 2,137,209 | .. |
| Period of the Continental System (1807–12) . . | 2,463,800 | 15·20 |
| First quinquennial period after the peace (1816–20). | 2,812,851 | 14·83 |

These figures do not in the least degree indicate that the rate of industrial development was retarded under the Continental System, but, on the contrary, they show that the growth was not greater even during the first years of peace; and the figures for the particular years give the same impression. For the cotton industry by itself we have no figures to go by save those referring to the imports of raw cotton; and as appears from the tables given in a preceding chapter,[2] the fluctuations here were very great from year to year. But a summary of the figures for net imports, on the same method as before, gives the following result :

| Year | Pounds | Per cent. increase over preceding period |
|---|---|---|
| 1801–5 . . . . | 56,662,421 | .. |
| 1807–12 . . . . | 79,744,529 | 40·73 |
| 1816–20 . . . . | 130,328,347 | 89·27 |

Here too, therefore, we are confronted with an increase which is even several times greater than in the former case, although it falls far short of the increase during the following peace period, which, of course, is only natural.

Nor does the rest of the somewhat scattered material that is available show any visible signs that the uniquely rapid industrial development which is characteristic of this period

---

[1] The figures have been collected on the basis of the table in Porter, *Progress of the Nation*, pp. 275–6. The other statistical data in this section have been taken, where nothing to the contrary is stated, from the same work.

[2] See *ante*, p. 242.

was retarded by the Continental System. The population of Great Britain and Ireland increased 13 per cent. between the years 1801 and 1811, as compared with 15¼ per cent. during the following decade; and naturally it was considerably greater for the industrial districts. Calico-printing works quadrupled their production between 1800–14, and the exports of iron increased. Nor did the years of the Continental System form an exception to the general transition to new technical methods which constituted the *primus motor* of the industrial revolution. Thus Cort's son stated in a petition to the House of Commons in 1812 that even at that date 250,000 tons of malleable iron were annually produced by puddling and that Cort's processes had obtained practically general acceptance.[1] The power-loom likewise made progress, though at a considerably slower pace. A great new revolution took place in calico-printing with the year 1808, in that the pattern was transferred to the cylinders from a little steel cylinder instead of being engraved direct; and the lace machine came into existence in 1809, &c.

There was certainly no pause in the industrial revolution, nor any tendency to a backward development of the industrial life of Great Britain toward increased self-sufficiency, such as, in accordance with our previous findings, would have been the consequence of complete success for the Continental System. But, of course, it was not in that way that Napoleon himself thought of the matter; his hopes were limited to dislocations in the system.

### EFFECTS OF DISLOCATION OF EXPORTS

It appears from the account in part iii that these hopes were not frustrated, but, on the contrary, were very nearly fulfilled through the British crisis of 1810–11. Also it appears equally clear that this crisis cannot be regarded wholly, or even mainly (though certainly in part), as a fruit of the blows of the Continental System against Great Britain; nor was the extent of its effects at all what Napoleon had imagined.

[1] Hansard, vol. xxi, p. 330.

On the whole, we have no reason to regard the economic effect of purely dislocation phenomena as particularly important. It is possible in this connexion that we are too much impressed by the unique experiences of the recent war in this direction; but even if we think of crises occurring during otherwise normal times—even crises of such an incalculable character as the cotton famine in England during the American Civil War—it is striking how soon their traces are swept away by subsequent development. The whole of Napoleon's plan on this point, made out at short sight as it was, cannot be regarded as having had any great prospect of attaining its object, that is, the crippling of Great Britain's military power by undermining the foundations of her economic life.

This, then, holds good of the purely economic effects of the dislocation; with regard to its social and political effects the matter assumes quite a different aspect. Here the political economist can really neither contest nor confirm the process of thought, for the result depends almost exclusively on the character of the people in question. An impulsive race, which has also become accustomed to receiving help from the state in all things great and small, may be led by a mere trifle to overthrow a government, a constitution, perhaps a whole order of society, while another people, which is more phlegmatic and less trained to rely on the state, may leave the conduct of the state entirely undisturbed even in times of serious distress and great difficulties. It is quite obvious that Englishmen, especially during the time of the Napoleonic wars, belonged to the latter category; and as Miss Cunningham has justly observed, the rage of the unemployed was directed in the " Luddite riots " against the new machinery (frame-breaking), but not really against the government.[1] One can easily imagine that Napoleon, with his experience of the continual *coups d'état* during the French Revolution, could not see this; but this makes no difference with respect to the fact that he made a thorough miscalculation.

But to all this must be added the fact—and this is a very

[1] Miss Cunningham, *British Credit*, &c., pp. 76–7.

important fact—that the particular kind of dislocation in Great Britain due to the Continental System which was most favourable to Napoleon, was necessarily of a comparatively superficial nature, just because it was a dislocation caused by obstacles in the way of exports and not of obstacles in the way of imports. A failure of exports can always be alleviated by production with a view to accumulating stocks—supported, if necessary, by public funds; but that is not the case with the failure of imports, for if irreplaceable commodities are irretrievably left outside no measures can be of any avail.[1]

Napoleon's thoughts certainly did not run in that direction, and the explanation lies in an attitude we have already learned to know, and which he shared not only with all his countrymen, but also, probably, with the majority of Englishmen. But even with due allowance for this, the position he took up was very peculiar; for what England would have needed to do was pretty much what he himself did at that very time. His own remedy for unemployment, in fact, was state support in different forms, in order to enable manufacturers to continue operations; and there is no reason to suppose that he ever ceased to believe in the efficacy of this remedy. In that case it would not have been a great flight of imagination to expect the same capacity on the part of his adversaries, whose fertility of resource and endurance he was not wont to deny.

In reality, it is true, these remedies were employed in Great Britain only to a very limited extent, owing to the fact that the principle of *laissez-faire* had already obtained a great influence over the classes that held political power in England. But we may certainly assume that Napoleon was not so familiar with his enemies or their economic views that he took such a factor into account. The British measures were limited to an issue of treasury bills for £6,000,000 for the support of embarrassed business men, chiefly manufacturers, the intention being to tide them over the time of waiting until the assets locked up in South America or elsewhere could be released.

---

[1] It may be allowable to point out how well this result, which was reached early in 1918, is in accordance with later German developments.

The proposal on this subject, based on a precedent of 1793, had been brought forward by a committee of the House of Commons in March 1811, but was not very enthusiastically received in any quarter.  None the less the plan was carried out, because no one really wished to be responsible for throwing obstacles in the way of anything that might possibly be helpful in an unusually ticklish situation.[1]

The arguments brought against the plan, especially by the economic authorities of the opposition, such as Huskisson, were especially that the crisis had been brought on by an excess of credit, which in its turn was connected with the excessive issue of notes by the Bank of England, and that these new loans would merely augment the speculation, the issue of notes and the rise of prices.  To what extent this diagnosis was correct is a question that does not pertain to our present subject. We need only observe that if obstacles in the way of sale arise that are really caused by blockade and not by excessive speculation, then the transition to that form of production which in such a situation would be the right one can be rendered easier by a granting of credit that permits of a limited production for stock during the period of transition.  Further, if this granting of credit is effected by *genuine* saving, that is to say, by a diminution of the demand for credit for other purposes— a thing which the banks can bring about by raising the rate of discount—then there do not arise the consequences alleged by Huskisson and by those who shared his views.  This implies that the dislocation at which Napoleon aimed by placing obstacles in the way of British exports could have been overcome without insuperable difficulties.  As things were, one may say that, on the whole, the dislocation was overcome by itself, without any measure at all worth mentioning ; and it is not impossible that this was the best way out of the difficulty.

The impenetrable conviction as to the harm of all kinds of state interference found unmixed expression when it was a question of the sufferings of the workmen.  With reference

[1] For this and the following paragraph, cf. the references given above (p. 239, note).

to petitions from the cotton operatives in Lancashire and Scotland, the House of Commons appointed, at the beginning of June 1811, a committee, which made its report after eight days. In that report it was stated, in the first place, 'that no interference of the legislature with the freedom of trade or with the perfect liberty of every individual to dispose of his time and of his labour, in the way and on the terms which he may judge most conducive to his own interest, can take place without violating general principles of the first importance to the prosperity and happiness of the community '—this as a reply to the petitions of the workmen for a regulation of the actual conditions of labour. In the second place, it was laid down that help in the form of money ' would be utterly inefficacious as to every good purpose, and most objectionable in all points of view ', and after this there was no alternative left. Nevertheless, it would be a misjudgment of the leading men of the time if we should choose to see in their position mainly indifference as to the welfare of the workers, who, on the contrary, had indisputably sincere spokesmen in both the House of Commons and in the committee in question, especially the great cotton manufacturer, Sir Robert Peel, the father of the statesman. The fact of the matter is, as far as one can judge, that they sincerely regarded any kind of relief to the workers as harmful—although, in striking contrast, relief in the form of loans was finally granted to the manufacturers—because it was calculated to raise hopes which could not be fulfilled and to bind the workers firmly to an industry which could not give them employment. One speaker in the House of Commons particularly emphasized the necessity of the transfer of labour to agriculture, with the object of making the country independent of the import of foodstuffs. This was precisely a demand for the reorganization of economic life with a view to increased self-sufficiency. But the very fact that the working classes of Great Britain acquiesced with comparative patience in their tremendously heavy sufferings, even in the presence of so uncompromising a rejection, shows how limited the possibilities in reality were of putting an end to British power of resistance by any social movements caused by economic dislocations. This will be particularly clear if we compare the attitude of the holders of political power at that time with the concessions that had to be made to the demands of the workmen during the recent war in order not to endanger their good-will toward a continuance of the struggle.

### POSSIBILITY OF PREVENTING IMPORTS

All that has just been said, however, applies only to obstacles in the way of exports, with their obviously limited possibilities of causing ruin in the economic life of a country. As the economic function of exports is absolutely limited to providing payment for imports, it is quite meaningless when there are no imports. Imports, on the other hand, are ends in themselves, because they satisfy the wants of the people directly, which is the final function of all economic activity. Consequently, we cannot possibly turn our backs on the question as to what chances Napoleon would have had for gaining his object if he had directed the point of his blockade against the imports of Great Britain instead of against her exports. It is indeed true that this was quite incompatible with the economic views that he shared with the majority of persons of political consequence, as has been shown throughout our previous account. But it does not necessarily follow from this that he could not have made his object the cutting-off both of imports and of exports, as, on the whole, took place during the recent war ; in any case the problem is so important that it cannot be ignored. What especially necessitates an investigation of the whole thing, including Napoleon's policy in the matter, is that the view which has been pretty generally accepted during the last decade happens to have been determined by a popular article by Dr. J. H. Rose, which was hastily drafted for a purely practical purpose and which scarcely gives sufficient, or even correct, guidance in the question.[1]

[1] ' Britain's Food Supply in the Napoleonic War,' in the *Monthly Review* (1902), reprinted in *Napoleonic Studies*, pp. 204 *et seq.* The later statement by Dr. Rose in his chapter on ' The Continental System ', in the *Cambridge Modern History*, vol. IX, p. 371, is in far better accord with the sources as I read them.

## British Imports of Foodstuffs

The question of the dependence of Great Britain on imports from the European mainland has generally been regarded as identical with the question of its provision with food.  To a large extent this is correct, inasmuch as the majority of industrial raw materials imported came from transmarine countries, and practically all industrial products of importance for the mass of the community could be manufactured within the country.  Yet it should be mentioned that both naval stores (especially timber) and wool formed exceptions from this general rule, inasmuch as they were taken from the Baltic lands (including Scandinavia) and from Spain or Germany, respectively;  and, as we have already mentioned, there was at times a scarcity of both these kinds of commodities during the course of the Continental System.  Consequently it is not impossible that two such fundamental sides of war requirements as shipbuilding and the clothing of troops might have offered difficulties if the supply from Europe had been cut off.  It is far from probable, however, that these factors would have been decisive, since timber, like other things required for ships, could have been obtained from Canada ;  and according to an estimate for the year 1800 more than nine-tenths of the wool required can be assumed to have been provided from domestic sources.  Obviously the question of foodstuffs went much further.

The importance of Great Britain's imports of foodstuffs, which can practically be regarded as identical with her imports of wheat, is anything but clear, it is true, as we have no information at all as to the agricultural production of the country itself.[1]  Nevertheless, there can be no doubt that the previously

---

[1] Cf. also, Porter, *op. cit.* ;  Tooke, *op. cit.* ;  Smart, *op. cit.* ;  Oddy, *op. cit.*, bk. III ;  McCulloch, *Dictionary, Practical, Theoretical, and Historical, of Commerce and Commercial Navigation* (new ed., London, 1852), article on 'Corn Laws and Corn Trade' ;  Cunningham, *Growth of English Industry and Commerce*, 3d ed., vol. II, pp. 703 *et seq.* The British figures corresponding to volume (quarters of 8 bushels) have been recalculated according to weight, 1 bushel being taken as equal to 28·2 kgs.

existing surplus available for export had been replaced, within the twenty years before the outbreak of the revolutionary wars at the latest, by a normal excess of imports, and that the self-sufficiency of the country had thus ceased to exist. In absolute figures the excess imports of wheat quite naturally varied much from year to year, according to the harvest. The British imports during the Napoleonic wars—always including what came from Ireland—attained their maximum in 1810 with 336,400 tons, while one solitary year (1808) even showed an insignificant excess of exports. The average figure during the period of the Continental System (1807–12) was an import excess of 104,000 tons. The absolute significance of this figure will be made clearer if in connexion with it we mention the fact that the wheat imports of a country such as Sweden, for instance, during the period immediately before the outbreak of the World War in 1914, was about 200,000 tons, and its combined imports of wheat and rye were about 300,000 tons, that is to say, two or three times as much, respectively. Thus there can be no doubt that the quantities in themselves were small according to our notions. It is more important, however, to form a clear notion of the relative importance of such imports for the total British consumption of wheat ; but unfortunately this is impossible, as we do not know the amount of the harvests. The majority of estimates, both contemporary and later, however, are based on a consumption per inhabitant in Great Britain, that is to say, excluding Ireland, of one quarter or about 225 kgs. per annum, not counting seed-wheat. This undeniably strikes one as a very high figure, as, for instance, the Swedish consumption of wheat and rye together before the outbreak of the World War, that is to say, a hundred years later, was only about 180 kgs. However, if we take British calculations as to consumption as our basis, we find that, according to the average population of Great Britain during the decade 1801–10 (about $11\frac{3}{4}$ millions) the total consumption of wheat would have been 2,655,000 tons, of which the average import excess during that decennial period (132,600 tons) formed just 5 per cent., or one-twentieth. This very modest amount would thus have been the normal import demand ; but if instead of this we wish to investigate the relative magnitude of the greatest shortage during the period, that for the year 1810, we find that not even that, in relation to the then greater population, rises to more than about 12 per cent. However, there also occurs a lower calculation of the consumption than one quarter (eight bushels) per inhabitant, namely, six bushels, which falls slightly short of the Swedish consumption of rye and wheat a hundred years later. As the home supply in Great Britain can only be obtained from a figure based on consumption, this gives a smaller amount for the harvest, and consequently a greater share for imports. On such a supposition, that share forms $6\frac{1}{2}$ per cent., or somewhat over one-sixteenth, on an average, for the decennial period of 1801–10, and a good 16 per cent., or scarcely one-sixth, for the year of maximum imports, 1810.

Even if the imports of wheat had been totally cut off, therefore, the deficiency, even in years of bad harvest and on the most unfavourable estimate, would have been a mere trifle in comparison with what we had to accustom ourselves to during the recent war. For Sweden the average imports during the quinquennial period before the outbreak of that war formed a good fourth of the total requirements of wheat and rye, while the total supply of cereals in Sweden during the bad year 1917–18 was probably less than half of the normal. This shows to what extent normal food requirements have been curtailed, even in neutral countries in our own day, and the shortage a hundred years ago consequently dwindles into comparative insignificance. In spite of this, the blockade during the revolutionary and Napoleonic wars was sufficiently effective both to stimulate the cultivation of corn in Great Britain,[1] and also to bring about a severely felt shortage of food, which was especially marked in the years 1795, 1800, and 1812, and which gave rise to constant apprehensions. A large number of the measures adopted during the recent war were

---

[1] Cp. Ricardo, *Principles of Political Economy and Taxation* (London, 1817), ch. XIX ; Malthus, *Principles of Political Economy* (London, 1820), ch. III, sec. IX.

also employed a hundred years ago, though not the most effective and far-reaching among them, and especially not rationing. These measures included a suspension of the corn duties, the prohibition of the distillation of spirits and the manufacture of starch, the postponement of the sale of bread until twenty-four hours after baking, incessant exhortations in royal proclamations and also organized agreements to reduce the consumption of bread by a third, as well as a prohibition against baking bread of unmixed fine bolted wheat flour, which is known as the Brown Bread Act of 1800. But the population found it much more difficult to put up with these interferences with their food habits than with other privations which, to our way of thinking, were considerably greater. It proved impossible to enforce the Brown Bread Act, so that it had to be repealed immediately; and serious food disturbances occurred both in 1800 and in 1812. So far, therefore, it is fairly evident that the placing of obstacles in the way of importing corn would have had far greater prospects of affecting public opinion and tranquillity in Great Britain than the barring of exports, in which Napoleon placed his confidence. On the other hand, the assumption that even the barring of imports would have forced the conclusion of peace, or overthrown the British government, is one which is more or less refuted by experience. During the year 1812, when the prices of wheat reached a record height and remained there until the last weeks of the old harvest year, there prevailed just that position which would have been the consequence of a blockade as complete as one can reasonably imagine to have been enforced. For owing to the bad harvest, which was general in Europe, as well as to immense purchases made by Napoleon as a preparation for the Russian campaign, the rise in prices in Great Britain did not cause any imports worth mentioning; for the whole year there entered the country only 55,000 tons, which is little more than half of the average figure for the sexennial period of the Continental System, and considerably less than half of the average figure for the preceding decennial period. Thus the fact that, despite all this, difficulties could be overcome indicates more or less plainly that not even a complete barring of imports would have attained its object, even apart from the fact that an effective blockade would probably have been able, after some time, to pave the way for some of the effective measures with which a much greater scarcity of food was met during the recent war.

Napoleon's chances of striking at British food supplies were evidently limited to what had to be taken from the mainland of Europe, or, in the case most favourable to him, from there and from the United States.   In sources accessible to me there do not exist figures relating to all the countries of origin of the wheat imported into Great Britain during this period.   But the American wheat went mainly to South Europe, especially to the Iberian peninsula during the tremendous struggles there, while all our information points to the idea that the Baltic lands formed the main source of supply of corn for Great Britain, with Danzig as the centre.   From the very full statistics on the Baltic seaports printed in Oddy's work, it appears that in the year 1800, when British imports of wheat were great, 47 per cent. came from the three ports, Königsberg, Elbing, and Danzig, 34 per cent. from Danzig alone.[1]   And besides these, other Baltic ports were of importance also.   Consequently, so far as Napoleon could make his will prevail, not only on the North Sea coast of Germany, but also upon the south and, to some extent, the east coast of the Baltic, he did not lack the possibility of hampering the food supply of Great Britain.   Accordingly, the question is, How did he really regard such a task and what steps did he take to accomplish it ?

### Food Policy of Napoleon and His Opponent

It is on this point that the accepted views have been determined by the conclusions of Dr. Rose in the article referred to above.   They come to this, that Napoleon not only did nothing to hinder British imports of foodstuffs, but actually sought to encourage the exports of corn to that country with the object of ruining the enemy through the unfavourable

[1] Computed on the basis of Oddy's figures, *op. cit.*, pp. 234-52 ; *passim.*

trade balance which would be the consequence thereof.  But
this account gives a misleading impression both of the measures
and of the motives of Napoleon, and it is not borne out by the
letters cited by Dr. Rose in its support.

It is true that the notion of ruining the enemy by imports
fitted in very well with the economic conceptions of Napoleon
and of many of his contemporaries, as has been sufficiently
shown in the foregoing pages.  But the matter of food supplies
here took an exceptional position, inasmuch as it was regulated
in the continental states, and especially in France, along the
lines of the mediaeval 'policy of plenty' rather than in accordance with the principles of mercantilism, in that it was desired,
primarily, to provide for an abundant supply and not for
profitable production and sale.  Napoleon did not swerve from
the economic traditions of France any more in this department
of economic policy than in others;  and it would have been
highly peculiar if he had allowed himself to be led by one set
of ideas where his own country was concerned and by another
set when the enemy was concerned.  Nor was that the case,
but, on the contrary, his opinion is quite consistent and not at
all difficult to explain.

The fundamental object of Napoleon's food policy was, as
has just been mentioned, to secure supplies within the country ;
and this not only from the same motives that actuated his
Bourbon predecessors, but also because of his desire to prevent
labour disturbances.  Consequently, he is always reminding
his French helpers of the danger of being insufficiently provided with foodstuffs, urging them to remember what it had
cost him in the Year X (1801–2) to procure a few thousand
*quintaux* of corn, and insisting that it would involve the greatest
danger if they had not a 'double supply'.  'You have not
sufficient experience in this matter,' he wrote in 1810 to Eugene,
the viceroy of Italy.  'The corn question is for sovereigns the
most important and the most delicate of all. . . . The first duty
of the prince in this question is to hold to the people, without listening to the sophisms of the landowners.'  During the
difficulties of the winter of 1812 he strove, by the distribution

of bread and soup, ' to make the most needy part of the
multitude independent' of food difficulties. Just as before,
therefore, he forbade the export of corn when scarcity was
apprehended, or even, as in 1810, while awaiting the results
of the harvest. And although on August 6, 1810, he had
authorized Eugene to permit the exportation of corn from
Italy, he wrote to him three weeks later (August 31) : ' It is
said that the Italian harvest is bad. Take care that not too
much corn is exported and that we do not get into difficulties.'
For this reason, too, he authorized his Italian minister of finance
in 1813 to permit the export of French and Italian products
with the exception of corn and rice, regarding which he wished
to have a report first—a policy that marks the special position
of food exports—and, in full analogy with this, Napoleon, in
January 1812, expressed the opinion that licences for the
importation of foodstuffs should be granted without conditions ;
that is to say, he waived the customary obligation of exporting
goods to the corresponding value.

The same point of view determined the whole series of
measures that the Emperor took in the winter and spring of
1811–12, when, according to his own declaration, there was
a real scarcity of corn in Paris. At the same time he deemed
it necessary to take more pains than usual to secure quiet in
Paris during his absence on the Russian campaign. His feverish
zeal to intervene and regulate drove his helpers, especially
Pasquier, the eminent prefect of police in Paris, to despair,
and afterwards led Chaptal to make the biting remark that
Napoleon took every measure that was calculated to further
the rise in prices and the shortage of foodstuffs. These measures
included the buying up and seizure of corn in the departments
adjoining Paris, the taking over of the mills, secret sales by the
agents of the government in order to force down prices when
they rose in consequence of the previous measures—the only
consequence of which was to raise them still farther, and the
final result, as the culmination of the abortive ' policy of
plenty ', was the establishment of maximum prices. It should
be obvious, on the face of it, that the whole of this series of

measures was totally incompatible with the notion that it would injure an enemy to provide him with food.[1]

On the other hand, it certainly did not follow from such a point of view that the export of foodstuffs would be considered inexpedient or even looked at askance, under all circumstances. As soon as the supply of food within the country was considered safeguarded, the general interest for exports showed itself at once ; and the ruler of such countries as North Germany, Italy, and France, which were distinctively countries that exported foods and stimulants, could hardly be imagined as adopting any other standpoint, when in other respects he favoured the mercantilist or ' bullionist ' policy. It was only natural, therefore, that Napoleon, in a letter of 1810 to Gaudin, his minister of finance, which has already been cited once or twice, spoke of his object of favouring, by means of smuggling, the export of French foodstuffs and the import of precious metals ; and that in the same year he caused Champagny to inform the French ambassador at St. Petersburg—evidently with reference to complaints on the part of Russia—that he granted licences for the exportation of wine and corn as beneficial to his territories, without inquiring too closely as to how the English afterwards treated the vessels provided with licences. Similarly, in a letter of July 28, 1809 (cited by Dr. Rose), to the acting home secretary, Fouché, he bitterly denounced the allegation that he discountenanced export in itself, which he, on the contrary, regarded as being hindered by the British and not by him. ' Exports occur,' he said, ' as soon as there is a possibility of sale.' Not one of these letters, or any other letter known to the writer, contains even a hint of an intention to injure England by the exports of foodstuffs, but, on the other hand, an evident intention to benefit France thereby. The real

---

[1] Letters to Archchancellor Cambacérès, Apr. 5 and 25, 1807 ; to Eugene, Aug. 6 and 31, Sept. 24, 1810 ; various ' notes ' (imperial dictated addresses) dated Jan. 13, Feb. 8, Mar. 11, 1812 (*Correspondance*, nos. 12,297 ; 12,470 ; 16,767 ; 16,855 ; 16,946 ; 18,431 ; 18,485 ; 18,568) ; Letters to the Italian minister of finance, Mar. 22, 1813 (*Lettres inédites de Napoléon Ier*, no. 972) ; Pasquier, *Histoire de mon temps : Mémoires* (Paris, 1893), vol. I, ch. XXI ; Chaptal, *Souvenirs, &c.*, pp. 291-2 ; Levasseur, *Histoire des classes ouvrières, &c., de 1789 à 1870*, vol. I, pp. 341, 477 note 5 ; Vandal, *op. cit.*, vol. III, pp. 339, 459.

motive stands out distinctly in the most celebrated cases when extensive exports of corn from France, Holland, and Flanders to Great Britain took place in the years 1809 and 1810. During 1809 it is stated that about 90,000 tons of wheat, besides other grain, came from those countries; and of the unprecedented imports in the following year—which, without deducting exports, amounted to 353,500 tons of wheat and 135,400 tons of other grain and represented a total value of more than £7,000,000—one-third of the wheat (evidently unground) and half of the flour were said to have come from Napoleon's empire, all by means of mutual licences. The remarkable thing in this connexion is that not only Napoleon but also many Englishmen considered these large imports from France, under the existing conditions, to be extremely advantageous for the French, and consequently open to grave objection from a British point of view. This was partly because it provided means of disposing of surplus products, and partly because it was an important source of income to Napoleon owing to the huge licensing fees, which, together with freight and insurance, were alleged to raise the price by 30–50s. per quarter, or from £6 15s. to £11 per ton. This mode of thought, which is just as much French as British, was given characteristic expression in a speech in the House of Commons (February 13, 1810) by the politician Marryat, the father of the famous novelist, from which we cite the following:

The benefit which the enemy derived from the present system of licensing the importation of his grain was much more than many gentlemen imagined. It was a fact that in July last the farmers of France were so distressed by the low price of grain, that they could not pay their taxes. The price was then so low as 27s. the sack, whilst it was known that the French farmer calculated upon a price of 36s. as a fair return for his expences. Buonaparté, being apprized of these circumstances, had no hesitation, of course [sic], in granting licences for the exportation of that grain, which our government readily granted licences to import; the consequence of which was the raising of the price of that article in France, by the last accounts, above 50 per cent. beyond the rate in July last. Thus were the French corn growers benefited, while Buonoparté's treasury derived at the rate of 18s. a quarter from the same means. He would then submit it to the serious consideration of the House whether some measures ought not to be immediately taken to put an end to a practice which so materially served the resources of the enemy.

This leads us to the third motive determining Napoleon's corn policy, the motive that had decisive weight for more and more of his economic measures the longer the war went on—the need of money. This, and nothing else, dictated the whole of the motley multitude of export licences for corn to French, Italian, and Neapolitan ports, the Hanse Towns, Mecklenburg, Danzig, &c., in combination with special export fees, especially in the last-named place, which was the most important export-ing port of all. This fact alone shows that there was no thought of flooding Great Britain with corn, for in that case there would have been no question of export dues, least of all to such amounts as now occurred, which, according to General Rapp, the French commander in Danzig, were 60 francs per ton in 1810, and were so high that they were quite expected to smother the trade of Danzig.

So far was Napoleon from believing that he was injuring England by the mere fact of supplying her with corn, that he evidently perceived the profit of that supply to his adversary, as indeed is obvious beforehand. In the above-mentioned instructions to Champagny, meant to be forwarded to Caulain-court, the ambassador in St. Petersburg, he expressly says : ' The English, having need of corn, will naturally let them (the vessels) enter and leave, because the corn is a prime necessity for them.'

Since that was the case, however, the question arises whether the Emperor had no thought of giving a new turn to his policy and making a direct effort to starve out England. Thus far we have had no knowledge of this matter ; but some contributions toward an answer to the question have become available through the publication, in 1913, of the first part of the work of the Russian historian, Tarle, entitled *Kontinental'-naja blokada*. Thus in a report dated July 17, 1810, Montalivet, the home secretary, wrote to Napoleon as follows : ' If our rival is eventually threatened with famine, it would seem to be

quite natural to close all ports to him. It would be beneficial
to the common cause if all the peoples of the North Sea and the
Baltic united to deprive Great Britain of her means of existence.'
But Tarle's supposition that Napoleon really entertained any
serious plans in that direction at the time seems to be refuted
by the fact that his licences for the export of corn were being
issued in torrents just then; and in any case he adhered to
exactly the opposite view in the following year, as appears from
a particularly illuminative imperial dictated utterance of
June 24, 1811, which Tarle has also brought to light. The
situation then was stated to be such that there was a scarcity
of corn in Great Britain at the same time as there was a surplus
thereof in Germany and Poland, which naturally caused the
British to import the commodity by sea. The question, therefore, was whether this should be prevented. Napoleon's answer
to this question was in the negative, for three reasons : In
the first place, he regarded it as useless because the English
would procure the corn from America if they could not get
it from the Baltic. Thus it was the limitations to his power
over the supplies that here blocked the way. In the second
place, it was, according to Napoleon's declaration, impossible,
even with all watchfulness, to prevent Prussia and Poland
from exporting. This is undeniably a surprising utterance on
the part of a man who was not wont to acknowledge economic
impossibilities ; but an explanation of it may possibly be found
in his conception that exports are always more natural, and
consequently more difficult to prevent, than imports. Finally,
in the third place, fiscalism stuck up its head as usual, in that
the Emperor debated the question of moving the exports to the
Hanse Towns, which were at that time·incorporated in his
empire, in order thereby to give the French treasury the benefit
of the export dues. It is obvious that these reasons do not
bear witness to any special zeal to prevent the importation of
foodstuffs into Great Britain ; but, like everything else, they
show that Napoleon did not overlook the utility to England of
those imports, but rejected measures against them owing to
their futility. The remarkable thing is that he recognized the

unfeasibility of the thing only in this case, while the argument might seem to apply with at least equally great strength to that kind of blockade which he tried to enforce.[1]

## GREAT BRITAIN AND NORWAY

Before leaving the subject of food supply, it may be asked whether the policy of Great Britain followed the same lines as that of Napoleon in regard to the unrestricted exportation of corn to enemy countries. It follows from what has previously been said that the question was hardly of importance in more than one case, namely, that of Norway, where, according to the recent work of Worm-Müller, about a quarter of the normal consumption of corn (raw materials for the distilleries not included) was covered by imports. The motives which guided British policy on this particular point hardly appear with the necessary clearness from hitherto-published materials; but at least the external facts are not open to doubt.

In the first years after the bombardment of Copenhagen, (1807–9) Great Britain maintained a rigorous blockade, but apparently with no object other than that of bringing about a relaxation of the rigours of embargo prevailing on the other side, and especially of securing a supply of Norwegian timber. When the needs of Norway prevailed over the somewhat quixotic loyalty of Frederick VI to the Continental System, the importation of food, as well as trade in general, was allowed to continue unhampered, upon the usual system of British licences, to such a degree that the situation was said to border on commercial relations in times of profound peace. So far British policy was apparently guided by the same principles which had dictated her earlier measures, e. g., the prohibitions on the exports of raw cotton and ' Jesuit's bark '. But in the last years of the struggle (1812–13) these methods were again reversed, and a food blockade was brought to bear on Norway—

[1] *Correspondance*, nos. 16,224, 16,508 ; *Lettres inédites*, nos. 491, 652 (to Montalivet, July 16, 1810) ; Hansard, vol. xv, pp. 396–7 ; Fisher, *Studies*, &c., p. 344 ; Stuhr, *op. cit.*, p. 355 ; Rambaud, *op. cit.*, pp. 426–7 ; Tarle, *Kontinental' naja blokada*, vol. i, pp. 486, 494–5.

so far as is known, the only serious instance of such a measure in the course of the revolutionary and Napoleonic wars. The blockade could be made exceptionally binding and effective, especially after Sweden and Russia had joined the anti-Napoleonic alliance. A contributory cause undoubtedly was that the need for Norwegian timber, as well as for exports to Norwegian markets, had lost their importance to Great Britain. In other words, the policy which made exports of vital interest had lost a great deal of its force since the palpable breakdown of the Continental System. But even if these conjectures prove to be correct, the incident shows that Great Britain was already at that time more willing than her adversary to use a food blockade as a weapon of war.

The weapon, however, came far from gaining general approval even among Englishmen, and naturally it called forth anathemas from the opposite side. The British *chargé d'affaires* in Stockholm, Foster, openly told the Swedish statesmen that ' the starvation system appeared to him to be blameworthy, difficult to execute, and conducive to numerous dangers '.

The result was that Norway came nearer to starvation than any other country during this period, so that her pitiful situation was alleged by Frederick VI as a reason for renouncing his rights to the country in the peace of Kiel in January, 1814. Had it not been possible for spirited Norwegians and Danes to break through the blockade with their small corn vessels, the situation would have appeared all but hopeless in the eyes of contemporaries.[1]

### British Support of the Continent

We may now return to the economic life of Great Britain herself. It has been shown that the more fundamental effects of the Continental System on her organism did not play a decisive part in the issue of the struggle. But as the reader may

---

[1] Cf. Worm-Müller, *op. cit.*, the greater part of which is devoted to this subject. For the later years, cf. Rubin, *op. cit.*, ch. x, and Holm, *Danmark-Norges Historie*, &c., vol. vii : 2 ; *passim*. The utterance of Foster may be found in Grade, *Sverige och Tilsit-Alliansen*, pp. 438-9.

remember from part I, chapter IV, it was assumed in French circles that there was a more immediate connexion between the self-blockade of the Continent and the political elimination of Great Britain than that which was provided by its general economic ruin.  It was thought, in fact, that, owing to the inability to export, Great Britain would be prevented from supporting the Continent either by means of subsidies or by the maintenance of troops.  Miss Cunningham, in the little study that has often been cited in this work, has not only successfully elucidated these ideas and their bearing on the policy of Napoleon but has also, with less success, so far as I can judge, sought to show the validity of that train of thought to such an extent as to prove the correctness of Napoleon's (falsely assumed) object of ruining Great Britain by supplying her with foodstuffs. Miss Cunningham's thesis, indeed, is that the excess of imports gave rise to an export of gold which came near to exhausting the metal reserve of the Bank of England and thus shaking ' the real foundation of the credit system '.[1]  This contention does not appear to give due weight to the real significance of international exchange as that was brought out, not only by Adam Smith, but more particularly by the leading economists, in the great currency debate which went on during the actual period of the Continental System.  To begin with, we must see whether that French line of thought was correct which made British exports the antecedent condition for the making of payments on the Continent ;  and in so doing we must connect the matter with the discussion in our first part to which reference has just been made.

The kernel of the question, then, is the point that Adam Smith maintained, namely, that both war and other functions are in reality paid for by goods and human efforts (services), and not by money or precious metals.  The subsidies that Great Britain had to pay on the Continent were intended to procure necessaries for her allies, and the same were required for the maintenance of the British troops after Great Britain had begun operations by land.  Consequently, the business in

---

[1] Miss Cunningham, *British Credit*, &c., pp. 4 *et seq.*, pp. 71 *et seq.*

hand was either to provide the necessaries direct or else to provide the means with which they might be purchased.

If, then, the situation was such that British goods could be imported into the Continent, the simplest arrangement of the matter was that described by Adam Smith, namely, an export of goods from Great Britain without corresponding imports. It was of no consequence whether the British goods were or were not precisely of the kind required by the troops or by the continental governments.  Their sale on the Continent created in the latter case British assets which could be used to pay for the domestic goods needed by the troops or by the allies ;  that is to say, the purchasers of the British goods in reality paid their debt, not to the British, but to the sellers of the domestic goods that were used by the British troops or by the governments supported by Great Britain.  But the fact that the matter was simplified by the possibility of exporting British goods to the Continent by no means implies that the support of the continental governments would have been impossible without the realization of such a condition.  If, for instance, we suppose, instead, that no British, but, only transmarine goods, could get into the Continent, the system only needed to be supplemented by the participation of a third country, for instance, the United States, in the operation.  At times this was undoubtedly the case with the payments on the Iberian peninsula, where American corn went in great quantities.  The assets that Great Britain acquired by her exports in transmarine countries went, under this supposition, to the European mainland in payment for continental imports of colonial goods, that is to say, British exports for the non-European countries paid for British support to the Continent of Europe.  In the one case as in the other it was a question of the exchange of commodities, and not of any need of payment in money or in gold and silver. When, therefore, it came about that Wellington wished to make cash payment during his campaigns in Spain and Portugal, this by no means meant that he had to have the requisite amount sent to him in precious metal.  The only thing necessary was that the British government should have assets on the Iberian peninsula, for instance, in the form of bills of exchange or claims on business establishments there, to an amount corresponding to the requirements of the British army, so far as those requirements could not be satisfied by the supply of goods on British account.

It is true that it is possible to imagine a situation in which Great Britain was cut off from exporting to transmarine countries as well as to the European Continent ; and it would then become a question of what possibilities there would be for supporting the Continent under such conditions. In that case the matter was manifestly hopeless ; for a completely isolated Great Britain—and a country without exports is practically the same as an isolated country—must, no less than a completely isolated European Continent, necessarily imply the impossibility of British help for the adversaries of Napoleon. But this connexion is self-evident to such a degree that it need scarcely be pointed out ; and what is more, the supposition of its existence is so devoid of practical importance that it can never have played any part in the conduct of Napoleon or any other statesman of the time.

The next question, then, is whether even a diminution of British exports would not have been able to place obstacles in the way of supporting the Continent, inasmuch as the assets held by Great Britain to pay for the support might in that case be expected to be smaller. But even this idea is incorrect, because the decisive thing is not the absolute amount of exports but the amount in relation to imports, *i. e.*, the excess of exports. If only imports were diminished to the same extent as exports, the possibility of giving support would be in no wise altered. It is in the nature of things that the support must be paid for by limitation of domestic consumption when a country cannot count upon borrowing abroad, a thing which was not to be thought of for Great Britain during the period of the Continental System. The general conclusion thus remains simply this, that exports (including carrying profits and other foreign trade profits) must exceed imports by the amount of the support given to foreign countries. It is true that British commercial statistics for this period are altogether too uncertain to admit of any positive arithmetical proof in such a question; but it may be mentioned that the British customs statistics for the years 1805–9 show an excess in the trade balance itself (that is to say, apart from freights, &c.) varying between 5,900,000 and 14,900,000 pounds sterling, or, as an average for those five years, amounting to almost precisely £10,000,000.[1]

However, still another possibility may be conceived, namely, that the European Continent might take no necessaries at all, either British or continental, or might take only money or precious metals. This was undoubtedly what Napoleon aimed at, although he never even approximately reached his goal. So far as Great Britain succeeded in carrying on military operations on the Continent, however, even this possibility was quite out of the question; for where troops could be landed, it is evident that goods could be landed with still greater ease. And as regards the allies, the matter would have been of importance only in the highly curious situation that the countries in question applied the Continental System strictly and received British subsidies at the same time. For the sake of completeness, however, this line of thought may be followed out. Here, too, the same thing holds good; the idea to which Adam Smith had given expression, namely, that the precious metals in this connexion were commodities like others and would have had to be purchased by means of British exports. The only difference in the situation from a British point of view would have lain in the fact that precious metals might prove difficult to obtain, as indeed was probably often the case. From the point of view of the Continent, on the other hand, such a form of payment meant that in reality nothing was imported that could serve military purposes; and consequently the thing could have been of importance only in case one or more of the individual continental states could thereby acquire necessary goods from other continental countries.

If we pause to consider the actual circumstances in greater

[1] *Report of the Select Committee on the High Price of Bullion* (1810 : House of Commons, 349, table 73).

detail, we are immediately impressed by the fact that it was precisely the flourishing period of the Continental System that was marked by quite insignificant subsidies to the continental states ; and the reason for this is closely connected with the fact just mentioned that efficacy of the self-blockade ceased as soon as Great Britain gained the support of allies on the Continent.   For the whole of the sexennial period 1807–12, the sum total of the cash subsidies subsequently reported to Parliament was £14,722,000 ;   and it is in the very nature of things that most of this amount fell to countries with which Great Britain had unimpeded intercourse, *e. g.* (in round numbers), Portugal (1809–12) nearly £6,000,000; Spain (1808–12) £3,660,000 ;   Sicily (1808–12) £1,700,000 ;   Sweden (1808–9 and 1812) £1,660,000 ;   and Russia (1807, before the Peace of Tilsit) £600,000.   Altogether these came to £13,580,000, or more than nine-tenths of the total amount.   There is no material available for estimating the total amount spent on British military operations on the Continent ;   but in 1808–10 the total payments of the British government abroad ran to something over £32,000,000.[1]   As has been observed above, however, the military expenses must always have been among those where the normal system of international payments could be employed.

As a matter of fact, however, we have the seemingly incompatible facts that, on the one hand, Great Britain had great difficulties with her payments on the Continent, and, on the other hand, was exposed to an outflow of precious metals, which constantly threatened the bank reserve and was usually connected with the heavy decline in the rates of exchange on England.   It might thus seem as if Napoleon was right after all in trying to read the success of his war against the credit of England in the decline of the exchanges and in the difficulties of payment.   But the true connexion was quite different.

First, as regards the difficulty of financing the military operations on the Continent, we may say that that difficulty was mainly due to bad financial organization, and also to an

---

[1] The figures are based on the tables in Porter, *op. cit.*, p. 507, and Tooke, *op. cit.*, vol. i, pp. 352.

apparently ineradicable notion of the unimportance of the war in the Iberian peninsula. Wellington had many occasions to complain of the inadequacy of pecuniary support and the shortage of the most necessary things, while at the same time huge sums were dissipated in far less important ways, even on the Continent, such as for the notorious and thoroughly abortive expedition to the island of Walcheren, off the coast of Holland, in 1809. As regards the *modus operandi*, Wellington had to obtain funds by drawing bills on the British treasury and selling them on the spot, that is to say, without there being any available British assets ; and as there was an entire lack of organization, this could not take place without a heavy decline in their value. Nathan Mayer Rothschild, the greatest financial genius of the house of Rothschild and its true founder, who at this time had already moved from Frankfurt to London, mentioned to Sir Thomas Fowell Buxton, in the course of a conversation many years afterwards, that once during this period he set about buying up, on the one hand, a great number of Wellington's bills on the British government, which were under par, and, on the other hand, gold, which was sold by the East India Company ; and by so doing he declared that he compelled the government to come to an agreement with him, on the one hand, to prolong the bills which it had no means to pay, and, on the other hand, to pass over the gold, for which Wellington was very hard pressed. ' When the Government had got the money,' he said, with well-founded contempt, ' they did not know how to get it to Portugal. I undertook all that, and I sent it through France. It was the best business I ever did.'

Apart from this scanty and late item, which is as meagre as most of the contributions to the history of the house of Rothschild, we seem to know hardly anything about the actual manner in which the Continent was financed by the British government under the Continental System. On the other hand, we have a somewhat fuller knowledge of the circumstances during the next period, that of the Wars of Liberation and of the Hundred Days in 1813-15, owing to the materials collected in a biography of the politician J. C. Herries, the commissary in chief in the British financial administration of that time (1811–16), on which the German economic historian, Professor Richard Ehrenberg, has based that part of his study of the house of Rothschild. Even at that time, with the greatly multiplied continental expenses for both subsidies and military requirements, the financing was at first managed partly by very cumbrous movements of silver from England, and partly, and more particularly, by bills drawn from the Continent on the British treasury in London. These last the continental governments and generals afterwards had the greatest difficulty in selling, and therefore they declined heavily in value. But now there was gradually carried out, through N. M. Rothschild, a change of system by which bills and coins were privately bought up on the Continent, with the result that difficulties of placing bills and the consequent dislocations in the exchanges almost ceased. Thus Herries states in his official report that during 1813 bills on Holland and Frankfurt for £700,000 were bought up without depressing the exchange, while a payment of £100,000 on the old methods would, in his opinion, have had ten times as great an effect upon the exchanges.[1]

The whole of this account shows clearly enough that the difficulties lay in the matter of technical organization and were not due to any profound economic obstacles in the way of payments on the Continent; for it is manifest that such obstacles, had they existed, would no less fully have lain in the way of Rothschild's purchases of commercial paper on the Continent, that is to say, his acquisition of continental assets on British account. What the change of system implied, therefore, was to organize the support in the main on the lines of international payments in general.

But it was recently mentioned that in the earlier stage Rothschild sent gold to Wellington on the account of the British government, and that the later payments on the Continent were partly effected by sending silver. One thus

---

[1] *Memoirs of Sir Thomas Fowell Buxton* (3d ed., London, 1849), ch. XXI. pp. 288 *et seq.* ; Ehrenberg, *Grosse Vermögen, ihre Entstehung und ihre Bedeutung* (Jena, 1903), vol. I, pp. 58 *et seq.*

gets the impression, in spite of all that has been said, that precious metals were necessary, at least at times, in order to support the Continent. This evidently needs explanation ; and the explanation mainly lies in the state of British currency during the Napoleonic wars.

## British Currency

As has been mentioned in part I, Great Britain had had an irredeemable paper currency ever since 1797 ; but before 1808 this currency had only in particular years shown any great deviations from its par value. The quotations for gold do not appear to have been very reliable at the time, but the rates of exchange on Hamburg and Paris, both of which, characteristically enough, were quoted in London without intermission during the whole course of the last Napoleonic war, make the matter sufficiently clear. In 1808, however, a great change set in. Especially from 1809 the exchanges began to show a very remarkable fall, i. e., the amount of foreign money to be obtained for £1 sterling declined heavily. The average depreciation for 1809 is given by Mr. Hawtrey as 21 and 23·3 per cent. as compared with Hamburg and Paris, respectively. This gave rise to a great controversy—which offers a number of points of contact with the discussion during the recent war—concerning the connexion between the changes in the value of gold and the rates of exchange, on the one hand, and the decline in the value of the British paper currency, on the other hand, and also concerning the true cause of the latter phenomenon. The first important contributions to this controversy were made by Ricardo in the late summer and autumn of 1809 in the form of three articles published in the *Morning Chronicle*, which were followed up in December by a celebrated pamphlet, the title of which, *The High Price of Bullion a Proof of the Depreciation of Bank Notes*, sufficiently expresses his point of view. In this pamphlet, Ricardo, who at that time was known only as a successful and highly respected broker on the Stock Exchange, laid down what is called the quantity theory of money and laid the foundation of his still unpresaged fame as the most acute of economic theorists. In order to test the question, the House of Commons in February 1810 appointed a committee, known as the Bullion Committee, whose report, framed entirely in the spirit of Ricardo, was announced in June but did not come before Parliament until the following spring. The discussion was carried on with great zeal outside Parliament as well, simultaneously with an almost continuous rise in the price of gold. According to the computations of Mr. Hawtrey, that rise was 36·4 per cent. in 1813 (that of silver being 36·7 per cent.), while the fall in the exchanges had already culminated in 1811 with 39·1 per cent. and 44 per cent. on Paris and Hamburg, respectively. During these long discussions there also arose the question of the cause of the export of gold and its connexion with payments on the Continent ; and it may be said that in the course of this discussion the connexion was made clear in all essentials, especially by Ricardo.[1]

As a starting-point in this discussion Ricardo took the case where a country, owing to failure of the harvest, has to embark upon unusually large imports of corn ; but he maintained that the payment of subsidies to a foreign power formed a still more marked instance of the same thing. Now, if the country in question, that is to say, Great Britain, had a metallic system of money and no ' redundant currency ', that is, not a greater quantity of money in relation to the quantity of commodities than other countries, there was, in his opinion, no occasion for the export of precious metals. In that case, corn, like the subsidies, would be paid for by exports of commodities in the usual way, as has been explained at length above. If, on the

---

[1] *Report of the Bullion Committee*, with examination of witnesses. Hansard, vol. XVII, pp. ccii *et seq.* The appendices, however, are printed only in the official separate edition (see *ante*, p. 352 note). Ricardo, *Works* (McCulloch ed., London, 1852), pp. 267 *et seq.*, 269 *et seq.*, 292 *et seq.* ; *Three Letters on the Price of Gold, A Reprint of Economic Tracts* (Hollander ed., Baltimore, 1903) ; *Letters to Thomas Robert Malthus, 1810–1823* (Bonar ed., Oxford, 1887), pp. 1, 15 *et seq.*, 19, 20 *et seq.* ; Anonymous [Malthus], in *Edinburgh Review* (Feb., 1811), pp. 342 *et seq.*, 361 *et seq.* ; Hawtrey, *The Bank Restriction of 1797*, loc. cit. (1918), vol. XXVIII, p. 64 ; Tooke, op. cit., vol. I, pp. 157 *et seq.*, 207 *et seq.*, 352 *et seq.*, 375 *et seq.* ; also, *A History of Prices from 1839 to 1847, inclusive* (London, 1848), pp. 100 *et seq.*

other hand, there prevailed a ' superabundant circulation ', that is, a greater quantity of money in the subsidy-paying country than in the country to which the subsidies were paid, it meant that the value of money was lower or the price-level of commodities higher in the former place than in the latter, in which case the precious metals flowed to the place where their value was highest; in other words, an export of gold took place.  Or, as also explained by him, if money or gold was exported instead of commodities, this was due to the fact that the transaction could be settled more cheaply in this way.  In that case gold or money was what stood relatively lowest in value in the paying country (Great Britain), as compared with its value in the other country, and consequently people fulfilled their obligations at a smaller sacrifice if they paid with money or gold than if they paid with commodities.  Otherwise, if the value of money was the same in both countries, the export of gold would never be worth while, but the payment must take the form of commodities.  Ricardo did not dispute absolutely, it is true, that the transmission of gold could take place in all events;  he considered it highly improbable, however, because in that case the gold would have gone to a country where its purchasing power was less, or at least not greater, than in the country from which it came.  But both he and his opponents were agreed that in that case the gold must soon flow back to the former country;  and even if this factor played a larger part than Ricardo supposed, it could never explain that one-sided movement of precious metal from Great Britain to the Continent that exhausted the gold reserves of the Bank of England and therefore gave rise to such great anxiety.

The outflow of gold was thus an evidence that money had a lower value in Great Britain than on the Continent.  But if Great Britain, like the Continent, had been on a metallic basis, this dissimilarity would have been removed by the outflow, inasmuch as the quantity of money would have been diminished in the former place and augmented in the latter.  As it was, Great Britain had a paper currency which stood far below its nominal value in gold;  and in that case the export of gold could continue for any length of time without restoring equilibrium, because the vacuum was constantly being filled with new notes. Thus it was not the payment of subsidies or any extraordinary export of corn that caused the outflow of gold, but ' the superabundant circulation ', or, in other words, the lower value of money in Great Britain.

This account, which goes to the root of the matter, can be regarded as conclusive in all essentials and needs to be supplemented only in one or two points, which are also touched upon by Ricardo. If the country in question has a mixed paper and gold circulation, as was the case with Great Britain, not only the paper money but also the metallic money declines in value within the country. In other words, prices rise in whichever currency they are quoted, inasmuch as they are both legal tender and their combined quantity has been increased. It is precisely this circumstance that drives out the ' better ', that is, the metallic money, because people get more goods for that in other countries.

If, then, it was the case, on the whole, that the export of gold had its root in the depreciation of British currency, it should nevertheless be added, in common fairness, that a payment of subsidies in itself, regarded as an isolated phenomenon and without any connexion with the depreciation of the currency, would also set going a definitive export of gold from the subsidy-paying country, inasmuch as it would diminish its stock of commodities ; and an unchanged relation between the quantity of money and the quantity of commodities—in other words, an unchanged comparative price-level—would thus require a corresponding diminution on the other side of the equation. But the quantity of goods is exposed to so many changes in different directions that this matter is probably of no practical interest whatever.

The argument brought forward against all this by Ricardo's opponents, especially by Malthus in the *Edinburgh Review*, in February 1811, was that a great export of corn, or claims to subsidies on the part of the continental states, need not evoke among them a greatly increased demand for ' muslins, hardware, and colonial produce ', and that, therefore, it might be necessary for Great Britain to pay instead with money, which was always welcome.  Applied to the payment of subsidies, however, this argument was particularly unfortunate, as the function of the subsidies was quite obviously that of procuring goods for the work undertaken by the continental powers, as has been explained at length above ;  and consequently for our purpose the objection can be dismissed without further ado.  For the sake of completeness, however, it may be added that the same conditions prevail in other cases.  No country sells corn except to get something else instead ;  and no country has so much of all commodities that it cannot use more.  The origin of these commodities is a matter of no importance, as we have already seen ;  and the limitation, in Malthus's instance, to the articles of British trade itself is consequently quite unjustifiable.  The only exception, which is scarcely treated by Ricardo, but which is discussed in detail, from a somewhat different standpoint, in the report of the Bullion Committee, would be if a country had some special reason to increase its stock of precious metals, e. g., to form a war fund or to pass from a paper to a metallic currency.  The Bullion Committee here showed the untenability of the supposition that the Continent had any such increased need of gold as could explain the course of development in Great Britain.

The gist of all this is, therefore, that the export of gold from Great Britain can be regarded neither as a necessary condition nor a necessary consequence of the payment of subsidies to the Continent, but had its essential cause in the deterioration of the currency.  From this, two conclusions follow.  In the first place, the British government could have prevented, not only the export of gold, but also the permanent fall in the rate of exchange (to be carefully distinguished from the temporary dislocation occasioned by especially large payments on the Continent) by raising the value of money.  Whether in that case the remedy would have been less harmful than the disease, after the depreciation had gone so far, it is not easy to say ;  but that matter need not be discussed in this place, as it is at all events clear that the Continental System, as such, was not the cause of the situation, or at any rate not one of its principal causes.

In the second place, from the standpoint of the payment of subsidies, it cannot even be regarded as having been necessary to let the export of gold or silver continue when the British government had once ceased to keep the currency at par with gold. From a purely formal point of view, it had obtained the possibility of independence in this respect by the Bank Restriction Act, that is to say, by making bank notes irredeemable; nor was there any insuperable obstacle in the way of this expedient in actual fact. Strictly speaking, the Continent needed no importation of either gold or silver; and it is far from the case, of course, that all the payments of the British government on the Continent were effected by the export of precious metal. For the moment it is not possible to state the relation between the total foreign payments and the transference of coin on behalf of the government except for the two years 1808 and 1809; but even the figures for those two years show how casual the proportion was.[1] In 1808 the foreign payments of the government (here, as elsewhere, the figures refer to all countries outside the British Isles, and not merely the Continent of Europe) amounted to £10,235,000, while the exports of precious metal on public account amounted to at least £3,905,000, or, if we include that sum which was paid for the purchase of silver dollars (without our being able to see whether they were purchased inside or outside the country) to £4,543,000, or over 44 per cent. of the whole. The principal part in this matter was played by over twenty remittances, principally silver, to the Iberian peninsula to a total of more than £2,666,000, and also £855,000 in silver to Gothenburg, sums which the British government could not contrive to provide in a more convenient fashion. In the year 1809, on the other hand, when the total payments abroad were larger than

---

[1] The figures for the exports of precious metal follow tables 69 and 79 in the appendices to the *Report of the Bullion Committee*, reduced, when necessary, to pounds sterling.

in the previous year (amounting to £12,372,000), the exports of precious metal on account of the government reached only £1,206,000, according to the lower calculation, and £1,290,000, according to the higher calculation ; that is to say, at the most only 12¼ per cent. of the total payments.  Now if it was regarded as necessary, out of regard for British ' prestige ' or for any other cause, not to let so much metal go out of the country as actually did, these mere figures make it clear (and the idea is confirmed by the experiences of the recent war) that it would have been quite possible to avoid sending out gold or silver.  Even if one had not been able to come to this conclusion by theoretical methods, it follows from the practical experience gained by Rothschild's rearrangement of the system of foreign payments in 1813, that these payments did not involve any inevitable need for the export of gold or silver ;  and for other purposes such export was, considering the general position of currency policy, a somewhat purposeless means of limiting the fall in value of British currency to a negligible extent, without restricting the circulation of bank notes.

### BRITISH CREDIT SYSTEM

The above largely supplies the answer to the question that still remains, namely, as to the importance of the Continental System in relation to the solidity of the British credit system. If it was considered that the credit of Great Britain stood and fell with the metallic reserves of the Bank of England, neither Napoleon's measures nor the depreciation of the currency would have prevented the preservation of the gold reserve, as has just been shown.  It is true that the very conception of the importance of the metallic reserves for the credit of a country with a paper currency lacks support both in theory and in experience, although popular notions to this effect have been diligently nourished at all times ;  and it is difficult to see what inconveniences would have followed if the metallic reserves of the Bank of England when it did not redeem its notes, had had to sink to the same level as at the Bank Restriction of 1797 or even lower.  But if it had been desired to avoid that state of things, then, as has been said, there would have been no insuperable difficulties, as is also shown by the experiences of the following years.

It is a quite different and far more searching question, to what extent the British credit system could have been thrown into disorder by the general difficulties and dislocations caused to British economic life by the Continental System in combination with a number of other factors.  As regards the credit of the state, nothing of the kind occurred.  The system of the national debt was so firmly founded that it resisted the strain without difficulty, though the cost of the revolutionary and Napoleonic wars certainly appears, for various reasons, to have been much greater than would have been the case if the borrowing had been effected in some other way.  The private credit system, on the other hand, had not yet attained the same vital position in the economic life of the country as it has now.  The new large-scale industry was to a predominant extent based on its own capital, and was mainly extended with the help of its own profits—a fact which is seldom properly emphasized.  Consequently, the harm that could be involved by a dislocation of credit can probably be measured by the results of the crisis of 1810–11—that is to say, bankruptcies by the merchants with reaction on the manufacturers from whom they bought their goods.  Besides, it is an open question whether the credit system of a country can be regarded as being so delicate as it has long been the fashion to make out.  The experience of the recent war has largely suggested that our credit organization has a much more robust physique than anyone had previously suspected.

# CONCLUSION

## COMPARISON WITH THE PRESENT DAY

THE Continental System had little success in its mission of destroying the economic organization of Great Britain, and most of the things it created on the Continent lasted a very short time. The visible traces that it left in the economic history of the past century are neither many nor strong. Indeed, it is difficult to find any more obvious and lasting effect than that of prolonging the existence of the prohibitive system in France far beyond what was the case, not only in Great Britain, but also in Prussia. Thus there are good grounds for doubting that the material development of our civilization would have been essentially different if this gigantic endeavour to upset the economic system of Europe had never been made. In general, it is true that what sets its mark on the course of economic development—largely in contrast with what is political in the narrower sense—is that which can be used as a foundation for further building, where cause can be laid to cause. Isolated efforts to destroy the texture of economic society, even if they are made with a giant's strength, can generally do little more than retard the process of development, and gradually they disappear under the influence of what may be called in the fine—perhaps too fine—phrase, 'the self-healing power of nature' (*vis medicatrix naturae*).

However, the Continental System mainly had immediate ends in view. It was in the first place a link in a life-and-death struggle, where, as is always the case under such circumstances, the thought of the future had to be relegated to the background. The fact that the future effects were small, therefore, is a thing which, strictly speaking, touches the heart of the Continental System no more than it touches the heart of other trade wars. It is true that in all such struggles people count on the most far-reaching and profound effects in the future from the victory that they wish to win to-day; but the only thing that they understand clearly is their desire to win the victory. First and foremost, therefore, the question is, to what degree the Continental System served this its immediate aim.

So far as the answer to this question lies in the sphere of economics—and the present book has no concern with what lies outside that sphere—the answer has already been given in the preceding pages, and is mainly in the negative. But no detailed explanations need be given as to why just the failure of the Continental System, even as a pure measure of trade war, makes it especially important to confront it with the phenomenon that corresponds to it in our own day, the trade war in the shadow of which we still live at the time of this writing. If any point should have stood out clearly from the foregoing survey, it is surely the paradoxical character of the Continental System; and so far the contrast with the present day has consisted in the very setting here given to the subject. But from a purely economic point of view every trade war is, strictly speaking, a paradox, for it is directed against intercourse which is profitable to both parties and therefore inevitably inflicts sufferings on its author no less than its intended victims. Consequently, the property of the Continental System of being an economic paradox does not render superfluous a comparison with the present time. Perhaps such a comparison derives still greater interest from the light it seems to cast over the general development of society during the past century in its connexion with economic conditions. But as the materials for such a survey have been largely given in the preceding chapters, these last few pages will to some extent have the character of a summary.

The relatively limited effect of the Continental System on the economic life of Europe was primarily due to the autarchy of the different countries, that is, their far-reaching economic self-sufficiency in all vital matters. The speedy conclusion of the blockade of France at the outbreak of the revolutionary wars was undoubtedly connected, not only with the particular ideas with which we have become acquainted, but also with the slenderness of the prospects of starving a country in the position of France ; and to a lesser degree the circumstances were the same with regard to a food blockade of the British Isles. On the other hand, it may be taken for granted that a blockade of the latter kind would now be effective if it could be carried out. But even with regard to its practicability the situation is altered. Nowadays such a blockade demands, almost inevitably, the command of the seas, as the countries that now produce corn are so many and so scattered that it can hardly be possible to command them all by land ; and the same holds good of the majority of products other than foodstuffs, even of the majority of raw materials. The possibility of blockading a country simply by power over the sources of supply has therefore been enormously reduced since the time of Napoleon with regard to all the main commodities of world commerce. Such a possibility is mainly reduced to a number of important, but quantitatively insignificant, articles, such as certain special metals, potassium, and indigo. Therefore, the possibilities of an effective blockade have been so far diminished that nowadays, to a much greater extent than a hundred years ago, they require power over the transport routes, while formerly there were greater possibilities of becoming master over production itself. In the opposite scale we have the fact that the damage done by blockade, when it can be carried out, is many times greater now than then. Consequently, it is obvious that the blockade of the Continent, which was never even attempted seriously during the Napoleonic wars, is now susceptible of a much wider range.

In addition to these fairly self-evident material reasons for the greater efficacy of a blockade in our own day, there are other reasons which lie in the social or spiritual sphere, and are therefore far less obvious and generally known, but by no means less important. Foremost among these should be placed the increased power of governments in comparison with a hundred years ago. If there is anything which forms the burden of all discussions under the Continental System it is the hopelessness of enforcing obedience to the blockade decrees. ' Why not prevent the skin from sweating?' was King Louis's despairing cry in answer to the threatening complaints about the smuggling in Holland; and an anonymous report of 1811 in the Berlin national archives expressed the matter in the following way : ' To keep the English away from the Continent by blockade without possessing fleets is just as impossible as to forbid the birds to build their nests in our country.' In the same way a French report to Bonaparte in 1802 declared it to be a hopeless undertaking to prevent the importation of English manufactures that everybody wanted; and as we know, Napoleon himself justified his failure to try to prevent the export of corn to England on the ground that such measures were futile.[1]   No one who has followed the foregoing account can doubt the correctness of these opinions; and as has been said already, the food supply of Norway during the years of rigid blockade depended on blockade-breaking. In contrast with all this, we are confronted with the fairly indisputable fact that during the recent war both the belligerent parties were able, without any noteworthy leakages, both to exclude the enemy's goods, when they deemed it expedient, and to prevent their own goods from leaving the country. No country has been able to get her food supply through blockade-breaking.

In a manner corresponding to the utterances just cited, Stephen speaks of the great difficulties involved in preventing the conveyance across the sea of enemy goods disguised as neutral; while, on the other side, those who had command of the sea during the recent war revealed a remarkable capacity to prevent, not only this, but also the exportation to the enemy from neutral territory of goods produced from imported raw materials, and even the exportation of a neutral country's own goods when they had to be replaced in some way or other by goods imported by sea. The ' import trusts ' that have been established in different countries created guaranties which were altogether lacking during the Napoleonic wars, and which

---

[1] Duboscq, *Louis Bonaparte en Hollande*, p. 48; Hoeniger, *op. cit.*, p. 19; Tarle, *Kontinental'naja blokada*, vol. I, p. 147.

fundamentally changed the nature of neutral trade. Highly significant, too, is the insurance of enemy cargoes, which developed into a perfect system under the Continental System, with a special provision for the underwriter that he should abstain from the right to have the insurance annulled on the ground of the enemy origin of the cargo, while there was no mention of anything of the kind during the recent war.

Most striking of all is the contrast with regard to the export of gold and transactions in gold at rates above par. There is a famous eighteenth-century utterance by Bishop Berkeley to the effect that it is impossible to make a prohibition of the export of precious metals effective without building a brass wall round the whole country; and the majority of writers on the monetary system a hundred years ago were agreed on this point. Thus, for instance, the somewhat lower value of gold in specie than gold in bullion in England was explained by the existence of somewhat greater risk of exporting the former, because it was forbidden by law ; ' but,' says Ricardo, ' it is so easily evaded, that gold in bullion has always been of nearly the same value as (i. e., very little above) gold in coin '.[1] During the recent war, on the other hand, in Germany and France, for instance, gold was seen pouring into the coffers of the banks of issue in spite of its far higher value than the paper money given in exchange ; and consequently there has been scarcely any mention of smuggling gold out of the country, although such export would have yielded a large profit if it could have been successfully performed.

This general weakness of governments a hundred years ago constitutes the constantly recurring justification for the frequent concessions toward disobedience to the prohibitive regulations existing on paper. Thus, for instance, Perceval in the House of Commons in 1812 justified the licences for the importation of lace and muslin on the ground that they would be imported illegally if permission were not given for it ; and about the same time Lord Bathurst declared in the House of Lords that the only effect of the abolition of licences would be

[1] Ricardo, *Works* (*High Price of Bullion*), p. 265.

that British subjects would continue the trade with neutral foreigners as dummies and resort to every conceivable dodge and device to avoid detection. ' In fact,' concluded the British minister of commerce, in words which might stand as a motto for the entire policy of licences, ' we only permitted him (the merchant) to do that openly which he would surely [*sic*] do clandestinely '.[1]

It is of great moment to determine the causes of this enormous difference in the effectiveness of governments then and now. Some of the causes are more or less temporary, that is to say, they are due to the peculiar conditions governing the carrying-on of wars both then and now, especially then ; but others, so far as one can judge, express a tendency in development which deserves particular attention. When, in discussions as to the possibilities of state intervention in some respect or other, reference has been made to older precedents, people have usually failed to see to what an extent those old measures were ineffective, and have therefore completely misunderstood the connexion between cause and effect.

The most profound change, so far as one can see, consists in the increased honesty and efficiency of public administration. In the preceding pages sufficient evidence has been given of the corruption of the executive powers under the Continental System, so that no further evidence is necessary. To some extent the situation was undoubtedly affected by the reluctance with which people conformed to the Continental decrees, which was especially the case in the non-French states of the Continent; however, this factor played no part at all in England, and only a small part in France. We must, therefore, search deeper for the causes, and in so doing we can scarcely avoid the conclusion that the majority of European states and also Great Britain— perhaps the latter above all—did not until the nineteenth century attain an executive organization on whose sense of duty and incorruptibility it was possible to rely. Therefore, while in our day it is possible to entrust an executive with functions

[1] Speeches in the House of Lords, Feb. 28, 1812 ; in the House of Commons, Apr. 17, 1812. Hansard, vol. XXI, p. 1055 ; vol. XXII, p. 435.

that put these qualities to the test, such was not the case a hundred years ago, and is even now not the case in countries with an executive organization of the older type. It need not be further elaborated what consequence this involves with regard to the possibility of state intervention and the state management of economic undertakings. As a matter of fact, these possibilities vary largely according to the nature of the executive in each individual country.

It is true that the palpable overstraining of government functions during the recent war has led to a more or less marked relapse both as to the law-abidingness of subjects and the integrity of officials; and it is quite conceivable that history will thus repeat itself. So far, however, the difference between now and then remains very great; and at least one factor appears to work in the direction of keeping up this distinction. For, furthermore, technical development has played into the hands of the governments to an extent that people in general have not fully appreciated. It is especially the network of cables and lines of communication of every sort, which practically form a completely new factor in the economic life of the nineteenth century, that have brought about this result; for it is obvious that power over this system creates a possibility of control over almost everything that falls under the head of intercourse, and over much that falls under the head of production. Within a country it is especially railways and high-pressure electric transmission lines that create this power, while both within and between countries a part of the same function is performed by the telegraph cables. The last-named have created a possibility for censorship and a possibility for counteracting revolutionary measures on the part of citizens or foreigners, and also on the part of the enemy; and with the help of the railways it is possible to throttle almost all domestic industrial production and most of the imports or exports that it is desired to hinder. It is true that quite recent events have served to show various features which point to a certain degree of emancipation from the supremacy of a rigid system of lines, namely, wireless telegraphy and aerial navigation.  But the latter is still, from an economic point of view, little more than the music of the future; and even the part played by wireless telegraphy during the war, though certainly not altogether insignificant, was remarkably restricted, while the former types of communication are the genuine reality which for the present place resources hitherto undreamt of in the hands of governments—so long as they can hold them. Of course, anarchy can throw the system into pieces, or factions can get hold of these engines of power and destroy them; but this in no wise alters the fact that they have increased enormously the strength of an undisputed government.

It is highly significant, in connexion with this increased strength of governments, that almost the only point one can speak of any real improvement in the treatment of the neutrals since the beginning of the last century is with regard to captures at sea.  Here, indeed, a strictly military governmental organization has not only taken the place of the purely private and acquisitive enterprises of the privateers, but at the same time has also put an end to the pecuniary interest of naval officers and crews in the seizure of neutral cargoes; and this means at least the abolition of that kind of high-handed treatment which had its sole root in the desire of private gain.

With these deeper dissimilarities between the past and the present may be associated others which have a more temporary character, but are nevertheless of great interest.  One of them, which must strike every careful observer, is how completely that character of 'a political war of religion', which was first noticed by Lars von Engeström, disappeared in the sphere of economics, and to what an extent an open and acknowledged intercourse existed among the belligerents.  The licence system as such is one huge example of this, but there are other still more striking ones.  Thus, for instance, it appears from many details that journeys to an enemy country were by no means unusual.  Napoleon told the deputies of the French Chamber of Commerce in his speech to them in March 1811, that he was well aware of these journeys; and he does not seem to have taken them at all with a tragic air.  From the continental states, of course, no feeling of hostility to Great Britain was to be expected ; but it is nevertheless remarkable that Englishmen seem to have lost hardly anything by their continental debtors. All this, however, referred to private individuals ; but the grandest example of economic co-operation between the enemies occurred on account of the governments themselves. This was what was known as the Ouvrard Affair, which pops up many times in the contemporary sources—most in detail in the memoirs of the great Parisian speculator, Ouvrard, but perhaps most authoritatively in Mollien's memoirs—and which is one of the most astounding of the economic events of the period. The affair had to do with what was, for the conditions of those times, a colossal remittance of silver to an amount of 37,000,000 francs, which Spain was to make to France from Mexico through the mediation of the Anglo-French-Dutch banking firm of Hope & Co. of Amsterdam, with which Baring Brothers of London and the ultraspeculative banker, Ouvrard of Paris, worked. As the British controlled the sea, however, the transference could only be effected by British war-ships fetching the money from Vera Cruz in 1807, and conveying it to a European port on Napoleon's account. Mollien's comment on this is : ' Thus three powers which were waging war *à outrance* could suddenly make a kind of local truce for an operation which did not seem likely to benefit more than one of them ' ; and he goes on : ' When Napoleon expressed to me some inquietude regarding the fate of such an important remittance, I was able to answer him, with a confidence that the result fully justified, that the enemy hands that I had chosen would not prove faithless hands.'[1] Even though future researches should reveal many transactions from the recent war of which we now suspect nothing, yet it must be regarded, to put it

---

[1] Mollien, *Mémoires*, &c., vol. I, pp. 434 *et seq.*, 490 *et seq.* ; vol. II, pp. 129 *et seq.*, 242 (the quotation being from vol. II, p. 132) ; Ouvrard, *Mémoires*, &c., vol. I, *passim*, especially pp. 107 *et seq.* ; Ehrenberg, *Grosse Vermögen*, &c., vol. I, pp. 72 *et seq.* ; vol. II (1905), pp. 120 *et seq.* Cf. also, G. Weill, *Le financier Ouvrard*, *loc. cit.* (1918), vol. 127, p. 39. An article on Pierre César Labouchère, the head of the Hope firm, in the *Revue d'histoire diplomatique* for 1913, gives no information on this or related subjects.

mildly, as improbable that any of them will prove to show such a measure of working agreement between deadly enemies.

One very important reason for this lively economic intercourse with the enemy is undoubtedly the distinctively mercantilist nature of the blockade. When exporting to the enemy was regarded as a patriotic action, regardless of the fact that the trade prohibitions with the enemy forbade it on paper, this really cut off the possibility of a political or economic war of religion ; and it was no longer possible in that case to avoid forming commercial ties with enemy subjects, so that governments had to take the consequences. Accordingly, the methods of the recent war in severing all commercial ties led, in quite another degree, to the establishment of a gulf between the combatants that was not merely material but also mental.

The most obvious difference between the past and the present, of course, is precisely this dissimilarity in the object of the blockade, which has been set forth and discussed in the foregoing account. It is impossible to deny that the blockade of the World War, conceived as a means to the end of undermining the enemy's power of resistance by economic pressure, had a far more correct economic object than had that of Napoleon. The recent blockade was primarily directed against the enemy's imports, which procure what can be replaced by neither financial dexterity nor credit, while the Continental System was directed against exports, and therefore had very small prospects of attaining its object. Saying this is not the same as saying under what conditions the present-day policy of trade war may have a chance of attaining its object. Economic life has exhibited a power of adaptation that was completely undreamt of, a possibility of changing its direction with the shortest preparation under pressure of external conditions, which should have greatly diminished hopes of conquering an enemy by such means. In consequence of this the problem of self-sufficiency also has passed into a new phase. The primary thing for a country is, or at any rate should be, no longer to be self-sufficient in peace, but to possess that elasticity throughout its economic organization which creates the power of becoming

self-sufficient in war or on the occasion of any other isolation ;
and in complete contrast to what most people have believed,
the development of modern industrial technique and a modern
credit system has increased, and not diminished, the prospects
of this.  But the discussion of these problems does not belong
to an historical account, but to an analysis of the economics
of the recent war.  Such an analysis has been attempted to
some little extent in a preceding work by the present writer
and therefore need not be repeated here.[1]

[1] *Världskrigets ekonomi : en studie af nutidens näringslif under krigets inverkan*
(Stockholm, 1915).

# BIBLIOGRAPHICAL NOTE

FINALLY, it seems expedient to give a rapid summary of the most important materials that throw light on the Continental System itself. The present writer's studies as regards the sources themselves, as well as the works in which those sources have been worked up, were necessarily limited to what was accessible in Swedish libraries, since it was practically impossible to obtain books from abroad during the period in which this book was in preparation ; nor had the writer either time or opportunity to visit foreign libraries. On the whole, the Swedish libraries cannot be regarded as poorly equipped for a subject such as the present one ; but the lack of contemporary British and American publications was nevertheless strongly felt. Consequently, in this book remarks to the effect that information of one sort or another was inaccessible mean simply that sources containing it were unknown to the author. The more important collections, in so far as they are known to the author, are included herein.

## BIBLIOGRAPHIES

Mr. Dunan's bibliography contained in *Revue des études napoléoniennes*, vol. III (Paris, 1913), merits study owing to its freshness and searching appreciation of the various works (it even contains corrections of mistakes in detail) ; but it is far from complete as regards the several countries, particularly as regards British and American literature. This, to a certain extent, is supplemented by a valuable article by Dr. Lingelbach in the *American Historical Review* (January 1914), vol. XIX, containing a discussion principally of manuscript sources, with copious extracts. An extensive and more comprehensive, but less copious, bibliography, together with a criticism of the manuscript sources, forms an introduction to the Russian work mentioned below, *i. e.*, Tarle, *Kontinental'naja blokada* (Moscow, 1913).

## SOURCE PUBLICATIONS

The collection of original documents which must always remain the principal source for the history of the Napoleonic age is *Correspondance de Napoléon Ier*, published on the initiative of Napoleon III in two parallel editions, both in thirty-two volumes, which are quite identical as to contents (Paris, 1858–69 and 1870, respectively). To facilitate the use of either edition, Napoleon's letters are referred to by number in the preceding pages. In the first fifteen volumes of the *Correspondance* practically everything of interest has been included ; but after that a selection was made out of regard to the prestige of the empire, a selection which applied especially to the letters written to Napoleon III's father, King Louis of Holland. This has led to a number of collections, among which the collection issued by Lecestre in two volumes, *Lettres inédites de Napoléon Ier* (Paris, 1897), would seem to be the only one offering anything of importance for the history of the Continental System. That collection includes certain of the most characteristic letters of Napoleon, but the general impression created through them is too one-sided and violent owing to their being compressed into two small volumes.

Besides these must be mentioned the well-known work of Martens, *Nouveau recueil de traités*, which in its first part, for 1808–14 (Göttingen, 1817), contains a fairly abundant collection of the various blockade decrees. Of perhaps greater value, however, are the documents collected in different parts of the original *Recueil*, including earlier declarations and instructions which are less accessible. The American official publication, *American State Papers (Foreign)*, vol. iii, is also supposed to contain a collection of the most important laws and regulations of all the belligerents governing neutral trade.

## GENERAL SURVEYS

These are not very numerous and are of less value than might be expected. The first of a serious tendency appears to be Kiesselbach's *Die Continentalsperre in ihrer ökonomisch-*

*politischen Bedeutung* (Stuttgart & Tübingen, 1850). It is very far from impartial and is sadly confused on the economic side; but a large number of what have been taken to be recent discoveries will be found there, especially in regard to the matters treated in part I, chapter IV, of the present work. The book is throughout dominated by the ideas of Friedrich List and advocates the necessity of combating England in order to free the Continent from the bondage of the ' agricultural state '. I know only by name the next work, by Sautijn Kluit, *Geschiedenis van het Continentaal stelsel* (Amsterdam, 1865). An Italian work by Baron Lumbroso, *Napoleone I e l'Inghilterra: Saggio sulle origini del blocco continentale e sulle sue conseguenze economiche* (Rome, 1897), should properly come next in chronological order. It is a somewhat undigested collection of abstracts and information gathered from different sources. Quite recently two general surveys on a fairly large scale have been attempted. One of them is a German-Austrian work by Peez and Dehn, *Englands Vorherrschaft*, vol. I, *Aus der Zeit der Kontinentalsperre* (Leipzig, 1912), an uncritical and biased work, mainly directed against England, which, however, does not lack information of value and may lead a critical reader to more authentic accounts. Of quite another kind is Tarle's *Kontinental'naja blokada* (Moscow, 1913), which is based on exhaustive studies, especially in the French archives, and contains a great mass of material; but the first part of it—and the only one that has so far appeared —treats of nothing but French commerce and industry. Owing to the language in which it is written I have been able to use the text only to a very limited extent, but the notes and appendices are accessible to everybody and contain an abundance of valuable information. Last in time probably comes the work of Dr. Frank E. Melvin, *Napoleon's Navigation System* (New York, 1919); but it had not reached me at the time of writing. There is yet another work, however, which, though dominated by a somewhat antiquated conception of history, as well as by a very obvious pro-British and anti-French bias, may probably be regarded as containing the best survey that

has so far appeared of the ideas of the Continental System
and their application, namely, the last three chapters of Mahan,
*The Influence of Sea Power upon the French Revolution
and Empire, 1793–1812*, vol. ii (London, 1893). Despite its
weaknesses, this work is still well worth reading. Its general
thesis has several times been discussed in the preceding pages.

Of general historical surveys of the time, two should be
named in this connexion, namely, Sorel, *L'Europe et la révolution
française*, vols. i–viii (Paris, 1885–1904), which has been
sufficiently characterized in the preceding pages ; and Thiers,
*Histoire du Consulat et de l'Empire*, the twelfth part of which
(Paris, 1855) contains bk. xxxviii, entitled *Blocus continental*,
which despite a highly uncritical admiration of Napoleon—
particularly surprising with regard to the Trianon policy—
is based upon materials which still give value to an unusually
absorbing account.

A contemporary source of great value in regard to commercial conditions, especially in the north of Europe, is Oddy,
*European Commerce, showing New and Secure Channels of Trade
with the Continent of Europe* (London, 1805), published little
more than a year before the Berlin decree. The full and greatly
needed particulars of the commerce and economic character of
the northern countries, particularly Russia, are supplemented
by a lengthy section on Great Britain, which is, however, more
in the nature of an economic pamphlet, and besides, distinctly
inferior to the rest.

FRANCE

With regard to source publications, of course, we have here
to take into consideration the *Correspondance de Napoléon Ier*,
the *Bulletin des lois*, &c., and *Le Moniteur*, all of them very
helpful. A contemporary, secondary, though very abundant
source is Chaptal, *De l'industrie françoise*, vols. i–ii (Paris,
1819). It suffers from the very obvious vanity and prejudices
of its author, who, however, probably had a better acquaintance
than most of his contemporaries with the economic life of
France under Napoleon. Of the almost innumerable memoirs

of the Napoleonic age scarcely more than two bear on the question in hand, both by ministers of Napoleon, namely, Mollien, *Mémoires d'un ministre du trésor public*, vols. I–III (1845—here used, Gomel ed., Paris, 1898); and Chaptal, *Mes souvenirs sur Napoléon* (Paris, 1893), of which the former is beyond comparison both the more useful and the more trustworthy. Chaptal's reminiscences have the same weaknesses as his book, and also exhibit a rancour toward Napoleon that is difficult to explain. Of Mollien, on the other hand, the words of Macaulay in reference to George Savile, Marquess of Halifax, hold good to an unusual extent, namely, that he saw the events of his own day ' from the point of view from which, after the lapse of many years, they appear to the philosophic historian '.

Of secondary works we must first refer once more to Tarle's book, which in the volume so far published chiefly falls under this section. A detailed survey of the economic history of France throughout this period is given in Levasseur, *Histoire des classes ouvrières et de l'industrie en France de 1789 à 1870*, 2d ed., vol. I (Paris, 1903). Darmstädter, who would seem to be the foremost living German authority of the administrative history of the Napoleonic age, has treated the economic life of France under the Continental System and during the crisis of 1810–11 in the first of his two treatises, *Studien zur napoleonischen Wirtschaftspolitik* in *Vierteljahrschrift für Social- und Wirtschaftsgeschichte*, vol. II (Leipzig, 1904). The only thing lacking there is a thorough grasp of the deeper economic character of the question in hand. An excellent monograph on one particular problem is Roloff's *Die Kolonialpolitik Napoleons I.* (*Historische Bibliothek*, vol. x; Munich and Leipzig, 1899). Moreover, the periodical *Revue des études napoléoniennes* (Paris) contains several minor contributions to the history of the Continental System in France. The periodical *Revue Napoléonienne*, edited from Rome by Baron Lumbroso, also contains some studies which bear on the subject, as does even more the *Revue d'histoire des doctrines économiques et sociales* (later called *Revue d'histoire économique et sociale*).

The literature concerning the various incorporated territories is treated below under the countries to which they belonged just before the World War of 1914.

## Great Britain

With regard to published sources there is a very perceptible scarcity of all collections. Naturally enough there is nothing corresponding to Napoleon's correspondence; but there is not even any collection of official documents or legal enactments other than statutes. This makes Hansard's *Parliamentary Debates* (after 1803) our main source in a very high degree, because it contains, in addition to the debates themselves, a number of official papers which otherwise appear only in the *London Gazette*, which was rather inaccessible to me. Besides Hansard, however, there is, so far as I can judge, very comprehensive and useful material in the great collection of Blue Books or *Parliamentary Papers*, of which, however, very few were accessible to me. The same is the case with the pamphlet literature of the period. Among the writings falling under this head is Stephen's *War in Disguise : or the Frauds of the Neutral Flags* (London, 1805 ; reprinted in 1917), which has been repeatedly cited in the preceding pages and needs only to be mentioned here. The many accessible volumes of Life and Letters, Memoirs and Correspondence, &c., which largely have the character of sources, owing to the number of original documents included, have proved to contain very little material of importance for the history of the Continental System.

As regards secondary works, the foremost place must be given to those of Dr. J. Holland Rose, of which, however, only the articles *Napoleon and British Commerce* (1893), *Britain's Food Supply in the Napoleonic War* (1902), both reprinted in his collection of essays, *Napoleonic Studies* (London, 1904), contain a somewhat detailed discussion of the problems that concern us ; and even these are based mainly on politico-historical studies. On the other hand, there are abundant economic materials, though but little worked up, in three books :

Smart, *Economic Annals of the Nineteenth Century*, vol. I, *1801-20* (London, 1910), which, as the name implies, is a purely chronological account of the more important economic events, based mainly on Hansard; Tooke, *A History of Prices, and of the State of the Circulation, from 1793 to 1837*, vols. I–II (London, 1838), in which the indispensable material is made to support certain rather dubious economic theories of the author; and finally Porter, *The Progress of the Nation* (many editions). The English work corresponding to Levasseur's work is Cunningham's *Growth of English Industry and Commerce*, vol. II, *In Modern Times*, 3d ed. (Cambridge, 1903); but this fundamental work gives much less on the Continental System than Levasseur's, simply because that incident takes a far more humble place in the economic history of Great Britain than in that of France. There is, therefore, really no comprehensive summary for the United Kingdom. A special problem is treated in Miss Audrey Cunningham's *British Credit in the Last Napoleonic War* (Girton College Studies, vol. II, Cambridge, 1910), which has been sufficiently discussed in the preceding pages. Two valuable short studies on the currency problems of the time have been published by Mr. R. G. Hawtrey in *The Economic Journal*, vol. XXVIII (London, 1918), and reprinted in the volume *Currency and Credit* (London, 1919); of these the *Bank Restriction of 1797* bears more directly upon the problems treated in this book.

## GERMANY

Here we find by far the greatest flood of literature; but the political conditions in Germany during that period rendered possible only investigations for particular areas so that many of the volumes are far too special to find a place here. There is no comprehensive survey of the economic history of Germany as a whole in modern times. Curiously enough, Prussia seems to be the important territory in Germany whose position with regard to the Continental System has been least fully treated.

A sort of substitute for a comprehensive survey is offered by the work which has been frequently cited in the preceding pages, namely, König's *Die sächsische Baumwollenindustrie am Ende des vorigen Jahrhunderts und während der Kontinental-sperre* (published in *Leipziger Studien aus dem Gebiet der Geschichte*, vol. v : 3, Leipzig, 1899). This has developed into a very detailed and useful study of the history of the Leipzig Fair during this period, based on excellent archive materials ; and owing to the importance of the Leipzig Fairs in the economic life of Germany, it contributes greatly to our knowledge of the position of the whole of Central Europe during the self-blockade. According to an announcement published in German periodicals, the Saxon Royal Commission for History at the end of 1915 awarded a certain sum to Dr. König for a work which he submitted on the influence of the Continental System on the industry of Saxony ; but of the fate of this work I have been unable to obtain information. With the work of König we may connect an article by Tarle, *Deutsch-französische Wirtschaftsbeziehungen zur napoleonischen Zeit* in Schmoller's *Jahrbuch für Gesetzgebung*, &c., vol. XXXVIII (Leipzig, 1914), which is also based on valuable archive material, with sections on Hamburg, the Grand-Duchy of Berg, and the rest of Germany.

For the Hanse Towns, which are the most important in this connexion, there is a particularly copious literature, of which we may mention : Servières, *L'Allemagne française sous Napoléon Ier* (Paris, 1904), a work which, despite its compre-hensive title, deals only with the Hanse Towns, but which, though written by an historical dilettante, is valuable owing to its employment of much French archive material ; Wohlwill, *Neuere Geschichte der Freien und Hansestadt Hamburg, insbeson-dere von 1789 bis 1815 (Allgemeine Staatengeschichte. Dritte Abt., Deutsche Landesgeschichten*, 10. Werk, Gotha, 1914), a comprehensive account by the leading authority on the modern history of the Hanse Towns, and especially Hamburg, but meagre in the sphere of economics ; Vogel, *Die Hansestädte und die Kontinentalsperre* in *Pfingstblätter des Hansischen Geschichtsvereins* (vol. IX, 1913), an unusually good little survey which suffers only from its popular form and its scanty references; Max Schäfer, *Bremen und die Kontinentalsperre*, in *Hansische Geschichtsblätter*, vol. xx, 1914, the chief value of which consists in the statistical materials included. Of contemporary accounts, Rist's *Lebenserinnerungen*, vol. ii (Poel ed., Gotha, 1880), and Bourrienne's *Mémoires sur Napoléon, le Directoire, le Consulat, l'Empire et la Restauration*, chiefly vol. vii (Paris, 1829), are the most important; but the former is in all respects the most useful and reliable.

For the states of the Confederation of the Rhine, König's work has already been mentioned. But by far the principal work, as an historical account, is Schmidt's *Le Grand-Duché de Berg, 1806–1813* (Paris, 1905), which casts more light on the Continental System as a whole than most works; the parts which are mainly concerned with the matter are chapters x and xi. Darmstädter's *Das Grossherzogtum Frankfurt* (Frankfurt-am-Main, 1901) has also an account of the Continental System in the small district covered by the book, which is excellent but much shorter and more anecdotal than Schmidt's.

There are three books dealing with the more important German territories that were incorporated in the French Empire: Zeyss, *Die Entstehung der Handelskammern und die Industrie am Niederrhein während der französischen Herrschaft* (Leipzig, 1907), is an impartial and helpful account of the Roer department on the left bank of the Rhine; Herkner, *Die oberelsässische Baumwollindustrie und ihre Arbeiter (Abhandlungen aus dem staatswissenschaftlichen Seminar zu Strassburg i. E.*, vol. iv, Strassburg, 1887), gives a somewhat meagre account of the extremely important Mülhausen district during this period, by way of an introduction to a social-political study of the present day. Darmstädter, *Die Verwaltung des Unter-Elsass (Bas-Rhin) unter Napoleon I., 1799–1814*, in *Zeitschrift für die Geschichte des Oberrheins*, N.F., vol. xix (Heidelberg, 1904), treats, in its last sections, the economy of the Strassburg district under the Continental System.

UNITED STATES

The principal work for the history of the United States during this period, namely, Henry Adams's *History of the United States of America during the Administrations of Thomas Jefferson and James Madison*, vols. I–IX (New York, 1889–91), has not been accessible to me. Good surveys of the general course of political events are given by Edward Channing, *The Jeffersonian System*, in *The American Nation ; a History*, vol. XII (ed. by Albert Bushnell Hart, New York, 1906), and J. B. McMaster in the *Cambridge Modern History*, vol. VII (Cambridge, 1903). For the actual course of the trade war, however, there is a work which largely makes the others superfluous, namely, Mahan's *Sea Power and its Relations to the War of 1812*, vol. I (London, 1905). In merits and defects alike it is similar to his better-known general work which has previously been mentioned.

SCANDINAVIA

The lack of any kind of comprehensive survey for Sweden makes itself felt very strongly ; but it may be hoped that the great history of Gothenburg that is now being planned will largely fill the gap. Moreover, a fairly complete collection of the letters of Governor von Rosen of Gothenburg from that time would probably prove to be of great value. A rather small number of them are available in Ahnfelt, *Ur Svenska hofvets och aristokratiens lif*, vol. V (Stockholm, 1882), Schinkel-Bergman, *Minnen ur Sveriges nyare historia*, vol. VI (Stockholm, 1855), and von Engeström, *Minnen och anteckningar*, vol. II (Tegnér ed., Stockholm, 1876) ; and, moreover, Fröding has based, mainly on such letters, an article bearing on our subject in his collection of essays, *Det forna Göteborg* (Stockholm, 1903). There are statistical materials for the exports of Gothenburg in Bergwall, *Historisk Underrättelse om Staden Götheborgs betydligaste Varu-Utskeppningar* (Gothenburg, 1821). Some contributions toward an English presentment of the period may be found in *Memoirs and Correspondence of Admiral Lord de Saumarez*, vol. II (Ross ed., London, 1838). The only comprehensive account, necessarily brief from the nature of the book, is offered by Clason, in Hildebrand's *Sveriges Historia intill tjugonde seklet*, vol. IX: A (Stockholm, 1910); and the same writer has illustrated a special point in the first of his collected essays published under the title of *Gustaf IV Adolf och den europeiska krisen under Napoleon* (Stockholm, 1913).

In comparison with this both Denmark and Norway are infinitely better represented in the literature. For Denmark we have Holm, *Danmark-Norges Historie fra den store nordiske Krigs Slutning til Rigernes Adskillelse (1720–1814)*, vol. VII (Copenhagen, 1912), which, however, treats only the external history, as the author did not live to conclude the only remaining part (vol. VIII), which was to have treated the internal history of the period 1800–14. But this inconvenience is considerably diminished by the fact that we may fall back on a very full and useful account of this very subject in Rubin, *1807–1814; Studier til Köbenhavns og Danmarks Historie* (Copenhagen, 1892).

The state of affairs in Norway has long been illustrated by a well-known work which has partly the character of contemporary source, namely, Aall, *Erindringer som Bidrag til Norges Historie fra 1800–1815*, vols. I–III (Christiania, 1844–5); and, moreover, there has recently appeared an exhaustive description for the first half of the period of the Continental System, by Worm-Müller, *Norge gjennem nödsaarene 1807–1810* (Christiania, 1918), largely based on manuscript sources and very rich in details.

OTHER COUNTRIES

Only the most important works can be mentioned in this place. For Italy, mention may be made of the second article in Darmstädter's *Studien* in *Vierteljahrschrift für Social- und Wirtschaftsgeschichte*, vol. III (1905), which treats of Napoleon's commercial policy, mainly with regard to the Kingdom of Italy (North Italy); and Rambaud's *Naples sous Joseph Bonaparte, 1806–1808* (Paris, 1911), in which, however, economic questions have been awarded an extremely limited amount of space.

For Switzerland, a doctoral dissertation by de Cérenville, *Le système continental et la Suisse, 1803–1813* (Lausanne, 1906), provides a full and many-sided survey, based partly on an abundant collection of Swiss monographs on the industrial development of different cantons, and partly on Swiss archive materials; but, on the other hand, the work almost completely lacks contact with the general literature on the Continental System and is far too biased against the French.

As regards Belgium, we may mention the extremely interesting historical introduction to the two volumes of Varlez, *Les salaires dans l'industrie gantoise* (Royaume de Belgique, Ministère de l'industrie et du travail, Brussels, 1901, 1904).

With regard to Holland, there is a fairly extensive collection of publications, especially as regards the reign of King Louis. Foremost among these, perhaps, is Rocquain's *Napoléon Ier et le Roi Louis* (Paris, 1875), with the correspondence of the two brothers, which, however, was not accessible to me; but Napoleon's side of the correspondence is contained in full in Lecestre's edition of *Lettres inédites*. Moreover, a valuable collection of letters from Louis, chiefly to his Dutch ministers, is contained in Duboscq, *Louis Bonaparte en Hollande ; d'après ses lettres* (Paris, 1911). Of secondary works can be mentioned only Wichers, *De regeering van Koning Lodewijk Napoleon, 1806–1810* (Utrecht, 1892).

For Russia there are scattered notices of the Continental System in Vandal, *Napoléon et Alexandre Ier*, vols. i–iii (Paris, 1891–6), and valuable particulars in Oddy's work ; but, on the whole, it would seem that the internal condition of Russia under the Continental System was a *terra incognita*, at least for students of Western Europe.

Finally, I would refer to my own work, *Världskrigets ekonomi* in *Skrifter utgifna af Handelshögskolan* (Stockholm, 1915) for general economic ideas and comparisons with the recent war.

# APPENDICES

# APPENDIX I

## THE BRITISH ORDERS IN COUNCIL, 1807 [1]

### I

#### First (Whig) Order

JANUARY 7, 1807.

*Order in Council; prohibiting Trade to be carried on between Port and Port of Countries under the dominion or usurped controul of France and her allies.*

AT the Court at the Queen's Palace, the 7th of January 1807 ; Present, The King's most excellent Majesty in council.—Whereas, the French government has issued certain Orders, which, in violation of the usages of war, purport to prohibit the Commerce of all Neutral Nations with his majesty's dominions, and also to prevent such nations from trading with any other country, in any articles, the growth, produce, or manufacture of his majesty's dominions : and whereas the said government has also taken upon itself to declare all his majesty's dominions to be in a state of blockade, at a time when the fleets of France and her allies are themselves confined within their own ports by the superior valour and discipline of the British navy : and whereas such attempts on the part of the enemy would give to his majesty an unquestionable right of retaliation, and would warrant his majesty in enforcing the same prohibition of all commerce with France, which that power vainly hopes to effect against the commerce of his majesty's subjects ; a prohibition which the superiority of his majesty's naval forces might enable him to support, by actually investing the ports and coasts of the enemy with numerous squadrons and cruisers, so as to make the entrance or approach thereto manifestly dangerous : and whereas his majesty, though unwilling to follow the example of his enemies, by proceeding to an extremity so distressing to all nations not engaged in the war, and carrying on their accustomed trade, yet feels himself bound by a due regard to the just defence of the rights

---

[1] The Orders in Council are here reprinted from Hansard, vol. x, pp. 126-48. Although the text, unfortunately, is not very good, it has been followed literally in all respects, including spelling, capitalization, &c. A collation, kindly undertaken at my request by Dr. Knut Petersson, with the text of the Orders as inserted in the *London Gazette* (all except II, III, VIII, X, and XII of the following series), has shown almost complete conformity with the rendering of Hansard. The chronological order of the original has been preserved ; but for the different Orders issued under the same date, the order of the original has been slightly changed to one more logical. The headings have been italicized by the editor for the sake of convenience, and signatures have been omitted. No. IV is signed ' Steph. Cottrell ' ; all the rest ' W. Fawkener' or ' Fawkner '.

and interests of his people, not to suffer such measures to be taken by the enemy, without taking some steps on his part to restrain this violence, and to retort upon them the evils of their own injustice : his majesty is thereupon pleased, by and with the advice of his privy council, to order, and it is hereby ordered, That no vessel shall be permitted to trade from one port to another, both which ports shall belong to or be in the possession of France or her allies, or shall be so far under their controul, as that British vessels may not freely trade thereat : and the commanders of his majesty's ships of war and privateers shall be, and are hereby instructed to warn every neutral vessel coming from any such port, and destined to another such port, to discontinue her voyage, and not to proceed to any such port ; and any vessel after being so warned, or any vessel coming from any such port, after a reasonable time shall have been afforded for receiving information of this his majesty's Order, which shall be found proceeding to another such port, shall be captured and brought in, and, together with her cargo, shall be condemned as lawful prize : and his majesty's principal secretaries of state, the lords commissioners of the admiralty, and the judges of the high court of admiralty, and courts of vice admiralty, are to take the necessary measures herein as to them shall respectively appertain.

## II

### February 4, 1807

*Order in Council; approving Draught of an additional Instruction to the Commanders of His Majesty's Ships of War and Privateers, directing that Neutral Vessels, laden with Cargoes consisting of the Articles therein enumerated, coming for importation to any Port of the United Kingdom (provided they shall not be coming from any Port in a state of strict and rigorous Blockade), shall not be interrupted ; and that in case any such Articles shall be brought for Adjudication before the High Court of Admiralty, or any Court of Vice Admiralty, the same shall be forthwith liberated, upon a Claim being given by or on behalf of the Merchant or Merchants to whom such Articles shall be coming for Importation.*

At the Court at the Queen's Palace, the 4th of Feb. 1807 ; present the King's most excellent Majesty in Council.—Whereas there was this day read at the Board, the annexed Draught of an Additional Instruction to the commanders of his majesty's ships of war and privateers, directing that they do not interrupt Neutral Vessels laden with Cargoes consisting of the Articles thereinafter enumerated, coming for importation to any port of the united kingdom (provided they are not coming from any port in a state of strict and rigorous Blockade) ; and in case any such vessel, so coming with such articles, shall be brought for adjudication before the high court of admiralty, or any court of vice admiralty, that the same shall be forthwith liberated, upon a claim being given by or on behalf of the merchant or merchants to whom such Articles are coming for Importation : his majesty taking the said Draught of Additional Instruction into consideration, was pleased, with the advice of his privy council, to approve thereof, and to order, as it is hereby ordered, That the right hon. earl Spencer, one of his majesty's principal secretaries of state, do cause the said Instruction to be prepared for his majesty's royal signature.

*Draught of an Additional Instruction to the Commanders of our Ships of War and Privateers.*

Our will and pleasure is, That you do not interrupt Neutral Vessels laden with cargoes consisting of the Articles hereinafter enumerated, coming for Importation to any port of our united kingdom (provided they are not coming from any port in a state of strict and rigorous blockade) ; and in case any such vessel so coming with such Articles, shall be brought for adjudication before our high court of admiralty, or any court of vice admiralty, we hereby direct that the same shall be forthwith liberated, upon a claim being given by or on behalf of the merchant or merchants to whom such Articles are coming for Importation.

### ENUMERATION OF ARTICLES

Grain, viz. corn, meal and flour, (if importable according to the provisions of the corn laws) ; rice, Spanish wool, Mohair yarn, madder and madder roots, malts, shumack, argol, galls, cream of tartar, safflower, valone, brimstone, Spanish wine, indigo, saffron, verdigrease, cochineal, orchella weed, cork, olive oil, fruit, ashes, juniper berries, barilla, organzined, thrown, and raw silk (not being of the production of the East Indies or China) ; quicksilver, bullion coined and uncoined ; goat, kid, and lamb skins, rags, oak bark, flax, seeds, oil of turpentine, pitch, hemp, timber, fir, oak, oak plank, masts, and yards.

## III

### FEBRUARY 18, 1807

*Order in Council ; approving Draught of Additional Instructions directing that the Ships and Goods belonging to the Inhabitants of Hamburgh, Bremen and other places and countries in the north of Germany, which Vessels and Goods shall be engaged in the Trade to or from the Ports of the United Kingdom, shall, until further Order, be suffered to pass free and unmolested, &c.*

AT the Court at the Queen's Palace, the 18th of Feb. 1807 ; present, the King's most excellent Majesty in Council.—Whereas there was this day read at the board the annexed draught of Additional instructions to the commanders of ships of war and privateers, and to the judge of the high court of admiralty, and the judges of the courts of vice-admiralty, directing, that the ships and goods belonging to the Inhabitants of Hamburgh, Bremen, and other places and countries in the north of Germany, which vessels and goods shall be employed in a trade to or from the ports of the united kingdom, shall until further order, be suffered to pass free and unmolested, notwithstanding that the said countries are or may be in the possession or under the controul of France and her allies ; and that all such ships and goods so trading, which may have been already detained, shall be forthwith liberated, and restored: his majesty, taking, *etc.* [almost identical with no. II].

*Additional Instructions to the Commanders of Ships of War and Privateers, to the Judge of the High Court of Admiralty, and the Judges of the courts of Vice Admiralty.*

Our will and pleasure is, That the ships and goods belonging to the inhabitants of Hamburgh, Bremen, and other places and countries in the north of Germany, which vessels and goods shall be employed in a trade to or from the ports of our united kingdom, shall, until further order, be suffered to pass free and unmolested, notwithstanding that the said countries are or may be in the possession or under the controul of France and her allies ; and all such ships and goods so trading which may have been already detained shall be forthwith liberated and restored.

## IV

### AUGUST 19, 1807

*Order in Council ; directing, that all Vessels under the flag of Mecklenburgh, Oldenburgh, Papenburgh, or Kniphausen, shall be forthwith warned not to trade in future at any hostile Port, unless such vessels shall be going from or coming to a Port of the United Kingdom, &c.*

AT the Court at the Queen's Palace, the 19th of August 1807 ; present, the King's most excellent Majesty in Council.—His majesty, taking into consideration the measures recently resorted to by the enemy for distressing the commerce of the united kingdom, is pleased, by and with advice of his privy council, to order, and it is hereby ordered, That all vessels under the flag of Mecklenburgh, Oldenburgh, Papenburgh, or Kniphausen, shall be forthwith warned not to trade in future at any hostile port, unless such vessels shall be going from or coming to a port of the united kingdom ; and in case any such vessel, after having been so warned, shall be found trading, or to have traded after such warning ; or in case any vessels or goods, belonging to the inhabitants of such countries, after the expiration of 6 weeks from the date of this order, shall be found trading, or to have traded after such 6 weeks have expired, at any hostile port, such vessel and goods, unless going from or coming to a port of the united kingdom, shall be seized and brought in for legal adjudication, and shall be condemned as lawful prize to his majesty : etc. [almost identical with no. i].

## V

### Principal (Tory) Order : Blockade Ordinance

NOVEMBER 11, 1807

*Order in Council ; declaring the Dominions of his Majesty's Enemies, and of Countries under their Controul, in a state of Blockade, under the Exceptions specified in the said Order.*

AT the Court at the Queen's Palace, the 11th Nov. 1807 ; present, the King's most excellent Majesty in Council.—Whereas certain Orders, establishing an unprecedented system of warfare against this kingdom, and aimed especially at the destruction of its commerce and resources, were some time since issued by the government of France, by which 'the British islands were declared to be in a state of blockade,' thereby subjecting to capture and condemnation all vessels, with their cargoes, which should continue to trade with his majesty's dominions.—And whereas by the same Orders, ' all trading in English merchandize is prohibited ; and every article of merchandize belonging to England, or coming from her colonies, or of her manufacture, is declared lawful prize : '—And whereas the nations in alliance with France, and under her controul, were required to give, and have given, and do give, effect to such Orders :—And whereas his majesty's Order of the 7th of January last, has not answered the desired purpose, either of compelling the enemy to recall those Orders, or of inducing neutral nations to enter- pose, with effect, to obtain their revocation ; but, on the contrary, the same have been recently enforced with increased rigour :—And whereas his majesty, under these circumstances, finds himself compelled to take further measures for asserting and vindicating his just rights, and for supporting that maritime power which the exertions and valour of his people have, under the blessing of Providence, enabled him to establish and maintain ; and the maintenance of which is not more essential to the safety and prosperity of his majesty's dominions, than it is to the protection of such states as still retain their independence, and to the general intercourse and happiness of mankind:—His majesty is therefore pleased, by and with the advice of his privy council, to order, and it is hereby ordered, That all the ports and places of France and her allies, or of any other country at war with his majesty, and all other ports or places in Europe, from which, although not at war with his majesty, the British flag is excluded, and all ports or places in the colonies belonging to his majesty's enemies, shall from henceforth be subject to the same restrictions, in point of trade and navigation, with the exceptions hereinafter mentioned, as if the same were actually blockaded by his majesty's naval forces, in the most strict and rigorous manner : and it is hereby further ordered and declared, that all trade in articles which are of the produce or manufacture of the said countries or colonies, shall be deemed and considered to be unlawful ; and that every vessel trading from or to the said countries or colonies, together with all goods and merchandize on board, and all articles of the produce or manufacture of the said countries or colonies, shall be captured and condemned as prize to the captors.—But, although his majesty would be fully justified, by the circumstances and considerations above recited, in establishing such system of restrictions with respect to all the countries and colonies of his enemies, without exception or qualification ; yet his majesty, being nevertheless desirous not to subject neutrals to any greater inconvenience than is absolutely inseparable from the carrying into effect his majesty's just determination to counteract the designs of his enemies, and to retort upon his enemies themselves the consequences of their own violence and injustice ; and being yet willing to hope that it may be possible (consistently with that object) still to allow to neutrals the opportunity of furnishing themselves with colonial produce for their own consumption and supply ; and even to leave open, for the present, such trade with his majesty's enemies as shall be carried on directly with the ports of his majesty's dominions, or of his allies, in the manner hereinafter mentioned :—His majesty is therefore pleased further to order, and it is hereby ordered, That nothing herein contained shall extend to subject to capture or condemnation any vessel, or the cargo of any vessel, belonging to any country not declared by this Order to be subjected to the restrictions incident to a state of blockade, which shall have cleared out with such cargo from some port or place of the country to which she belongs, either in Europe or America, or from some free port in his majesty's colonies, under circumstances in which such trade from such free port is permitted, direct to some port or place in the colonies of his majesty's enemies, or from those colonies direct to the country to which such vessels belong, or to some free port in his majesty's colonies, in such cases, and with such articles, as it may be lawful to import into such free port ;—nor to any vessel, or the cargo of any vessel, belonging to any country not at war with his majesty, which shall have cleared out from some port or place in this kingdom, or from Gibraltar or Malta, under such regulations as his majesty may think fit to prescribe, or from any port belonging to his majesty's allies, and shall be proceeding direct to the port specified in her clearance ;— nor to any vessel, or the cargo of any vessel belonging to any country not at war with his majesty, which shall be coming from any port or place in Europe which is declared by this Order to be subject to the restrictions incident to a state of blockade, destined to some port or place in Europe belonging to his majesty, and which shall be on her voyage direct thereto : but these exceptions are not to be understood as exempting from capture or confiscation any vessel or goods which shall be liable thereto in respect of having entered or departed from any port or place actually blockaded by his majesty's squadrons or ships of war, or for being enemies' property, or for any other cause than the contravention of this present Order.—And the commanders of his majesty's ships of war and privateers, and other vessels acting under his majesty's commission, shall be, and are hereby instructed to warn every vessel which shall have commenced her voyage prior to any notice of this Order, and shall be destined to any port of France, or of her allies, or of any other country at war with his majesty, or to any port or place from which the British flag as aforesaid is excluded, or to any colony belonging to his majesty's enemies, and which shall not have cleared out as is hereinbefore allowed, to discontinue her voyage, and to proceed to some port or place in this kingdom, or to Gibraltar or Malta ; and any vessel which, after having been so warned, or after a reasonable time shall have been afforded for the arrival of information of this his majesty's Order at any port or place from which she sailed, or which, after having notice of this Order, shall be found in the prosecution of any voyage contrary to the restrictions contained in this Order, shall be captured, and, together with her cargo, condemned as lawful prize to the captors.—And whereas, countries, not engaged in the war, have acquiesced in the Orders of France, prohibiting all trade in any articles the produce or manufacture of his majesty's dominions ; and the merchants of those countries have given countenance and effect to those prohibitions, by accepting from persons styling themselves commercial agents of the enemy, resident at neutral ports, certain documents, termed ' Certificates of Origin,' being certificates obtained at the ports of shipment, declaring that the articles of the cargo are not of the produce or manufacture of his majesty's dominions ; or to that effect :—And whereas this expedient has been directed by France, and submitted to by such merchants, as part of the new system of warfare directed against the trade of this kingdom, and as the most effectual instrument of accomplishing the same, and it is therefore essentially necessary to resist it :—His majesty is therefore pleased, by and with the advice of his privy council, to order, and it is hereby ordered, That if any vessel, after reasonable time shall have been afforded for receiving notice of this his majesty's Order at the port or place from which such vessel shall have cleared out, shall be found carrying any such certificate or document as aforesaid, or any document referring to or authenticating the same, such vessel shall be adjudged lawful prize to the captor, together with the goods laden therein, belonging to the person or persons by whom, or on whose behalf, any such document was put on board.—And the right hon. the lords commissioners of his majesty's treasury, etc. [almost identical with no. 1].

## VI

### NOVEMBER 11, 1807

*Order in Council ; containing certain Regulations under which the Trade to and from the enemies Country shall be carried on.*

AT the Court at the Queen's Palace, the 11th Nov. 1807 : present, the King's most excellent Majesty in Council.—Whereas articles of the growth and manufacture of foreign countries cannot by law be imported into this country, except in British ships, or in ships belonging to the countries of which such articles are the growth and manufacture, without an Order in council specially authorizing the same :—His majesty, taking into consideration the Order of this day's date, respecting the trade to be carried on to and from the ports of the enemy, and deeming it expedient that any vessel, belonging to any country in alliance or at amity with his majesty, may be permitted to import into this country articles of the produce or manufacture of countries at war with his majesty :—His majesty, by and with the advice of his privy council, is therefore pleased to order, and it is hereby ordered, That all goods, wares, or merchandizes, specified and included in the schedule of an act, passed in the 43rd year of his present majesty's reign, intituled, ' an act to repeal the duties of customs payable in Great Britain, and to grant other duties in lieu thereof,' may be imported from any port or place belonging to any state not at amity with his majesty, in ships belonging to any state at amity with his majesty, subject to the payment of such duties, and liable to such drawbacks, as are now established by law upon the importation of the said goods, wares, or merchandize, in ships navigated according to law : and with respect to such of the said goods, wares, or merchandize, as are authorized to be warehoused under the provisions of an act, passed in the 43rd year of his present majesty's reign, intituled, ' an act for permitting certain goods imported into Great Britain, to be secured in warehouses without payment of duty,' subject to all the regulations of the said last-mentioned act ; and with respect to all articles which are prohibited by law from being imported into this country, it is ordered, That the same shall be reported for exportation to any country in amity or alliance with his majesty.—And his majesty is further pleased, by and with the advice of his privy council, to order, and it is hereby ordered, That all vessels which shall arrive at any port of the united kingdom, or at the port of Gibraltar, or Malta, in consequence of having been warned pursuant to the aforesaid order, or in consequence of receiving information in any other manner of the said Order, subsequent to their having taken on board any part of their cargoes, whether previous or subsequent to their sailing, shall be permitted to report their cargoes for exportation, and shall be allowed to proceed upon their voyages to their original ports of destination (if not unlawful before the issuing of the order) or to any port at amity with his majesty, upon receiving a certificate from the collector or comptroller of the customs at the port at which they shall so enter (which certificate the said collectors and comptrollers of the customs are hereby authorized and required to give) setting forth, that such vessels came into such port in consequence of being so warned, or of receiving such information as aforesaid, and that they were permitted to sail from such port under the regulations which his majesty has been pleased to establish in respect to such vessels : but in case any vessel so arriving shall prefer to import her cargo, then such vessel shall be allowed to enter and import the same, upon such terms and conditions as the said cargo might have been imported upon, according to law, in case the said vessel had sailed after having received notice of the said Order, and in conformity thereto.—And it is further ordered, That all vessels which shall arrive at any port of the united kingdom, or at Gibraltar, or Malta, in conformity and obedience to the said Order, shall be allowed, in respect to all articles which may be on board the same, except sugar, coffee, wine, brandy, snuff, and tobacco, to clear out to any port whatever, to be specified in such clearance ; and, with respect to the last mentioned articles, to export the same to such ports and under such conditions and regulations only as his majesty, by any licence to be granted for that purpose, may direct.—And, etc. [identical with no. v].

## VII

### NOVEMBER 11, 1807

*Order in Council ; declaring the future Sale and Transfer of enemies Vessels to the Subjects of a Neutral Country, to be invalid.*

AT the Court at the Queen's Palace, the 11th Nov. 1807 ; present, the King's most excellent Majesty in Council.—Whereas the sale of ships by a belligerent to a neutral, is considered by France to be illegal : —and whereas a great part of the shipping of France and her allies has been protected from capture during the present hostilities by transfers, or pretended transfers, to neutrals :—And whereas it is fully justifiable to adopt the same rule, in this respect, towards the enemy, which is applied by the enemy to this country :—His majesty is pleased, by and with the advice of his privy council, to order, and it is hereby ordered,

That in future the sale to a neutral of any vessel belonging to his majesty's enemies shall not be deemed to be legal, nor in any manner to transfer the property, nor to alter the character of such vessel : and all vessels now belonging or which shall hereafter belong to any enemy of his majesty, notwithstanding any sale or pretended sale to a neutral, after a reasonable time shall have elapsed for receiving information of this his majesty's Order at the place where such sale or pretended sale was effected, shall be captured and brought in, and shall be adjudged as lawful prize to the captors.   And, etc. [identical with no. v].

## VIII

### November 18, 1807

*Order in council ; approving Draught of Instructions to the Commanders of his Majesty's Ships of War and Privateers, &c. to act in due conformity to and execution of the Order in Council of the 11th of November, declaring the Dominions of his Majesty's Enemies and of Countries under their Controul, in a state of Blockade.*

At the Court at the Queen's Palace, the 18th Nov. 1807 ; present, the King's most excellent Majesty in Council.—Whereas there was this day read at the Board, the annexed Draught of Instructions to the Commanders of all ships of war and privateers, and to the judge of the high court of admiralty, and the judges of the courts of vice admiralty, strictly charging and enjoining them to act in due conformity to and execution of his majesty's Order in Council of the 11th of this instant, declaring the dominions of his majesty's enemies, and of countries under their controul in a state of blockade, under the exceptions specified in the said Order : his majesty, taking the said draught of instructions into consideration, was pleased, with the advice of his privy council, to approve thereof, and to order, as it is hereby ordered, That the right hon. lord Hawkesbury, one of his majesty's principal secretaries of state, do cause the said instructions (a copy whereof is hereunto annexed) to be prepared for his majesty's royal signature.

*Draught of Instructions to the Commanders of his Majesty's Ships of War and Privateers, and to the judge of the High Court of Admiralty, and Judges of the Courts of Vice Admiralty.*

Whereas by our Order in Council of the 11th Nov. instant, it is recited and ordered as follows ; to wit, &c. [Here the said Order is recited, as in no. v, *ante*, p. 393.]   Our will and pleasure is, and we do hereby direct, by and with the advice of our privy council, that the commanders

# THE BRITISH ORDERS IN COUNCIL, 1807 399

of our ships of war and privateers do act in due conformity to and execution of our aforesaid Order in Council ; and we do further order and declare, That nothing in the said Order shall extend or be construed to extend to prevent any vessel, not belonging to a country declared to be under the restrictions of blockade as aforesaid, from carrying from any port or place of the country to which such vessel belongs, any articles of manufacture or produce whatever, not being enemies property, to any port or place in this kingdom.—And we do further direct, That all articles of British manufacture, upon due proof thereof, (not being naval or military stores) shall be restored by our courts of admiralty or vice admiralty, on whatever voyage they may have been captured, to whomsoever the same shall appear to belong : and we do further direct, with respect to vessels subject only to be warned, that any vessel which shall belong to any country not declared by the said Order to be under the restrictions of blockade and which shall be proceeding on her voyage direct to some port or place of the country to which such vessel belongs, shall be permitted to proceed on her said voyage ; and any vessel bound to any port in America or the West Indies, to which port or place such vessel does not belong, and which is met near to America or the West Indies, shall be permitted, at the choice of the master of such vessel to proceed either to Halifax, or to one of our free ports in the West Indies, at the option of such master, which choice of the master, and the port chosen by and assigned to him, shall be written on one or more of the principal ship's papers ; and any vessel subject to warning, met beyond the equator, shall in like manner be permitted to proceed, at the choice of the master of such vessel, either to St. Helena, the Cape of Good Hope, or the island of Ceylon, and any such vessel which shall be bound to any port or place in Europe, shall be permitted, at the choice of the master of such vessel, to proceed either to Gibraltar or Malta, or to any port in this kingdom, at the option of such master, which request of the master, as well as the port chosen by and assigned to him, shall be in like manner written upon one or more of the principal ships' papers : and we do further direct, that nothing in the above Order contained, shall extend or be construed to extend to repeal or vacate the additional instructions of the 4th day of February last, directing that neutral vessels laden with cargoes consisting of the articles therein enumerated, coming for importation to any port of our united kingdom (provided they are not coming from any port in a state of strict and rigorous blockade) shall not be interrupted.

## IX

NOVEMBER 25, 1807

*Order in Council ; establishing certain Regulations as to Vessels clearing
out from this Kingdom, with reference to the Order of the 11th of
November instant.*

AT the Court at the Queen's Palace, the 25th Nov. 1807 ; present,
the King's most excellent Majesty in Council.—Whereas his majesty,
by his Order in council, dated 11th of Nov. instant, respecting the
trade to be carried on with his majesty's enemies, was pleased to exempt
from the restrictions of the said Order all vessels which shall have
cleared out from any port or place in this kingdom under such regulations
as his majesty may think fit to prescribe, and shall be proceeding direct
to the ports specified in the respective clearances : his majesty, taking
into consideration the expediency of making such regulations, is pleased,
by and with the advice of his privy council, to order, and it is hereby
ordered, That all vessels belonging to countries not at war with his
majesty, shall be permitted to lade in any port of the united kingdom
any goods, being the produce or manufacture of his majesty's dominions,
or East India goods or prize goods (all such goods having been lawfully
imported) and to clear out with, and freely to convey the same to any
port or place in any colony in the West Indies or America, belonging
to his majesty's enemies, such port or place not being in a state of
actual blockade, subject to the payment of such duties as may, at the
time when any such vessels may be cleared out, be due by law on the
exportation of any such goods, or in respect of the same being destined
to the ports of the colonies belonging to his majesty's enemies, and likewise to lade, clear out with, and convey as aforesaid, any articles of
foreign produce or manufacture which shall have been lawfully imported
into this kingdom, provided his majesty's licence shall have been previously obtained for so conveying such foreign produce or manufactures :
and it is further ordered, That any vessel, belonging as aforesaid, shall
be permitted to lade in any port of the united kingdom any goods, not
being naval or military stores, which shall be of the growth, produce,
or manufacture of this kingdom, or which shall have been lawfully
imported, (save and except foreign sugar, coffee, wine, brandy, snuff,
and cotton) and to clear out with, and freely to convey the same to
any port, to be specified in the clearance, not being in a state of actual
blockade, although the same shall be under the restrictions of the said
Order, and likewise to lade, clear out, and convey foreign sugar, coffee,
wine, brandy, snuff, and cotton, which shall have been lawfully imported,
provided his majesty's licence shall have been previously obtained for
the exportation and conveyance thereof : and it is hereby further

ordered, That no vessel shall be permitted to clear out from any port or place in this kingdom, to any port or place of any country subjected to the restrictions of the said Order, with any goods which shall have been laden, after notice of the said Order, on board the vessel which shall have imported the same into this kingdom, without having first duly entered and landed the same in some port or place in this kingdom ; and that no vessel shall be permitted to clear out from any port or place in this kingdom to any port or place whatever, with any goods, the produce or manufacture of any country subjected to the restrictions of the said Order, which shall have been laden, after notice as aforesaid, on board the vessel importing the same, without having so duly entered and landed the same, or with any goods whatever which shall have been laden after such notice in the vessel importing the same, in any port or place of any country subjected to the restrictions of the said Order, without having so duly entered and landed the same in some port or place in this kingdom, except the cargo shall consist wholly of flour, meal, grain, or any article or articles the produce of the soil of some country which is not subjected to the restrictions of the said Order, except cotton, and which shall have been imported in an unmanufactured state direct from such country into this kingdom, in a vessel belonging to the country from which such goods have been brought, and in which the same were grown and produced : and it is further ordered, That any vessel belonging to any country not at war with his majesty, may clear out from Guernesy, Jersey, or Man, to any port or place under the restrictions of the said Order, which shall be specified in the clearance, not being in a state of actual blockade, with such articles only, not being naval or military stores, as shall have been legally imported into such islands respectively, from any port or place in this kingdom direct ; and with respect to all such articles as may have been imported into the said islands respectively, from any port or place under the restrictions of the said Order, it shall not be permitted to any vessel to clear out with the same from any of the said islands, except to some port or place in this kingdom. And, etc. [identical with no. v].

## X

### November 25, 1807

*Order in Council ; approving Draught of Additional Instructions to the Commanders of Ships of War and Privateers, &c. for protecting Goods going from and coming to any Port of the United Kingdom, to whomsoever the Property may appear to belong.*

At the Court at the Queen's Palace, the 25th Nov. 1807 ; present, the King's most excellent Majesty in Council.—Whereas there was this day read at the Board, the annexed Draught of Additional Instructions to the commanders of all ships of war and privateers, and to the judge of the high court of admiralty, and the judges of the courts of vice admiralty, for protecting goods going from and coming to any port of the united kingdom, to whomsoever the property may appear to belong : his majesty, taking the said Draught of Instruction into consideration, was pleased, with the advice of his privy council, to approve thereof, and to order, as it is hereby ordered. That, etc. [almost identical with no. VIII].

*Draught of an Additional Instruction to the Commanders of Our Ships of War and Privateers, and to the Judge of Our High Court of Admiralty, and the Judges of Our Courts of Vice Admiralty.*

Our will and pleasure is, that vessels belonging to any state nor [*not*] at war with us, laden with cargoes in any ports of the united kingdom, and clearing out according to law, shall not be interrupted or molested in proceeding to any port in Europe (except ports specially notified to be in a state of strict and rigorous blockade before our order of the 11th Nov. instant) or which shall hereafter be so notified, to whomsoever the goods laden on board such vessels may appear to belong : and we do further direct, that vessels belonging as aforesaid, coming from any port in Europe (except as before excepted) direct to any port of the united kingdom with goods for importation, shall not be interrupted in the said voyages, to whomsoever the goods laden on board the said vessels may appear to belong : and in case any vessel which shall be met with, and asserted by her master to be so coming, shall be detained, on suspicion of not being really destined to this kingdom, such vessel shall be brought to the most convenient port in the course of her asserted destination, and the captors are hereby required to enquire, with all convenient speed, into the alledged destination, and in case any vessel and goods so brought in and detained shall be proceeded against in our high court of admiralty, or in any courts of vice admiralty, we hereby direct that the same shall be forthwith restored, upon satisfactory proof being made that the cargo was coming for importation to a port of this kingdom.

## XI

### NOVEMBER 25, 1807

*Order in Council ; respecting Enemies Produce and Manufacture on board British Ships.*

AT the Court at the Queen's Palace, the 25th Nov. 1807 ; present, the King's most excellent Majesty in Council.—Whereas his majesty, by his Order in Council of the 11th Nov. inst. was pleased to order and declare that all trade in articles which are of the produce or manufacture of the countries and colonies mentioned in the said order, shall be deemed and considered to be unlawful (except as is therein excepted): his majesty, by and with the advice of his privy council, is pleased to order and declare, and it is hereby ordered and declared, That nothing in the said Order contained shall extend to subject to capture and confiscation any articles of the produce and manufacture of the said countries and colonies, laden on board British ships, which would not have been subject to capture and confiscation if such Order had not been made.    And, etc. [identical with no v].

### XII

#### November 25, 1807

*Order in Council ; appointing Times at which Notice shall be presumed to have been received of the Order of the 11th instant at the different places specified in the said Order.*

At the Court at the Queen's Palace, the 25th Nov. 1807 ; present, the King's most excellent Majesty in Council.—Whereas it has been represented that it would be expedient to fix certain periods, at which it shall be deemed that a reasonable time shall have elapsed for receiving information, at different places, of his majesty's Order in council of the 11th Nov. instant, respecting the trade with his majesty's enemies, and in their produce and manufactures : his majesty, taking the same into consideration, and being desirous to obviate any difficulties that may arise in respect thereto, and also to allow ample time for the said Order being known to all persons who may be affected thereby, is pleased, by and with the advice of his privy council, to order and declare, and it is hereby ordered and declared, That information of the said Order of the 11th Nov. instant, shall be taken and held to have been received in the places hereinafter mentioned, at the periods respectively assigned to them ; namely, ports and places within the Baltic, Dec. 21st 1807 ; other ports and places to the northward of Amsterdam, Dec. 11th 1807 ; from Amsterdam to Ushant, Dec. 4th 1807 ; from Ushant to Cape Finisterre, Dec. 8th 1807 ; from Cape Finisterre to Gibraltar, inclusive, Dec. 13th 1807 ; Madeira, Dec. 13th 1807 ; ports and places within the Streights of Gibraltar, to Sicily and Malta, and the west coast of Italy, inclusive, Jan. 1st 1808 ; all other ports and places in the Mediterranean, beyond Sicily and Malta, Jan. 20th 1808 ; ports and places beyond the Dardanelles, Feb. 1st 1808 ; any part of the north and western coast of Africa, or the islands adjacent, except Madeira, Jan. 11th 1808 ; the United States, and British possessions in North America and the West Indies, Jan. 20th 1808 ; Cape of Good Hope, and the east coast of South

America, March 1st 1808 ; India, May 1st 1808 ; China, and the coast of South America, June 1st 1808 ; and every vessel sailing on or after those days from those places respectively, shall be deemed and taken to have received notice of the aforesaid Order : and it is further ordered, That if any vessel shall sail within twenty days after the periods above assigned respectively, from any of the said places, in contravention of the said Order of the 11th Nov. instant, and shall be detained as prize on account thereof ; or shall arrive at any port in this kingdom, destined to some port or place within the restriction of the said Order, and proof shall be made to the satisfaction of the court of admiralty, in which such vessel shall be proceeded against, in case the same shall be brought in as prize, that the loading of the said vessel had commenced before the said periods, and before information of the said Order had actually been received at the port of shipment, the said vessel, together with the goods so laden, shall be restored to the owner or owners thereof, and shall be permitted to proceed on her voyage, in such manner as if such vessel had sailed before the day so specified as aforesaid ; and it is further ordered, That no proof shall be admitted, or be gone into, for the purpose of shewing that information of the said Order of the 11th Nov. instant had not been received at the said places respectively, at the several periods before assigned.  And, etc. [identical with no. v].

## XIII

### NOVEMBER 25, 1807

*Order in Council ; establishing certain Regulations as to Vessels clearing out from the Ports of Gibraltar and Malta, with reference to the Order of the 11th Nov. instant.*

AT the Court at the Queen's Palace, the 25th Nov. 1807 ; present the King's most excellent Majesty in Council.—Whereas his majesty, by his Order in Council, dated the 11th Nov. instant, respecting the trade to be carried on with his majesty's enemies, was pleased to exempt from the restrictions of the said Order all vessels belonging to any country not at war with his majesty, together with their cargo, which shall be coming from any port or place in Europe which is declared in the said Order to be subject to the restrictions incident to a state of blockade, direct to some port or place in Europe belonging to his majesty ; and also all vessels which shall be cleared out from Gibraltar or Malta under such regulations as his majesty may think fit to prescribe, and which shall be proceeding direct to the ports specified in their respective clearances :  and whereas it is expedient to encourage the trade from Gibraltar and Malta to countries under the restrictions of the said Order subject to regulations to be made in respect thereto :

his majesty is therefore pleased to prescribe the following regulations in regard to such trade accordingly, and, by and with the advice of his privy council, to order, and it is hereby ordered, That all sorts of flour and meal, and all sorts of grain, tobacco, and any other article in an unmanufactured state, being the growth and produce of any country not being subjected by the said Order to the restrictions incident to a state of blockade (except cotton, and naval and military stores) which shall have been imported into Gibraltar or Malta, direct from the country where the same were grown and produced, shall, without any licence, be permitted to be cleared out to any port or place, not being in a state of actual blockade, without the same being compelled to be landed : but neither the said article of cotton, however imported, nor any article which is not the growth, produce, or manufacture of this kingdom, or which has not been imported in a British ship, or from this kingdom direct, (except fish), and which shall have been laden at the port of original shipment, after the period directed by an Order of this date to be taken as the time at which notice of the said Order of the 11th Nov. shall be considered as having been received at such port of shipment, shall be permitted to be exported from Gibraltar or Malta, except to some port or place in this kingdom : and all other articles of the growth, produce and manufacture of this kingdom, or which shall have been imported into Gibraltar or Malta in a British ship, or from some port or place in this kingdom, together with the article of fish, however imported, may be exported to any ports or places in the Mediterranean or Portugal, under such licence only as is hereinafter directed to be granted by the governor of Gibraltar and Malta respectively : and it is hereby further ordered, That licences be granted by the governors, lieutenant governors, or other persons having the chief civil command at Gibraltar or at Malta respectively, but in his majesty's name, to such person or persons as the said governors, lieutenant governors, or persons having the chief civil command shall think fit, allowing such person or persons to export from Gibraltar direct, to any port in the Mediterranean or to any port of Portugal, or to any port of Spain without the Mediterranean, not further north than Cape Finisterre, and from Malta direct to any port being within the Mediterranean, with any articles of the produce or manufacture of his majesty's dominions ; and any articles which shall have been imported into Gibraltar or Malta from this kingdom, to whomsoever such articles shall appear to belong (not being naval or military stores) in any vessel belonging to any country not at war with his majesty, or in any vessel not exceeding one hundred tons burthen, and being unarmed, belonging to the country to which such vessel shall be cleared out and going ; and also to import in any such vessel or vessels as aforesaid, from any port within the Mediterranean, to Gibraltar or Malta, or from any port in

Portugal or Spain as aforesaid, to Gibraltar, such port and such destination respectively to be specified in such licence, any articles of merchandize, whatsoever and to whomsoever the same may appear to belong, such articles to be specified in the bill of lading of such vessel, subject however to such further regulations and restrictions with respect to all or any of the said articles so to be imported or exported, as may be inserted in the said licences by the governors, lieutenant governors, or other persons having the chief civil command at Gibraltar or Malta for the time being respectively, as to them shall from time to time seem fit and expedient.—And it is further ordered, That in every such licence shall be inserted the names and residence of the person or persons to whom it shall be granted, the articles and their quantities permitted to be exported, the name and description of the vessel and of the master thereof, the port to which the vessel shall be allowed to go, which shall be some port not under actual blockade ; and that no licence so to be granted, shall continue in force for longer than two months from its date, nor for more than one voyage, or any such licence be granted, or acknowledged to be valid, if granted, to permit the clearance of any vessel to any port which shall be actually blockaded by any naval force of his majesty, or of his allies.—And it is further ordered, That the commanders of his majesty's ships of war and privateers, and all others whom it may concern, shall suffer every such vessel sailing conformably to the permission given by this Order, or having any licence as aforesaid, to pass and repass direct between Gibraltar or Malta and such port as shall be specified in the licence, in such manner, and under such terms, regulations, and restrictions, as shall be expressed therein.—And it is furthered ordered, That in case any vessel so sailing as aforesaid, for which any such licence as aforesaid shall have been granted, and which shall be proceeding direct upon her said voyage, shall be detained and brought in for legal adjudication, such vessel, with her cargo, shall be fortwith released by the court of admiralty or vice admiralty, in which proceedings shall be commenced, upon proof being made that the parties had duly conformed to the terms, regulations, and restrictions of the said licence ; the proof of such conformity to lie upon the person or persons claiming the benefit of this Order, or obtaining or using such licence, or claiming the benefit thereof.—And it is hereby further ordered, That no vessel belonging to any state on the coast of Barbary, shall be prevented from sailing with any articles of the growth or produce of such state, from any port or place in such state to any port or place in the Mediterranean or Portugal, such port or place not being actually blockaded by some naval force belonging to his majesty, or his allies, without being obliged to touch at Gibraltar or Malta.—And, etc. [identical with no. v].

## XIV

DECEMBER 18, 1807

*Order in Council ; declaring that his Majesty's Orders of the 11th of Nov. shall not extend to permit the Produce of enemies Colonies in the West Indies to be brought direct to any British Port in Europe.*

AT the Court at Windsor, the 18th Dec. 1807 ; present, the King's most excellent Majesty in Council :

His majesty is pleased, by and with the advice of his privy council, to order, and it is hereby ordered, That nothing in his majesty's Order in Council of the 11th of Nov. last, shall extend or be construed to extend, to permit any vessel to import any articles of the produce or manufacture of the enemy's colonies in the West Indies, direct from such colonies to any port of this kingdom, and it is further ordered, That all vessels which may arrive in the ports of this kingdom direct from the colonies aforesaid, shall nevertheless be released, upon proof being made that the charter-party or other agreement for the voyage was entered into before notice of this Order. And, etc. [identical with no. v].

# APPENDIX II

## FRENCH CUSTOMS DUTIES ON COLONIAL PRODUCE, 1802–10 [a]

| Commodities | From French colonies | | | | | | From foreign colonies | | | | | |
|---|---|---|---|---|---|---|---|---|---|---|---|---|
| | 1802 [b] | 1803 [b] | 1804 | 1805 | 1806 | 1810 | 1802 | 1803 | 1804 | 1805 | 1806 | 1810 |
| Sugar, raw | 30 | 30 | .. | .. | 45 | 300 | 45 | 45 | .. | .. | 55 | 300 |
| clay | 50 | 50 | .. | .. | 80 | 400 | 75 | 75 | .. | .. | 100 | 400 |
| refined | 100 | .. [c] | .. | .. | .. | .. | 100 | .. [d] | .. | .. | .. | .. |
| Molasses | 16 | 16 | .. | .. | .. | .. | 75 | 75 | .. | .. | .. | .. |
| Coffee | 50 | 50 | .. | 75 | 125 | 400 | 75 | 75 | .. | 100 | 150 | 400 |
| Cocoa | 50 | 50 | .. | 95 | 175 | 1,000 | 75 | 75 | .. | 120 | 200 | 1,000 |
| Tea, green (kilo.) | .. | .. | .. | (+5%) [e] | (+10%) [e] | } 600 | .. | .. | .. | (+5%) [e] | (+10%) [e] | } 600 |
| other sorts (kilo.) | .. | .. | .. | 2 | 3 | 150 | .. | .. | .. | 2 | 3 | 150 |
| Preserves | 50 | 16 | .. | .. | .. | .. | .. | .. | .. | .. | .. | .. |
| Tafia (hectolitre) | 10 | 10 | .. | .. | .. | .. | 1·50 | 1·50 | .. | .. | .. | .. |
| Liqueurs (litre) | 1 | 1 | .. | .. | .. | .. | 9 | 9 | .. | .. | .. | .. |
| Ginger | 6 | 6 | .. | .. | .. | .. | .. | .. | .. | .. | .. | .. |
| Cloves (kilo.) | .. | .. | .. | 3 | 3 | 600 | .. | .. | .. | 3 | 3 | 600 |
| Pepper, white | .. | } 30 [f] | } 40 [f] | 80 | 135 | } 600 | 9 | } 60 | } 40 [f] | 100 | 150 | } 600 |
| black | 6 | | | .. | .. | 400 | .. | | | .. | .. | 400 |
| Cassia | .. | .. | .. | .. | .. | .. | .. | .. | .. | .. | .. | .. |
| Cinnamon, ordinary | .. | .. | .. | .. | .. | 1,400 | .. | .. | .. | .. | .. | 1,400 |
| fine | .. | .. | .. | .. | .. | 2,000 | .. | .. | .. | .. | .. | 2,000 |
| Nutmeg | .. | .. | .. | .. | .. | 2,000 | .. | .. | .. | .. | .. | 2,000 |
| Cochineal | .. | .. | .. | .. | .. | 2,000 | .. | .. | .. | .. | .. | 2,000 |
| Hyswin | .. | .. | .. | .. | .. | 900 | .. | .. | .. | .. | .. | 900 |
| Annatto | 4 | 4 | .. | .. | .. | .. | 6 | 6 | .. | .. | .. | .. |
| Indigo | 10 | 10 | .. | .. | .. | 900 | 15 | 15 | .. | .. | .. | 900 |

FRENCH CUSTOMS DUTIES ON COLONIAL PRODUCE 1802-10 [a]

| Commodities | From French colonies | | | | | | From foreign colonies | | | | | |
|---|---|---|---|---|---|---|---|---|---|---|---|---|
| | 1802 [b] | 1803 [b] | 1804 | 1805 | 1806 | 1810 | 1802 | 1803 | 1804 | 1805 | 1806 | 1810 |
| Madder | .. | .. | .. | 2, 6, 15[g] | 2, 6, 15[g] | .. | .. | .. | .. | 2, 6, 15[g] | 2, 6, 15[g] | .. |
| Pernambuco | .. | .. | .. | .. | .. | 120 | .. | .. | .. | .. | .. | 120 |
| Logwood | .. | .. | .. | .. | .. | 80 | .. | .. | .. | .. | .. | 80 |
| Dyewood, ground | .. | .. | .. | .. | .. | 100 | .. | .. | .. | .. | .. | 100 |
| Mahogany and Marquetry wood | 10 | 10 | .. | 20 | 20 | 50 | 15 | 15 | .. | 25 | 25 | 50 |
| Tortoise shell | 30 | 30 | .. | .. | 120 | .. | 45 | 45 | .. | .. | 120 | .. |
| Hides, dry, with hair on (per hide) | 0·25 | 0·25 | .. | .. | .. | .. | 0·40 | 0·40 | .. | .. | .. | .. |
| Raw cotton | 2 | 2 | 1 | .. | 60 | {200[h] / 800} | 3 | 3 | 1 | .. | 60 | {200[h] / 800} |

[a] The tariffs referred to are: Thermidor 3, year x; Floréal 8, year xi; Ventôse 22, year xii; Pluviôse 17, year xiii; February 22, March 4, April 30, 1806; August 5, 1810 (Trianon tariff). Duties are given in francs per quintal métrique (100 kilograms), unless otherwise stated. Consumption duty is always included.

[b] In the tariffs of 1802 and 1803 non-specified commodities pay half duty when coming from French colonies.

[c] Refined sugar prohibited in 1803; export bounty 50 francs.

[d] Molasses prohibited in 1803; when coming from foreign colonies.

[e] Tea, 1805: value below 10 fr. per kg.; value from 10 fr. per kg. upward: 2 fr. + 5 per cent. ad valorem. Tea, 1806: value below 8 fr. per kg.: 3 fr. per kg.; value from 8 fr. per kg. upward: 3 fr. + 10 per cent. ad valorem.

[f] Pepper, 1803: the lower duty when coming from Cayenne or the French colonies in the east, in French bottoms. Pepper, 1804: colonial duty as above when imported through French commerce from beyond the Cape except from Isle-de-France (Mauritius) and Réunion.

[g] According to different stages of manufacture.

[h] Raw cotton: from Brazil, Cayenne, Surinam, Demerara and Georgia long staple 800 fr.; from the Levant by sea, 400 fr.; from the Levant by Cologne, Coblenz, Mainz, Strassburg, 200 fr.; from other countries except Naples, 600 fr.; from Naples, old duty, 60 fr.

# INDEX